THE PRESIDENT'S CZARS

THE PRESIDENT'S CZARS

UNDERMINING CONGRESS AND THE CONSTITUTION

Mitchel A. Sollenberger and Mark J. Rozell

University Press of Kansas

Published by the University Press of Kansas (Lawrence, Kansas 66045), which was organized by the Kansas Board of Regents and is operated and funded by Emporia State University, Fort Hays State University, Kansas State University, Pittsburg State University, the University of Kansas, and Wichita State University

Library of Congress Cataloging-in-Publication Data

Sollenberger, Mitchel A.
   The president's czars : undermining Congress and the Constitution / Mitchel A. Sollenberger and Mark J. Rozell.
      p.   cm. —(Studies in government and public policy)
   Includes bibliographical references and index.
   ISBN 978-0-7006-1835-4 (cloth : alk. paper) — ISBN 978-0-7006-1836-1 (pbk. : alk. paper) 1. Executive power—United States—History. 2. United States—Officials and employees—Selection and appointment—History. 3. Presidents—Staff—Selection and appointment—United States—History. 4. United States. Congress. Senate—Powers and duties. 5. Separation of powers—United States. I. Rozell, Mark J. II. Title.
   JK585.S64 2012
   352.2'64—dc23   2012007605

British Library Cataloguing-in-Publication Data is available.

Printed in the United States of America
10 9 8 7 6 5 4 3 2 1

The paper used in this publication is recycled and contains 30 percent postconsumer waste. It is acid free and meets the minimum requirements of the American National Standard for Permanence of Paper for Printed Library Materials Z39.48-1992.

For my son, Will (born December 31, 2010)

—MAS

In memory of my mother, Josephine Rozell (1926–2010)

—MJR

CONTENTS

PREFACE

The analysis in this book is contrary to trends in political science scholarship and conventional wisdom about the presidency. It is grounded in a public law analysis at a time when much of the political science discipline increasingly has turned its back on such an approach.[1] And it counters a continually growing and now widespread preference among many scholars and political observers for a powerful presidency with relatively limited constraints. We agree with Louis Fisher that these trends are connected: "The neglect of public law coincided with, and helped encourage, the belief that presidential power was our best hope for promoting the public good and should be unfettered by constitutional and statutory restrictions."[2] With such a widespread preference that presidents act in ways to gain and maintain power, czars fit comfortably within the framework of an executive-dominated system of government.

These trends are having a substantial impact on the contemporary controversy over presidents using what have become known as executive branch czars. Without public law guidance, the criteria for judging presidential actions are largely utilitarian. In this case, the guiding consideration would be whether czars help to facilitate the president's tasks of leading the agenda and managing the government. While there is value to using the prevailing political science methods to study the presidency and the role of executive branch czars, approaches that emphasize advancing the needs of presidents have limitations and often perpetuate a distorted view of the constitutionally based system of separated powers. For the study of executive branch czars, a public law approach can fill important gaps and also provide a much-needed scholarly corrective to the more conventional approaches.

With little emphasis on the role of public law analysis, the major contemporary debates over presidential use of executive branch czars are mostly partisan-based. The best-known critics of czars today are conservative popular talk show hosts with a large partisan axe to grind against a Democratic president, Barack Obama. Yet prior to the Obama administration, there were loud protests from the Left against President George W. Bush having appointed a number of powerful czars, and hardly a word from the Right. If the objective is to enhance presidential powers to achieve desired policy ends, then it is no surprise that critics of czars are selective in their criticisms, depending upon who just happens to be chief executive at the time.

That is not to suggest that there are no serious analysts writing about czars.

Our colleagues José Villalobos and Justin Vaughn are simultaneously undertaking a study of the czar phenomenon. Congress has held hearings on the subject, at which such respected scholars as James P. Pfiffner, Bradley Patterson, and Harold C. Relyea testified. Nonetheless, other than the mere handful of political science colleagues and some law faculty writing on the subject, we have found very little constitutionally based analysis on the czars controversy.

The other challenge in undertaking this topic is that the term *czar* has been used very loosely without any guiding definition. Much of that circumstance is media driven of course. News reports and analyses have labeled all kinds of executive branch officials as czars—some of whom are in Senate-confirmed executive branch offices, others in nonconfirmed positions. We posit a working definition of executive branch czars that we hope will lend clarity to this important area. We then follow with a broad overview of the history of executive branch czars and provide both an analysis of this phenomenon and a recommendation for reform.

Neither of us is given to engaging in polemics in our academic research. Nonetheless, that does not hold us back from taking a firm position on constitutional issues. If we come across as engaged in an exercise to undermine the practice of presidents appointing czars, it is because we have strong feelings on the subject based on our own long period of investigating the evidence. We find that evidence weighs heavily in a particular direction. And thus, we declare executive branch czars to be a constitutional aberration, a practice that violates the core principles of a balanced governing system based on democratic controls. Whatever utility presidents may see in appointing czars, we believe that the overall damage to our constitutional system is great and that this practice needs to stop. In our conclusion we present what we consider the best way out of the current situation and toward a restoration of the principles of democratic controls and accountability.

We are grateful for the insights of a number of scholars who have shared their ideas and offered helpful suggestions to us on the topic of this volume, particularly Louis Fisher, Herbert Fenster, Morton Rosenberg, and two anonymous reviewers for the University Press of Kansas. Over the years Lou has been extraordinarily generous with his time and has provided many helpful insights and suggestions to both of us on multiple books and articles. He read drafts of all the chapters of this volume and offered extensive comments from which we have benefited substantially. We are proud to have such a selfless colleague and very good friend. It was also Lou who urged us to consult Herb and Mort for their insights, as both have extensive knowledge on topics directly related to our analysis here. We drew significantly from our many exchanges with both of them over the past year. Any errors, of course, are our own responsibility.

To date, our research on executive branch czars has resulted in two journal articles: one published in *Presidential Studies Quarterly* and the other forthcoming in *Congress & the Presidency*. Portions of this book appear with permission in those articles.

Both of us are fortunate to work in supportive and collegial academic environments. We thank Department of Social Sciences Chair Martin Hershock of the University of Michigan–Dearborn, as well as Dean Edward Rhodes and Associate Dean Ann Baker of the School of Public Policy at George Mason University, for their academic leadership and support of our scholarship. In addition, we are grateful to Drew Buchanan, who, as director of the University of Michigan–Dearborn's Office of Research and Sponsored Programs, provided us with a faculty development grant. We also thank the library staffs at the University of Michigan–Dearborn and George Mason University who helped acquire the books and articles necessary for this study. Finally, we want to express our appreciation to the editors and staff at the University Press of Kansas, especially Fred Woodward, who took an immediate interest in this project and provided his usual steady guidance throughout the process of developing and writing this study. Each of us has previously written a book published by the press. Based on our past good experiences and the plain fact that University Press of Kansas is the recognized leading publisher in U.S. presidential studies, we never considered for a minute to send this volume anywhere else.

The period of writing this book corresponded with major changes in our lives, both joyful and sad. It is therefore dedicated to William Sollenberger (born December 31, 2010) and to the memory of Josephine Rozell (1926–2010).

Mitchel A. Sollenberger, University of Michigan–Dearborn
Mark J. Rozell, George Mason University

THE PRESIDENT'S CZARS

1. Czars and the U.S. Constitution

As the worst environmental disaster in U.S. history devastated the livelihoods of many Gulf Coast residents, in June 2010 President Barack Obama directed his "pay czar" Kenneth Feinberg to oversee a $20 billion oil spill victims' fund that had been established by British Petroleum (BP), the company responsible for the largest oil spill ever in the Gulf of Mexico.[1] One year earlier, the president had appointed Feinberg to the pay czar position under the auspices of the Department of Treasury.[2] The Obama administration charged Feinberg with establishing and enforcing executive pay guidelines for companies—including banks, insurance companies, and automobile makers—that had received federal bailout money from the $700 billion Troubled Asset Relief Program (TARP).[3] Regarding the BP oil spill victims' fund, Feinberg also became known as the "claims czar."

Feinberg, unelected and in positions that do not require Senate confirmation, exercised some of the most significant powers of any official in the federal government, with the ability to promulgate executive pay within companies that received government loans through TARP and to exercise discretion over the distribution of once unimaginable sums of taxpayer and also private industry money. Although he possessed vastly expansive policy powers, his positions did not fit anywhere in the constitutional scheme of checks and balances. In fact, the White House seemed uncertain of the legal basis for the claims czar position even weeks after Feinberg's appointment had been made. During a press conference on June 21, 2010, White House Deputy Press Secretary Bill Burton did not know if Feinberg's compensation would come from BP or another source (perhaps the federal government).[4] On June 29, in a question to White House Press Secretary Robert Gibbs, a reporter wanted to know if what Feinberg had said about the White House and BP agreeing "to give him jurisdiction over claims from individuals and businesses" was true. Gibbs's response was muddled at best, saying that "there is confusion" on the matter and that he would "get an answer in our transcript."[5] A few days later Gibbs was equally dumbfounded by a reporter's straightforward question concerning the legal language pertaining to the BP oil spill victims' fund, as he replied, "Let me check. I don't know the answer."[6] The answer that Gibbs eventually placed in the June 29 transcript reads: "The fund is administered by BP. How that fund is distributed, whether through a foundation, a charity or through Ken Feinberg is for them to decide."

On the Obama White House blog entry concerning the BP oil victims' fund, the administration gives a different impression. From that entry it is clear that the White House is deeply involved in the process. The blog noted that the president and vice president were meeting with BP executives "to ensure that families and businesses in the Gulf Region are not shortchanged for their losses." It also provides a fact sheet that highlights a structure that appears to be mimicking a government-like administrative claims process or leaves the impression that all claims are governed by federal law. First, the fact sheet notes that "a new, independent claims process will be created with the mandate to be fairer, faster, and more transparent." Next, it explains that a "panel of three judges will be available to hear appeals" of Feinberg's decisions. Finally, after noting that dissatisfied claimants can "go to court" or to the federal government's Oil Spill Liability Trust Fund, the fact sheet states: "Decisions under current law by the independent claims facility shall be binding on BP."[7]

The entire document is vague and confusing but the general impression is that the federal government is an active participant or even running most, if not all, of the claims process. A panel made up of "three judges" sounds like some sort of administrative appeals court. Who appoints the judges and what laws or rules are in place to ensure a "fairer, faster, and more transparent" process? The "go to court" language and Oil Spill Liability Trust Fund also point to a government-controlled claims process. Far from clarifying the legal status of Feinberg's position, the White House blog only confused the issue even more. In a statement announcing the creation of the oil fund, President Obama gave the impression that Feinberg's appointment and the claims process were made not by BP alone but with his administration helping to set it up. "We have mutually agreed," Obama declared, "that Ken Feinberg will run the independent claims process we are putting in place."[8] At no point since Feinberg's appointment has the Obama administration made clear the legal authority used to create the claims czar position.

If Feinberg were the only executive branch czar who exercised substantial powers while operating independently of legislative controls, then that would be adequate justification for alarm. But he is just one of a growing number of high-level executive branch individuals acting on their own without any constitutional or statutory backing let alone clear checks on their powers. Increasingly the practice of presidents unilaterally creating positions of authority is being accepted as an ordinary function of the federal government. Typically when crises strike at home or abroad, there are often calls for presidents to appoint a person, without seeking legislative approval, to coordinate, direct, or otherwise take control of a policy area. Criticisms of this practice are often dismissed as partisan efforts to weaken presidents or as failures to recognize that there is substantial precedent for czars in the federal government.

LIMITING CZARS: DEMOCRATIC CONTROLS

We are deeply troubled by these developments. Czars are a constitutional aberration, a direct violation of the core principles of a system of separation of powers and government accountability. Presidents may find some utility in having czars. Many members of Congress may even be content to defer to the executive branch to undertake complex policy problems and the responsibility for any outcomes. Organized groups and many concerned citizens may also appreciate the seriousness that a president attaches to their issues when he appoints one person to solve them. None of that should override the rule of law. The constitutional framers did not create this delicately balanced system of separated powers for the convenience of officeholders or to achieve efficiency or immediate gratification of citizens. Different forms of government can better achieve those ends; ours should stay true to its principles of balanced and constrained powers. Czars do severe damage to our principles and the practice of creating and appointing them should be stopped.

We reach this conclusion based on the understanding that republican and structural safeguards such as the principles of separation of powers and of checks and balances matter when assessing governing relationships. These principles, which are rooted in the Constitution, are what we call the democratic controls that guide government actions. One of the key components of democratic controls, and a cornerstone of the Constitution, is the belief that a fully functional government must be based on the idea of representation. In *The Federalist* no. 49, James Madison confirmed this view. "The people are the only legitimate fountain of power," Madison declared, "and it is from them that the constitutional charter, under which the several branches of government hold their power, is derived."[9] Alexander Hamilton agreed, arguing in *The Federalist* no. 9 that republican government is maintained through "the representation of the people in the legislature by deputies of their own election."[10] At the founding, opponents of the Constitution likewise supported this point. Anti-Federalist author "Brutus" wrote that "in a free republic . . . all laws are derived from the consent of the people."[11] Another Anti-Federalist, Melancton Smith of New York, said that "the scheme of representation had been adopted, by which the people deputed others to represent them."[12] Both sides in the ratification controversy agreed that the people were at the heart of government authority, giving it energy, direction, and legitimacy.

Equally important to the concept of republicanism is the notion that Congress possesses significant governing power and is the first branch of the national government. "In republican government," Madison declared in *The Federalist* no. 51, "the legislative authority necessarily predominates."[13] That is why the Constitution first provides for the structure and powers of Congress and then moves to the presidency, where nearly no executive power functions without the consent of the legislative branch. The framers viewed Congress as the primary institution for carrying out the will of the people. "The genius of republican liberty seems to demand on one side, not only that all power should be derived from the people," Madison noted in *The Federalist* no. 37, "but that those intrusted with it should be kept in dependence on the people, by a short duration of their appointments; and that even this short period the trust should be placed not in a few, but in a number of hands."[14] Congress, not the president, offers the protection of the many over the few that Madison's republican liberty commands. Even Hamilton, more committed to executive power, argued in *The Federalist* no. 77 that protection against executive influence is best secured by placing power in the hands of the many.[15] Republicanism therefore helps guide the actions of the federal government by ensuring that the legislative branch has a significant say in the process of creating, defining duties, appointing, and funding officers and employees.

Republican government also provides a link between citizens and their government. As the elected representatives of the people, members of Congress have a constitutional duty to express the people's opinions on various matters including appointments. Not only does this arrangement provide protection against unworthy candidates from taking office, it also gives indirect public support for the unelected officials within the federal government. As an early nineteenth-century U.S. senator once explained, no branch of government "can exist without the affections of the people," and if any is "placed in such a situation as to be independent of the nation," it "will soon lose that affection which is essential to its durable existence."[16] Therefore a close link between the elected and unelected helps to assure citizens that the government is responsive to their wishes. Perhaps nothing is more important in a republican form of government.

The framers wanted to do more to guard against the concentration of power than merely making the people the ultimate source of government structure and authority. Further safeguards against misguided government actions were needed. To be sure, in a republican government the people's voice must prevail. The question was how to do that but still protect against the accumulation of power. "In framing a government which is to be administered by men over men," Madison memorably declared in *The Federalist* no. 51, "the great difficulty lies in this: you must first enable the government to control the governed; and in the next place oblige it to control itself." Rejecting the idea that merely relying on popular control of the government would be enough, Madison argued in support of separation of powers, checks and balances, and federalism, or what he called "auxiliary precautions," which would help guard against the concentration of power.[17]

Along with republicanism, these structural safeguards make up the core principles of democratic controls. As they relate to the executive branch czars, the most important protections are separation of powers and checks and balances. One of the initial objections concerning the Constitution centered on the claim that the framers violated Montesquieu's separation of powers maxim in not adequately dividing the powers of government among the branches. James Winthrop of Massachusetts, opposing the Constitution under the pen name "Agrippa," pointed out, "It is now generally understood that it is for the security of the people that the powers of the government should be lodged in different branches."[18] At the Pennsylvania ratification convention, the dissenting delegates protested "the undue and dangerous mixture of the powers of government; the same body possessing legislative, executive, and judicial powers."[19] There is much to be said against the accumulation of power in the hands of a small group of individuals or one person. For this reason, the framers purposely designed a system of government where each branch could check the others through the use of shared powers.

Again, the framers did not create a government where power rested in one branch. Instead of separate departments each possessing its own unique powers, the framers designed a system where the branches shared power to better check one another. As Madison said in *The Federalist* no. 51,

> the great security against a gradual concentration of the several powers in the same department, consists in giving to those who administer each department the necessary constitutional means and personal motives to resist encroachments of the others. The provision for defence must in this, as in all other cases, be made commensurate to the danger of attack. Ambition must be made to counter ambition. The interest of the man must be connected with the constitutional rights of the place.[20]

The Constitution therefore calls on each branch to defend itself and to protect its own interests.

This book thus has the straightforward purpose of addressing the growing problem that presidents are circumventing democratic controls by unilaterally forming, implementing, and changing public policy through the use of czars. We address this issue by first defining executive branch czars. The term *czar* is often used very loosely. The lack of a common definition causes enormous confusion. A clear definition is needed in order to properly analyze this subject. Second, we identify and analyze the constitutional issues surrounding the use and growth of executive branch czars. Third, we trace the history and the evolution of the use of executive branch czars. Only through such a comprehensive review is it possible to provide an analysis of how we arrived at the current state of affairs regarding the growth of czars in government. Fourth and finally, we offer what we consider a way out of the current situation. There have been some legislative attempts at controlling the powers of czars. We believe a more firm and definitive response than offered so far is needed.

DEFINING EXECUTIVE BRANCH "CZARS"

No official title of executive branch "czar" appears in the U.S. Constitution, federal laws, or government manuals. The 2005 edition of the *Merriam-Webster* dictionary defines *czar* as the emperor or ruler of Russia until the 1917 revolution. It also provides a secondary definition: "one having great power or authority."[21] A 1964 dictionary on political terms notes that the *czar* title is "applied to public men of dictatorial tendencies."[22] The take-away from those definitions appears to be that the term applies to those who exercise powers not necessarily checked by others. As a result, the very use of the word to depict executive branch officials seems inappropriate in a constitutional republic. However, it has been popularized by mass media, political observers, and elected leaders who have used it as shorthand for describing a variety of positions in the federal government.

In his 2000 book *The White House Staff*, Bradley H. Patterson Jr. provides one of the first academic accounts of the term. He notes that "when an overwhelming problem lands in the president's lap or a new initiative is aborning, he can bring in a White House assistant—perhaps a 'czar' or 'czarina'—to add the new, needed focus and energy to deal with it."[23] Although Patterson proceeds to detail various positions considered to be czars during Bill Clinton's administration, he does not venture a working definition of the term. More recently James P. Pfiffner offers a helpful starting point when he described czars as "members of the White House staff who have been designated by the president to coordinate a specific policy that involves more than one department or agency in the executive branch; they do not hold Senate confirmed positions; nor are they officers of the United States."[24]

Czars have certainly been placed within the White House, which provides them with some measure of protection from congressional oversight. However, czars are also found—as in the case of Feinberg and others—within a department or agency. Some of them have even had dual appointments—as a part of the White House staff and also within a department or agency.[25] In all three scenarios, many czars have made significant policy, regulatory, and budgetary decisions, while largely operating independently of the normal constraints built into our constitutional system.

In a system of government that seeks to prevent tyranny by ensuring each branch can check the others, there are dangers in allowing executive branch officials with far-reaching powers to be isolated from legislative oversight and controls. The text and underlying principles embodied in the Constitution are essential starting points when analyzing the propriety of executive branch czars. We are mindful that presidents have many difficult responsibilities and that they need substantial assistance to do their jobs. But that reality does not give presidents the leeway to override constitutional constraints placed on them by appointing czars to carry out policy, regulatory, and budgetary duties without being authorized by law and subject to legislative checks.

By our definition a czar is an executive branch official who is not confirmed by the Senate and is exercising final decision-making authority that often entails controlling budgetary programs, administering/coordinating a policy area, or otherwise promulgating rules, regulations, and orders that bind either government officials and/or the private sector. In addition, any persons who carry out the traditional functions of an ambassador or consul—some of whom qualify as czars—similarly need to be confirmed by the Senate, although many are not. An overwhelming number of czars owe their positions to unilateral presidential appointments without statutory authority. Nonetheless, some czar positions have been established by statute. As we explain below, the Constitution does not provide presidents with independent power to create offices. The framers understood that the British monarch possessed that power, and they gave detailed explanations why the U.S. president would be denied its use. Although we do not attempt to classify czars based on executive branch structure, typically they would include heads, assistant heads, deputies, and any other top-level personnel within departments and agencies appointed solely by the president.[26] We do not consider government officials or employees who merely advise or assist in the formation of policy to be czars. They do not require Senate confirmation. A czar's duties go well beyond merely advising to include a level of command and execution over a policy area that is not present with traditional support staff and advisers. We are mindful that the number of executive branch officials whom we would label as czars would greatly increase if policy planning/development functions were part of our definition. However, we believe that such duties do not create a constitutional or legal issue. This distinction allows for a more uniform and consistent definition to be applied throughout our analysis.

We also do not think that the staff of czars should be defined as such. Staff members provide support to their superiors. They do not make final decisions on policy and therefore they are in a support role and a similar position as presidential advisers. Finally, since we consider the non-delegation doctrine to be an important feature of a constitutional republic, czars can be found in some Senate-confirmed and statutorily grounded positions but, as explained later in this chapter, may be in violation of the Constitution by exercising powers not properly delegated to them. Not only do we regard some Senate-confirmed officials as czars, but the same analysis even applies to some of the nation's vice presidents. The length of service of czars is not a factor as government officials can and do certainly serve for short periods of time or for many years.

Similar to Feinberg, many contemporary czars are officials appointed solely to nonconfirmed positions and yet possess policy, regulatory, and spending authority. But as our coverage of the history of czars shows, there are also some officials who have held, for example, cabinet-level appointments, and then been given additional substantial duties outside the framework of their confirmed positions. Such additional duties pose no problem when they are in conformity with the framework that Congress set in place in 1950 with the Presidential Subdelegation Act, which permits a president to delegate to Senate-confirmed officers statutory authority unless otherwise prohibited from doing so.[27] Yet in some cases, presidents have assigned to Senate-confirmed officials and even vice presidents additional, nonstatutorily authorized duties that have included the ability to coordinate, regulate, or otherwise direct the outcomes of certain policy areas. Since such extra-legal duties are not authorized by Congress, they do not fall under the Subdelegation Act. Therefore it is possible that an official may simultaneously possess both legitimate and czar authority.

Our definition of an executive branch czar is rooted in the text and underlying principles of the Constitution, which caution against czars since they often violate (1) the Appointments Clause by exercising substantial policymaking functions without the need for nomination and confirmation, but can also run into conflict with (2) the non-delegation doctrine, and (3) the principle that a president cannot unilaterally establish offices without legislative authorization. After highlighting these issues in the following sections we also address the danger of concentrating executive power into the hands of a select few offices that have not been statutorily created and that presidents have attempted to insulate from the traditional democratic controls of governing.

Appointments Clause

The Appointments Clause provides the framework for understanding the central component to our *czars* definition: the requirement that executive branch officials who have final decision-making authority to control budgetary programs, administer/coordinate a policy area, or otherwise can promulgate rules, regulations, or any orders that bind either government officials and/or the private sector must receive Senate confirmation. This proposition stems from the constitutional dictate that all federal offices established by the Congress and president must adhere to Article II, section 2, clause 2, which reads:

> [The President] shall nominate, and by and with the Advice and Consent of the Senate, shall appoint Ambassadors, other public Ministers and Consuls, Judges of the supreme Court, and all other Officers of the United States, whose Appointments are not herein otherwise provided for, and which shall be established by Law: but the Congress may by Law vest the Appointment of such inferior

Officers, as they think proper, in the President alone, in the Courts of Law, or in the Heads of Departments.

There are two primary appointment methods contemplated by this clause. First, the president may nominate by and with the advice and consent of the Senate several named positions and all other principal officers of the United States. This appointment process is referred to as presidential appointed and Senate confirmed (PAS). The second method permits Congress to establish "inferior Officers" that can be appointed by the default PAS process; by the president alone (PA); by federal courts; or by department and agency heads (Schedule C and noncareer SES [Senior Executive Service]).

Officers of the United States are subject to the Appointments Clause processes. However, not all government workers are officers. The practice has been that non-officers and employees may secure their positions using other methods than PAS, PA, or appointment by the federal courts or department and agency heads. Many individuals enter government service after passing a civil service exam. In 1823, Chief Justice John Marshall, sitting as a circuit court judge, presented one of the first statements on the distinction between officers and employees: "Although an office is an employment, it does not follow that every employment is an office. A man may certainly be employed under a contract, express or implied, to perform a service without becoming an officer."[28] More recently the Supreme Court has stated that the term *officers* does not encompass everyone employed by the federal government. Instead, the Court reasoned, "employees are lesser functionaries subordinate to officers of the United States."[29]

In 1867, the Supreme Court attempted to clarify the differences between an officer and an employee by arguing that the former "embraces the ideas of tenure, duration, emolument, and duties."[30] As in many of its ensuing opinions, the Court definition of an officer is vague. For example, employees and officers each receive some sort of emolument as compensation for service. The fact that an emolument is provided does not create a clear distinction. Later, in *United States v. Germaine* (1878), the Court defined duties by noting that they should be "permanent, not occasional or temporary."[31] Many employees have permanent, not temporary, positions. Federal service can last twenty or thirty years or longer, and the duties of an employment can remain regardless of the individual officeholder. In the end the *Germaine* definition lacks clarity. Not until 1976 in *Buckley v. Valeo* did the Supreme Court provide substantial guidance. In that case, the Court explained that an officer is "any appointee exercising significant authority pursuant to the laws of the United States" and as a result "must, therefore, be appointed in the manner prescribed by" the Appointments Clause.[32] The Court did not provide a detailed assessment of what constituted significant authority.

The Office of Legal Counsel (OLC) within the Department of Justice has tried to provide its own definition. One effort in 1996 raised more questions than it answered and required OLC to prepare a second analysis a decade later. In the initial effort, OLC said that an "officer's duties are permanent, continuing, and based upon responsibilities created through a chain of command rather than by contract."[33] Next, OLC pointed to the need to assess "the extent of the authority" of a government worker's responsibilities.[34] Citing *Buckley* it noted that an officer, unlike an employee, would exercise "significant authority," which meant some level of "independent discretion."[35] The OLC explained that "an employee may not exercise independent discretion [but that] does not, of course, mean that his or her duties may not encompass responsibilities requiring the exercise of judgment and discretion under the ultimate control and supervision of an officer."[36] Finally, it reasoned that an officer must be appointed to a position of employment within the federal government. The OLC surmised that the "delegation to private persons or non-federal government officials of federal-law authority . . . can raise genuine questions under other constitutional doctrines, such as the non-delegation doctrine and the general separation of powers principle," but that does not mean the Appointments Clause is implicated.[37] All three features needed to be met for a position to be considered an officer.[38]

The OLC's definition of an officer is inadequate and confusing. The focus on the permanency or continuing nature of the position misses a key point. Federal employees can have long careers that often outlast those of presidents or department and agency heads. The creating of "responsibilities" through a contract does not seem to add much, either. Since employees can be hired, and protected, by the civil service system, the contract language is not comprehensive enough. The OLC does not sufficiently define "significant authority." Instead, it attempts to provide some clarity by noting that employees may not use their own discretion, but their duties could require "judgment and discretion" as long as there is a supervising officer. The distinction makes no sense. Regardless of whether a person is an employee or an officer, unless he is the president (and even then the people ultimately control him as well), everyone is subject to the command of a higher official. Even cabinet heads report to the president. In the end the distinction does not make a difference. The OLC does, however, correctly note that the delegation of federal authority to nongovernment officials or private citizens raises non–Appointment Clause concerns, which we address later in this chapter.

In 2007, the OLC revisited its analysis of the Appointments Clause and noted that in order to be considered an officer there needs to be a delegation of sovereign authority and the position must be "continuing."[39] It explained that the sovereign authority language is no different in meaning from the Supreme Court's use of "significant authority" in *Buckley*.[40] The OLC, however, provided more detail than it had in 1996 by stating that sovereign/significant authority means "power lawfully conferred by the Government to bind third parties, or the Government itself, for the public benefit." In addition, OLC said it "primarily involves the authority to administer, execute, or interpret the law," which includes the ability "to arrest criminals, impose penalties, enter judgments, and seize persons or property."[41] As for the "continuing" requirement: First, the office must not be "limited by time or by being of such a nature that it will terminate 'by the very fact of performance.'" Second, the office could be temporary so long as: (1) its functions continued regardless of the officeholder; (2) it is not "transient" and more likely to be seen as a "seat of power"; and (3) it does not exercise "incidental" duties "to the regular operations of government." The OLC admitted that the transient and incidental aspects of the "continuing" definition, although referenced in the early case law, "escape precise definition."[42]

The OLC made what may be the first attempt to provide a substantial definition of significant/sovereign authority. We agree that actions that bind third parties or the federal government itself are functions of sovereign/significant authority. The OLC detailed some of the specific responsibilities that such authority entails, including the ability to administer, execute, and interpret the law. Yet the OLC's definition breaks down over the "continuing" characteristic. It defies logic that a position can be temporary but still "continuing." The "incidental" feature also is bewildering as it has nothing to do with whether an office is continuing. This part of the OLC's definition does not clarify the differences between officers and employees.[43]

The Constitution also does not define the responsibilities or duties of principal and inferior officers. In 1988, the Supreme Court tried to draw a line between principal and inferior officers in *Morrison v. Olson*. The Court cited four factors that would help to determine if an officer is inferior. Those factors were that the officer is subject to removal by a higher-level executive branch official other than the president, and that the scope of the office is limited in duty, jurisdiction, and tenure.[44] What exactly are limited duties, jurisdiction, and tenure? The tenure component even parallels the "continuing" requirement that is supposed to distinguish officers from employees. The Court's definition remained imprecise. One legal scholar commented that "the Court declined to give much content to these four factors" and "discussed neither the amount of supervision required nor the limits on duties, jurisdiction, or tenure necessary to qualify as an inferior officer appointable without the advice and consent of the Senate."[45] Indeed, the Court even acknowledged that it would "not attempt here to decide exactly where the line falls between the two types of officers."[46]

Nearly a decade later the Supreme Court tried again. In *Edmond v. United States* (1997), the Court said that "*Morrison* did not purport to set forth a definitive test for whether an office is 'inferior' under the Appointments Clause."[47] For that reason it crafted another standard: "the term 'inferior officer' connotes a relationship with some higher ranking officer or officers below the President: Whether one is an 'inferior officer' depends on whether he has a superior. . . . We think it evident that 'inferior officers' are officers whose work is directed and supervised at some level by others who were appointed by Presidential nomination with the advice and consent of the Senate."[48]

The Court's new focus places less emphasis on the duties, jurisdiction, or even tenure of an office and more on whether there is a supervisor between an office-holder and the president. If the position does have a supervisor then, according to the Court, most likely it is an inferior officer. The Supreme Court tried to further clarify the differences between principal and inferior officers;[49] however, as in *Morrison,* much of its definition lacked substantive details. There are lingering issues concerning the Appointments Clause that the Court has left open. First, is the "significant authority" requirement provided in *Buckley* still good law? If so then does it remain a key element in defining a principal officer? Second, to what extent would direction and supervision need to be given to make an officer inferior? Finally, how long does an office have to remain in existence to be of suitable tenure for its occupant to actually be considered an officer?

The Supreme Court's current standard is difficult to follow. The focus on a supervisor allows for the appointment of individuals—by the president alone, or the courts and heads of departments and agencies—who exercise any type of authority, as long as they are supervised by a PAS officer or the president.[50] There is a fundamental conflict with the basic principles of democratic controls by maintaining an appointment system that does not attempt to ensure certain officeholders remain answerable to more than just the president or their immediate supervisors.

A consequence of the Supreme Court's analysis is that Congress could very well be left out of the appointment process for positions exercising vital and significant government functions. That circumvents the intended governing checks and balances structure. Congress has traditionally required Senate confirmation for all department and agency heads. Presidential advisers have typically been appointed by the president alone but their functions were considered to be only advisory. In establishing the Executive Office of the President (EOP), even President Franklin D. Roosevelt confirmed this view by noting that his assistants would "have no authority" and they could not interpose themselves between him and the heads of departments and agencies.[51] Congress has supported this understanding since not only did it accept the creation of the EOP but it did not provide non-PAS presidential personnel with the authority to issue orders or regulations or to otherwise direct policy areas.[52] The current federal law still reflects this view on presidential personnel.[53] Longstanding practice has shown that when Congress delegates important functions to executive branch officials it also incorporates necessary checks, which include Senate confirmation, reporting requirements, and other controls.

An appointment process that is faithful to the Constitution should require Senate confirmation of all officers who have the final decision-making authority to control budgetary programs, administer/coordinate a policy area, promulgate rules, regulations, or any orders that bind either government officials and/or the private sector. Moreover any executive branch official who exercises duties traditionally carried out by ambassadors or consuls would also need to receive Senate confirmation. As previously mentioned, our definition would not include officers who merely advise or assist in the formation of policy and other decisions of their departments and agencies. They would presumably have no authority to issue orders or rules that bind others, and therefore their positions would not require Senate confirmation.

Non-Delegation Doctrine

Although not the central element to our definition of czars, presidents can come into conflict with the non-delegation doctrine as well. This part of our analysis is a delicate matter as many academics have concluded that the non-delegation doctrine is an inoperative concept for purposes of constitutional analysis. Yet, the principle remains germane today and does impact the exercise of delegated functions carried out by presidents and various executive branch officials.

Article I, section 2 of the Constitution provides the textual basis for this doctrine: "All legislative powers herein granted shall be vested in a Congress of the United States."[54] The underlying principle from that clause is that no one branch of government should have absolute power. In a system of government that separates powers between the branches any unnecessary concentration could be potentially dangerous, which is why British political philosopher John Locke aptly warned that the "legislative neither must nor can transfer the power of making laws to anybody else, or place it anywhere but where the people have."[55] Locke's concern over the delegation of legislative power derived from his belief in government accountability. In a republican government, the people hold elected officials responsible for their actions through frequent elections. If Congress delegates its legislative power to nonelected and nonconfirmed officials, the link between citizens and leaders is undermined.

Nonetheless, over time Congress has found it necessary to entrust some discretionary authority in officials within departments, agencies, and commissions. The complexity of modern life aided in the growth of the delegation movement, especially during and after the New Deal. However, despite the practical need to delegate some authority, there are limits. In 1928, the Supreme Court attempted to provide guidance to this matter in *Hampton v. United States*—a case dealing with custom duties on imported goods—by arguing that "if Congress shall lay down by legislative act an intelligible principle to which the person or body authorized to fix such rates is directed to conform, such legislative action is not a forbidden delegation of legislative power."[56] In short, the Court left it to Congress to provide guidance to executive officials when delegating its powers.

Since *Hampton*, the Supreme Court has continually applied the intelligible principle doctrine when considering the issue of delegation of legislative authority. In the 1935 decisions of *Panama Refining Company v. Ryan* and *A.L.A. Schechter Poultry Corporation v. United States*, the Supreme Court held that Congress had unconstitutionally delegated its legislative functions when it passed the National Industrial Recovery Act (NIRA).[57] Chief Justice Charles Evans Hughes in *Panama Refining* acknowledged that the Constitution provides Congress leeway to deal with modern problems:

> Undoubtedly legislation must often be adapted to complex conditions involving a host of details with which the national legislature cannot deal directly. The Constitution has never been regarded as denying to the Congress the necessary resources of flexibility and practicality, which will enable it to perform its function in laying down policies and establishing standards, while leaving to selected instrumentalities the making of subordinate rules within prescribed limits and the determination of facts to which the policy as declared by the legislature is to apply. Without capacity to give authorizations of that sort we should have the anomaly of a legislative power which in many circumstances calling for its exertion would be but a futility.[58]

However, Hughes cautioned that "the constant recognition of the necessity and validity of such provisions, and the wide range of administrative authority which has been developed by means of them, cannot be allowed to obscure the limitations of the authority to delegate, if our constitutional system is to be maintained."[59] Congress had failed to set limits and thus, Hughes determined that NIRA violated the non-delegation doctrine as it did not provide any standards to guide executive action.

Similarly in *Schechter* the Supreme Court stated that it had "repeatedly recognized the necessity of adapting legislation to complex conditions involving a host of details with which the national legislature cannot deal directly."[60] Again the Court determined that NIRA unconstitutionally delegated legislative power since it supplied "no standards" nor undertook "to prescribe rules of conduct to be applied to particular states of fact."[61] Concurring, Justice Benjamin Cardozo confirmed that the authority Congress delegated had been "unconfined and vagrant" as it established "a roving commission to inquire into evils and upon discovery correct them."[62]

Since 1935 the Supreme Court has not used the non-delegation doctrine to strike down a federal law, but this does not mean it is a dead principle. In 1980, the Court expressed concerns about delegation when it declared that the Occupational Safety and Health Administration (OSHA) could not promulgate a business regulation under the Occupational Safety and Health Act.[63] In a concurring opinion, Justice William Rehnquist argued that the non-delegation doctrine needs to be given teeth primarily because it would force Congress, "the branch of our Government most responsive to the popular will," to make important policy decisions.[64] "It is the hard choices," he explained, "and not the filling in of the blanks, which must be made by the elected representatives of the people." Rehnquist believed that "fundamental policy decisions underlying important legislation" are to be made by "Congress and the President insofar as he exercises his constitutional role in the legislative process."[65]

In 2001 the Supreme Court assessed the constitutionality of the Environmental Protection Agency's (EPA) rules on air-quality standards for ozone that were based on the Clean Air Act (CAA).[66] Speaking for the Court, Justice Antonin Scalia noted that the non-delegation doctrine requires Congress to "lay down by legislative act an intelligible principle to which the person or body authorized to [act] is directed to conform."[67] However, Scalia refused to strike down the EPA regulation and determined that the CAA did contain an "intelligible principle" for setting air-quality standards.[68]

The reluctance of the Supreme Court in that case and in recent years to use the non-delegation doctrine to strike down federal laws should not be taken as a sign that this principle has no merit. Even if it is wise to transfer discretionary authority to independent agencies and commissions, Congress should not so freely give away power to executive branch agents or czars who are not elected and have not been vetted through the Senate's confirmation process. Members of Congress should take seriously their responsibility to provide more exacting standards when empowering executive branch officials. Ultimately the constitutionality of delegation should rest with lawmakers, as the Supreme Court has "almost never felt qualified to second-guess Congress regarding the permissible degree of policy judgment that can be left to those executing or applying the law."[69]

Congress has not always followed the practice of including clear or even general guidance when it delegates authority. That certainly was the case when it granted economic powers to President Richard M. Nixon in the early 1970s.[70] Through two executive orders Nixon created a number of czar positions that included the heads of the Cost of Living Council, Pay Board, and Price Commission to exercise those powers.[71] Aware of its mistake Congress quickly amended the economic powers delegated to Nixon, but it still fell short of clarifying the extent of the president's authority.[72]

As delegation relates to czars the central issue is not often about whether an "intelligible principle" has been provided in law. Instead, it largely focuses on the re-delegation of authority that a president grants to executive branch officials. The framework for understanding and adhering to this aspect of the non-delegation doctrine is the Subdelegation Act, which, as stated previously, authorizes a president to delegate his statutory authority only to Senate-confirmed officers. As explained in more detail in chapter 5, a violation of this statute arose after Congress had reorganized and expanded the powers of the Bureau of the Budget. In that case Nixon delegated to Director George P. Shultz of the renamed and retailored Office of Management and Budget (OMB) authority that was in violation of the Subdelegation Act.[73] Although other issues arose directly impacting the OMB (including the improper impounding of appropriated funds), we consider Shultz to have been a czar as he held a non-Senate-confirmed position when Nixon delegated statutory authority to him. Congress quickly acted to require Senate confirmation of the OMB director and several other agency officials primarily out of concern for the abuse of power experienced during the impoundment crisis.

Finally, the risks of a loss of accountability and oversight are much greater when a president delegates authority to non-Senate-confirmed officials, especially ones placed within the White House Office or EOP. To take one example, we revisit Nixon's decision to delegate his economic powers to various officials including the Cost of Living Council executive director Donald Rumsfeld, who also served as counselor to the president. As a dual appointee Rumsfeld used his status as a White House adviser to refuse to appear before Congress.[74] On at least two occasions Rumsfeld argued that he did not have to testify before a congressional committee in his role as executive director because of his "confidential relationship" with Nixon.[75] Other examples abound of White House aides refusing to testify despite possessing more than just advisory powers.[76]

Currently the lack of even a clear delegation of authority is a troubling occurrence with czars. We have already noted that Obama's pay/claims czar Feinberg has no express statutory authority to control over a billion dollars of funds. In fact, in Feinberg's position as claims czar there is no clear evidence that his position has any grounding in law. Even if the claims czar post had been statutorily authorized, neither it nor the pay czar position required Senate approval. Another example is Obama's former health czar, Nancy-Ann DeParle, who was charged with integrating "the President's policy agenda concerning health reform across the Federal Government . . . ; work[ing] with State, local, and community policymakers and public officials to expand coverage . . . ; [and] develop[ing] and implement[ing] strategic initiatives under the President's agenda to strengthen the public agencies."[77] Not only were DeParle's duties stated in a broad manner, but her position also placed her in a role very much like that of the Health and Human Services (HHS) Secretary, who by statute is authorized to carry out healthcare functions and is accountable to Congress. There is no reason that a president should be permitted to create positions in the White House that mimic the role and responsibilities of cabinet officers, who have been given the actual statutory authority to implement and execute policy. In no way should Congress allow non-elected and nonconfirmed officials who have little if any congressional oversight to exist through executive whim.

Turning to the issue of spending, the delegation of Congress's appropriations power to non-Senate-confirmed officials is especially troubling. No one—particularly a person in a position that does not require routine testimony before Congress and the issuing of periodic reports—should have complete discretion over public funds. Again the pay/claims czar is only the most prominent example. In September 2009, Obama appointed Ron Bloom as the car czar, taking over for Steven Rattner, who left the administration when New York Attorney General Andrew Cuomo's investigation into a state pension fund scandal began to heat up (see chapter 7 for more details).[78] As Obama's second car czar Bloom—a non-Senate-confirmed official—had the primary role in negotiating a deal to provide government loans to General Motors and Chrysler. After negotiations fell apart between Chrysler and Fiat, Bloom made a call to Fiat CEO Sergio Marchionne, at which time the lingering issues were resolved.[79] As a sign of the power and influence Bloom held in the Obama administration, *Time* magazine named him one of the world's 100 most influential people for 2010.[80] Obama also made Adolfo Carrion the urban affairs czar "to ensure that Federal Government dollars targeted to urban areas are effectively spent on the highest impact programs."[81] Senator John Cornyn (R-TX) correctly protested that "it is inappropriate for them to steer the distribution of taxpayer funds without congressional oversight."[82] Indeed, it is constitutionally and legally troublesome for any individual, especially one who is not Senate confirmed, to control federal appropriations without congressional authorization.

Legislative Establishment of Office

The unilateral creation and modification of offices without legislative approval is a device employed by modern presidents to shape public policy. When combined with the absence of Senate confirmation, such offices have the potential to do great damage to a governing system built on democratic controls. To be sure, under the British governing system, the king had the ability to create offices and appoint his special favorites to them.[83] As Alexander Hamilton explained, the "king of Great Britain is emphatically and truly styled the fountain of honor. He not only appoints to all offices, but can create offices."[84] Such power was based on the prerogative theory of chief executives, which did not limit the British monarch's ability to create new offices without Parliament.[85] The framers of the Constitution rejected that model and settled on a system that protects the power of the legislative branch.[86] Article II of the Constitution provides the president with the ability to make appointments subject to Senate confirmation, of ambassadors, ministers, consuls, judges, and other officers whose offices have been "established by law" (full text quoted above).[87] In addressing the differences between the British monarch and the president, even a strong presidential supporter such as Hamilton noted that there "is evidently a great inferiority in the power of the President, in [creating offices], to that of the British king."[88]

Subsequent interpretations of legislative authority confirmed the framers' goal of ensuring that Congress established government structures. Speaking during the First Congress, James Madison declared that the "legislature creates the office, defines the powers, limits its duration, and annexes a compensation."[89] In 1819, Chief Justice John Marshall explained in *McCulloch v. Maryland* that Congress has the ability through the Necessary and Proper Clause to create government structures which "shall be necessary and proper for carrying into Execution" its express powers.[90] Four years later Marshall, sitting as a circuit court judge, again supported Congress's ability to create offices but this time based its authority on the Appointments Clause. As he explained, the most proper interpretation of that clause, which "accords best with the general spirit of the constitution," places the creation of office with Congress. Marshall said clear textual direction is provided by the second section of Article II, section 2, which "directs that all offices of the United States shall be established by law." That language can be interpreted to mean only that Congress, not the president, can create offices. Finally, he noted that "the practice of the government has been for the legislature" to organize a method for executing policy by authorizing the president "to employ such persons as he might think proper, for the performance of particular services."[91]

On at least three occasions, U.S. attorneys general have supported Marshall's judgment. In 1849, Attorney General Reverdy Johnson issued an opinion instructing Interior Secretary Thomas Ewing Sr. that he did not have the authority to appoint a building superintendent because Congress acted to abolish the office. Johnson stated that President Zachary Taylor concurred in his assessment.[92] Twelve years later, Attorney General Edward Bates said that the president has no authority to create a bureau in the War Department without Congress's approval. The president and Congress "may exercise the powers conferred by the Constitution in the appropriate sphere," Bates reasoned, "but neither may assume the powers which belong to the other."[93] Referencing Chief Justice Marshall's own assessment, Attorney General Augustus Hill Garland said in an 1885 opinion that "an officer of the United States presupposes an office duly created by law; and the offices to which the President is authorized under the Constitution to appoint are only those established or recognized by the Constitution or by act of Congress." He even declared that since "the president cannot create an office, I am of opinion he cannot appoint honorary commissioners" as well.[94]

Even in the otherwise pro-presidential-power decision of *Myers v. United States,* Chief Justice William Howard Taft, a former president himself, stated: "To Congress under its legislative power is given the establishment of offices, the determination of their functions and jurisdiction, the prescribing of reasonable and relevant qualifications and rules of eligibility of appointees, and the fixing of the term for which they are to be appointed, and their compensation—all except as otherwise provided by the Constitution."[95] Taft's words were reinforced by constitutional scholar Edward S. Corwin, who reasoned that the "Constitution by the 'necessary and proper' clause assigns the power to *create offices* to Congress." Any appointment, he argued, would therefore have to be "to an *existing* office, one that owes its existence to an act of Congress."[96]

More recently, President Ronald Reagan's Office of Legal Counsel (OLC) within the Department of Justice issued a legal memorandum addressing the question of whether a president could create new executive branch structures independent of Congress. The OLC concluded that "the President lacks constitutional and statutory authority to do so." It said that the text of the Appointments Clause and "the historic practice of the Executive and Legislative Branches suggests strongly that offices of the United States must be created by Congress."[97] The traditional division of responsibilities, the OLC argued, has been for Congress to provide for the establishment of executive branch structure by statute and presidents or department and agency heads to select individuals to fill various positions.[98] The OLC highlighted that presidents have responded to such governing realities by continually seeking "reorganization legislation in order to restructure or consolidate agencies within the Executive Branch." Finally, the OLC touched on the statutory language that provides a president "shall designate" agency or department officers to administer a new program. It argued that unless Congress provides additional authority, a president cannot create new offices in such cases. "On its face," the OLC concluded, the "shall designate" language contemplates that the assistance will come from an existing department or agency.[99]

A claim could be made that Congress in appropriating funds for the salaries and resources of new government structures has provided its consent to presidents to have created these structures on their own. That is a constitutionally and legally dubious argument. Today presidents have available to them discretionary accounts that add up to millions of dollars. Presidents have often used such funds to create new offices without seeking the approval of Congress. The end around of the legislative appropriations process is a direct assault on the duties and responsibilities of lawmakers.[100] The House of Representatives and the Senate have established a two-step process for the creation and funding of new executive branch structures. Each chamber can authorize the establishment of an agency or program that will be signed into law by the president. For example, Congress set up the Department of Homeland Security detailing its leadership personnel and functions along with its subunits and agencies in the Homeland Security Act of 2002.[101] The funding for the new department, however, came later through an independent appropriations law.

The rules of the House and Senate specifically require the two-step authorization-appropriations process with clear distinctions between each part.[102] During the U.S. war in Vietnam, Lyndon B. Johnson's administration argued that Congress had authorized the military conflict by appropriating funds. In 1970, various academic experts challenged that theory in *Beck v. Laird*, a U.S. District Court case in the Eastern District of New York, by reasoning that policy cannot be set through the legislative appropriations process.[103] The court concluded, however, that if Congress funded the war then it had been legislatively authorized. Many federal judges backed away from the view that appropriations can mean legislative endorsement of war policy.[104] Later, through section 8 of the War Powers Resolution, Congress expressly stated that appropriations do not authorize a war unless there is language in a spending bill that clearly provides legislative approval for a president's military actions.[105] The assumption that Congress has somehow authorized unilateral executive action through appropriations is false.

Certainly presidents can seek advice, but once they establish a new government structure independent of Congress, they are in violation of the Constitution. We are not ready, however, to place the czar moniker on such presidentially created positions unless they also exercise significant authority without Senate confirmation or have powers improperly delegated to them. Primarily we are hesitant to do this because an exclusion of offices set up solely by presidents would greatly expand the number of czars to include positions with only advisory powers. That is why we do not consider most of the chairs or members of presidential commissions (see chapter 2) to be czars.

Presidents who act independently of Congress to unilaterally establish government structure are assuming a potentially dangerous power. The checks built into the Constitution that limit one branch from gaining complete control over governing mechanisms are lost if such actions are allowed to continue. Potentially the act of creating offices that exercise significant authority would entail appointment without the consent of the Senate. That is an assumption of power not contemplated by the framers nor can it be reasonably inferred by the express or implied authority granted to presidents by the Constitution. In the end, the unilateral act of creating offices is an unconstitutional exercise of inherent power that not only encroaches on legislative responsibilities but seeks to break the safeguards created to promote accountability in government.

The importance of a statutory grounding of government structure and positions should not be dismissed. A regulatory agency created by statute is permanent and a continuing body. Czars, on the other hand, are usually temporary creations, existing for perhaps a few years or months. As a result, the former is better equipped to develop consistent principles that can be adopted as policy and rules that regulated industries and individuals can understand. That is nearly impossible in the case of presidentially created czars. Moreover, laws embody the collective wisdom of representatives, and presidents, in a battle of ideas concerning which policies the nation should adopt. Of course such debates never die and consistently evolve, but they should not be short-circuited by way of presidential decree.

POTENTIAL IMPLICATIONS OF EXECUTIVE BRANCH CZARS

The fact is that many of the executive branch czars exert substantial policy authority and yet reside outside the normal constraints of a governing system built on the checks and balances principle. It violates constitutional principles that some temporarily appointed czars may be empowered to manage public policy that is supposed to be handled by Senate-approved department or agency heads who are accountable to Congress and the laws it creates. Even well-intentioned czars can do much damage to that legal and constitutional structure. Confirmed department or agency officials have a duty to the law. Temporary czars do not have that same commitment. Indeed, their commitment often may not be to statutory programs but rather to the campaign promises of the president and his aides. In a February 23, 2009, letter to President Barack Obama, Senator Robert C. Byrd (D-WV) raised the key point:

> The rapid and easy accumulation of power by White House staff can threaten the Constitutional system of checks and balances. At the worst, White House staff have taken direction and control of programmatic areas that are the statutory responsibility of Senate-confirmed officials. They have even limited access to the president by his own cabinet members. As presidential assistants and advisers, these White House staffers are not accountable for their actions to the Congress, to cabinet officials, and to virtually anyone but the president.[106]

CZARS AND THE ABUSE OF EXECUTIVE PRIVILEGE

It hardly makes for a system of openness and accountability when there are such officials lurking in a White House, unconfirmed, not subject to testimony, and apparently, in some cases, not even knowable. Czars can raise significant executive privilege concerns when, because of their proximity to the president, they seek to wall themselves off from public and congressional scrutiny. In particular, an individual who serves in a dual appointment as an official within a department or agency and also as a White House aide raises checks and balances concerns. Of course any executive branch official can try to avoid legislative oversight; however, a dual appointee could potentially invoke a form of executive privilege that is much more difficult for Congress to overcome and have significant implications for ensuring accountability in all parts of government. The Supreme Court case of *U.S. v. Nixon*, several post-Watergate circuit court cases, and interchanges between the executive and legislative branches over the years have established the broad contours of executive privilege.

Specifically, the two primary legal claims of privilege are based on presidential communications and the deliberative process. The presidential communications privilege is one of the strongest areas to make an executive privilege claim but is limited by fundamental threshold concerns. It is based on the constitutional separation of powers principle and the president's unique position in the governing system. The privilege claim applies to a president's decision making when carrying out a "quintessential and non-delegable Presidential power" such as the nomination or pardon authority.[107] A privilege claim will cover all documents, whether pre-decisional or post-decisional, but is not an absolute barrier. The claim only protects the communications of those who are personally advising, or preparing to advise, the president (i.e., White House staff). Congress may overcome this privilege with a showing of corruption or need or by providing evidence that the information sought cannot be found elsewhere. The executive branch has traditionally, but not always, yielded to the legislative branch when Congress is carrying out its legislative and oversight functions.

The deliberative process privilege, as defined by the D.C. Court of Appeals, has a much lower threshold to overcome, partially because it is based on common law.[108] All executive branch officials are protected generally; however, only pre-decisional documents are covered and not those that state a policy decision or only contain factual information. In addition, like the presidential communications privilege, a showing of corruption or other wrongdoing will wipe away any protection that results from a deliberative process claim.

Although Congress should use all of its latent constitutional powers to force stonewalling executive branch officials to testify before its committees, recent cases—particularly the claims of absolute immunity by Harriet Miers and Joshua Bolten during George W. Bush's presidency—have shown that the federal courts' interpretation of executive privilege plays a significant role in such interbranch disputes.[109] If an official who serves in the White House makes a claim of executive privilege then it is one that perhaps has a higher threshold to overcome. Presumably White House aides are only advising the president, not issuing orders or otherwise directing others. Individuals pulling double duty as both a White House staffer and a department or agency official create not only the problem of providing a clear line of authority for officeholders in carrying out their tasks, but also the more troubling accountability concern of claims to the presidential communications privilege.

Most statutory top-level officers within a department or agency require Senate confirmation, and the performance of their duties is subject to clear direction and control by Congress. But White House advisers are appointed directly by the president and are usually afforded greater executive privilege protections than other executive branch officials. The risk in dual appointment arrangements is that a president might try to claim presidential communications privilege to protect the duties and responsibilities the appointees carry out as department or agency officials. Such a concern is not imaginary. As we explain in chapter 5, President Richard M. Nixon implemented a plan to create super-secretaries who would hold dual roles as department heads and White House advisers. At least two senators—Jacob Javits (R-NY) and Charles H. Percy (R-IL)—raised concerns over the potential for individuals serving as cabinet officers and White House counselors to stonewall Congress by asserting executive privilege against congressional committee requests to testify despite having already been confirmed by the Senate. Such concerns were realized when Nixon's White House aide in charge of economic affairs, Kenneth Rush, who also served as deputy secretary of state, refused to even appear before a congressional committee citing separation of powers concerns that prevent testimony of a president's direct staff. Incredibly, while making the executive privilege claim, Rush answered economic questions on several television programs and even spoke at the National Association of Manufacturers.

We are mindful of the need to preserve a degree of separation between the branches, especially when a congressional investigation touches a president's inner circle of advisers. However, any perceived or actual right to "autonomy" within the White House depends on the actions of the president and his advisers.[110] Since the creation of the modern White House staff system in 1939, Louis Fisher and Harold C. Relyea argue that presidential advisers "have become highly conspicuous, multiple in number, possessed of great power, and virtually unaccountable to anyone but the Chief Executive for their actions."[111] What White House aides do should be of great importance to Congress.[112] As originally envisioned, they were intended to function as mere advisers to the president and not supervisors of statutory programs or administrators of policy. When White House aides, dual appointees or otherwise, not only begin to compete with but also take over the responsibilities of department and agency heads, then greater legislative scrutiny and control is required.[113] At such a point, however, the issue is not one of whether a president is willing to allow his aides to testify (i.e., not making an executive privilege claim), but of how Congress needs to create institutional mechanisms that prevent program responsibilities and policy controls from being exercised within the White House or provide greater accountability and legislative oversight requirements.

SUMMARY: THE NECESSITY OF LEGISLATIVE OVERSIGHT AND ACCOUNTABILITY

Given the lack of confirmation and oversight checks, czars pose a serious problem for the principles embodied in democratic controls. Unlike established permanent positions that carry over from one administration to another, such as the director of the Office of Management and Budget, czars usually hold temporary posts, but nonetheless ones that sometimes have exercised even more policymaking power than many cabinet secretaries and agency heads. And some czar positions, though initially slated to be temporary, have carried over from one administration to another over a period of many years.

Presidents find the use of czars helpful in that Congress can be bypassed and policy can be overseen and managed independent of legislative oversight. Often the duties of czars will overlap, and sometimes conflict with, statutory programs of departments and agencies. The absence of a PAS appointment process for such positions is especially troubling. Presumably, a shared appointment power provides another check against presidents appointing high-end officials who lack proper qualifications or basic credibility to exercise vast governing powers.

Take the example of Obama's former "green jobs czar" Van Jones, who had to resign under criticism for overheated comments he had made about Republicans and for reports that he had advocated a review of whether former president George W. Bush had advance knowledge of the 9/11 attacks and had allowed them to happen.[114] There is no guarantee that the Senate confirmation process will stop unqualified persons or conspiracy theorists from achieving high-ranking office, but it is certainly much more likely that the process will expose such persons. The Obama green jobs czar's past comments were easily available, but he achieved his post without the benefit of Senate review. With a confirmation hearing and the customary investigative measures, the administration would possibly have avoided public embarrassment and the resignation of its official. Especially troubling is that Jones had the authority to make decisions about the distribution of billions of dollars on green initiatives, all outside the immediate overview of Congress.[115]

The vast duties given to the Obama White House pay/claims czar are also troubling. Assigning the responsibility of distributing large sums of private money from the BP spill victims' fund effectively allows the president to engage in significant expenditures without congressional authorization or oversight. All can understand the necessity of BP compensating the victims, but that should happen either through voluntary direct payment by the company itself or through litigation. The pay/claims czar is exercising policy and regulatory authority without being required to appear before Congress or account for expenditure decisions. That constitutes nothing less than an end run around the constitutional system and should never happen, no more than, for example, Exxon Corporation deciding to contribute billions of dollars to the government to set up a private nonappropriated fund to be administered by the president and a designated administrator who is not subject to Senate advice and consent, and then having the president and the corporation negotiate over how to spend the money.[116] Of course, the very idea is patently absurd, but not significantly different from what is taking place among the president, the pay/claims czar, and BP.

Regarding the pay/claims czar's authority as it relates to the TARP legislation, the *Wall Street Journal* included the following telling description in its report: "Mr. Feinberg will report to Treasury Secretary Timothy Geithner, but he is expected to have wide discretion on how the rules should be interpreted. Firms likely won't be able to appeal decisions that Mr. Feinberg makes to Mr. Geithner, according to people familiar with the matter."[117] What was reported in such an ordinary fashion is, on closer look, rather stunning. First, the TARP law prohibits injunctions or other forms of equitable relief to be issued against the pay czar for regulations he makes under the executive compensation section. Second, apart from legal actions that charge the pay czar with making final decisions that are "arbitrary, capricious, an abuse of discretion, or not in accordance with the law," no suit can be brought by a person or company that sells assets to TARP.[118] Thus, with such broad-scoped and largely unchallenged power, judicial authority is greatly diminished. We cover the various constitutional and legal issues with the Obama era czars in chapter 7.

It is a long-recognized principle that presidents cannot fulfill their many varied duties without significant assistance from staff. The Brownlow Committee famously expressed the view in 1937 that "the president needs help."[119] But as the White House Office and staff grew tremendously along with the increased role of the federal government, by 1975 scholar Thomas Cronin cleverly posited that "the president needs help merely to manage his help."[120] The claimed utility of the czar position is that it somewhat fulfills the need that the president has to manage his help and agenda. Nonetheless, that an office may have utility for our system does not make it constitutional. There is no constitutional foundation for having a position of czar in our government, as the reality is that many of these unelected and unconfirmed officers have been yielded substantial policymaking authority.

The primary problem with this or any study that attempts to analyze White House structure and presidential aides is the historical and continuing lack of accountability and congressional oversight. To a large degree, it is sometimes difficult to pinpoint when an adviser to the president crosses the magical threshold and becomes a supervisor of a program or administrator of a policy area. The statutory reporting provisions established by the White House Authorization Act of 1978 (see the Jimmy Carter section in chapter 5 for more details) do not even require the full accounting of presidential staffing numbers let alone the names, titles, general job descriptions, and salaries of everyone who works within the White House. We acknowledge up front this problem when researching and analyzing czars within the White House and understand that our study may not necessarily include every presidential—or even executive branch—official who should otherwise be classified as a czar.

What follows is an overview of the history of executive branch czars in the United States. The chapters on the various presidencies describe and analyze a variety of czar positions, as well as those mistakenly defined as czars in media coverage, and detail the differences. Tables provided in the appendix identify, by president, all of the media-labeled and actual czars and their periods of service, as well as their bases of authority.[121] Throughout that presentation it becomes clear that although the czar controversy has been especially heated in the Obama era, the presidential use of czars in the United States actually has a long history. We turn now to the origins and the development of executive branch czars.

2. The Origins and Growth of Executive Branch Czars

We begin our analysis of czars by tracing their origin and development along with identifying key positions in various presidential administrations that are in violation of the Constitution. This overview includes detailing a varied spectrum of government positions, which at times results in our discussion and analysis of media-labeled czars. However, we have made it a point to clearly explain which positions we consider to be czars and the ones that are not, independent of how media reviews might use the label. Although we provide a president-by-president account of czars for much of this book, here we first offer stand-alone accounts of presidential commissions and special envoys—two types of executive branch structure that have a long-lasting history, which are more properly covered uniformly.

The detailed coverage of commissions and envoys that follows is necessary to understand the development and growth of czars over time. Czars did not arise as an isolated phenomenon but are a part of a larger overall pattern in the evolution of presidential use of officers who operate outside the normal system of democratic controls. Without these other nonaccountable offices, czars stand out as a clear constitutional aberration. But with them, czars became accepted by many as almost an ordinary extension of a system that upholds the power of presidents to appoint various nonconfirmed officers to carry out policy-oriented duties. We conclude that commissioners actually do not meet the czar criteria; nonetheless, it is not possible to fully understand the czar phenomenon without examining the presidential use of commissioners as well as special envoys.

Commission heads and special envoys are sometimes labeled czars, and some envoys have exercised government functions better left to executive officials who are presidentially nominated and Senate confirmed. The origins of each of these positions date back to George Washington's administration, and they have been used by various presidents up to and including Barack Obama. We begin by analyzing the constitutional and legal issues involving presidential commissions and special envoys. Then we turn to the historical origins and the evolution of executive branch czars in the United States.

PRESIDENTIAL COMMISSIONS

At times of crisis or a perceived need to act, presidents have created without legislative approval what are known as presidential commissions to investigate an issue or develop a plan of action for a particular policy. Membership to such commissions varies as presidents have selected private citizens, government officials, and even members of Congress to serve. In his study of presidential commissions, Carl Marcy explained that presidents often create such entities based upon their "own authority" and for their "own purposes," such as guiding public opinion and influencing Congress. The activities of presidential commissions have the potential to "profoundly affect the life of the nation." At the extreme, Marcy argues, presidents have used commissions "to confuse the public and to avoid important issues."[1]

The first presidential commission dates to 1794 when President Washington created one, "unauthorized by law," to attempt to negotiate a settlement with protesting Pennsylvania distillers—known as the Whiskey Rebellion—who opposed a federal liquor tax.[2] In 1833, President Andrew Jackson set up a commission, headed by John P. Van Ness and Amos Kendall, to investigate fraud and corruption charges within the Navy Department.[3] A congressional committee in 1837, looking into various irregularities within the executive departments, raised the question of Jackson's constitutional authority to create the Van Ness/Kendall commission.[4] Jackson failed to provide any official response, but he did go on to charge Kendall with leading another commission to negotiate the terms for private banks to receive the deposits of the Bank of the United States.[5] Likewise, President Martin Van Buren created two commissions: one to study the postal systems of various European countries and another to do the same with their armies.[6]

In 1841 President John Tyler decided to create a three-person commission, led by former Mississippi senator George Poindexter (Anti-Jacksonian), to investigate a scandal involving the embezzlement of government funds by two custom collectors at the New York Custom House.[7] At the time lawmakers were not happy with Tyler's action. In February 1842, the House of Representatives issued a resolution requiring Tyler to clarify under what authority he created the commission. "I have to state that the authority for instituting the commission mentioned in said resolution," Tyler responded, "is the authority vested in the President of the United States to 'take care that the laws be faithfully executed, and to give to Congress from time to time information on the state of the Union, and to recommend to their consideration such measures as he shall judge necessary and expedient.'"[8] Senator Henry Clay (Whig-KY) protested Tyler's actions and answered: "If this practice should be persisted in, hosts of officers might be appointed for any other purpose, and the powers of Congress thereby be in great degree superseded by the act of the Executive."[9] By the end of the summer of 1842, Congress passed a general appropriations bill that included a rider amendment by Rep. Joseph R. Underwood (Whig-KY) that forbade the payment of any government account "growing out of, or in any way connected with, any commission or inquiry, except courts martial or courts of inquiry in the military or naval service" unless otherwise provided by law.[10]

Shortly after the passage of the Underwood Amendment, two attorneys general provided strict interpretations of the law. President Tyler's attorney general, Hugh S. Legare, stated in October 1842 that he thought "it impossible to put any construction upon the [Underwood Amendment] which shall authorize the executive departments to pay for any inquiry whatever, without a previous appropriation for that purpose by the legislature. The words of the law are too comprehensive to admit of any exception, and too express to warrant any relaxation."[11] Nearly a year later, Attorney General John Nelson said that Congress may "limit the exercise of [the appointment] power by refusing appropriations to sustain it, and thus paralyze a function which it is not competent to destroy." He went on to note that "this would seem to be the purpose of the [Underwood Amendment]." Finally, Nelson reasoned that the authority to seek funding for salaries "cannot be safely implied from the general terms of an appropriation law, which should always be interpreted in subordination to the limitations imposed by the existing and qualifying enactments."[12]

By the early twentieth century various officials continued to support Legare and Nelson's interpretation of the Underwood Amendment. In 1915 Comptroller of the Treasury George E. Downey argued that the amendment "prohibit[s], indirectly, the creation of commissions by the executive department of the Government through [Congress's] inherent power to make appointments."[13] Eleven years later Comptroller General of the United States J. R. McCarl rendered a similar understanding: "The creation of the [coordinating commission on national parks and national forests] here involved was not authorized by law and neither the appropriations from which it is proposed to pay the claim specifically authorizes the expense of a commission of this character." McCarl concluded that payment for the commission is therefore "not authorized."[14] The Underwood Amendment remains in effect today.[15]

The creation and use of presidential commissions through the nineteenth century "was sporadic and relatively unimportant," most likely because presidents viewed their constitutional powers as being limited along with their general adherence to the restrictions of the Underwood Amendment.[16] As a result not until Theodore Roosevelt became president were commissions used extensively and for policy development.[17] In total Roosevelt created six commissions addressing the following issues: inland waterways, national conservation, country life, organization of government scientific work, and department methods.[18] The Underwood Amendment restrictions had no impact on limiting Roosevelt's actions as Congress appropriated funds to pay for the presidentially established commissions. At the end of Roosevelt's presidency, Rep. James A. Tawney (R-MN) attached an amendment to a sundry civil expenses bill that sought to prohibit any appropriations from being used for a commission unless it had been authorized by law. In addition, it stipulated that no "personal services" from any department or agency could be used to support a "commission, council, board, or other similar body."[19]

Although Roosevelt did not veto the bill, he attached a memorandum to it (what would now be called a signing statement) outlining his thoughts on the prohibition of funding provision. In doing so Roosevelt attempted to redefine his actions as not violating the Constitution or law but providing a service to government for the public interest. As such he argued that "Congress cannot prevent the President from seeking advice. Any future President can do as I have done, and ask disinterested men who desire to serve the people to give this service free to the people through these commissions."[20] Tawney, author of the amendment, defended Congress's action against what he deemed unfair and misguided attacks by Roosevelt and his allies. "To condone such a usurpation or encroachment upon the powers and functions of the legislative branch, upon the theory that the executive is more representative of the interests and more responsive to the sentiment of the people," he declared, "is to invite disaster, for the greatest abuses of executive authority most often arise from the usurpation of power upon the pretense of serving the people." Tawney explained that the country was not willing to revert back to the British model of government where the executive is infallible and provides the sole source of governing authority. Nor are people ready, he said, "to believe that the legislative branch of our Government is so unresponsive to the needs of the people that the extreme remedy of government by executive choice and discretion is warranted."[21]

The Tawney Amendment remains in effect today having been combined with the prohibitions stipulated in the Underwood Amendment.[22] Roosevelt's successor, William Howard Taft, accepted the restrictions on appropriations and refused to create any commissions without congressional approval.[23] Since then the law has largely been circumvented by presidents in a variety of ways.[24] Some presidents have created commissions and used private sources of funds to support them. For example, President Herbert Hoover received over $2 million from private donors in order to pay for his commissions.[25] Such actions do not violate the spending restrictions, but they do destroy the intent of the law along with going against the proposition that Congress, not the president, creates and supports government structure. Taken to the outermost limits a president could build up an account from private contributions, separate from congressional appropriations, to carry out government functions Congress refuses to approve.[26] In effect a president would become a governing force without need to consult or go to Congress to carry out his intentions. If commissions can exist without the consent of Congress, can a president then create any position and fund it through other means? In a world where appropriations no longer provide limits to executive action, Congress would have to resort to impeachment to stop a runaway president.

Presidents have also justified the creation of commissions by giving a loose interpretation to the Tawney Amendment. In 1909 President William Howard Taft's attorney general, George W. Wickersham, issued an opinion arguing that "Congress did not intend to require that the creation of the commissions, etc., mentioned should be specifically authorized by a law of the United States, but that it would be sufficient if their appointment were authorized in a general way by law."[27] U.S. Comptroller General Elmer Staats gave a similar construction of the amendment in 1970 when he explained to a congressional committee that his office, along with the attorney general's, has interpreted the "authorized by law" language to "not necessarily require that a committee be specifically provided for by statute." He argued that as long as a presidential commission is carrying out "an authorized function," then it will be "considered to be authorized by law."[28] This statement is a regrettable interpretation of the Tawney Amendment, seeing that even President Roosevelt acknowledged that had the law "been enacted earlier *and complied with*, it would have prevented the appointment of" the commissions he created. However, Roosevelt acknowledged that he would have simply not complied with the law.[29]

Besides using private funds and rather dubious legal interpretations, presidents have found government-based financial support for their commissions through the use of special appropriations accounts established by Congress. For instance, there is a long history of departments and agencies being provided contingency funds subject to certain legislative controls.[30] Other discretionary accounts—including the Emergency Fund for the President (est. 1942) and the Special Projects Fund (est. 1955)—have from their beginning been exempt from federal expenditure laws with annual appropriations reaching roughly $1 million for use at the president's discretion.[31] President Harry Truman relied heavily on the Emergency Fund to create a variety of commissions.[32] The Special Projects Fund (now the Unanticipated Needs Fund within Title 3 of the U.S. Code) permits presidents to spend up to $1 million "to meet unanticipated needs for the furtherance of the national interest, security, or defense . . . without regard to any provision of law regulating the employment or compensation of persons in the Government service or regulating expenditures of Government funds."[33] These laws, however, do not stipulate that presidents can create executive branch structure or ad hoc commissions for the development of public policy or to investigate issues of public interest.

Aside from the statutory restrictions on appropriations and the unconvincing proposition that presidents have the constitutional authority to create government structure, there is the issue of lawmakers serving on presidential commissions. Throughout the twentieth century and beyond there have been a variety of commissions that have included members of Congress: the Hoover Commission (under Truman and Dwight D. Eisenhower), the Kestnbaum Commission, the Randall Commission (both under Eisenhower), and, more recently, President Barack Obama's National Commission on Fiscal Responsibility and Reform. There is a constitutional restriction under the Ineligibility Clause that prohibits lawmakers from holding federal office while serving in Congress.[34] Edward S. Corwin noted that one possible argument for bypassing the clause is to hold that the position a lawmaker is serving in is not actually an "office" under the Constitution.[35]

Even if such an argument can be sustained, and we believe it cannot, a practical concern remains. A member of Congress holding another office or position of responsibility is unreasonable on its face. Depending on the particular commission's functions a lawmaker would have to supervise its staff, read and generally become familiar with a new policy area, travel around the country and possibly internationally, conduct hearings, and assist in the writing of a report. Any one of these duties would most likely impede, or even prevent, a member from doing the job the people of a district or state had elected him or her to actually perform. Even if a defender of the practice believes that the functions of a commission are similar to a congressional committee, then, for all practical purposes, presidents are usurping the duties and responsibilities of Congress. Neither proposition works well in our constitutional system of government.

The simple fact is that presidents have created commissions without constitutional authority and have violated the statutory prohibitions Congress established to curtail such unilateral actions. Even today various chief executives continue to set up commissions to analyze important policy areas for the country, such as controlling the federal government's debt. We believe that any government structure, including presidential commissions, not sourced in law, violates the Constitution. With that said we are not ready to place the czar moniker on presidential commissions as no one position has been given clear authority over a policy area. In fact, members of a commission mainly advise and help create policy, not implement it. Although presidential commissioners should not be called czars, we do urge Congress to eliminate the unrestricted presidential accounts and clarify the existing laws so that legal loopholes used by various administrations are finally closed.[36]

SPECIAL ENVOYS

Congress has experienced similar difficulties with special envoys that are not based on statutory authority. At various points in the nation's history presidents have employed special envoys, often without the input or sanction of Congress, to negotiate treaties or manage a likely or actual international crisis. Such actions have tended to displace ambassadors who hold Senate-confirmed positions. As a result, E. Wilder Spaulding could write by the mid-twentieth century: "It has been too easy for the White House to appoint a whole bevy of second-rate chiefs of mission and fill the near-vacuum later on when an emergency arose with special agents. Little wonder that the skeptics look upon the ambassador as a non-essential."[37] The use of special envoys by presidents does more damage than lessening the prestige of a few ambassadors. In fact, it creates an end around in our constitutional system of government where presidents can conduct foreign policy with agents that have not been vetted or approved by the Senate.

Special envoys also date to the beginning of the republic. In October 1789 Washington named Gouverneur Morris as a "private agent" to represent the United States to the British government.[38] Five years later Washington made Supreme Court Chief Justice John Jay a special envoy to Great Britain and later he sent two different sets of commissioners to negotiate a treaty with France.[39] Elmer Plischke notes that the record and number of special envoys during the nineteenth century are "less impressive than was the case during the early era of U.S. diplomacy." Although there were a few presidentially named envoys, the secretaries of state or statutorily created diplomats generally managed high-level negotiations during the nineteenth century.[40]

By the twentieth century the use of special envoys increased largely as a result of improvements to transportation as presidents could send their trusted advisers around the globe at a moment's notice.[41] During World War I, President Woodrow Wilson's close adviser and personal friend Colonel Edward M. House became a roving unofficial ambassador of sorts to Britain, Germany, and France.[42] Arthur D. Howden Smith notes that during that time there had been a "quiet usurpation" of many of the prerogatives of Secretary of State William Jennings Bryan.[43] Wilson even permitted Colonel House to continually go "over the head of Ambassador Walter Hines Page in London."[44] President Franklin D. Roosevelt likewise employed his own special envoys. In December 1939 he sent Myron C. Taylor to the Vatican as his personal representative.[45] By the early 1940s, Roosevelt repeatedly bypassed his ambassador to Russia, William H. Standley, through the use of a number of special envoys. Standley even claimed that Roosevelt told them "not to show the Ambassador anything, not to tell him about the nature or progress of negotiations."[46] At the end of World War II Roosevelt's close White House adviser,

Harry L. Hopkins, became his personal envoy representing the president in discussions with Winston Churchill and Joseph Stalin.[47]

President Dwight Eisenhower made the former Chamber of Commerce president Eric A. Johnston his Middle East envoy with the rank of ambassador. Other individuals who served Eisenhower as special envoys to various regions of the world included: Milton Eisenhower, James P. Richards, Loy Henderson, and Richard M. Nixon.[48] More recently, President Bill Clinton made Kenneth H. "Buddy" Mackay his special envoy to the Americas with a particular focus on Peru. He also named the Rev. Jesse Jackson the special envoy to Africa, and Bill Richardson became a roving envoy for the president managing high-level negotiations in Iraq and North Korea. President George W. Bush also had his own set of envoys to Northern Ireland (Richard Haass) and Afghanistan (Zalmay Khalilzad). Today President Obama has employed a number of private citizens as special envoys to the Middle East (former Democratic senator George Mitchell of Maine), Afghanistan and Pakistan (Richard Holbrooke—now deceased), North Korea (Stephen W. Bosworth), Sudan (J. Scott Gration—now ambassador to Kenya), Guantanamo Bay (Daniel Fried), the Persian Gulf and Southwest Asia (Dennis Ross—currently a National Security Council staff member), and for climate change (Todd D. Stern).[49]

Early in the nation's history the justification for presidents creating offices of consuls and envoys was based on the theory that they were merely following the law of nations. James Madison announced such a view in an 1822 letter to President James Monroe.[50] In 1855, Attorney General Caleb Cushing issued an opinion noting that a president's ability to "appoint diplomatic agents" derives from the law of nations.[51] Of course when the Constitution refers to the law of nations it appears in Article I, section 8, clause 10, not Article II. In addition, this earlier practice requires congressional appropriations for the diplomats' salaries.[52] Senate confirmation of diplomats, even if never formally established by statute, was very much a part of the process of fulfilling such offices. Even Cushing acknowledged that the upper chamber's consent is a controlling feature of our constitutional system.[53]

Other examples support the view that both branches understood Senate confirmation to be a necessary requirement of diplomatic service in the early part of the U.S. history. In May 1810, President Madison even signed a law that expressly stated that no compensation shall be allowed to any envoy without having been confirmed by the Senate.[54] Between December 1825 and March 1826, President John Quincy Adams sent two letters to Congress, one asking that the Senate confirm his nominations of ministers to an assembly of American nations at Panama and another requesting that appropriations be made for the mission.[55] In 1831 the Senate considered the nominations of Charles Rhind, David Offley, and James Biddle after President Andrew Jackson had sent them on a mission to negotiate a treaty with the Ottoman Empire during a congressional recess. A fierce congressional debate occurred and ended with the Senate attaching the following provision to an appropriation bill offsetting the cost of the said agents: "That nothing in this act contained shall be construed as sanctioning, or in any way approving, the appointment of these persons, by the President alone, during the recess of the Senate, and without their advice and consent, as commissioners to negotiate a treaty with the Ottoman Porte."[56] The House eventually removed the language from the bill.[57] In 1843, Congress provided appropriations for an agent to China and stipulated that the position could not be filled without the advice and consent of the Senate.[58]

Aside from basing the creation of special envoys on international law, an early twentieth-century scholar on American foreign relations, Quincy Wright, stated that the source of the president's authority to name special envoys derives from his "inherent power."[59] Whether one bases the source of a president's authority on the law of nations or on inherent powers, we believe each should be rejected as adequate justification for unilateral executive action. The framers were familiar with the writings of English legal thinker William Blackstone, who broadly construed the king's power to include the ability to create, send, and receive ambassadors without parliamentary input. Like Madison and Cushing, Blackstone noted that the law of nations is controlling on the "rights, the powers, the duties, and the privileges of ambassadors." However, he went on to associate those remarks with the ability of ambassadors to be free from prosecution in the nation to which they had been appointed. In fact, Blackstone made clear that an ambassador "ought to be independent of every power, except that by which he is sent."[60] The framers clearly broke with the governing norms of England. No longer would the executive be the source of sovereign authority, nor would the appointment of ambassadors be subject to the whims of a king. Far from leaving every aspect of foreign relations with the president, subject to only the direction of the law of nations, the framers decided to provide clear guidance that all "Ambassadors, other public Ministers and Consuls" would be confirmed by the Senate along with needing Congress to provide for their salaries and diplomatic expenses.[61]

Not only had the framers placed clear constitutional restrictions on the use of diplomatic agents, but they also rejected the view that the chief executive would exercise inherent powers. It is true that presidents have the ability, like Congress, to carry out their duties based on the express and implied powers coming from the Constitution. Express powers are provided directly in the Constitution, whereas implied powers, although not specifically mentioned, are reasonably inferred from them. Some scholars—such as Steven G. Calabresi and Christopher S. Yoo— have used the terms *implied* and *inherent* interchangeably.[62] However, there are significant differences between the two. Inherent powers are not derived from the text of the Constitution but, instead, are justified through the status or position of the president. In a system of government that seeks to prevent tyranny by ensuring each branch can check the other, any claim to inherent powers can potentially create a runaway presidency. Louis Fisher explains that the "claim and exercise of inherent powers move a nation from one of limited powers to boundless and ill-defined authority. The assertion of inherent power in the president threatens the doctrine of separated powers and the system of checks and balances. Sovereignty moves from the constitutional principles of self-government, popular control, and republican government to the White House."[63]

Congress has pushed back against the idea that the president can create ambassadors and envoys at whim. In 1813, President Madison sent Albert Gallatin, John Quincy Adams, and James A. Bayard as agents to negotiate the Treaty of Ghent.[64] Federalist Senator Christopher Gore (MA) protested Madison's actions and entered a resolution stating that the offices necessary to fill those positions did not exist and that "the Senate had not advised and consented to their appointment."[65] He continued that an "office is created by the constitution, or by some power under it. Prior to its being so created, it does not exist." Any authority regarding diplomatic agents, Gore declared, is in the Appointments Clause, which provides for them expressly. He explained that the placement of individuals in such offices must be done through "an actual appointment, and that can be only by the President and Senate."[66] Although the Senate never acted on Gore's protest, most likely the sensitivity and importance of a treaty to end the War of 1812 with Britain greatly colored the debate.

The same situation occurred in 1848 when the Senate considered a treaty with Mexico to end the Mexican-American War. A presidential agent, Nicholas P. Trist, who had been recalled by the president and Congress, had negotiated the treaty, which caused the entire Senate Foreign Relations Committee except for the Chair Ambrose H. Sevier (D-AR) to object to it. They argued that Trist had no authority under the Constitution to negotiate for the United States since he had been recalled.[67] The committee wanted to reject the Trist treaty and send a commission to renegotiate a new treaty with Mexico. Polk believed such a course to be senseless: "the Treaty itself was the subject for consideration and not [Trist's] conduct, and . . . if the provisions of the Treaty were such as could be accepted, it would be worse than an idle ceremony to send out a grand commission to re-negotiate the same Treaty."[68] The committee accepted Polk's rationale and quickly approved the treaty, which was subsequently amended and ratified by the Senate. As a result of the amended treaty, Polk followed the constitutionally prescribed course and nominated two commissioners, Senator Sevier and Attorney General Nathan Clifford, to finish negotiations with Mexico.[69]

Eventually Congress began creating statutory qualifications.[70] In 1855, it stipulated that "envoys extraordinary and ministers plenipotentiary" shall be confirmed by the Senate along with requiring presidents to nominate only "citizens of the United States."[71] Although Attorney General Cushing believed that the citizenship provision should be treated as "recommendatory only, and not mandatory," the law remained on the books well after he left office.[72] A subsequent law passed in 1893 not only specified the grades for envoys and ministers but also statutorily created the ambassador position for the first time in the nation's history.[73] By 1909 Congress passed legislation stipulating that "no new ambassadorship shall be created unless the same shall be provided for by an act of Congress."[74] Although presidents have not subsequently created or tried to appoint ambassadors without Senate confirmation, they have bypassed the intent of the law by employing special envoys to diplomatic missions through executive direction alone. In fact, none of President Obama's current envoys has had to appear before the Senate, submit financial disclosure forms, or otherwise experience any kind of legislative review of his or her qualifications to serve and represent the country around the world.

Another related matter to the constitutional question of special envoys is the naming of members of Congress to such positions. As with presidential commissions there is a constitutional conflict when lawmakers serve in another governmental office during the time for which they were elected. The Ineligibility Clause, which reads "no person holding any office under the United States shall be a member of either House during his continuance in office," prevents senators or representatives from serving as officers.[75] As such, it also excludes their use as ambassadors or other named diplomatic agents. Plischke notes that there appeared to have been a great deal of respect for this constitutional prohibition as "a good many members of Congress gave up their seats to accept diplomatic appointment" during the nineteenth century.[76]

During President William McKinley's administration, Senator George F. Hoar (R-MA) protested the use of members of Congress as commissioners in treaty and other negotiations with foreign governments. Hoar rejected the claim that such posts are not offices for purposes of the Ineligibility Clause, noting that they "exercise an authority, they are clothed with a dignity equal to that of the highest and most important diplomatic officers, and far superior to that of most of the civil officers of the country." He proceeded to decry the hypocrisy of forbidding lawmakers from serving as a "postmaster in a country village" but approving their missions abroad "as a representative of the United States, with all his expenses paid, and a large compensation added, determined solely by the executive will." Concluding, Hoar declared that "to hold that the framers of the Constitution would for a moment have tolerated that seems to me utterly preposterous."[77]

McKinley accepted Hoar's criticism and decided not to select lawmakers as diplomatic agents. No president named a sitting member of Congress to a similar post until Warren Harding sent two senators to the Disarmament Conference in 1921. After that, Plischke explained, "members of Congress have regularly been included in U.S. delegations to negotiate important treaties and agreements."[78] We do not believe there is a constitutional problem with lawmakers serving on U.S. delegations for purposes of negotiating treaties and other important issues. However, the Ineligibility Clause would be violated if a senator or representative served as an ambassador or a special envoy during the time for which he or she had been elected.

In recent years special envoys have been frequently labeled czars and properly so.[79] Sometimes, however, envoys are not given a czar designation in media reports despite their diplomatic status and ability to negotiate with heads of state. For example, there is little question that few if any ambassadors had a much more important diplomatic status or role than Bill Richardson during Bill Clinton's administration. In 1996, Clinton sent Richardson to Iraq as a sitting member of the House of Representatives to conduct one-on-one negotiations with Saddam Hussein. Richardson performed this role before he served as ambassador to the United Nations. We do not expect that there will be overall consistency in the use of labels in the media. Nonetheless, the use of the czar label has a substantial history in the United States and it is important to identify and explain its origins in order to better understand the eventual widespread use and acceptance of a constitutionally dubious position in government.

CZAR: ORIGINS OF THE TERM

Within the United States, the term *czar* for government positions and officials dates to at least the early nineteenth century when politicians began using it in a pejorative manner to describe their political enemies. During the 1830s President Andrew Jackson and his allies labeled the Bank of the United States president Nicholas Biddle a czar.[80] In the 1860s President Andrew Johnson's Republican opponents made similar attacks, referring to him as Czar Andrew.[81] By the late nineteenth and early twentieth centuries, political rivals of Speakers Thomas Reed (1889–1891 and 1895–1899) and Joseph Cannon (1903–1911) called them czars during their respective reigns over the House of Representatives.[82]

None of those individuals, however, meets our definition of czar. Biddle headed a congressionally chartered government corporation that had several built-in features to promote democratic controls. For example, the authorizing legislation establishing the Bank of the United States called for twenty-five directors to manage "the said corporation . . . five of whom, being stockholders." Each director would be appointed by the president and confirmed by the Senate. In addition, Congress created a number of statutory qualifications: no more than three directors "shall be residents of any one state"; twenty directors "shall be annually elected at the banking house" in Philadelphia; and none of the directors "shall be a director of any other bank." The law also called on the directors to annually elect a bank president from their numbers.[83] President Andrew Johnson, as a constitutional officer, had been elected through the Electoral College, albeit not as president, and Congress initiated impeachment proceedings against him for allegedly abusing the powers of his office. Although not removed from office for the remainder of his presidency, Johnson had little say over major public policies of the day. Speakers Reed and Cannon may have amassed great power during their times in office, but they were elected members of the House of Representatives and thus subject to the will of the people.

During the early twentieth century the czar title was popularized, and given a positive connotation, outside of government. After the 1919 Black Sox Scandal, the owners of the Major League Baseball teams made federal court Judge Kenesaw Mountain Landis commissioner of baseball with unlimited authority to act in the "best interests" of the game. Landis ruled with absolute control and helped to restore the public's faith in baseball. Through his time as commissioner (1920–1944), Landis held the unofficial title of baseball czar.[84] In 1922 the Hollywood studios formed the Motion Picture Producers and Distributors of America (now titled Motion Picture Association of America) and made President Warren Harding's postmaster general, Will H. Hays, its head. During his tenure as president (1922–1945) Hays earned the title of film/movie czar by enforcing a strict self-censorship code, which stopped the implementation of any federal government regulations of the industry.[85] After seeing the successes of Landis and Hays in office, many other industries considered appointing or did appoint their own czars.[86]

WOODROW WILSON

At the same time the czar title started to be viewed in a positive light, it also began to be linked to various government positions, one of the first being the position of internal revenue commissioner within the Treasury Department. In 1919 Congress, through the newly passed National Prohibition Act (popularly known as the Volstead Act), gave the commissioner authority to enforce the federal prohibition on alcohol that was required by the Eighteenth Amendment. Congress charged the internal revenue commissioner, whom the media called the dry law czar,[87] with the duty to investigate and report violations of the prohibition laws to the

U.S. attorneys.[88] Some members of Congress were unhappy with the amount of power and appropriations given to the internal revenue commissioner for enforcing prohibition. In 1922, Rep. James A. Gallivan (D-MA) decried the $10 million request of Commissioner Roy A. Haynes:

> to meddle with the private affairs of the people as did the czar of Russia in the days of the Black Watch. Some think our Presidents are extravagant with a $75,000 salary, house rent free, and other luxuries; but the whole estimate for the executive department proper was only $227,000, while Maj. Haynes demanded nearly forty times as much for prying and snooping through the land and holding up innocent men and women, sometimes killing them, because of the natural suspicion of the spy of all other people on the face of the earth.[89]

Although the internal revenue commissioner exercised great enforcement powers, that fact in itself did not make the position a "czar" under our definition. From 1919 to 1927 the appointment of the internal revenue commissioner was subject to presidential nomination and Senate confirmation. The National Prohibition Act made all searches subject to judicial warrants.[90] No additional law enforcement powers were given that were not subject to the supervision of the local U.S. attorney or a federal judicial magistrate. In March 1927 Congress created the Bureau of Prohibition within the Treasury Department, directed by a commissioner of prohibition. Congress also modified the existing appointment arrangement and gave the treasury secretary the sole power to appoint.[91] Three years later, after much complaining and lobbying by Treasury Secretary Andrew Mellon,[92] Congress transferred the Prohibition Bureau to the Justice Department and gave the appointment authority to the attorney general.[93] However, the position's powers, as originally constituted in 1919 under the National Prohibition Act, remained unchanged and as a result do not meet our definition of a czar.

The prohibition era and the increased police powers within the executive branch, especially in the form of the prohibition commissioner, can be viewed as part of a slow but successful attempt by the progressive movement to boost executive power in order to secure the growth of the federal government in all areas of social and economic activity.[94] Progressives had broad aims of using government to make improvements in economic and social affairs, and they favored executive over legislative power and influence to accomplish their goals.[95] Historian Richard Hofstadter said that progressives "scoffed at the inherited popular suspicion of executive power as an outmoded holdover from the days of the early Republic when executive power was still identified with royal government and the royal governors."[96] Instead, progressives wanted government to be reorganized so that "responsibility and authority could be clearly located in an executive" to ensure that their reform efforts would be possible.[97] For that reason progressives, as political scientists Raymond Tatalovich and Thomas S. Engeman explained, "were the nearest to presidential absolutists of any theorists and practitioners of the presidency."[98] As a result the progressives worked to break the hold of democratic controls on the presidency and favored a bureaucracy within the executive branch staffed by national experts free from congressional fetters.[99] Progressives were therefore the first true, and successful, advocates of executive branch czars.

A significant part of that movement can be seen in the agencies established during World War I that were intended to coordinate and direct the war effort in the United States. The most vital agency for those purposes was the War Industries Board (WIB), which was created by the Council of National Defense (CND). In 1916 Congress had set up the CND to aid in the likely involvement of the United States in World War I. Specifically, Congress empowered the CND to advise President Woodrow Wilson and the heads of executive departments on the placement of railroads and highways to better coordinate the shipment of military supplies and troops. In addition, Congress tasked the CND with increasing the "domestic production of articles and materials essential to the support of armies and the people during the interruption of foreign commerce" along with the "development of seagoing transportation" and the facilitation of military supply needs to private producers and manufactures, "which will render possible in time of need the immediate concentration and utilization of the resources of the Nation."[100]

In July 1917, the CND created the WIB to carry out the coordination of domestic production.[101] The WIB, however, did not have the authority required to fulfill its duties. As a result, President Wilson asked Congress to give him the ability to reorganize and redistribute the functions of the executive branch departments, agencies, boards, and other entities to better meet the demands of war.[102] Some lawmakers resisted.[103] Senator Albert B. Cummins (R-IA) proclaimed: "When I am convinced that it is necessary to save the Union that this sort of power shall be given to the President, I am willing to give it, and would without hesitation give it; but I not only believe that it is not necessary to grant such power to the President in order to save the Union, but I believe that if granted it would be an influential step toward destroying the Union."[104] More lawmakers, however, supported the measure. Senator Charles S. Thomas (D-CO) believed that Congress specified too many of its expenditures and thought giving the president the responsibility to control spending when he consolidated agencies would bring accountability to the executive branch.[105] Senator James Kimble Vardaman (D-MS) proclaimed that "we have granted so many unusual powers to the Executive—we have had to add so many things in faith—that I am afraid if we should stop right now the patient might suffer from the change of treatment. And I do not want to be responsible

. . . for the enactment of any measure or failure to enact any measure that would in any way hinder or embarrass the President in the performance of his great function in this emergency."[106]

Congress eventually passed the Overman Act, which gave President Wilson the authority "to make such redistribution of functions among executive agencies as he may deem necessary, including any functions, duties, and powers hitherto by law conferred upon any executive department, commission, bureau, agency, office, or officer." The act also authorized Wilson "to utilize, coordinate, or consolidate any executive or administrative commissions, bureaus, agencies, offices, or officers now existing by law."[107] The only provision that gave Wilson the authority to establish a new office was section 3, which said the president could create "an executive agency which may exercise such jurisdiction and control over the production of aeroplanes, aeroplane engines, and aircraft equipment." Finally, Congress limited the president's reorganization authority to "matters relating to the conduct of the present war" along with restricting the use of federal funds to only the purposes they had been appropriated for and requiring the submission of a report to Congress when a bureau would be abolished.[108] Nowhere in the law did Congress provide Wilson with the power to create government structure, excepting an agency to manage the production of aircraft. If Wilson wanted the statutory authority to establish new agencies or positions then he would have to go to Congress.

Eight days after passage of the Overman Act, Wilson formally established through an executive order the WIB as a separate executive branch agency acting under his direction with Wall Street financier Bernard Baruch as its chair.[109] Wilson charged Baruch with increasing the production of materials needed for the war effort. In issuing his executive order Wilson cited no constitutional or statutory authority. As a result we consider the WIB chair to be a czar. At the time, the WIB's general counsel, Albert C. Ritchie, even questioned the legal basis for the creation of the agency:

> The Overman Act . . . does not seem to me to authorize the President to do anything more than transfer existing functions from one board or department to another, and in creating the War Industries Board, the President delegated to it functions which no other board or department had previously exercised. There was, therefore, no transfer, and for this reason I have doubted whether the War Industries Board was really created under the authority of the Overman Act, although as I say, this is supposed to have been the case.[110]

Others were more supportive of Wilson's actions at the time. In an article in the *Journal of Political Economy*, the assistant secretary of the CND, Curtice N.

Hitchcock, praised the establishment of the WIB as an executive agency. Hitchcock believed Wilson's changes would produce "more effective results" because, first,

> the President, far more definitely and emphatically than before, has thrown the vast prestige of his office behind the agency and has delegated to Mr. Baruch in no uncertain terms many functions of an extra-legal but widely extended character which the presidency has gradually assumed during the past fifteen years and especially since the beginning of the war. This in itself is a guaranty that the influence of the War Industries Board will be determined by no narrow legalistic interpretation of its powers.

Second, Hitchcock explained that "the final decision as to the action of the Board is vested by the President in the chairman exclusively instead of as hitherto in the Board as a whole. This gives hopeful promise of quick and decisive action and opens the way to a courageous and effective assumption of leadership by the man to whom he has delegated the functions which his letter defines." Finally, Hitchcock argued that the passage of the Overman Act "giving the President power to redistribute the powers of the executive departments in any way which he may wish, will undoubtedly make available to the President the power to remove any existing legislative obstacles to the assumption of full control over governmental industrial policy by the War Industrial Board and its investment with any or all necessary prerogatives now held by the several existing production and contracting bureaus and departments."[111]

No clearer statement could be offered by any progressive or presidential absolutist. Hitchcock's summary of the benefits of the WIB highlights the dangers when there is a concentration of power within an unelected, non-Senate-confirmed official, along with the removal of the traditional democratic controls found in the U.S. governing system. Wilson's actions in this case align perfectly with the vision of the presidency and Constitution first articulated by President Theodore Roosevelt that would have been foreign to most presidents dating back to the founding of the republic. Roosevelt championed an aggressive model of the presidency where the chief executive became "a steward of the people bound actively and affirmatively to do all he could do for the people." He explained that the president not only has a right but a "duty to do anything that the needs of the Nation demanded unless such action was forbidden by the Constitution or by the laws."[112] As a result, Roosevelt reasoned that "the actions of the executive offers the only means by which the people can get the legislation they demand and ought to have."[113] He even suggested that if the legislative branch failed to govern, its power might need to be exercised elsewhere: "as in any nation which amounts to anything, those in the end must govern who are willing actually to do the work of governing; and insofar as the Senate becomes a merely obstructionist body it will run the risk of seeing its power pass into other hands."[114] Although Roosevelt did not elaborate on where the Senate's power would ultimately rest, it is reasonable to assume he meant that the presidency would be the primary actor.

Wilson's vision of the presidency was no less expansive. In his book *Constitutional Government*, Wilson argued that the president is "predominant and the 'center' of national leadership and representation." The Constitution could evolve to "express the changing temper and purposes of the American people from age to age." Wilson also thought that the presidency was the only institution that could provide active political leadership by channeling public opinion "independent of any constitutional grant of authority, or of constitutional constraints." He went on to describe this new governing norm:

> The nation as a whole has chosen him, and is conscious that it has no other po-
> litical spokesman. His is the only national voice in affairs. Let him once win the
> admiration and confidence of the country, and no other single force can with-
> stand him, no combination of forces will easily overpower him. His position takes
> the imagination of the country. He is the representative of no constituency, but of
> the whole people. When he speaks in his true character, he speaks for no special
> interest. If he rightly interpret the national thought and boldly insist upon it, he
> is irresistible.[115]

Wilson placed independence and power of a president above all other considerations. Because the president represents the "whole people," he should be free to govern with force since the "object of constitutional government is to bring the active, planning will of each part of the government into accord with the prevailing popular thought and need, and thus make it an impartial instrument of symmetrical national development."[116]

Wilson could not fully implement his vision of the Constitution and presidency under normal conditions. However, during war he convinced Congress to give him more reorganization authority than any president had ever received. By using the Overman Act as statutory cover, Wilson claimed fidelity to the law while drastically expanding presidential power to unilaterally create czars. Wilson not only independently set up the WIB, he also gave it a tremendous amount of power, which Baruch used to command the wartime economy. With no statutory basis for the WIB, Baruch would even sometimes press the boundaries of the powers Wilson granted.[117] In one case WIB General Counsel Ritchie issued a legal opinion making an argument that Baruch "was operating beyond his legal authority and was personally vulnerable to lawsuit."[118] Members of Congress were troubled by the methods used by the WIB. As Baruch biographer Carter Field recounted:

On Capitol Hill there were grave wonderings about all this. Never had the senators and representatives seen so much power exercised without their having made the grants of authority, approved the appropriations to exercise them, and had something to say about the personnel. There was criticism in the cloakrooms, not of the actual deeds of the War Industries Board, but of this method of governmental functioning. Critics insisted that Congress had signed its life away when it passed the Overman bill.[119]

Under the Constitution, Congress has the primary role of reorganizing the executive branch. With the Overman Act, Congress went from the branch with near complete control over executive branch structure and powers to a nonexistent player that sat on the sidelines watching the president rearrange and redistribute government functions.[120] If the war would have continued Baruch had plans, among other things, to reduce the number of shoe styles to three with fixed prices and require civilians to wear service uniforms.[121] After the war Baruch lobbied Wilson and Congress to continue the WIB or create another agency with "powers necessary to coordinate and synchronize the economic resources of the country" when an "emergency arises," but his suggestions were not adopted.[122] Yet, overall industrial production peaked in May 1917, a full year before President Wilson's reorganization order occurred and two months before the CND created the first WIB.[123] More importantly the WIB signified that Congress was willing to modify the traditional democratic controls established by the framers in order to meet emergency conditions. If that meant giving near total power to the president and executive officials with little real checks, then so be it.

Of course the WIB was not the only agency created to aid in the war effort. On April 13, 1917, Wilson issued an executive order setting up the Committee on Public Information (CPI), which consisted of Secretaries of State, War, and Navy serving as ex officio committee members and "a civilian who shall be charged with the executive direction of the Committee." Wilson appointed journalist George Creel to chair the committee and charged him with establishing a propaganda campaign that would persuade the American public to support the war along with ensuring that certain military information was not disseminated in the press or by private citizens.[124] Although the committee consisted of various department heads and "a civilian," the management and operation of it rested with the chair as Creel held only one meeting and "never convened it again."[125]

Creel's position as CPI chair meets our definition of a czar. First, Creel was not confirmed by the Senate. Second, Wilson created the position without any constitutional or statutory backing. Even if defenders of this action believed that the Overman Act somehow authorized the creation of the CPI—which it did not—there were no existing laws that provided the kind of propaganda authority that Creel would exercise. As a result, Wilson could not redistribute functions that had not been provided by law. Third, Wilson had direct control over the appointment and direction of the committee. Structurally the CPI was not an independent agency but a creature of the president. What makes this aspect of the committee so troubling was the statutory authority Creel used to support his propaganda campaign.

On June 15, 1917, Wilson signed into law the Espionage Act. Section 3 of Title I of the act made punishable by a fine up to $10,000 and/or a twenty-year prison sentence the making of "false reports or false statements with intent to interfere with the operation or success of the military or naval forces of the United States or to promote the success of its enemies" or causing the "insubordination, disloyalty, mutiny, or refusal of duty, in the military or naval forces of the United States" or obstructing "the recruiting or enlistment service of the United States."[126] Although nowhere in the Espionage Act was the CPI mentioned, authors of a 1939 study of the CPI explained that section 3 of Title I of the Act "is what gave teeth to the Committee on Public Information."[127]

Nearly a year later Congress amended the Espionage Act by modifying section 3 of Title I to include the prohibition on various forms of speech including "any disloyal, profane, scurrilous, or abusive language about the form of government of the United States, or the Constitution . . ., or the military or naval forces . . ., or the flag . . ., or the uniform of the Army or Navy . . ., or any language intended to bring the [U.S. government, Constitution, armed services, or flag] into contempt, scorn, contumely, or disrepute, or shall willfully utter, print, write, or publish any language intended to incite, provoke, or encourage resistance to the United States, or to promote the cause of its enemies," among other things.[128] Certainly these additional prohibitions gave the CPI added "teeth."

Although Creel largely carried out the censorship functions of the CPI by encouraging voluntary restrictions on speech by the press and public, Mock and Larson noted that even if the "censorship power was employed with moderation" that should "not detract from its significance in American history." They argued that Creel, with President Wilson's support, could "have imposed an almost complete censorship on the utterances and publications of all Americans during the war."[129] In terms of the CPI's propaganda activities, Creel "stirred up hatred of all things German" and pushed the public into believing that anyone "voicing the least sympathy for anything German might well be a traitor in disguise."[130] The success of Creel's efforts would be used as a model for Adolf Hitler's propaganda minister, Joseph Goebbels, before and during World War II.[131] The public and Congress eventually had enough of Creel's overzealous use of his powers. At the end of the 1919 fiscal year Congress decided not to fund the CPI and, as a result, it was disbanded.[132]

Another example of Wilson's willingness to act unilaterally without constitutional or statutory authority was his creation of the Food Administration with Herbert Hoover functioning as its chief administrator. At the time Congress had not acted to give Wilson the ability to establish such an agency nor did he receive Senate confirmation for Hoover's appointment. Therefore we consider Hoover to have been a czar.[133] Nearly four months after Wilson acted, Congress passed the Food and Fuel Control Act, also known as the Lever Act, which authorized the president to set prices on food and fuel throughout the country. Congress also gave Wilson the authority to create "any agency or agencies" to carry out the functions of the law.[134] One scholar noted: "Never before had such sweeping powers of economic control been granted by Congress to the President."[135] After passage of the statutory authority Wilson also established the Fuel Administration, headed by Harry A. Garfield (son of former president James Garfield).[136]

Even with the statutory authority provided by the Lever Act there were several problems with the Food and Fuel Administrations that made their administrators czars. Wilson failed to specify if either entity was an independent agency or office placed under the presidency. Most likely, since they were creations of the president, neither was an independent agency. Wilson even stated in his executive order creating the Food Administration that it would be "directly responsible to him."[137] However, most importantly, neither Hoover nor Garfield received Senate confirmation and they were selected solely by the president. In addition, the Food and Fuel administrators exercised significant authority based on the Lever Act.[138] For example, at one point Garfield ordered a fuel holiday for all businesses east of the Mississippi, requiring them "to reduce their daily fuel usage to customary Sunday quantities during the five days from January 18 through January 22 and on each of the following nine Mondays" in order to conserve fuel for munitions ships.[139] Hoover chose to establish "state, county, and municipal offices" that were staffed by volunteers "who exhorted, intimidated, or simply forced their neighbors to comply with numerous food regulations" established by the Food Administration. In one local newspaper the Food Administration's county representative issued a food schedule that required people to not eat wheat on Mondays and Wednesdays, no meat on Tuesdays, and a variation of the two from Thursday to Sunday.[140]

President Wilson also created czars of trade along with labor negotiations. On August 21, 1917, Wilson issued an executive order setting up the Exports Administrative Board (EAB) claiming authority under Titles V, VI, and VII of the Espionage Act.[141] To head the new agency Wilson chose Democratic National Committee Chair Vance McCormick (who remained in that position throughout his time as trade czar) and charged him with regulating and enforcing export licenses.[142] After the passage of the Trading with the Enemy Act in October 1917,

Wilson abolished the EAB and merged its export regulatory functions into the presidentially created War Trade Board (WTB), which had added authority over the country's imports.[143] McCormick stayed on as the head of the WTB, functioning as a general czar of trade with the primary duty to see that shipments to the enemy were eliminated.[144] Although Congress had delegated to Wilson the ability to regulate exports and imports, it had not provided him the authority to create new agencies. More importantly Wilson invested in McCormick significant regulatory authority without the requirement of Senate confirmation.

As for Wilson's labor czar there were actually two individuals who occupied the position. In an attempt to minimize conflict, Wilson chose to placate both business and labor interests and established the National War Labor Board (NWLB) to sit as the "Supreme Court" for labor cases within the United States.[145] Instead of trying to appoint an individual that neither business nor labor would likely accept, Wilson allowed each group to recommend a candidate who would preside as chair on alternate days.[146] Former Republican president William H. Taft (representing employers) and progressive labor lawyer Frank P. Walsh (representing employees) became co-chairs of the NWLB. Neither Taft nor Walsh received Senate confirmation. In addition, Wilson failed to cite any statutory authority when giving life to the new agency.[147] One contemporary account of the NWLB noted that "the board was not created by statute." Instead, it "was the result of voluntary agreement of leading representatives of the three great parties in interest,—employers (capital), organized labor, and the public,—expressly sanctioned by the executive arm of the national government with all its ordinary and extraordinary war powers."[148] Of course the word *voluntary* carried with it the full force of the executive branch. In one case the gun company Smith & Wesson refused to honor the NWLB's ruling, which resulted in the president ordering its takeover.[149] After seizing the company, Wilson declared: "It is of the highest importance to secure a compliance with reasonable rules and procedure for the settlement of industrial disputes."[150] The problem with the system put in place was that the rules were purely executive in origin and the people deciding their application were solely responsive to the president, not Congress.

The final World War I czar established by Wilson was head of the Price-Fixing Committee (PFC), a sub-unit to the WIB, who reported directly to the president and exercised regulatory functions without the need to receive Senate confirmation.[151] Of course, like most of Wilson's czars, the PFC had no statutory authority.[152] As its Chair Robert S. Brookings explained, there was no need to seek approval from Congress as "he would much rather rely upon close association with the president of the United States for power than upon any congressional statute."[153] This point underscored the rising influence of the president's bully pulpit; he could not only influence how his agenda was perceived by the public and Congress but also how executive branch officials, with little to no statutory authority, could exercise vast amounts of power to control policy areas based solely on the dictates coming from the White House. In fact, Brookings and other executive branch officials—most notably Baruch, Garfield, Hoover, and McCormick—were aided greatly by "presidential announcements" that strengthened their positions against industries and individuals that they sought to regulate.[154]

THE TWENTIES

With the start of the 1920s the executive branch saw the elimination of many of the agencies created during World War I.[155] Aiding in the decline of executive branch agencies and czar-like officials was the election of conservative presidents who generally deferred to Congress and did not seek to concentrate power within the White House.[156] Both Presidents Warren Harding and Calvin Coolidge sought to curb the Roosevelt-Wilson conception of the presidency. In fact, during his acceptance speech for the Republican nomination for president, then senator Harding (OH) clearly rejected the Roosevelt-Wilson theory of presidential governance and representation. "No man is big enough to run this great Republic," he declared. What had occurred over the last few years, he explained, "was the surrender of Congress to the growing assumption of the executive before the world-war imperiled all the practices we had learned to believe in; and in the war emergency every safeguard was swept away. In the name of democracy we established autocracy." Harding's prescription against executive governance would be "the restoration of representative popular government, under the Constitution," with Congress, not the president, leading the way.[157] Likewise Coolidge resisted concentrated power within the presidency: "I have never felt that it was my duty to attempt to coerce Senators or Representatives, or to take reprisals. The people sent them to Washington. I felt I had discharged my duty when I had done the best I could with them. In this way I avoided almost entirely a personal opposition, which I think was of more value to the country than to attempt to prevail through arousing personal fear."[158]

Of course there were media claims of czar-type officials during the 1920s. For instance, the director of Public Buildings and Public Parks, Clarence O. Sherrill, was known as the Washington czar.[159] Appointed by President Coolidge, Sherrill oversaw the upkeep of the White House and executive offices, Lincoln Memorial, Washington Monument, Grant Memorial, and other public buildings and land in the District of Columbia, along with the construction of the Arlington Memorial Bridge. Charges of czar-like and dictatorial powers by Sherrill were primarily made by Rep. Thomas L. Blanton (D-TX), who claimed: "To my surprise evidence of great probative conclusiveness has forced me to the opinion that no czar has ever been in more complete control than you are of over one-seventh of the District of Columbia." Blanton said that he had gathered evidence that indicated Sherrill "arrogantly and pompously preside[s] as the sole and exclusive granter, employee hirer, employee discharger, money disburser, judge, jury, and executioner, from whose iron decree there is no way of escape."[160] The problem with Rep. Blanton's remarks was that the duties of the director of Public Buildings and Public Parks were equivalent to those exercised by the Architect of the Capitol and the General Services Administration.

In 1925 Congress provided that the Public Buildings and Public Parks director be given "all authority, powers, and duties" relating to the "construction, maintenance, care, custody, policing, upkeep, or repair of public buildings, grounds, parks, monuments, or memorials in the District of Columbia."[161] As a result, Sherrill exercised no significant authority that would place his position in the same class as the directors and administrators of the World War I agencies. Even considering the fact that the president had the sole power to appoint the director of Public Buildings and Public Parks, the House Committee on Public Buildings and Grounds had direct supervision and control over all aspects of the public buildings and land in the District of Columbia.[162]

The only other position to have been referred to as a czar during this period was the flood relief coordinator appointed by President Coolidge.[163] Coolidge named Secretary of Commerce Herbert Hoover to the position after the Mississippi River flood disaster of 1927.[164] As the designated recovery coordinator, Hoover possessed the power "to direct disaster response, relief, and reconstruction" of the flood-damaged areas.[165] In total, Hoover had at his disposal approximately $32 million in public and private funds—or roughly $346.7 million in today's dollars—for relief expenses.[166] Although at the time Hoover had been confirmed to a cabinet-level position as secretary of commerce, the position should still be considered czar-like since the office and powers used were based on the commands of the president and not any statutory authority coming from Congress. As a result, the recovery coordinator position raises serious constitutional concerns as its creation was based on no law; Hoover's placement into that office received no Senate confirmation; and part of the money spent on reconstruction came from private sources.

SUMMARY

Although some individuals were considered czars during the nineteenth century, the wide use of the term did not occur until the early twentieth century. Even then the media did not start applying the term to executive branch positions—except for the president—until Woodrow Wilson's administration. Our study, however, does not accept media definitions of czars as necessarily accurate. Media accounts generally lack a consistent standard. Oftentimes, such accounts involve the use of the label *czar* for some powerful executive branch official with a long and complicated title. Thus, at times the label is a mere media shorthand and its casual use causes considerable confusion.

Executive branch czars have origins dating back to the presidency of George Washington. But aside from the occasional use of special envoys during the nineteenth century, not until World War I did the country see a full-fledged use of czars. Bernard Baruch became the most powerful czar during this period with the ability to issue orders, regulations, and otherwise direct other government agents and the private sector. If power were the only consideration to being a czar, then Baruch should perhaps be considered the most influential.

Although President Wilson acted unilaterally in bestowing on Baruch such powers, Congress provided a measure of political and legal cover as it delegated to the president reorganization authority by way of the Overman Act. One scholar called the delegation "unprecedented."[167] Yet others have downplayed Wilson's use of the Overman Act. Kendrick A. Clements, biographer of Wilson, said that any "charge of dictatorship was ridiculous, since Wilson made little use of the Overman Act."[168] In his book *Constitutional Dictatorship*, Clinton Rossiter made the same point: "resorts to [the Overman Act] for authority were scarce."[169]

The danger, however, had nothing to do with the number of times Wilson employed the Overman Act. Instead, Wilson's view of the presidency allowed him to adopt a very expansive interpretation of the law that had little basis in any of its statutory provisions. The creation of executive branch structure, including Baruch's agency and position, had not been contemplated by Congress. Nothing in the Overman Act permitted Wilson to establish new executive structure, but he did so regardless and, combined with the absence of a Senate confirmation requirement, Baruch and others were czars during World War I.

Lawmakers were partially to blame. On matters of reorganizing and consolidating the executive branch, Wilson no longer had to go to Congress for legislative support. As one important study of World War I explained, the passage of the Overman Act "signified the beginning of the end of Wilson's effective relationship with Congress."[170] The delegation of so much wartime authority did much to concentrate power within the president and his chosen agents.[171] Why would Wilson go back to Congress and request authorization for wartime czars if his liberal interpretation of a law that already gave him tremendous authority to reorganize the executive branch seemed to be sufficient? After the initial resistance to the Overman Act there were no legislative attempts to stop Wilson from using his reorganization authority to create new agencies. Instead Congress seemed happy to place a sunset provision on the law and leave the heavy lifting to the president.

Only one czar would be created during the twenties. That most likely resulted from a period of normalcy that returned after the war when the country was in no mood for expansive international or domestic actions on the part of the federal government.[172] Both Presidents Harding and Coolidge sought a return to a less energetic chief executive and the restoration of Congress to its traditional place in the governing system. In addition, the lack of a law similar to the Overman Act, which delegated to presidents significant reorganization authority, contributed to the absence of czars during this time. Only in a natural disaster could a president find an opening to establish a czar through emergency action. But the 1930s and 1940s saw the emergence of a vastly expanded presidential office and powers. As he did in so many other areas, President Franklin D. Roosevelt substantially increased the use of executive branch czars and established key precedents for the exercise of such positions by his successors.

3. Franklin D. Roosevelt: Czars in the Modern Presidency

By the early 1930s the life of the czar position had been relatively quiet, except for the brief experience of the federal government during World War I. However, the ongoing Great Depression created the perfect political environment for the reemergence of czars. Franklin D. Roosevelt, as the newly elected president, took control of the national crisis and pushed Congress to pass laws that either created new agencies or presumably gave him the authority to do so. The offices established during World War I became useful models for Congress and Roosevelt when deciding the breadth and scope of these New Deal agencies.[1] As historian William E. Leuchtenburg has noted: "There was scarcely a New Deal act or agency that did not owe something to the experience of World War I."[2]

FDR drew on earlier precedents to create a variety of executive branch czars. Scholars often refer to FDR's administration as having established the origins of the modern presidency characterized by vastly expanded executive powers. FDR indeed broke new ground in the exercise of many aspects of executive powers. He established new czar positions and set into motion many of the conditions for future presidents to continue, and to expand, the use of executive branch czars. Given the actions of President Wilson during World War I, FDR did not make up the use of such offices completely out of thin air. FDR himself had precedents from which he could draw.

Franklin D. Roosevelt's admiration of both Woodrow Wilson's and Theodore Roosevelt's style of governing is well documented.[3] Even though the two had infrequent contact, Roosevelt learned much from working in Wilson's administration.[4] One scholar of the period explained: "A veteran of the Wilson era, Franklin Roosevelt clearly cherished his progressive roots."[5]

An often-used example of FDR's view of the presidency comes from his 1942 speech demanding that Congress act to repeal a provision of the Emergency Price Control Act. He stated that inaction by Congress "will leave me with inescapable responsibility to the people of this country to see to it that the war effort is no longer imperiled by threat of economic chaos." Continuing, he declared: "In the event that Congress should fail to act, and act adequately, I shall accept the responsibility, and I will act."[6]

Edward S. Corwin found Roosevelt's remarks to be alarming and wrote that they could "only be interpreted as a claim of power on the part of the President to suspend the Constitution in a situation deemed by him to make such a step necessary."[7] Roosevelt's claim to such power to nullify the law at will had never been asserted so boldly by a president. Even English monarchs had been unable to exercise such authority since before the Glorious Revolution.[8] The framers were well aware of British history and rejected the ability of chief executives to ignore law. Instead, they placed within the Constitution a duty on presidents to "take care that the laws be faithfully executed."[9] Asserting the right to dispense with duly enacted laws thus goes well beyond even the most expansive views of the presidency that Theodore Roosevelt and Woodrow Wilson asserted.

FDR's tenure in office thus represents the last significant step to what is now considered to be the model for the modern presidency. Given his belief in expansive and unilateral presidential powers, it is no surprise that his presidency played a key role in the evolution and development of the use of executive branch czars. We now turn to the key events during the FDR years that would do much to institutionalize the use of executive branch czars.

THE NEW DEAL

The New Deal, an economic program designed to alleviate the devastation of the Great Depression, became the initial stomping grounds for Roosevelt to put in place his conception of the presidency. Congress mostly followed FDR's lead and agreed to his measures.[10] Even with the legislative sanction, the media used the czar moniker for statutorily established, and Senate-confirmed, positions. Roosevelt's secretary of agriculture, Henry A. Wallace, would be one of the first officials to be mistakenly given the title of czar by the media.[11] The basis of the designation was the Agricultural Adjustment Act passed in May 1933. Under that law Congress delegated to Wallace the authority to reduce the production of any agricultural commodity, regulate the private storage of nonperishable agricultural commodities, issue licenses restricting the shipment of agricultural commodities in interstate commerce, and assess a processing tax, among other responsibilities.[12] In addition, Congress established the Agricultural Adjustment Administration (AAA) within the Department of Agriculture to assist Wallace in administrating the responsibilities delegated to him. To head the new agency, Wallace appointed George N. Peek, whom the media labeled the agriculture czar.[13]

Neither Wallace nor Peek was an actual czar. Although Congress failed to provide the precise language with some of the provisions of the original act, it did go back and pass amendments that "clarified the particular powers" delegated to the agriculture secretary.[14] At all times the AAA was in operation, that office did not have any independence from the agriculture secretary. That was one of the repeated sources of friction between Wallace and Peek. The latter believed that he worked directly for President Roosevelt, not Secretary Wallace. Historian Dean Albertson once wrote that Peek, "determined to run his own show, . . . beguiled himself into believing he had direct administrative access around Wallace to the President."[15] Regardless of the tension, Congress had properly delegated its powers and created the AAA. In *United States v. Butler* (1936), the Supreme Court declared the processing tax provision of the Agricultural Adjustment Act to be unconstitutional but did not find problems with other parts of the law, particularly the general delegation of authority to Wallace or the creation of the agency.[16] Two years later Congress passed legislation that addressed the constitutional problems found in *Butler*.[17]

The first true New Deal czar of FDR's presidency would be National Recovery Administration (NRA) administrator Hugh S. Johnson, whom the president appointed in June 1933 after creating the agency by way of an executive order.[18] In setting up the new agency Roosevelt did not, however, act unilaterally. Congress had passed the National Industrial Recovery Act (NIRA) giving him the authority to approve fair competition codes that would be created by various industries. If no voluntary agreement could be reached, the president had unilateral power to establish compulsory codes. Roosevelt also had the ability to create a licensing system for all businesses in industries with fair competition codes. Any business without a license or that had violated one of the codes could be subject to a $500 fine. Finally, Congress permitted FDR to establish such agencies as he deemed necessary to carry out the above-stated functions.[19] Soon after Johnson took office, one historian remarked that the NRA administrator "was entreating, cajoling, and threatening the large industrial groups to hasten the submission of proposed codes of fair competition."[20] Eventually Johnson adopted hundreds of codes concerning work hours, wages, employment numbers, and child labor for various industries.[21]

In 1935, the Supreme Court declared the NIRA to be unconstitutional in *Schechter Poultry Corp. v. United States*. It explained that the NIRA violated the non-delegation doctrine in that Congress failed to establish adequate standards. The Court asked: "What is meant by 'fair competition' as the term is used in the Act?"[22] Nowhere in the NIRA did Congress attempt to define it. In concluding the act was unconstitutional, the Court declared that "the discretion of the President in approving or prescribing codes, and thus enacting laws for the government of trade and industry throughout the country, is virtually unfettered."[23] The Court's analysis of the NIRA hit the mark. Congress failed to provide for adequate democratic controls when delegating its legislative functions. In addition, delegating lawmaking authority to the president instead of an independent commission meant bestowing on the chief executive a combination of power (making laws and enforcement) that the framers rightly tried to separate and balance between the two branches. Effectively, Congress made Johnson a czar by delegating without legislative guidance its authority to Roosevelt and permitting the president to create the NRA.

Another New Deal czar to be created by way of statutory authority was the Federal Coordinator of Transportation, a position established in the Emergency Railroad Transportation Act. The coordinator would be responsible for organizing the railroad companies into three groups or committees (eastern, southern, and western) with the purpose of avoiding duplication of unnecessary services and facilities. In addition, the position had the authority to eliminate railroad lines and to investigate the internal operations of all carriers, including the right to access their accounts and records. Refusal to adhere to the transportation coordinator's rules could result in a fine of up to $20,000. Finally, Congress created a limited right to appeal the coordinator's orders (as long as they had not gone into effect) to the Interstate Commerce Commission (ICC).[24]

Appointment of the transportation coordinator could be made by the president "by and with the advice and consent of the Senate," or an ICC member could be designated for the assignment. FDR designated ICC commissioner Joseph B. Eastman to the position.[25] Eastman's unofficial media title would be the railroad czar.[26] Even Roosevelt's close adviser Felix Frankfurter wrote to Eastman upon his appointment: "Who would have thought that you would end up as one of the country's czars?"[27] Eastman not only possessed significant authority under the president's direct command but also expressed the wish that the federal government would eventually own and operate all railroads in the United States.[28] In fact, Eastman helped draft a Senate bill that would have created a federal corporation to take over all railroads in the nation.[29]

Constitutional historian Carl Brent Swisher remarked that Eastman had "a considerable amount of coercive power over the railroads," but he chose "for the most part not to exercise it."[30] Aside from getting past Swisher's qualifying words "for the most part," there is the larger issue of Congress delegating significant authority to such a position in the first place. As the railroad coordinator, Eastman was a creature of the executive branch and under the direct control of the president. Eastman said to Congress that he would not be a "czar of railroads." Instead, his duty would be "to aid and promote and, if necessary, require the cooperation" of railroads.[31] The fact that Eastman could back up his request for cooperation by requiring it through the use of government orders and regulations counters his claims of not being a railroad czar. In addition, a president designating an official to a position of significant authority is not the same as having that person go through the Senate confirmation process as provided by the Appointments Clause. There is a measure of accountability in requiring Senate confirmation that was lost in allowing FDR to designate Eastman as railroad coordinator. Finally, the creation of a limited appeals process should be seen as a direct attempt to remove another government check. Like Congress, the federal courts play an important role in limiting executive power. Removing them from an important area of public policy—federal transportation issues—should only be considered and done with great care and caution.

Eastman would be the only other New Deal czar. Johnson and Eastman became czars not by way of unilateral executive action, but from the carelessness with which lawmakers crafted the New Deal authorization statutes. Both positions speak more to congressional ambivalence and a desire to cede power to the executive branch than to Roosevelt's motives or actions. In each case Congress delegated to FDR either the ability to create an agency or designate any existing government official, which greatly limited traditional democratic controls, especially for positions that possessed significant authority to regulate or otherwise bind others with their orders. Such statutorily established positions can add to the confusion over czars. Some czars do have a foundation in law, but many others do not. Even when Congress creates legislation providing the legal framework for a president or agency to act, there need to be constraints attached to the delegation of authority. For positions with regulatory powers Senate confirmation should be required.

Media-labeled czars add considerable confusion. Aside from Wallace and Peek, many in the media continued the use of the term for other non-czar positions. At the beginning of FDR's administration, the nation repealed the Eighteenth Amendment, which effectively ended the Volstead Act and the existing prohibition enforcement agency (see chapter 2 for more details). In order to placate fears of the remaining prohibition supporters, Roosevelt established the Federal Alcohol Control Administration (FACA) by an executive order based on authority granted to him under Title I of the National Industrial Recovery Act. The president named Joseph H. Choate Jr., an internal revenue officer, as the chair and director of FACA, giving the agency the ability to "make investigations and studies with reference . . . to the taxation, control, and regulation of alcohol and alcoholic beverages."[32] Like the prohibition commissioner before him (see chapter 2), reporters referred to Choate as the liquor czar.[33] However, the position lacked any real authority to regulate or otherwise control the liquor industry, and therefore does not meet our definition of a czar.[34] After the Supreme Court's *Schechter* decision, which held the NIRA to be unconstitutional, President Roosevelt acknowledged that "new legislation would be necessary for the continuance" of FACA.[35]

Two months later Congress passed the Federal Alcohol Administration Act, which established the Federal Alcohol Administration within the Treasury Department and provided that its administrator would be appointed by presidential nomination and Senate confirmation. In addition, Congress created a statutory qualification to appointment where no person would be eligible to be administrator who had owned or worked for a liquor business.[36] The administrator had the power to promulgate regulations that were "subject to the approval of" the Treasury Secretary. Annual reporting to Congress of the administrator's actions along with the names and compensation of all employees was required by the law.[37] Although this new position had significant authority, Congress decided to qualify the power delegated and as a result the administrator was not a czar.

No one reason will likely explain why the media used the czar moniker even on statutorily established and Senate-confirmed officials. Perhaps reporters found the label an easy and appealing way to make clear to their readers that a government official possessed great power or was someone of importance. Regardless, the New Deal era saw the use of czars through legislative grants of authority, not unilateral power grabs by FDR. Terry M. Moe and William G. Howell explained: "Much of Roosevelt's New Deal was designed and implemented under delegations so broad that he could do virtually anything he wanted."[38] In part, this circumstance can be explained as just one unique aspect of the modern presidency where the chief executive set the legislative agenda and Congress merely ratified it. As a result, czars were born through the negligence of lawmakers in protecting their own institutional interest and their failure to adequately control the power that they delegated to the executive branch.

REORGANIZATION ACT OF 1939

The origin of the czar position within the White House began with the establishment of the President's Committee on Administrative Management on March 22, 1936. President Roosevelt appointed Louis Brownlow as chair and charged him with designing a governing structure that would enhance the president's control over the executive branch.[39] FDR had questionable legal authority to even set up such a committee, as the comptroller general of the United States, J. R. McCarl, refused to permit the allocation of money to fund it. Only when Roosevelt went to Congress and received a specific appropriation did McCarl finally approve the expenditure.[40] In 1937, the Brownlow Committee issued its report recommending, among other things, the reorganization of the executive branch and the creation of six administrative assistants to the president.

The committee declared that the president's "immediate staff assistance is entirely inadequate" and that "a small number of executive assistants who would be his direct aides in dealing with the managerial agencies and administrative departments of the government" should be established. The committee reasoned that these assistants:

> would have no power to make decisions or issue instructions in their own right. They would not be interposed between the President and the heads of his departments. They would not be assistant presidents in any sense. Their function would be, when any matter was presented to the President for action affecting any part of the administrative work of the Government, to assist him in obtaining quickly and without delay all pertinent information possessed by any of the executive departments so as to guide him in making his responsible decisions; and then when decisions have been made, to assist him in seeing to it that every administration department and agency affected is promptly informed. Their effectiveness in assisting the President will, we think, be directly proportional to their ability to discharge their functions with restraint. They would remain in the background, issue no orders, make no decisions, emit no public statements.[41]

As a result, White House aides were supposed to play a passive role in our governing system. They would make no decisions and issue no instructions. Primarily they would be tasked with gathering information for the president and helping him do his job "with restraint." Although many of the Brownlow Committee's recommendations were rejected, Congress eventually passed the Reorganization Act of 1939, which authorized the president to appoint six administrative assistants who could be assigned various duties.[42] It also permitted the president to reorganize the executive branch—with several agencies and bureaus exempted—by submitting his plan to Congress, at which point it would become law within sixty days unless a concurrent resolution finding objection to the proposal passed. The law expressly forbid the president from establishing new departments and provided no new authority for him to create offices or agencies through executive orders.[43]

Shortly after passage of the law, FDR submitted two reorganization plans, which became law on July 1, 1939.[44] On September 8, Roosevelt, through Executive Order 8248, established the Executive Office of the President (EOP) and transferred to it the White House Office, the Bureau of the Budget, the National Resources Planning Board, the Liaison Office for Personnel Management, the Office of Government Reports, and "in the event of a national emergency, or threat of a national emergency, such office for emergency management as the President shall determine." FDR reconfirmed the principles stated in the Brownlow report as they related to the newly established administrative assistants in the White House Office: "These Administrative Assistants shall be personal aides to the President and shall have no authority over anyone in any department or agency, including the [EOP], other than the personnel assigned to their immediate office.

In no event shall [they] be interposed between the President and the head of any department or agency, or between the President and any one of the divisions in the" EOP.[45]

ROOSEVELT PREPARES FOR WAR

The depth and breadth of FDR's use of unilateral executive action was not fully realized until the early 1940s when he began creating a number of agencies and offices for war-related purposes. The New Deal agencies and positions of the 1930s, however, did not disappear during this time. Instead, many of these new war agencies and positions were a natural continuation of the New Deal, albeit through presidential, not legislative, action. Andrew H. Bartels explained that "strands of the New Deal continued into the war years, metamorphosing over old issues of economic balance and social justice and coalescing around new concerns like civil rights, foreign policy, and postwar employment."[46] Unlike the New Deal, for which Roosevelt managed to easily convince Congress to pass legislation at his direction, during the lead-up to World War II he exercised powers not provided by the Constitution or law to create government structure and delegate extensive powers to presidentially appointed offices. No president before had so frequently acted without statutory support to fulfill his policy goals.

Even as the United States watched the war in Europe progress, Roosevelt began to slowly build the country's defensive capacities.[47] One of the problems with the mobilization effort centered on the haphazard nature of the czars and agencies Roosevelt established, which can be initially attributed to the country's uncertain objective.[48] Should the nation plan to only protect itself from attack or would it contemplate active involvement in the war? What level of planning and commitment of resources would be required? For that matter, should planning, defensive or otherwise, even be pursued if the stated goal of the country was to remain neutral? Whatever Roosevelt did he had to act judiciously, as his 1940 presidential campaign platform promised: "We will not participate in foreign wars, and we will not send our Army, naval or air forces to fight in foreign lands outside of the Americas, except in case of attack. . . . The direction and aim of our foreign policy has been, and will continue to be, the security and defense of our own land and the maintenance of its peace."[49] To add to his problems, much of the country—particularly members of Congress from both political parties—held isolationist views and did not want to become involved in what they considered a European war.[50]

Roosevelt decided to prepare for the country's involvement in World War II largely through unilateral executive action, thus bypassing any legislative resistance. His first step was to activate the Office of Emergency Management (OEM), which had been part of his 1939 reorganization plan, and place it within the EOP. The new agency was nothing more than a buffer between the presidentially created, and legally questionable, czars and Congress.[51] Aside from being a "buffer" by placing new presidentially created agencies within the EOP framework, Roosevelt ensured they would remain dependent on him.

Next FDR worked to marshal the nation's resources for war by establishing the Office of Production Management (OPM), which he placed in the OEM. As the first agency within the OEM, the OPM was headed by two officials: General Motors President William S. Knudsen as director general and Amalgamated Clothing Works President Sidney Hillman as associate director general, both appointed by the president.[52] However, in practice Knudsen would be the actual leader of the agency. As one scholar explained: "Knudsen made policy and Hillman only advised."[53] Roosevelt tasked Knudsen with increasing defense production in anticipation of the country's involvement in World War II.[54] Although unsuccessful in accomplishing the task (primarily because of Knudsen's unwillingness to force the private sector to curtail civilian production), FDR established the first czar of the prewar era in the OPM director.[55] Unilateral action benefited the president's governing style as he could not only appoint without the need for Senate review, but also quickly abolish an agency he believed was ineffective. Statutory agencies and offices, however, are not so easily swept under the rug.

There initially was some congressional pushback to Roosevelt's creation of the OPM without statutory authority. Herbert Emmerich, the executive secretary of the OPM, noted that the "Senate sub-committee on Appropriations did not like this method of creating new agencies, and senators, at a hearing in the spring of 1941, raised sharp questions as to whether they had been legally authorized." However, as soon as Knudsen—who was at the height of his "prestige" and fame as the former president of General Motors—"entered the room the senators rose to greet him, forgot their inhibitions, and passed the appropriations for the [OPM]."[56] With congressional resistance receding, FDR could focus on using his newly discovered power to unilaterally create, modify, and abolish government structure for war purposes at his choosing. A year after its creation, Roosevelt abolished the OPM because of its ineffectiveness in increasing defense production and transferred its functions to the War Production Board (discussed below).[57]

FDR soon began adding more war agencies, along with czars to head them, to prepare for a potential worldwide military conflict. In January 1941, Roosevelt created the Division of Defense Housing Coordination (DDHC) and made Charles F. Palmer, the chair of the Atlanta Housing Authority, the first czar of the new agency. As head of the DDHC, Palmer had responsibility for coordinating the development of defense, and even private, housing.[58] We consider Palmer to have been a czar since he exercised coordination functions under the direct control of the president without having been confirmed by the Senate.[59] Two months later FDR created, by presidential letter, the President's Committee on War Relief Agencies, which he charged with advising and recommending ways to promote efficiency within civilian relief organizations by avoiding duplication of charity work. Joseph E. Davis, a presidential appointee, chaired the committee. Initially, however, Roosevelt did not provide Davis with enforcement powers.[60] After Pearl Harbor nearly every community and private organization wanted to carry out charity work.[61] The war relief situation became chaotic, which caused FDR in the summer of 1942 to reconfigure Davis's agency (re-titled the President's War Relief Control Board) and powers. These now included the ability to issue licenses to private organizations for fund-raising activities along with regulating their operations, which included the selling of merchandise or services and the distribution of funds and contributions.[62] Like Palmer, Davis was certainly a prototypical World War II czar, whose powers Roosevelt could create and modify, all without having to go to Congress for statutory backing or guidance.

In other areas of the war effort Roosevelt chose to act unilaterally instead of working with Congress to find policy solutions. In the course of a year FDR would create two czars for purposes of labor dispute mediation. On March 19, 1941, he established the National Defense Mediation Board within the OEM, chaired by the former director of the Selective Service System Clarence A. Dykstra. Dykstra worked to settle any labor disputes that the secretary of labor determined would likely disrupt the production or transportation of equipment and supplies for national defense purposes and that could not be mediated by the U.S. Conciliation Service.[63] In January 1942 FDR abolished the board and transferred its functions to the newly created National War Labor Board (NWLB), a revival of a similar agency set up by President Woodrow Wilson during World War I (see chapter 2 for more details), which was also placed within the OEM. The new board, chaired by William H. Davis, possessed similar responsibilities of mediating labor disputes as it could initiate a settlement on its own after consulting with the secretary of labor.[64] As was true for its World War I predecessor, the NWLB could count on the president to enforce its rulings, as Roosevelt in several cases issued orders that shut down a recalcitrant employer's production facility or sent troops into an area to pressure striking workers to go back to work.[65]

Roosevelt also began to create agencies with responsibilities that conflicted with those of existing czars. Four months after setting up the OPM, he decided to establish a price czar position charged with taking "all lawful steps necessary or appropriate" to prevent price increases caused by "the diversion of large segments of the Nation's resources to the defense program" as well as stopping commodities speculation and stimulating the production of military defense needs.[66] Leon Henderson, a former NRA adviser, became the first presidentially appointed price czar as head of the Office of Price Administration and Civilian Supply (OPACS), an agency placed within the OEM.[67] Many of the price czar's responsibilities were somewhat conflicting as Henderson was charged with setting the maximum prices, based on presidential backing, that the federal government would pay for wartime supplies and materials while also trying to increase production.[68] For the most part, Henderson provided various industries with price schedules and nonenforceable price ceilings that most companies followed. According to Bartels: "Industry members generally complied with these ceilings for reasons of self-interest, patriotism, or fear of bad publicity or loss of [government] contracts."[69]

In August 1941, Roosevelt changed the name of the OPACS to the Office of Price Administration (OPA).[70] At the same time, Henderson submitted to Congress a price control bill that would provide the OPA with statutorily based authority to regulate prices as well as specific legislation creating it.[71] Although several lawmakers questioned the powers being contemplated, Congress eventually passed the Emergency Price Control Act of 1942 to make the OPA into an independent agency.[72] In passing the Emergency Price Control Act, Congress ensured that the OPA administrator would not thereafter be a czar by first requiring that the position be subject to the Senate's "advice and consent."[73] In addition, Congress delegated to the administrator the ability to regulate prices on commodities[74] but placed several limitations on that authority. First, the administrator needed to give due consideration to the prevailing prices "between October 1 and October 15, 1941." Second, the companies of the affected industry were to be consulted before the adoption of a regulation. Finally, the administrator had to establish an industry advisory committee whenever requested by members of the regulated industry. The committee functioned as an advisory unit for the administrator to consult about proposed regulations.[75]

Other powers of the OPA administrator centered on issuing declarations that recommended rent prices for "defense-area housing." Congress required a right of protest to the administrator of any regulation within a sixty-day period after its enactment. If the administrator denied the protest, the aggrieved party could appeal the decision to the Emergency Court of Appeals (created by the law). The Supreme Court had final right of review of the Emergency Court's decision.[76] In 1944, the Supreme Court found no constitutional issue with the delegation of authority to the administrator or the congressionally established review process. The Court declared that the "standards prescribed by the present Act, with the aid of the 'statement of the considerations' required to be made by the Administrator, are sufficiently definite and precise to enable Congress, the courts and the public to ascertain whether the administrator, in fixing the designated prices, has conformed to those standards. . . . Hence we are unable to find in them an unauthorized delegation of legislative power."[77]

The OPA would be the only World War II agency that Congress established through specific statutory language until the end of the war.[78] Even when Congress provided statutory authority for a particular policy area and required that it could only be exercised through "such department, agency, or officer as [the president] shall direct," FDR ignored the particular provision and created a czar instead.[79] For example, the president established within the OEM the Division of Defense Aid Reports managed by Army Major General James H. Burns and charged the new czar with overseeing the lend-lease program, which had been authorized by Congress through the Lend-Lease Act.[80] Six months later Roosevelt decided to eliminate Burns's position and create a new czar and agency in Edward R. Stettinius, who headed the Office of Lend-Lease Administration.[81] Again the lack of statutory grounding of the World War II czars and agencies gave FDR the ability to quickly modify how he implemented policy.

In other areas of concern for the nation's military needs, the president placed additional responsibilities on his department heads. For example, Roosevelt sent a letter to Interior Secretary Harold L. Ickes naming him the Petroleum Coordinator for National Defense.[82] The media and at least one scholar have referred to Ickes as the oil czar.[83] We do not, however, consider Ickes to have been a czar since his responsibilities were largely advisory and consisted of duties he already possessed as the interior secretary.[84] Later, FDR made a minor change to the position's title when he renamed it the Pe troleum Coordinator for War after the start of World War II, but the president provided no new authority.[85] From May 1941 until December 1942, the coordinator position had no real power to control the oil industry and therefore was not an actual czar. Regardless, that should not negate the fact that the president had no constitutional or statutory authority to designate Ickes the nation's petroleum coordinator.

Roosevelt continued to employ unilateral executive action to set up agencies in an attempt to prepare for war. Between May and September 1941, Roosevelt created three czars to head agencies—the Office of Civilian Defense (OCD), the Office of the Coordinator of Inter-American Affairs (OCIAA), and the Office of Defense Health and Welfare Services (ODHWS)—which were all placed within the OEM. Established on May 16, the OCD would be responsible for the coordination of civilian defense activities among the federal government, states, and local governments. Its first director would be New York Mayor Fiorello LaGuardia.[86] Nelson Rockefeller, who was named to head the OCIAA—created only a few days after the OCD—had the responsibility of overseeing the "cultural and commercial relations of the Nation affecting Hemisphere defense."[87] Later Roosevelt changed the position's title from coordinator to director and renamed the agency the Office of Inter-American Affairs.[88] Finally, FDR set up the ODHWS in July and made the Federal Security Administrator Paul V. McNutt its director. McNutt's agency would function as the coordination center for health and welfare services of the federal government.[89] To give some indication of the size of these new White House entities, Rockefeller's agency had a budget of $45 million with approximately 500 staffers.[90] The heads of the OCD, the OCIAA, and the ODHWS, all presidentially appointed, functioned as coordinators of policy areas without any constitutional or statutory backing. We therefore consider them to have been czars.

FDR continued to struggle with how to obtain the resources that would be necessary for war. He was eventually forced to establish a much more significant coordination agency in response to the increased attention paid by Congress to the problems with defense production. For example, in March 1941, the Senate established the Committee to Investigate the National Defense Program, known as the Truman Committee for its chairman, Senator Harry S Truman (D-MO), who held several high-profile hearings on the failings of the administration's defense preparations.[91] Eventually Roosevelt "had beat back proposed legislation that would have established a Director of Priorities, appointed by the president but subject to senatorial confirmation."[92] FDR first acted to create an advisory body in the Economic Defense Board (EDB)—later he changed the title to the Board of Economic Warfare—consisting of various department heads and chaired by Vice President Henry A. Wallace.[93] The board had the responsibility of developing an economic defense plan, which centered on acquiring strategic materials from around the world.[94] We do not consider Wallace to have been a czar since the EDB had only planning responsibilities.

Less than a month later, however, FDR would augment Wallace's duties by making him the chair of the Supply Priorities and Allocations Board (SPAB), which had the task of coordinating defense production.[95] After that, the OPM came under the direction and control of the SPAB. Although Wallace headed the SPAB, he could not devote full attention to his new responsibilities, so Executive Director Donald Nelson, the former head of Sears, Roebuck and Company, assumed day-to-day responsibilities for the agency. We consider both positions to have been czars. In his executive orders creating the EDB and SPAB, Roosevelt cited no statutory authority and claimed he was empowered "by virtue of the existence of an unlimited national emergency." That is false. Neither the Constitution nor federal law at the time provided the president powers in an "unlimited" matter. FDR acted unilaterally to prepare for war most likely because Congress would not go along as the country still held widespread isolationist views.

WORLD WAR II

The Japanese attack on Pearl Harbor not only prompted the United States to enter World War II but also convinced Congress to delegate to the president substantial wartime authority under the First War Powers Act. Throughout the war FDR repeatedly cited the law as justification for creating executive branch agencies along with czars. For example, on December 19, 1941—twelve days after the Japanese attack on Pearl Harbor—Roosevelt, through an executive order, created the Office of Censorship (OC) with Associated Press editor Bryon Price as its director.[96] FDR justified his actions under Title III of the First War Powers Act, which amended the Trading with the Enemy Act of 1917 and provided the president authority to issue such rules as he deemed necessary to censor communications between the United States and any foreign country. The penalty for evading the codes could be a fine up to $10,000 and/or imprisonment for ten years.[97] No provision within Title III, however, authorized Roosevelt to establish an agency or create new federal positions.

In so acting FDR unilaterally created a censorship czar, a position that had no legislative approval or chance for Senate review.[98] Perhaps sensing the potential public backlash to his creation of a censorship czar, Roosevelt issued a statement to the press declaring that all "Americans abhor censorship, just as they abhor war." However, he explained that "some degree of censorship is essential in wartime, and we are at war."[99] The same day FDR issued his executive order making Price the censorship czar and giving him "absolute discretion" to censor all communications coming and going to a foreign country.[100] Although many of Price's powers went unused as he implemented a voluntary domestic censorship program, the cooperation from the press came by way of threat of government takeover of its industry.[101] In the end, the position was a purely presidential creation. No one person, regardless of the self-restraint he or she might possess, should be left unchecked when exercising such powers.

The primary vehicle Roosevelt used to justify additional czars would be Title I of the First War Powers Act, which was a reenactment of the redistribution and coordination provisions of the Overman Act of 1918 (see the Woodrow Wilson section in chapter 2 for more details). Like Wilson, FDR could only exercise his redistribution and coordination powers "in matters relating to the conduct of the present war" along with placing the same spending restrictions on appropriations and requiring him to submit a report to Congress when he concluded that any bureau be abolished. In addition, Congress created an additional restriction in placing off-limits the consolidating or abolishing of the General Accounting Office.[102] Nothing in Title I or anywhere else in the First War Powers Act authorized the president to create new agencies or offices. In his book *The President: Office and Powers*, Edward S. Corwin also confirmed this understanding of the law. He argued that the act "authorize[d] the President, not to create new offices, but only to 'make such redistribution of functions among executive agencies as he may deem necessary.'"[103] Political scientist Albert L. Sturm as well said of the new law that "there is no power here to create new agencies with new functions."[104] Regardless of the statutory language provided, Roosevelt based the establishment of new agencies on the First War Powers Act.

In addition to setting up the OC, FDR used the First War Powers Act as justification to create the Office of War Information (OWI) within the OEM. To head the OWI, he named *New York Times* reporter Elmer Davis and charged him with providing the public with information about the war and coordinating with all departments and agencies the federal government's "war informational activities." In addition, Roosevelt provided Davis with the power to issue binding directives on all federal departments and agencies necessary to carry out an effective propaganda campaign. By creating two separate offices dealing with information control, FDR chose to split the functions which were given solely to the Creel Committee during World War I (see the Woodrow Wilson section in chapter 2 for more details). Roosevelt, however, directed the OWI and the OC to work together to help disseminate "all available information which will not give aid to the enemy."[105]

Despite FDR's decision to split the functions of the Creel Committee, we consider Davis to have been a czar over information/propaganda.[106] Davis possessed the ability to issue binding orders on other federal officials that had the effect of controlling the dissemination of government information to the public and press. The First War Powers Act also authorized presidents only to reorganize agencies, not to create new ones. Not only did Congress need to place the OWI on a solid legal foundation, but Senate confirmation of the director position was required as well. Having the OWI housed within the OEM did much to remove the agency from congressional oversight and control. Executive branch propaganda campaigns should be closely monitored and controlled by the legislative branch. The OWI structure established by Roosevelt failed to create the adequate checks needed to ensure proper democratic controls. Within two years of the OWI's creation, Congress finally took seriously the domestic propaganda functions of the agency. Various lawmakers began to view it as a way for FDR to promote his fourth-term reelection. In the 1944 election, conservative Republicans and southern Democrats united to slash the budget of OWI's domestic operations to just under $3 million, which effectively killed the administration's propaganda effort within the United States.[107]

Roosevelt next turned his attention to securing the transportation needs of the federal government.[108] He did so by creating a transportation czar to run the newly created Office of Defense Transportation (ODT), a presidential agency placed within the OEM. Joseph B. Eastman, the former Railroad Transportation Coordinator and current ICC commissioner, became the first czar of the new agency.[109] FDR bestowed on Eastman sweeping powers to manage the nation's transportation infrastructure. Eastman biographer Claude Moore Fuess acknowledged: "the director had broad, although somewhat vague, authority not only over railroads but also over other transportation agencies, including automotive highway vehicles, water carriers, pipe lines, and air carriers." Like his earlier position as railroad transportation coordinator, Eastman primarily relied on cooperation with various companies to promote his policy objectives. His ability to ensure cooperation, however, was backed up by the "ultimate power and authority" that was bestowed on his office. Eastman was subject to the Senate's advice and consent for his post as ICC commissioner (a position he held for over twenty-five years), but Roosevelt had subsequently given him additional powers. The president, not Congress, created and therefore controlled the ODT.[110] In the end, Congress not only had no say in the agency's creation, but FDR was able again to set up a new executive branch entity and place it under his direct control within the OEM.

As the U.S. involvement in World War II progressed and the OPM along with the SPAB proved to be ineffective in increasing the production and procurement of goods essential for the war, Roosevelt again seized the opportunity to unilaterally change government structure by abolishing the two agencies and replacing them with a new more powerful czar. On January 16, 1942, FDR created the War Production Board (WPB) within the OEM. The WPB consisted of a chairman, whom the president appointed, secretary of war, secretary of navy, and other federal officials. Roosevelt authorized the chair to determine "the policies, plans, procedures, and methods of . . . war procurement and production" for all departments and agencies.[111] Donald Nelson became the first chair of the WPB. Like heads of other federal entities that FDR had created by executive order, the media labeled Nelson a czar.[112] The reasons for the czar title were clear. Roosevelt created the WPB and placed in its chair substantial powers over the production and procurement of war goods.[113] Doris Kearns Goodwin wrote that Roosevelt's executive order "was the greatest delegation of power the president had ever made."[114] Of course the president must possess such power in the first place in order to delegate it. Roosevelt's executive order raises serious doubts that that was the case.

For some of Nelson's primary functions, either FDR specifically granted him the authority to delegate them to others or he chose to do that himself. Political scientist James Q. Wilson noted that Nelson "created 'czars' to manage" the various programs under his control.[115] For example, Roosevelt granted Nelson "full responsibility for and control over the Nation's rubber program" with the ability to appoint a rubber director to carry out the delegated authority.[116] Nelson proceeded to name Union Pacific Railroad president Bill Jeffers as the WPB's rubber director, prompting the media to call him the rubber czar.[117] In fact, Nelson acted to name a rubber director within the WPB to keep Congress from statutorily establishing such a position and making it independent of the White House.[118] Later, Nelson created another czar in the director of the Office of War Utilities (OWU), who would develop and manage the policy and administrative functions relating to "producing, transmitting and distributing electricity, manufactured gas, water and central steam heating" along with "natural gas."[119] Nelson made WPB employee Julius Krug, whom the press called the power czar, the first War Utilities director.[120] Since Roosevelt never had authority to create the WPB in the first place, the legal status of the directors of rubber and OWU was dubious. In effect, what occurred was that one czar, with his own questionable legal authority, created two additional positions and delegated to them authority that none of them, including the president, possessed. On top of that none had to receive Senate confirmation.

Besides production, wartime shipping became another pressing concern for Roosevelt, who created another czar to head the War Shipping Administration (WSA), which—like most of the other WWII agencies—was set up unilaterally by the president and housed within the OEM. FDR stipulated that the WSA administrator, whom he appointed, would manage the American merchant marine and "the operation, purchase, charter, requisition, and use of all ocean vessels under the flag or control of the United States," except military vessels and those controlled by the Office of Defense Transportation.[121] In early 1942, Emory S. Land became the shipping czar.[122] Like most of the positions Roosevelt established through executive order, the WSA administrator had no basis in law. Even if the statutory authority was not at issue, there were the additional problems of the position exercising significant authority and doing so under the complete supervision and control of the president.

The most repugnant czar FDR created had the chief responsibility for planning and overseeing a program for the removal, relocation, and detention of citizens and noncitizens of Japanese ancestry. In March 1942 Roosevelt acted to set up the War Relocation Authority (WRA)—placed within the OEM—and to be led by a director "appointed by and responsible to the President."[123] Aside from the constitutional problems of detaining without due process U.S. citizens during a war, FDR never received formal congressional approval for creating the WRA. Nothing in the First War Powers Act or any other statute passed by Congress provided such authority. In *Korematsu v. United States*, the Supreme Court gave its own approval of the detention program, but the case did not address WRA's constitutionality.[124] Roosevelt thus acted outside his constitutional and legal authority in creating the WRA and as a result its director, Milton S. Eisenhower (later succeeded by Dillon S. Myer), should be considered a czar.

Labor shortages and production needs that resulted from the military draft increasingly became a pressing concern for the war production effort.[125] In April 1942, FDR established the War Manpower Commission (WMC) within the OEM to devise policy on the recruitment and employment of additional labor for the war effort.[126] He named Federal Security Administrator Paul V. McNutt to chair the WMC with committee members coming from the War, Navy, Agriculture, and Labor Departments; the WPB; the Selective Service System; and the Civil Service Commission. McNutt, who became known by the media as the manpower czar, promulgated rules and standards to be used by the federal government in the hiring and management of workers for the war effort.[127] One scholar wrote that McNutt had assumed "the most extensive power over the American people ever held by any individual except the President."[128] The WMC chair should be considered a czar. McNutt chaired a presidentially created commission and was under Roosevelt's direct supervision exercising significant regulatory power. As for the position's legal standing, FDR might have been able to argue that he redistributed the hiring and management regulatory authority to McNutt in his capacity as head of the Federal Security Administration (which was a Senate-confirmed position). Doing so would clearly have been within the realm of the delegated authority Congress granted Roosevelt in the First War Powers Act. However, that did not occur. Instead, Roosevelt created the WMC and its chair based on no statutory authority.

Other wartime issues ranging from the economy to food shortages resulted in FDR creating even more czars. For example, in October 1942 Roosevelt made Supreme Court Justice James F. Byrnes the director of the Office of Economic Stabilization (OES), an agency he created through an executive order within the OEM. The media began calling Byrnes the economic czar.[129] FDR charged Byrnes as OES director with regulating the wages and prices within the economy.[130] The president based his actions on an amendment to the Emergency Price Control Act. However, that measure did not give him the authority to create the OES. Instead, it permitted Roosevelt to "promulgate such regulations as may be necessary and proper to carry out any of the provisions of this Act"; and to "exercise any power or authority conferred upon him by this Act through such department, agency, or officer as he shall direct."[131] No other part of the law provided for the creation of an office. Even before Congress acted to amend the Emergency Price Control Act, FDR had almost decided to unilaterally create a czar to regulate prices and wages. Eventually Byrnes and others persuaded Roosevelt not to act alone and to submit his proposal to Congress, but the incident highlights the initial lack of concern the president had for controlling legal authority.[132] In the end, Byrnes qualifies as a czar because he exercised regulatory authority under the direct control of the president without the need for Senate confirmation. Not to mention that

Roosevelt permitted him to function as a czar of czars in that Byrnes could referee jurisdictional disputes between presidentially created agencies.[133]

FDR did not always create new czars to manage wartime affairs. In December 1942, as a result of the country's defense oil and gas needs, he chose to issue an executive order establishing the Petroleum Administration for War (PAW) and made Interior Secretary Ickes its administrator.[134] Roosevelt specified no statute in his executive order but granted Ickes powers that Congress never contemplated in charging the interior secretary with formulating necessary policies and rules for the "most effective development and utilization of petroleum." He also gave Ickes the ability to "appoint such general, regional, local, or functional petroleum industry committees or councils" as he found necessary. Unlike FDR's previous designation of Ickes as the petroleum coordinator, here the president delegated to the interior secretary significant authority. The delegation, however, had no basis in any statute, which means that Ickes should be considered a czar even though he received Senate confirmation as interior secretary. Also, we consider PAW deputy administrator Ralph K. Davies to have been a czar since he ran the day-to-day operations of the agency as a non-Senate-confirmed official.[135]

In another case Roosevelt chose to grant Agriculture Secretary Claude Wickard the "responsibility for and control over the Nation's food program" because of increased food shortages after the country had entered the war.[136] Specifically, FDR charged Wickard (designated food czar by the media)[137] with the power to determine the food requirements for the nation, "formulate and carry out a program designed to furnish a supply of food adequate to meet such requirements," assign "food priorities" for all human and animal consumption, determine the food purchasing policies of federal agencies, and create a civilian rationing program.[138] Roosevelt's executive order cited no legal authority—other than various executive orders he had already issued—and made only general claims of constitutional support for the creation of a national food program. Because Congress passed no law that provided the president with the authority to create a national food program, we believe that Wickard was a czar since his newly acquired duties went beyond the statutory confines of the agriculture secretary.[139]

After several months of Wickard's ineffectual leadership, Roosevelt removed him as head of the nation's food production efforts.[140] In his place FDR created the Administration of Food Production and Distribution—later renamed the War Food Administration (WFA)—within the Agriculture Department and appointed the former head of the Agricultural Adjustment Administration, Chester C. Davis, as its administrator.[141] Davis lasted only a few months in the position, and Roosevelt named former Texas Democratic congressman Marvin Jones as his replacement. Media reports were accurate in describing both Davis and Jones as food czars.[142] In his executive order, FDR transferred all the powers he had earlier conferred onto Wickard to the War Food administrator. In doing so, Roosevelt made both Davis and Jones independent of the agriculture secretary by specifically mandating that the War Food administrator would "be directly responsible to" the president.[143] That meant FDR had complete control over the WFA, which he had unilaterally established and placed within the Agriculture Department. Finally, Roosevelt cited the First War Powers Act as the legal justification for the formation of the WFA. Such repeated statutory invocations on the part of the president do not somehow generate the authority required to create federal offices and agencies. That law did not authorize the president to create new executive branch structure or to appoint officials without additional statutory backing.

CONGRESS STEPS IN

During this time Congress became increasingly concerned with FDR's management of the war production effort and began considering a bill to establish "a giant administrative body" to manage and oversee the country's war mobilization. The congressionally proposed agency "would have encompassed all or parts of fourteen existing agencies," most of which had been created unilaterally by the president.[144] Roosevelt acted to put in place another czar who could take command of the wartime production effort, something the president had been reluctant to do since the start of the war. On May 23, 1943, he created the Office of War Mobilization (OWM) within the OEM to placate the growing calls for legislative action by lawmakers.[145] Again FDR justified his unilateral action in establishing the OWM by referencing the First War Powers Act, but, as explained earlier, that law only gave him the authority to consolidate agencies, not create new ones.

Roosevelt named James F. Byrnes, who then ran the OES, as the head of the OWM and chief czar of mobilization. Many considered the move a reconfirmation of Roosevelt's confidence in Byrnes "as second only to the President on the home front."[146] As the new mobilization czar, FDR tasked Byrnes with developing a program to maximize "the nation's natural and industrial resources for military and civilian needs," overseeing the nation's nonmilitary manpower, and stabilizing the economy. In addition, Byrnes could issue "directives on policy or operations to the Federal agencies and departments as may be necessary to carry out the programs developed."[147] As a non-Senate-confirmed official responsible to the president alone Byrnes would be the most powerful World War II czar, possessing a sweeping amount of power over all parts of the executive branch and nearly every aspect of domestic life in the United States.

Some members of Congress also became concerned that too many executive officials were in violation of specific constitutional provisions. In the spring of 1943, the Senate Judiciary Committee approved a bill that would require Senate confirmation for certain executive branch officers making more than $4,500 a year. In its report, the committee acknowledged that in recent years Congress had delegated vast amounts of powers to the president to cope with the "emergency conditions confronting the country." In turn, the president created many agencies through executive orders; but, the committee argued, it "does not follow ... nor is it true that the staffing of these executive agencies has been consummated pursuant to the Constitution or the laws of the United States."[148] Instead, many of the "so-called employees in the executive agencies, by virtue of authority which has been either assumed, or subsequently delegated to them, are in effect enacting legislation by means of rules and regulations which drastically affect the entire Nation" and that result in an unconstitutional system of governance.[149] FDR voiced his opposition to the bill, but support in the Senate ensured an easy passage in that chamber.[150] The president had better luck in the House, where the Senate bill was referred to the Committee on the Civil Service and never acted on.[151]

Even after the attempt by Congress to restrain presidential power, Roosevelt continued to create new czars and agencies without statutory backing. On September 25, 1943, he established the Foreign Economic Administration (FEA) within the OEM and made Leo T. Crowley its head.[152] Crowley as the foreign economic czar had the "responsibility for and control of all activities of the United States Government in liberated areas with respect to supplying the requirements of and procuring materials in such areas."[153] Like most of the czars established during World War II, FDR provided significant authority to a non-Senate-confirmed official. Another czar created after Congress's failure to require Senate confirmation for a number of executive branch positions was William L. Clayton, who headed the Surplus War Property Administration (SWPA)—an agency placed within the OWM. Roosevelt charged Clayton, a non-Senate-confirmed official, with beginning the disposal process of the defense property held by the government as the war began to come to a close.[154]

Congress, however, did not let FDR's final czar stand for long as it acted to bring statutory control and accountability to the disposal of government property. Within a year it passed the Surplus Property Act of 1944, which created the Surplus Property Board. All three members of the board served two-year terms and required Senate confirmation for appointment.[155] In a signing statement Roosevelt said he approved of the law "with considerable reluctance," noting that he believed many parts of the bill will "make extremely difficult" the disposal of surplus property. However, he said that the process needed to begin, so "it would be best to let the bill become law in the hope that" subsequent changes would be made.[156]

Later in 1944, Congress finally succeeded in limiting executive power by passing the Independent Offices Appropriation Act, which, among other things, denied appropriated funds if the president created an agency that had been in existence for one year and lacked a clear statutory basis.[157] Senator Richard Russell (D-GA) proposed the measure.[158] He stated that the rationale for it was "to retain in the Congress the power of legislating and creating bureaus and departments of the Government, and of giving to Congress the right to know what the bureaus and departments of the Government which have been created by Executive order are doing." No agency, Russell believed, "which has power to issue orders affecting the lives and business of the American people should stay in existence for more than 12 months unless the Congress has passed upon an appropriation for such agency."[159] Senators Millard E. Tydings (D-MD) and Walter George (D-GA) spoke in support of the measure. Senator George declared that "human liberty cannot exist in any democratic country anywhere, any time[sic], when the people fall under the rule of bureaucracies created by Executive order."[160] Russell's proposal eventually passed, and FDR signed the bill into law. However, as William G. Howell explained: "It is unclear why Roosevelt did not veto the appropriation."[161] Indeed, the president could have chosen instead to veto the bill as an incursion into presidential power. Regardless of the reason for his decision to not veto, the new law limited Roosevelt and future presidents from acting unilaterally in creating executive branch structure.[162]

Finally, Congress again turned to the matter of managing the war and economy.[163] Lawmakers wanted to find ways to provide a statutory framework for the eventual reconversion of the country from war to peace, along with introducing elements of accountability into the rapidly growing government structure. By the summer of 1944, Congress began drafting a bill to provide "proper legislative backing" for the OWM. As Senator Harley Kilgore (D-WV) noted, the mobilization czar's legal authority is derived solely from "a Presidential directive." Even in acknowledging the benefits of a centralized wartime coordination agency, Senator Claude Pepper (D-FL) expressed a need to provide "statutory authority" rather "than executive authority." In an exchange with Pepper, Senator Kilgore explained that the purpose of the bill was to ensure that wartime agency personnel "would have to come to the Congress for authority to carry out any of their functions, and would have to make regular reports to the Congress as to what they have done, and what they recommend, and the Congress then would act upon their recommendation through the passage of specific laws."[164]

On October 3, 1944, Congress passed the War Mobilization and Reconversion Act, which created the Office of War Mobilization and Reconversion (OWMR) as an independent agency and subjected its director to Senate confirmation with a two-year term. The OWMR director was empowered to formulate plans to address the "problems arising out of the transition from war to peace" and to issue orders/regulations to carry out those plans.[165] Although at first blush the director's powers appear unchanged from what FDR had provided, there were a great number of democratic controls included in the law. Aside from senatorial confirmation, the director under section 101 of the act had to gain congressional approval "to carry out plans" that the OWMR developed. The director was also required to submit a study to the president and Congress of the various agencies in the area of manpower along with developing a program for reorganizing and consolidating those agencies. In addition, quarterly reports summarizing the director's activities had to be given to the president and Congress. Finally, Congress stipulated that the director could not delegate his authority to issue orders and regulations to others.[166] Based on the statutory backing and added democratic controls, the OWMR director was not a czar under the new law.

SUMMARY

The practice of using executive branch czars grew rapidly throughout Franklin D. Roosevelt's administration. Like the Overman Act under President Woodrow Wilson, FDR mostly used the First War Powers Act to justify the creation of new executive branch structure and, as a result, czar positions proliferated. Neither act, however, provided the president in question with the express authority to establish offices on his own. Yet, both presidents did so by making questionable claims to constitutional and statutory authority.

Roosevelt did not stop with the unilateral creation of new executive branch structure. Many of his executive orders contained explicit language that new offices and positions would be independent of existing departments and placed within the EOP. Corwin, in analyzing the dubious claims on a statutory grant of office-creating authority by the First War Powers Act, said that FDR's administration "was clearly aware of these constitutional difficulties [as] is shown by its endeavor to evade them through the device of grouping its various creations under the rooftree of the oldest of them, the Office of Emergency Management, which was in turn installed in the 'Executive Office of the President.'"[167] As a result, Roosevelt created the first true White House czars without legislative consent and therefore vastly expanded his powers through executive orders.[168] At one point even the *Washington Post* mocked Roosevelt's rapid creation of so many new federal offices: "executive orders creating new czars to control various aspects of our wartime economy have come so thick and fast in the last week that it is difficult for the public to remember all of them." It concluded that "the galaxy of czars is now complete, unless the President should decide to appoint a czar over the czars."[169] FDR did just that when he made Byrnes the director of the Office of Economic Stabilization.

Although this study does not focus on the policy outcomes that czars produce, we would be remiss if we did not highlight the general ineffectiveness of Roosevelt's mobilization efforts. Repeatedly presidential advocates have called for increased presidential power so that the chief executive can bring energy and efficiency to government. However, the World War II experience shows that a strong president acting in isolation of Congress does not necessarily produce effective management decisions. A number of scholars have made this point before. Marc Landy and Sidney M. Milkis have said that FDR's "success in centralizing power in the White House came at the expense of a systematic coordination of a nationwide mobilization effort."[170] Likewise, Stephen Hess explained: "The needs of massive warfare were not as well served by improvisation and redundancy."[171] Perhaps the benefits of deliberation among a large group of elected officials with diverse backgrounds and experiences would have been a better course than ad hoc planning by an isolated few individuals within the White House.

Of course Congress did act to prevent the unilateral creation of agencies by presidents through executive orders. However, later it passed a measure that weakened its earlier prohibition. In section 214 of the 1946 Independent Offices Appropriation Act, Congress permitted appropriations from executive departments and agencies to be used for interagency groups as long as they are "engaged in authorized activities of common interest of such departments and establishments and composed in whole or in part of representatives thereof."[172] This loophole, which in practice blew a huge gap into the 1944 Russell amendment, would be exploited by future presidents to create various commissions, boards, and groups not specifically authorized by Congress. Presidents would do so even if they were in violation of the clear intent of the Russell Amendment by unilaterally establishing government agencies but instead calling them offices, groups, councils or commissions.[173] The fact is that the law never authorized the creation of any new government structure, just the appropriation of funds to support interagency groups. The Russell Amendment remains in effect today along with other statutory prohibitions against presidents using appropriated funds (see the presidential commissions section of chapter 2 for more details).[174]

Existing scholarship already shows that Roosevelt profoundly changed the office of the U.S. presidency and its powers. In fact, his leadership is widely admired by historians and political scientists, many of whom believe that FDR's accumulation and exercises of independent powers made him a model for future presidents.[175] Roosevelt indeed did much not only to aid in the acceptance of czars, but also to substantially expand their use as this executive branch practice took hold.

Not all scholars agree that FDR's actions deserve such widespread admiration, for his successful efforts to concentrate presidential powers have had varied consequences for our constitutional republic. Power has become heavily concentrated in the presidency. While presidents are expected to do more and more to lead the national agenda, Congress and democratic controls have weakened substantially. Few advise presidents to do less, to downsize the executive branch, to engage in more regular and genuine collaboration with Congress in policymaking. But rather, more commonly presidents are counseled to manage the government by adding more staff, more layers of support, and further walling themselves off from the process of accountability in order to further the national interest. The growth of the use of czars over time is a consequence of these developments. In what follows, we examine the evolution of the use of czars in the post-FDR modern presidency.

4. Harry S. Truman–Lyndon B. Johnson: Consolidating the Use of Czars

The centralization of power within the executive branch—particularly the Executive Office of the President—through the use of czars did not stop with Franklin D. Roosevelt. Congress had tried to reverse some of the more egregious abuses by passing the Independent Offices Appropriation Act in 1944, but that did little to stop the continued use of czars since a significant loophole had been passed a year later. In fact, far from ceding power back to Congress or to the people, President Harry S. Truman largely adopted his predecessor's practice of unilaterally creating czars to carry out his policy goals. This assessment conforms well to what the general academic literature details in that Truman adopted and reinforced various precedents established by Roosevelt.[1]

Indeed, as the following makes clear, FDR's use of emergency-based powers to create various czars had a lasting impact on the system of separated powers. His immediate successors institutionalized the practice of appointing executive branch czars, even in nonemergency situations. With Roosevelt's precedents and then Truman's actions, the exception slowly developed into a norm.

The following analysis of czars showcases the problems of allowing presidents to reach beyond the constitutionally based limits of their powers. Once certain precedents are established by one presidential administration, the next rarely turns back additional powers. If appointing a temporary czar to facilitate managing a crisis seems benign at the time, the following presentation and analysis of czars in the mid-twentieth century should give serious pause.

It's not that these presidents spun out large numbers of czars as became the practice years later—and one, John F. Kennedy, appointed no new czars—but they normalized the practice as an ongoing feature of the executive branch. The slow withering away of traditional democratic controls in a system of separated powers can be just as dangerous, and sometimes even moreso, than a sudden presidential power grab.

HARRY S TRUMAN

After Truman assumed the presidency, there remained a number of czar positions established under his predecessor. But in some cases media reports mistakenly labeled other officers in Truman's administration as czars. Truman's director of the Office of War Mobilization and Reconversion (OWMR), John Snyder, was known as a czar despite the fact that Congress had statutorily created his position and provided significant checks to control his powers.[2] Truman disbanded some czar positions established by Roosevelt. For example, he issued an executive order eliminating the War Food Administration and transferring its duties to Agriculture Secretary Clinton P. Anderson.[3] But so doing merely gave the czar authority to Anderson since he gained the functions of an agency not previously authorized by law.

Under Truman's watch, at least one of the special assistant positions created by the Reorganization Act of 1939 began to accumulate enough significant power to be considered a czar. In 1945 Truman made John R. Steelman his special assistant "to act in any field in which I want to use him."[4] Primarily, Truman made the appointment because of the ineffectiveness of Labor Secretary Lewis Schwellenbach in negotiating the various ongoing strikes and the fact that Steelman had successfully headed the U.S. Conciliation Service within the Labor Department to provide mediation services for labor disputes.[5] In empowering Steelman to negotiate with striking workers, Truman cited no constitutional or statutory authority. One scholar said that Truman acted out of a sense of necessity: "The president perceived the urgency, and he didn't have the patience to wait, and observe strict protocol, or bureaucratic courtesy. He would rather have some action. And John Steelman could give him the action, he felt."[6]

In June 1946, Truman nominated Steelman to direct the OWMR, while still retaining his White House Office position.[7] The Senate confirmed Steelman for a two-year term as the OWMR director.[8] Despite its statutory creation as an independent agency, historian Alfred Sander noted that by 1946 the OWMR "had become virtually a part of the White House staff."[9] Certainly that appeared to be the case, with one of Truman's closest White House aides confirmed to head the agency. A month later, Truman assigned all the functions of the Office of Economic Stabilization—a World War II agency Roosevelt created by executive order— to Steelman as well.[10] After making the announcement one reporter asked Truman: "How many jobs does that give Mr. Steelman?" The president replied, "Well, you'll have to ask him. I don't know."[11] Truman expanded Steelman's duties yet again by ordering that he chair the newly created President's Scientific Research Board, which would review the allocation of federal scientific research resources.[12]

Not all of Steelman's responsibilities would last. Republican victories in the November 1946 elections, combined with the end of wartime hostilities, convinced Truman to dissolve the OWMR. Through an executive order, Truman created the Office of Temporary Controls (OTC) to liquidate the OWMR along with several other war agencies.[13] Truman acted to eliminate war agencies in the absence of any controlling constitutional or statutory authority despite his reference to the First and Second War Powers Acts. In fact, Congress had provided a termination date for the OWMR of June 30, 1947, not December 12, 1946—the day Truman specified in his order.[14]

The elimination of the OWMR, however, did not mean that Steelman's role as director of that agency ceased. At a press conference, Truman stated that Steelman would continue to carry out the OWMR director's duties.[15] The problem with Truman's order was that Steelman no longer had the statutory authority that Congress delegated to the OWMR director.[16] Instead, he would be a White House aide exercising powers based on a president's decree. Not only did Steelman retain the residual authority of the OWMR, but he also gained responsibilities to coordinate federal agency programs and served as liaison for the President's Commission on Higher Education.[17] To signify Steelman's increased powers within the White House, his title changed from "Assistant to the President" to "The Assistant to the President."[18] In 1948, Truman designated Steelman as the acting chair of the National Security Resources Board—an entity created by the National Security Act of 1947. It was his duty to prepare plans for economic and manpower mobilization in the event of war—a position he held until 1950.[19] In 1949, Truman directed Steelman to coordinate federal projects with an emphasis on alleviating unemployment.[20] At that time the media labeled Steelman the U.S. project czar.[21] Finally, in 1952 Truman made Steelman the acting director of the Office of Defense Mobilization.[22]

Any one of several functions and responsibilities exercised by Steelman would qualify him as a czar under our definition. Even Patrick Anderson, author of *The President's Men*, once remarked that there "has never again been anyone quite like Steelman in a position of such authority in the White House."[23] The OWMR, created as an independent agency by Congress, should not have been placed within the White House. In addition, the transfer of negotiating functions from the Labor Department to Steelman's office without statutory authority is another example of the creation of a White House czar. Perhaps the First War Powers Act provided the president with sufficient authority to transfer those functions. However, additional constitutional and legal concerns arose. In March 1948, a subcommittee of the House Committee on Education and Labor served two subpoenas on Steelman in his role as White House labor negotiator.[24] Steelman returned the subpoenas with a letter stating that "in each instance the President directed me, in view of my duties as his assistant, not to appear before your subcommittee."[25] The incident highlights the transparency and accountability problems that can arise when presidents grant greater and greater powers to their White House aides. Not only is there an issue concerning the propriety of the legal authority of czars, but also one of the need of Congress and the public to know what they are doing.

Truman not only began to place significant authority within his immediate White House staff, but he also continued the practice of creating czars and placing them within the Office for Emergency Management (OEM)—something his predecessor FDR had repeatedly done. In some cases Truman created a czar to head a new agency with similar powers as a wartime one, but with a new title that was intended to signify its peacetime role. For example, Truman decided to terminate the War Production Board—a presidentially created war agency established to provide greater direction for the production and procurement of goods—and transfer its functions to the newly established Civilian Production Administration (CPA) headed by John D. Small, a presidentially appointed czar. Truman ordered Small to "further a swift and orderly transition from wartime production to a maximum peacetime production in industry free from wartime Government controls."[26] When asked what his new agency would do, CPA Administrator Small said: "It will use its authorized powers to expand the production of materials which are in short supply; limit the use of materials which are still scarce; restrict the accumulation of inventories so as to avoid speculation, hoarding and unbalanced distribution which would curtail total production," among other duties.[27]

Truman also created a presidentially appointed czar to dispose of defensive materials from the war. In January 1946 Truman established the Director of Liquidation within the OEM and appointed Robert L. McKeever, a former chief division head of the Office of Censorship, to run it. Truman charged McKeever with the "orderly and timely winding up of the affairs" of all temporary (i.e., presidentially created) war agencies. He also set up a Liquidation Advisory Committee, consisting of representatives of various departments and agencies, to advise the director in the performance of his duties.[28] Later Truman set up the Philippine Alien Property Administration within the OEM to oversee enemy alien property located in the Philippines. Truman stated that he possessed statutory authority under the Trading with the Enemy Act, the Philippine Property Act of 1946, and the First War Powers Act.[29] None of those laws, however, authorized Truman to create the new agency and appoint an administrator to operate it. The Trading with the Enemy Act permitted the president to appoint an alien property custodian to "receive all money and property in the United States due or belonging to an enemy, or ally of enemy."[30] The Philippine Property Act of 1946 only reauthorized the use of the Trading with the Enemy Act and allowed the president to delegate the authority to "such officer or agency as he may designate."[31] The "may designate" language, as explained earlier, anticipates that the assistance will come from an existing department or agency. Finally, the First War Powers Act only allowed presidents to consolidate, not create, agencies. The administrator, James M. Henderson, should therefore be considered a czar because the position lacked legal authority. The statutes Truman cited did not permit him to set up an agency.

Finally, the growing concern over a nuclear attack from the Soviet Union along with another prolonged military conflict, particularly in Asia, caused Truman to create a civil defense czar.[32] In early December 1950 Truman appointed former Florida governor and representative Millard Caldwell (D) to head the Federal Civil Defense Administration (FCDA), which had responsibility to coordinate and promote defense preparedness.[33] Created by executive order, Truman placed the FCDA within the umbrella of the OEM. Although in January 1951 Congress passed the Federal Civil Defense Act, we consider Caldwell to have been a czar during the nearly six weeks that he ran the presidentially established FCDA. The reasons are clear. Caldwell was a presidentially appointed official with coordination functions for purposes of strengthening the country's civil defense. Only when the Federal Civil Defense Act became law did Caldwell cease to be a czar as the FCDA became an independent agency and its head was required to receive Senate confirmation. In addition, the law provided a statutory direction set by Congress, not the president, and a number of democratic controls, including guidance on its emergency powers, reporting requirements, and certain prohibitions on the use of existing government entities.[34]

Truman did not always place executive branch czars within the White House structure. In the case of his housing czar he chose to locate the position within the OWMR, not the OEM. Truman named Wilson Wyatt to be the housing expediter and charged the new czar with making "the machinery of housing production run as smoothly and speedily as possible" for returning military veterans.[35] Truman announced Wyatt's appointment in December 1945 but did not officially establish, through an executive order, the position until six weeks later.[36] As a non-Senate-confirmed official created by Truman, Wyatt was a creature of the president, not Congress. Wyatt could issue orders to executive agencies and recommend legislative proposals for aiding in the carrying out of his duties.[37]

Working exclusively under the power granted by Truman, Wyatt held a series of meetings "with veterans' organizations, real estate officials, labor leaders, and experts on the housing industry" to produce a proposal to manage the nation's housing crisis.[38] Despite opposition from Republicans and conservative Democrats, Congress passed the Veterans Emergency Housing Act in May 1946 to formally establish the Office of the Housing Expediter.[39] Congress subjected the new position to Senate confirmation unless the president appointed "an existing official" within the federal government. In regard to powers, the housing expediter could issue orders to executive agencies—including the Office of Economic

Stabilization and the Office of Price Administration—to ensure the purposes of the act; set maximum sales prices for homes; and reallocate the distribution of construction materials.[40]

One assessment of the delegated authority provided by Congress noted that "Mr. Wyatt is armed with a grant of power perhaps more expansive than that provided any other single bureaucrat."[41] That might have been true, but Congress statutorily created the housing expediter and placed democratic controls on the authority delegated to that position, such as laying out a definition for maximum sales prices for homes. In addition, the emergency housing act provided guidance to the housing expediter when issuing reallocation orders. Finally, Congress set a termination date of December 31, 1947, for the powers conferred along with all orders and regulations issued by the housing expediter.[42] The guidance and controls Congress established meant that the post–May 1946 statutorily established housing expediter was not a czar.

Another czar not placed within the OEM structure was the director of central intelligence (DCI), who led the Central Intelligence Group (CIG), which Truman created, by directive, in early 1946. The purpose of the CIG was to better coordinate and manage foreign intelligence activities conducted by the United States. Truman stated that he acted to ensure that another Pearl Harbor attack never happened and to counteract threats from the Soviet Union.[43] Sidney W. Sourers, a rear admiral of the Navy, became the first DCI.[44] Since Truman appointed Sourers without Senate confirmation and empowered him to run the new agency for central intelligence, we consider him to have been a czar. In fact, one recent study of the Central Intelligence Agency reported that the president created "the CIG without consulting Congress or obtaining congressional approval."[45]

Not only did Truman appoint a czar but he was also in violation of the Independent Offices Appropriation Act of 1944 by creating a new agency through an executive order. As a result, the CIG would cease to function within a year because federal law required a statutory basis for the creation of all agencies or they would not receive continued appropriations.[46] Truman deceptively bypassed those restrictions by calling the CIG a "group" instead of an agency and created it by using a directive rather than an executive order.[47] He did this because the Russell Amendment specified "any agency" and "executive order."[48] Administration lawyers would eventually argue, however, that authorizing legislation would be needed to make the CIG legal.[49] By early 1947 CIG funds should have been cut off, but the Bureau of the Budget concluded that appropriations could continue because the administration "intended to seek statutory authorization later in the year."[50] Yet, the Independent Offices Appropriation Act did not include an extension provision for funding. Even if it had, the Truman directive made the DCI position a czar. Only after the passage of the National Security Act of 1947, which created the Central Intelligence Agency and required Senate confirmation of its director, were those lingering legal issues resolved.[51]

Various media reports claimed some officials during the Truman administration were czars. In early 1946 a nationwide meat-packing strike occurred as a result of price control measures established by the Office of Price Administration.[52] Truman quickly ordered Agriculture Secretary Clinton P. Anderson to seize and operate the meat-packing facilities based on authority present in the War Labor Disputes Act.[53] Section 3 of the act gave the president the power to "take immediate possession of any plant" required for the war effort and designate any department or agency to do so.[54] The law did have a sunset provision for "six months following the termination of hostilities of the present war."[55] Truman had proclaimed the cessation of hostilities just a month before issuing his order, which meant that he had authority to take over the meat plants.[56] Secretary Anderson assigned the takeover and operation responsibility of the meat industry to Agriculture Department employee Gayle C. Armstrong, who became known in the media as the meat czar.[57] Neither Armstrong nor Anderson, however, was actually a czar. Both operated under congressional authority when Truman ordered the takeover of the meat-packing facilities.

Another media-labeled czar who does not meet our definition was the director of guided missiles, a position that Defense Secretary George C. Marshall decided to establish as part of the military buildup for the Korean War.[58] The first director, Chrysler CEO K. T. Keller, was charged with providing Marshall with "competent advice to help him direct and coordinate activities connected with research, development and production of guided missiles."[59] The reason Keller does not meet our definition of a czar has to do with his advisory functions concerning the guided missile program along with the fact that Marshall had authority to make such appointments.[60] Specifically, the defense secretary was authorized "to appoint and fix the compensation of such civilian personnel as may be necessary for the performance of the functions of the Department of Defense other than those of the Departments of the Army, Navy, and Air Force."[61] Finally, Keller could not issue orders or control appropriations but, instead, was expected to work with the existing service departments on guided missile development without impacting their own assigned responsibilities.[62]

In other cases Truman acted unilaterally to establish government structure, but for reasons stated below we do not consider the various positions he created to have been czars. By the summer of 1950, Truman began preparing the nation for a military conflict in Korea, requiring the mobilization of the country's resources in a manner similar to World War II. In early September, Truman issued an executive order empowering the secretaries of Agriculture, Commerce, and Interior along with the commissioner of the Interstate Commerce Commission to set "priorities and allocations of strategic materials."[63] The order also established the Economic Stabilization Agency (ESA) as an independent agency led by an administrator to be nominated by the president and confirmed by the Senate. The ESA administrator would "seek to preserve and maintain the stabilization of the economy" by developing short- and long-range price and wage policies, informing the various industries of the need for stabilization, and establishing price ceilings along with standardizing wages and salaries. Housed within the ESA was a presidentially nominated and Senate-confirmed director of price stabilization, who would act to maintain low prices and receive general direction from the agency's administrator. In addition, a nine-member Wage Stabilization Board (WSB), appointed by the president and led by a chairman, would provide the ESA administrator with recommendations on wages. Finally, the chairman of the National Security Resources Board (NSRB), an existing agency, was charged with assisting the president in coordinating mobilization activities.[64]

Truman based his executive order on the Defense Production Act of 1950, which delegated to the president a substantial amount of authority to mobilize the country for purposes of national security. The law authorized Truman to set priorities and allocations of materials and facilities, to stabilize prices and wages, to settle labor disputes, and to regulate loan programs for consumer and real estate construction.[65] The delegation of some of those powers to department secretaries and the ICC commissioner appears to have been within Truman's legal authority. However, the act did not permit the president to reallocate and modify powers formally established by law. For example, the National Security Act of 1947, which created the NSRB, specifically stated that "the Board," not the chair alone, would advise the president "concerning the coordination of military, industrial, and civilian mobilization."[66] Truman had changed the allocation of responsibilities within the NSRB without any legal authority, which resulted in the chair operating outside his statutory functions. The positions created by Truman, however, do not meet our definition of a czar. The ESA administrator and price stabilization director each received Senate confirmation and exercised powers provided in law. As for the chair of the WSB, that position could only recommend wage prices to the ESA administrator and possessed no regulatory authority. On June 30, 1952, Congress statutorily established the WSB.[67]

Finally, on the same day Truman declared the existence of a national emergency "to prevent aggression and armed conflict" in Korea, he also issued an executive order that created the Office of Defense Mobilization (ODM).[68] The new agency, placed within the EOP, would be led by a presidentially nominated and Senate-confirmed director whom Truman charged with providing greater mobilization control in the areas of "production, procurement, manpower, stabilization, and transport activities." Truman subjected the ESA and its subunits to the "direction and control of the" ODM director. The move effectively transformed the ESA from an independent agency to an arm of the ODM and the president.[69]

Truman nominated, and the Senate confirmed, General Electric President Charles E. Wilson to be the ODM's first director, a job he would hold for two years.[70] Quickly the media began calling Wilson the nation's mobilization czar.[71] Wilson possessed the same "sweeping" powers as James F. Byrnes did in his capacity as director of the Office of War Mobilization at the end of World War II.[72] However, we do not consider Wilson to have been a czar as he was appointed with Senate confirmation and possessed authority provided by the Defense Production Act.

Later Truman would add more structures within the ODM as he created the Defense Production Administration (DPA) led by William H. Harrison, a presidentially nominated and Senate-confirmed administrator. The DPA was given the responsibilities for setting priorities and allocations of materials along with the expansion of production, capacity, and supply. Although Truman did not specify where the DPA would be located, he provided that its administrator "shall perform his duties subject to the direction, control, and coordination of the" ODM director. As a result, the DPA would be under the umbrella of the ODM.[73] Truman also created the Defense Mobilization Board (DMB) within the ODM, consisting of the secretaries of Defense, Treasury, Interior, Commerce, Agriculture, and Labor in addition to the chairs of the Reconstruction Finance Corporation, the Federal Reserve, and the NSRB. The ODM director would chair the board, which would advise the president on defense mobilization matters and effectively replaced the NSRB as a coordinating agency.[74] As with the ESA, none of the ODM officials should be considered czars as they either were Senate-confirmed or possessed only advisory duties.

DWIGHT D. EISENHOWER

As in the Truman era, the czars established during Dwight D. Eisenhower's presidency centered on managing defense policy. However, unlike his predecessor, Eisenhower did not use the OEM to place new presidentially created agencies under direct White House control. Instead, Eisenhower sought to govern through his cabinet, which meant not creating a large number of new White House agencies to control various public policy areas.[75] The size of the White House Office and EOP did greatly increase during the 1950s. However, as Stephen Hess explained: "Eisenhower's White House showed that a large staff need not be operational, at least if it is balanced with tenacious cabinet officials."[76] The Eisenhower-era czars were instead housed within the Defense Department and were a natural result of the growing Cold War conflict with the Soviet Union along with the increasing pressure from lawmakers to undertake a greater coordination effort of the country's guided missiles programs.

In early 1956, acting under instructions from Eisenhower, Defense Secretary Charles E. Wilson created the position of special assistant for guided missiles and appointed Eger V. Murphree to it.[77] The media quickly began calling Murphree a czar but the moniker did not accurately represent his actual duties.[78] Murphree had a place of importance within the department, but he merely advised and assisted the defense secretary in determining the direction of the guided missile program. Murphree had no authority to coordinate or direct others.[79] The statutory basis for the special assistant position was a provision of the 1951 supplemental appropriations act, which permitted the defense secretary to employ ten individuals of "outstanding experience and ability" to work "without compensation" within the department.[80]

Eisenhower strengthened the advice he received concerning missile defense within the White House by naming a special assistant for science and technology in MIT President James Killian.[81] The media quickly referred to Killian as the missile czar.[82] One newspaper even complained that the country is "giving birth to more czars than the Romanoffs."[83] In his memoirs, Killian denied the media accounts of his czar status, saying he "was an adviser and catalyzer, not a government administrative officer, much less a 'czar.'"[84] Killian's assessment was accurate.[85] Specifically, Eisenhower tasked Killian with advising him on scientific and technology matters as they related to national security, not managing, coordinating, or otherwise directing a missile program.[86] Before this time the Science Advisory Committee (SAC) of the Office of Defense Mobilization served as the White House's formal science advisory body.[87] Aside from creating the new special assistant position, Eisenhower transferred the SAC to the White House and renamed it the President's Science Advisory Committee (PSAC).[88] In part, Eisenhower acted out of a concern that "too much power might be centralized" in the special assistant position.[89] Killian became chair of the PSAC and the Federal Council for Science and Technology.[90]

The two actual czars of the Eisenhower administration did not come into being until after the Soviet Union launched its *Sputnik* satellites in October and November of 1957. A few days after *Sputnik 2* went into orbit Eisenhower delivered a television address to the country seeking to calm fears about the state of the national security situation. In one part of his speech Eisenhower spoke of "an official" in the Defense Department who was "in charge of missile development." Eisenhower added that he had directed the secretary of defense to "make certain that the Guided Missile Director is clothed with all the authority that the Secretary himself possesses in this field, so that no administrative or interservice block can occur."[91] A week later Defense Secretary Neil H. McElroy, who had replaced Charles E. Wilson, followed Eisenhower's order by abolishing the special assistant position and creating the Office of Director of Guided Missiles, which would "direct all activities in the Department of Defense relating to research, development, engineering, production, and procurement of guided missiles." In order to ensure that the various missile programs within the Defense Department came under centralized control, McElroy empowered the director to issue letters of instructions to the service secretaries.[92]

McElroy proceeded to appoint William M. Holaday as the director, a position the media began calling the military missiles czar.[93] One assessment of the director position said it had been created in "response to vocal demands for a missile 'czar' to find a surer way through the Pentagon maze and guide the national missile effort with a firmer hand."[94] We also consider Holaday to have been a czar within the Defense Department. Secretary McElroy based the establishment of the new office on the National Security Act of 1947, as amended, and Reorganization Plan No. 6 of 1953. The former provided McElroy with the authority to "perform any function vested in him through or with the aid of such officials or organizational entities of the Department of Defense as he may designate."[95] The 1953 reorganization plan permitted McElroy to delegate his functions to any officer, agency, or employee of the department.[96] Neither act authorized the creation of the director position but under Title 5 of the U.S. Code the defense secretary could appoint civilian personnel "as may be necessary for the performance of the functions of the [department]."[97]

More importantly for the purpose of determining the czar status is the fact that Holaday possessed significant authority over the nation's missile programs without having received Senate confirmation. McElroy specifically provided Holaday with the ability to give commands to the secretaries of the Air Force, Army, and Navy. At a Senate hearing, Holaday even said he functioned much like "a vice president of a corporation," who could issue orders to the service secretaries like they were managers.[98] Holaday not only oversaw the guided missiles programs but also had budgetary control over appropriated funds for the research and development of them.[99] The director position eventually reverted back to special assistant status by order of the defense secretary in April 1959.[100]

Despite the creation of new positions to provide greater information, coordination, and control of the nation's missile systems, there was still pressure to do more. On February 7, 1958, Defense Secretary McElroy, acting on orders from President Eisenhower, issued a directive creating another czar to head a new agency within the Defense Department called the Advanced Research Projects Agency (ARPA). This czar, whom the defense secretary appointed, would be responsible for ensuring that the United States remained ahead of the Soviet Union in space technological research, particularly as it related to the country's defense needs.[101] With such a broad mandate the media naturally began calling ARPA's first director, Roy W. Johnson, the defense or military space czar.[102] We agree, as Johnson controlled over $500 million in appropriations and had a budget plan to develop $2 billion in new research programs.[103] McElroy justified the creation of new department structure by citing the National Security Act of 1947, as amended, and the Reorganization Plan No. 6 of 1953.[104] Several days after the creation of ARPA, Congress passed legislation that authorized the defense secretary or "his designee" to engage in the research and development of weapons systems or other military requirements.[105] None of those laws, however, specifically provided the Defense secretary with the authority to create a new agency within the department.

A clear sign of Johnson's influence occurred when McElroy ordered the transfer of some of the functions of Guided Missiles Director Holaday to ARPA.[106] The new director became the symbol of the Defense Department's commitment to keeping pace with and surpassing the Soviet Union in defense space technology. By August 1958, Congress decided to provide a more accountable management structure over research programs. The Department of Defense Reorganization Act of 1958 established a Director of Defense Research and Engineering, appointed by the president and confirmed by the Senate, who would be the principal adviser to the defense secretary on scientific and technical matters along with taking control of all research and engineering activities of the department. Johnson began immediately reporting and taking orders from the Defense Research and Engineering director.[107] Only then do we consider Johnson to no longer have been a czar. Later space programs would be transferred to the National Aeronautics and Space Administration, and the military services again regained control over defense research, which left ARPA with a substantially reduced area of influence.[108]

JOHN F. KENNEDY

President John F. Kennedy entered the White House as the first president to style himself after FDR. One scholar explained: "Roosevelt's style was attractive to one who was fascinated by the techniques of wielding power, at which Roosevelt was a master."[109] Nonetheless, Kennedy did not adopt FDR's proclivity for creating czars for the following reasons: First, JFK initially did not face a prolonged world war with the need to mobilize the nation's resources. Second, his domestic agenda—which he called the New Frontier—could be implemented through existing government structure. In particular, he strengthened civil rights enforcement through the Department of Justice, and his goal of landing a man on the moon could be accomplished through the National Aeronautics and Space Administration. Finally, Kennedy's assassination in November 1963 cut short his presidency.

Despite the absence of actual czars during this time, continued use of the term by the media likely causes confusion in the contemporary debate over the issue. For instance, Kennedy continued the special assistant for science and technology position created by Eisenhower and named MIT Professor Jerome B. Wiesner to the post. Despite Wiesner's advisory status and his lack of operational control over government programs, the media began calling him a czar.[110] Along with his duties as special assistant, Wiesner chaired the PSAC and the Federal Council for Science and Technology.[111] Although Wiesner's position did not rise to the level of a czar, there were certainly problems with his status as presidential adviser. By the early 1960s, Congress bitterly complained about the lack of access it received from Wiesner and his predecessors. Lawmakers argued that the special assistant and PSAC "were conducting studies and making recommendations that were of great moment, and that the Congress was handicapped by not having access to their studies."[112]

Under this congressional pressure, Kennedy in June 1962, acting through Reorganization Plan No. 2, created the Office of Science and Technology (OST) within the EOP, to be led by a director who would be subject to Senate confirmation.[113] Kennedy nominated Wiesner to the OST director position, and in that capacity he made his first appearance before a congressional committee.[114] Kennedy's action, however, had little basis in law as his reorganization authority only permitted him to restructure, consolidate, and reduce the size of executive branch departments and agencies, not create new structures.[115] The result is that Kennedy created a new EOP agency not properly grounded in a statute. Even if there had been express language in the Reorganization Act permitting a president to create new executive branch structure, there would still have been a major constitutional concern with doing so. Reorganization plans were not approved by both chambers of Congress. Instead, the law called for a one-house veto of a president's plan.[116] The creation of new government structure should be accomplished through the constitutionally prescribed process of both chambers of Congress acting to pass legislation and the president signing it into law.[117]

Another position that the media mistakenly labeled a czar was Kennedy's special assistant on regulatory matters, James M. Landis, who had the responsibility of providing advice for overhauling the federal government's regulatory system.[118] Specifically, Kennedy tasked Landis with convincing Congress to pass legislation giving the president power to reorganize various regulatory agencies, subject to a congressional veto. The legislation would have had the Interstate Commerce Commission and the Federal Power Commission chairs serve at the pleasure of the president, removable by him without cause.[119] Lawmakers, however, balked at the plan.[120] As one newspaper described it, the "proposals were widely criticized in Congress as aimed at destroying the autonomy of the agencies and subjecting them to White House dictation. The agencies were all created by Congress and their members are appointed by the President, subject to Senate confirmation."[121] Despite the ill-conceived proposal, Landis only provided Kennedy with regulatory advice along with preparing the administration's reorganization proposals as they related to regulatory matters.[122] Landis was not a czar because he had no authority over government agencies or any other nonadvisory role. He served less than a year before being forced to resign after personal scandals involving an alleged affair with his married secretary and failure to pay taxes emerged.[123]

Finally, Kennedy's Special Representative for Trade Negotiations, Christian A. Herter, earned the czar moniker as well.[124] That characterization was not apt, though. Congress created the position, with the rank of ambassador, to be the nation's chief representative for trade negotiations, when it passed the Trade Expansion Act of 1962. The law required the special representative to be confirmed by the Senate. For purposes of trade negotiations, Congress also stipulated that the special representative should "seek information and advice . . . from representatives of industry, agriculture, and labor, and from such agencies as he deems appropriate."[125] Congress not only provided a legal basis for the new post but placed several democratic controls on it.

LYNDON B. JOHNSON

Lyndon B. Johnson's presidency highlights some of the challenges in determining the czar status of certain executive branch officials, particularly ones within the White House. The reason is the gradual movement of policy planning and even what bordered on operational control of programs to presidential aides.[126] Since we do not consider officials to be czars when their role is merely to provide advice or to develop policy, it is sometimes not absolutely clear when a particular White House staffer crosses the magical threshold and becomes a czar. Joseph A. Califano Jr. is a case in point. He served as Johnson's special assistant for domestic affairs, working on a variety of policy issues. During the late 1960s, the *New York Times Magazine* observed that "Califano has come to be, in function if not in title, the Deputy President for Domestic Affairs."[127]

In researching Califano's White House role and duties, it is often difficult to tell if and when he went from adviser to executor of policy. Much of the confusion has to do with Johnson's habit of expecting his staffers to be "general handymen."[128] But more importantly the president expected his aides to be involved in various activities and programs within the departments. As one Johnson administration official explained:

> Confusion is created when men try to do too much at the top. In order to know what decisions are being made elsewhere in government, the White House tends either to spend time reviewing programs or to take more and more decisions on itself. The separate responsibilities of the White House, the Executive Office, and the agencies are fudged, and the demarcations of who does what become uncertain. The result is a blurring of the distinction between staff and line, between program and policy.[129]

Despite the lack of clear lines of authority we do not believe Califano was a czar since his duties appear to have resembled those of a policy adviser and planner.[130]

There were actual czars in the Johnson administration. In February 1964, Johnson pushed ahead on one of his major domestic agenda items of fighting poverty by making Peace Corps Director Sargent Shriver his special assistant of the war on poverty programs, a position the president had announced during a January 8 prime-time television address and at the State of the Union later that same month.[131] In the formal letter of appointment, Johnson said that Shriver would "direct the activities of all executive departments and agencies involved in the program against poverty." In addition, Shriver would coordinate and integrate the poverty program "with the activities of state and local governments and of private persons, including the Foundations, private business and industry, labor unions, and civic groups and organizations."[132] Shortly after Johnson made his announcement the media began calling Shriver the country's poverty czar.[133] That label was appropriate as Johnson bestowed on his aide authority to direct departments and agencies that never had been contemplated for presidentially appointed White House aides. Such positions were intended to advise the president, not direct other officials within the executive branch.

For the first half of 1964 Johnson allowed Shriver to run the poverty program without seeking to create a new agency. During a television and radio interview in March, the president even declared that the White House could manage the poverty program and that no additional government structure was needed.[134] However, that same month Johnson proposed legislation to create the Office of Economic Opportunity (OEO) with Shriver as director.[135] Some members of Congress were concerned that the proposed OEO director would actually be a poverty czar "who could ride roughshod over established agencies." The department and agency heads assured worried lawmakers that "jurisdictional prerogatives were inconsequential compared to the larger issue of fighting poverty."[136] By August Congress passed, and Johnson signed into law, the Economic Opportunity Act of 1964, which formally established the OEO as a new agency within the EOP.[137]

Johnson placed Shriver at the head of the OEO, but Shriver could no longer be considered a czar. Congress not only authorized the creation of an agency to administer the poverty program but subjected the director and his deputy and assistants to Senate confirmation. In addition, lawmakers required that the director provide a report to Congress for each fiscal year. Other democratic controls placed on the OEO were the guiding principles that the director would use in making decisions to provide grants for the agency's community assistance program.[138]

Johnson was not beyond creating a temporary czar to confront an emergency situation. That is what occurred when on March 27, 1964, an earthquake of 9.2 on the Richter scale hit Alaska. The resulting devastation produced, according to one account, "one of the greatest natural disasters ever recorded in North America."[139] Soon various federal departments and agencies were working to provide aid to the state. However, within a day of the earthquake, "it had become clear that the existing machinery at all three levels of government could not begin to cope with the complexity, magnitude, and urgency of the physical and economic recovery faced by Alaska."[140] Newspapers began reporting that Johnson would name a "czar" with broad emergency powers to direct the Alaska relief effort. There was even some discussion that Johnson would request congressional authorization for dealing with the disaster.[141] Johnson made no such request.

Instead, on April 2, 1964, Johnson issued an executive order creating the Federal Reconstruction and Development Planning Commission as a temporary relief agency.[142] Led by Clinton P. Anderson, then a Democratic senator from New Mexico, as chair and Dwight Ink (the assistant general manager of the Atomic Energy Commission) as executive director, Johnson charged the new agency with developing coordination plans for reconstruction purposes and making recommendations to the president. Although Johnson stipulated in the last section of his executive order that the commission had no legal authority over any federal agency or officer, in the preceding section he ordered all agencies represented on the commission to cooperate with and provide information to it.[143] Senator Anderson later remarked that Johnson "authorized powers which exceeded even my conception of what was necessary for meeting the Alaskan challenge."[144]

In his review of Johnson's executive order, Bradley H. Patterson Jr. said that the "unwritten message was that Anderson and Ink were the president's personal deputies—the agencies were to follow their instructions."[145] It is accurate that any presidential aide has a measure of influence that is not reflected in law. But that begs the question whether Anderson and Ink possessed the legal authority to carry out their functions under Johnson's executive order. Johnson failed to state the statutory backing for his order. Does that make them czars? Patterson answered in the affirmative and explained that Anderson and Ink were backed by the president's standing, which "is every White House czar's not-so-hidden secret:

outwardly, they abjure the power that inwardly they carry—and that power is the president's, not their own."[146]

Even relying on the appropriations provision of the 1946 Independent Offices Appropriation Act does not provide adequate statutory backing to create the commission (see the summary section in chapter 3).[147] Although we usually do not place the czar designation on presidential commissions, as no one position has been given clear authority over a policy area, and members of a commission mainly advise and help create policy, we feel confident to label Anderson and Ink czars since they were implementing policy by directing departments and agencies.[148] Finally, we believe that Anderson violated the constitutional restriction under the Ineligibility Clause that prohibits lawmakers from holding federal office while serving in Congress. As a sitting senator he should have been barred from serving on the commission or in any other federal office (see our discussion of the Ineligibility Clause in the presidential commissions and special envoys sections in chapter 2).[149] In his autobiography Anderson admitted that his appointment was "the first time that a member of the legislative branch had been put in charge of a powerful executive agency." He went on to explain that "some jurists might even have argued that the arrangement was an unconstitutional violation of the separation of powers, but to Lyndon Johnson, this was no time to quibble over legalities."[150]

Johnson's final czar came after his landslide election victory in November 1964, when he decided to bestow on Vice President Hubert Humphrey the responsibility for coordinating the administration's civil rights effort, including the enforcement of the Civil Rights Act of 1964. Johnson also tasked Humphrey with coming up with specific recommendations for how the administration would manage civil rights activities.[151] Immediately after the assignment became known, the media began calling Humphrey the civil rights czar.[152] Johnson appointed Humphrey as head of the President's Council on Equal Opportunity (PCEO), which functioned as a coordination and advising agency.[153] As a result, Humphrey, even though in a position that requires election by the Electoral College, exercised coordination authority not established by law. In fact, by bestowing on Humphrey such powers, Johnson had modified and circumvented clear statutory language provided by the Civil Rights Act of 1964, which directs various departments to carry out the country's civil rights laws.

Humphrey's role as civil rights coordinator and chair of PCEO did not last. By September 1965 Johnson had lost confidence in his vice president and disbanded the PCEO.[154] Two executive orders restated the authority various departments and agencies statutorily had over civil rights enforcement.[155] As one scholar explained, "Given that Humphrey had never gotten on top of his assignment and given that responsibility finally resides in those charged by statute with a policy's execution, the outcome was probably inevitable."[156]

As with his predecessors, some of President Johnson's appointments were mistakenly considered czars by the media. In one case Johnson named Thomas C. Mann coordinator of the Alliance for Progress—a 1961 initiative started under President Kennedy that sought to promote economic growth in Latin America.[157] Many in the media referred to Mann as the Latin American policy czar.[158] Mann, however, was not a czar as he held the position of Assistant Secretary of State for Inter-American Affairs. In 1944, as a result of Congress increasing the number of assistant secretaries from four to six, Secretary of State Edward Stettinius Jr. designated one of them assistant secretary of state for American Republic Affairs.[159] In October 1949, Secretary of State Dean Acheson had redesigned the position to its current title: the Assistant Secretary for Inter-American Affairs.[160] Congress did not specify through legislation such a position. However, in an 1874 general appropriations law, it did authorize the Secretary of State to "prescribe duties for Assistant Secretaries" among other responsibilities.[161] That authority has largely remained unchanged, which meant that in 1944 and 1949 the secretary of state had the ability to designate and assign whatever duties to the department's assistant secretaries.[162] Finally, all assistant secretaries within the State Department are subject to Senate confirmation. Besides Mann, Jack Hood Vaughn, Lincoln Gordon, and Covey Oliver would serve as Assistant Secretary of State for American Republic Affairs.[163]

Another official whom many in the media considered a czar was Special Assistant for Consumer Affairs Esther Peterson.[164] In January 1964 Johnson appointed Peterson to the White House and also named her chair of the President's Committee on Consumer Interests.[165] Those moves were designed to give consumer affairs issues a higher profile in the Johnson administration. Peterson, however, had little influence in the Johnson White House even as a policy adviser for consumer affairs let alone a person with operational authority. Although her title might have indicated a place of prominence, Johnson gave her an office in the Executive Office Building, not in the White House. In addition, Peterson had only one secretary and no additional staff or budget. And even if a cabinet meeting discussed consumer affairs, Peterson was "not necessarily in attendance."[166]

Although we disagree with Peterson's unofficial czar title, there were other aspects of her status within government that we do find troubling. Admittedly Peterson had little authority or influence in the Johnson White House, but she did retain her position as assistant secretary within the Department of Labor.[167] The double duty as both a White House adviser and assistant secretary fails to provide a clear line of authority for officeholders to carry out their duties. More troubling is the accountability concern. As a statutory officer within the Labor Department, Peterson had to be confirmed by the Senate, and her performance was also subject to congressional oversight. But as a White House adviser, she was appointed directly by the president and afforded greater executive privilege protections than department officials. The risk in this arrangement is that a president might try to claim executive privilege with a dual appointee to protect her department duties from congressional oversight. The solution to ensure that divided loyalties or unjustified executive privilege claims are not made is to statutorily forbid dual appointments in the first place (see our discussion of reform proposals in chapter 7).

SUMMARY

Since the early part of the twentieth century, various presidential administrations have made use of executive branch czars. By the 1960s presidents became accustomed to the idea and practice of centralizing power and moving away from a reliance on department heads and the traditional cabinet governing system.[168] In fact, White House aides even began to issue orders to cabinet heads and their assistants. As Frederick Mosher noted: "Presidential aides afflicted with hubris, from at least the Johnson administration on, have given orders to Cabinet departments, sometimes contradictory orders from different assistants. Often they have given orders directly to subordinate officials in the departments, bypassing the secretaries."[169]

The creation and use of czar positions worked well with the greater hierarchal structure of the executive branch. Presidents no longer justified the concentration of power and the creation of czars by citing an economic crisis (the Great Depression) or war (World Wars I and II). By Johnson's administration presidents had a much larger White House staff that could develop and implement their policy goals. Stephen Hess explained some of the reasons for these changes:

> There was a president who was impatient with the pace of government and distrustful of those beyond his immediate reach. The programs that Johnson had pushed through Congress, grander in scale and more complex than ever to carry out, threatened to overwhelm the traditional machinery of government. And the prevailing view of public administration—nurtured by scholars who had come of age during the New Deal—approved centralizing the management of the executive branch in the Office of the President.[170]

The ratification of many of the Brownlow Committee's recommendations in the Reorganization Act of 1939 greatly aided in the centralization of power within the White House, but by mid-century presidents sought more. Continually they acted as if the only solution to governing problems was to create additional White House staffing positions and executive office structures.

President Johnson represented the centralization tendencies in modern chief executives.[171] Almost immediately after assuming the presidency, Johnson established the Task Force on Government Organization to consider the reorganization of top-level executive branch personnel, departments, and the executive office of the president.[172] Chaired by Don K. Price, the dean of what is now called the John F. Kennedy School of Government, the Price Task Force recommended a major overhaul of the executive branch by creating five new departments mainly through consolidation of existing ones.[173] The task force called for the creation of powers that would enhance the president's ability to manage and direct the executive branch. In particular, it recommended the establishment of a number of cabinet-level positions, subject to Senate confirmation, which the president could assign for various duties at his discretion. One observer called the proposed cabinet officers "secretaries without portfolio."[174] The task force also suggested that the president should be able to make a number of super-grade appointments, independent of the Senate, and have the ability to move them among the agencies. Finally, it recommended that the president be given complete control over the organization of the EOP and permanent reorganization authority of the executive branch.[175]

The Price Task Force ended with an assessment of the inter-branch relationship between Congress and the president that echoed the views of early twentieth-century administrative reformers: "The President shares with Congress the Constitutional responsibility for the general organization of the Executive Branch." However, the task force observed that the president "alone has the perspective to visualize the complex problems of Government organization, and to appreciate how greatly the success of his policies depends on the soundness of the administrative system by which they must be carried out." The task force reasoned that the president should be given complete control over executive branch reorganization. "If the Congress will in general support his initiative in the improvement of executive organization and in particular grant him permanent authority to initiate reorganization plans," the task force concluded, "the Nation will find fewer pitfalls ahead in the path that leads toward the Great Society."[176]

The general tenor of the Price Task Force's recommendations was to concentrate more power in the presidency and remove longstanding democratic controls. Most of the task force's recommendations were based on rather faulty assumptions. Why does the president alone have "the perspective to visualize the complex problems of Government organization"? Modern presidents are in office at most eight years and many for half that. Members of Congress often have much longer careers in national government and have more varied and rich perspectives for understanding the complexities of government. From 2001 to 2009, did President

George W. Bush really have a better understanding of government than Senators Robert C. Byrd (D-WV) and Ted Kennedy (D-MA)? A president might also be limited by the information he possesses. Rather than enhancing decision making, shielding a president from normal democratic controls will limit his access to useful information and hinder his understanding of complex issues.[177] A distant or misinformed president does not have the vantage point to provide a useful analysis or perspective for assessing government functions.

The Price Task Force's recommendations were not enacted, and the report had little immediate impact on administrative reform. When Chairman Price and the rest of the task force members met with the president in the fall of 1964, Johnson spent the meeting talking about the U.S. war in Vietnam instead of their report and recommendations. Johnson wanted to expend his political capital on his Great Society programs and a war against communism, not some piece of legislation on executive branch reorganization.[178] Ironically, over the next two years Johnson's administration came under attack for its management of the Great Society and its conduct of the U.S. war in Vietnam.[179]

By October 1966 Johnson responded to his critics by establishing another Task Force on Government Organization, this time chaired by Northwest Industries President Ben M. Heineman (known as the Heineman Task Force). Charged with bringing efficiency and greater coordination to the executive branch, the Heineman Task Force recommended the creation of the Office of Program Coordination (OPC) within the EOP, led by a presidentially appointed director with ten regional offices to provide a field-level force.[180] The OPC's director would have the power to "anticipate, surface, and settle jurisdictional and program arguments between Federal departments," among other duties.[181] Another recommendation called for the promotion of "a program development and evaluation capacity" for the president.[182] The Heineman Task Force asked that an Office of Program Development be created within the Bureau of the Budget (now the Office of Management and Budget) and run by a presidentially appointed director to provide the president and his staff with the ability to construct "a domestic legislative program."[183] Finally, it warned Johnson and future chief executives to resist the "perpetual political pressures" to dilute presidential power by creating more and more departments and agencies. "Unchecked, these pressures to widen the President's span of control will eliminate the possibility of meaningful direction from, and contact between, the President and the major line officials of his Administration," the task force argued. It recommended consolidating the twelve existing departments into four super-departments: Social Services, National Resources and Development, Economic Affairs, Science and Environmental Preservation.[184]

The Heineman Task Force recommendations not only would have provided the president with additional administrative support but also would have transformed the executive branch into a pyramid-like structure that concentrated power within the White House.[185] Certainly this outcome is what Johnson wanted. As Ronald C. Moe explained, the president "saw reorganization as an instrument to increase presidential power."[186] Coming so late in Johnson's administration (the president announced his decision to not run for reelection just six months after the report was submitted) and with the U.S. war in Vietnam taking more and more of his attention, the president did not act on the task force's report.[187] Eventually an executive branch reorganization task force established by Richard Nixon adopted many of the same recommendations, which were even implemented for a short time.[188] In the end government reform was not needed since Johnson, and future presidents, could use czars to control public policy without legislative interference.

5. Richard M. Nixon–Jimmy Carter: Congress's Feeble Response

The trend of presidents using czars as powerful instruments of executive action endured into the early 1970s but temporarily ceased that decade during the backlash against the "imperial presidency." Like Lyndon B. Johnson, President Richard M. Nixon became comfortable with the centralization tendencies embodied in every modern presidential administration.[1] The beginning of the temporary halt to the use of executive branch czars, however, came with Nixon's overreach of presidential powers and then the Watergate scandal.

As Arthur M. Schlesinger Jr. explained it, Nixon "had produced an unprecedented concentration of power in the White House and an unprecedented attempt to transform the Presidency of the Constitution into a plebiscitary Presidency."[2] Although Schlesinger displayed a bit of hyperbole, he did succinctly capture the pressing problem of the growth in presidential power during the twentieth century. The Watergate scandal that brought down the Nixon presidency was a symptom of an increasingly unchecked presidency that had been developing for decades.

In the immediate aftermath of the Watergate scandal and Nixon's resignation, lawmakers, academics, and the public pushed back against the trend toward expansive presidential powers. There would be much less acceptance of unilateral presidential governance in the years immediately following Nixon's exit from office. As a result, presidents Gerald R. Ford and Jimmy Carter cautiously exercised presidential powers in their efforts to accomplish their goals and to manage domestic policy issues of the day. Neither created any czars during their tenures, largely because of their desire to reverse the trends of the Nixon presidency, and also because they clearly understood the limits of their powers in the post-Watergate environment.

But even in this circumstance, Congress made only a half-hearted attempt to rein in the White House staff and to therefore provide more effective democratic controls over executive branch czars. Congress's inability or perhaps unwillingness to tackle this key matter of executive branch accountability meant that future presidents would be free to create czars, even if Ford and Carter chose not to do so. The post-Watergate backlash had thus only temporarily interrupted the trendline of expanding presidential powers and declining democratic controls. Eventually czars would again become a regular feature of the executive branch.

RICHARD M. NIXON

When Nixon entered the White House, he sought to decentralize power by re-turning traditional cabinet duties to department heads. As Nixon's chief of staff Bob Haldeman said: "Our job is not to do the work of government, but to get the work out to where it belongs—out to the Departments."[3] However, that plan did not last, and eventually Nixon resorted to centralizing power within the White House and creating czars to oversee various policy areas.

As during other administrations, however, the media continued to label some of Nixon's key officials as czars, even when the label clearly did not fit. For exam-ple, even before Nixon assumed the presidency various press outlets began call-ing Herbert G. Klein, the former *San Diego Union* editor, the information czar after the president announced that Klein would hold the newly created position of communications director within the White House.[4] Nixon actually intended Klein to promote transparency and greater access to executive branch information, but he was not placed in a position of authority with the power to issue orders or promulgate regulations.[5] As a result the communications director position func-tioned as an information staffer and should not be considered a czar.

Also at the start of his administration, Nixon named Henry Kissinger as the assistant to the president for national security affairs (more commonly known as the national security adviser).[6] The position dates back to the National Security Act of 1947, which calls on the president to appoint an "executive secretary" who shall function as the head of the staff of the National Security Council—an en-tity within the Executive Office of the President (EOP) charged with advising the president on national security matters along with coordinating the Departments of Defense and State, the military services, and related agencies.[7] President Harry S Truman used the executive secretary as a nonpartisan assistant as Congress had intended. However, Joseph G. Brock explains that President Dwight D. Eisen-hower turned the position into "a political appointee in order to vest him with greater authority in his dealings with departmental and agency officials."[8] As a re-sult, instead of naming a person to fill the executive secretary position, presidents have since entitled it the Assistant to the President for National Security Affairs.

During Nixon's administration, Kissinger dominated the debate over foreign affairs and national security, which resulted in what scholar John P. Burke de-scribed as "the almost total exclusion of Secretary of State William Rogers."[9] The decreased influence of the State Department seemed apparent from the begin-ning as Nixon tasked Kissinger, even before Rogers had been named as a cabinet member, to devise a White House policymaking process with the NSC leading the charge.[10] After he was named secretary of state, a sign of Rogers's early exclusion came in early 1969 when Nixon and Kissinger met with Soviet Ambassador to the United States Anatoly Dobrynin without Rogers. For the rest of the Nixon administration Rogers found himself pushed aside on most major foreign policy issues, which led one senator to quip: Kissinger became "secretary of state in everything but title."[11]

Rogers grew frustrated over his lack of influence and resigned in September 1973. Nixon quickly turned to Kissinger to fill the State Department post but also allowed him to keep his old job as national security adviser. Kissinger remained in both positions until November 1975.[12]

As previously stated, we find dual appointments to be constitutionally objectionable. We also believe that the national security adviser should be a Senate-confirmed official because of the important nature of foreign policy and national security affairs. However, foreign policy advising is not the same as implementation. Nothing about our argument against czars means that the White House is prevented from developing policy initiatives; just that the president and his aides must do so under the constraints placed on them by the Constitution and federal laws. We also acknowledge that Kissinger was not the first national security adviser to achieve prominence in the development of foreign policy. McGeorge Bundy had a considerable influence on Presidents John F. Kennedy and Lyndon B. Johnson during his tenure in the White House.[13] One account of Bundy's role noted that his "dominant personality largely defined the nation's idea of a national security adviser even down to the present. He remains the yardstick for measuring others."[14] The NSC–State Department disputes did not end with Kissinger and Rogers. There were significant disputes as well during the Carter administration between NSC adviser Zbigniew Brzezinski and Secretary of State Cyrus Vance.[15] Like Kissinger, neither Bundy nor Brzezinski, however, met our definition of a czar.

Nixon's first actual czar rose out of a reorganization plan to expand and alter the Bureau of the Budget (BOB), which had been established in 1921. Specifically, the renamed and retailored Office of Management and Budget (OMB) would not only retain the budgetary authority possessed by the BOB but also provide increased program oversight and regulatory review over the executive branch. Since the first OMB director, George P. Shultz, did not receive Senate confirmation, we consider him to have been a czar.

Nixon also added a Domestic Council placed within the EOP and gave it the responsibility to determine policy goals.[16] Almost immediately some members of Congress opposed the plan, particularly the changes to the BOB. Rep. Clarence Brown (R-OH) said: "As one Member of Congress, I do not intend to sanctify the establishment of a permanent new layer of power in the White House which will be able to operate under the protection of executive privilege which will protect it from being called to account by Congress."[17] Others viewed the plan more favorably. Senator Abraham Ribicoff (D-CT), the chair of the Senate Subcommittee on Reorganization, welcomed the "opportunity to take some of the function of the Budget Bureau and put it in the office of the Presidency where it belongs."[18] Even with significant opposition, after considerable lobbying by the White House, the House of Representatives approved the plan by a 193–164 vote.[19]

Once the reorganization of the OMB had been completed, the new budget unit became involved in policymaking along with its originally conceived management role.[20] In addition, the president illegally delegated authority to the OMB director through the use of the Presidential Subdelegation Act of 1950.[21] Under that law a president can only delegate his statutorily prescribed functions to officials who receive Senate confirmation.[22] Lawmakers became mindful of this development along with the fact that Nixon used the OMB to impound appropriated funds against the clear intent of Congress.[23] By 1973, members of Congress sought to provide greater oversight and accountability over the OMB. The Senate Government Operations Committee, which reported a bill to require Senate confirmation of the OMB director, remarked that the agency had "developed into a super department with enormous authority over all of the activities of the Federal Government. Its Director has become, in effect, a Deputy President who exercises vital Presidential powers."[24] The House equally became adamant about requiring confirmation as it declared:

> The decisions of the Director of the Office of Management and Budget are in most instances the final Executive Branch decisions on budget requests and on the legislative policy of the Executive Branch. To contend that the Director is nothing more than the President's technician on budgetary matters and that he does not exercise tremendous power and authority on his own initiative is to blind one's self to the real facts of governmental life and present-day realities. Next to the President, the Director is the most powerful person in the Executive Branch. To require Senate confirmation of departmental Assistant Secretaries and minor agency heads and board members and at the same time to leave the all-powerful office of Director of the Office of Management and Budget without this requirement, defies good sense and logic.[25]

After Nixon vetoed one version of the bill, Congress eventually succeeded in securing the passage of legislation that required Senate confirmation of the OMB director but did not call for the current officeholder's immediate removal.[26] Although we believe that the director should have been confirmed by the Senate since the creation of the Bureau of the Budget, once the 1970 reorganization changes occurred that position operated as a genuine czar until four years later when Congress required Senate confirmation.

Nixon next moved to create a drug czar within the EOP because of a combination of concerns over domestic crime, returning servicemen from the U.S. war in Vietnam who might have been addicted to drugs, and an upcoming presidential election.[27] In June 1971, he issued an executive order establishing the Special Action Office for Drug Abuse Prevention, with Dr. Jerome Jaffe as its first director. Nixon empowered Jaffe to develop policies "to combat drug abuse" along with coordinating all federal drug abuse programs.[28] Mindful that Jaffe lacked legal authority as he had no statutory backing, Nixon sent a special message to Congress asking that it legally set up the new agency.[29] In March 1972, Congress passed the Drug Abuse and Treatment Act, which formally established the Drug Abuse Office within the EOP and subjected the director and deputy director to Senate confirmation. The law also created the National Institute on Drug Abuse headed by a director appointed by the Health, Education, and Welfare secretary.[30] During Nixon's administration the director of the Drug Abuse Office also served as director of the National Institute on Drug Abuse. From June to March, since Jaffe operated as the chief planner and director of federal drug abuse programs and did not receive Senate confirmation, we consider him to have been a czar.

Nixon also attempted to use czars to better manage the economy, particularly rising prices, in the summer and fall of 1971.[31] In August, he issued an executive order freezing prices, rents, wages, and salaries for a ninety-day period. To aid in the price-control effort, Nixon established the Cost of Living Council (CLC) composed of the heads of the major economic departments and agencies with Treasury Secretary John Connally serving as chair.[32] The executive director, Donald Rumsfeld, however, managed the day-to-day operations of the council.[33] Two months later, Nixon created the Pay Board to help stabilize salaries and the Price Commission to set policies for prices and rents. Both were placed within the CLC and, respectively, chaired by George H. Boldt and C. Jackson Grayson Jr.[34] Almost immediately media reports began calling Connally, Boldt, and Grayson czars.[35]

Not only were the czar titles appropriate for several reasons, but the designation should be placed on Rumsfeld's position as well. The two executive orders were primarily based on the Economic Stabilization Act of 1970, but the law did not authorize the creation of new executive branch structure. Section 203 of the act permitted the president to delegate any function to "such officers, departments, and agencies of the United States as he may deem appropriate." However, nowhere else did Congress grant authority to create the Cost of Living Council or its subunits.[36] That meant Rumsfeld, Boldt, and Grayson were exercising authority improperly granted to them as czars. But under the law Nixon appears to have properly delegated to Connally price control duties. Such a delegation is permitted under the Presidential Subdelegation Act of 1950, which allows a president to delegate to Senate-confirmed officers statutory authority.[37] However, we consider the Economic Stabilization Act to have been flawed since Congress did not provide guidance to the president when it delegated its emergency price, rent, wage, and salary stabilization powers. In order to delegate authority Congress must provide "an intelligible principle," but it failed to do that.[38]

In May 1971, Congress amended the act by adding a subsection but still fell short of clarifying the extent of the president's authority or how it would be exercised.[39] Later in 1971, the U.S. District Court for the District of Columbia rejected a non-delegation doctrine challenge to the constitutionality of the Economic Stabilization Act. Judge Harold Leventhal held that "we cannot say that in the Act before us there is such an absence of standards that it would be impossible to ascertain whether the will of Congress has been obeyed." He reasoned that the May 1971 amendment narrowed the president's authority under the act and that legislative history could be used as guidance.[40] Remarkably, Leventhal argued that stabilization standards developed by the president would be the basis for limiting "the latitude of subsequent executive action."[41] Citing *Yakus v. U.S.* (see chapter 3), he concluded that his reasoning conformed to "the purpose of the constitutional objective of accountability."[42] We disagree. The Constitution does not call for the creation and execution of public policy through one branch of government. In making his final point, Leventhal placed complete trust in the president to provide useful guidance to the CLC, Pay Board, and Price Commission. Allowing that kind of latitude does more to limit accountability than promote it. Because we believe that the delegation of authority was constitutionally objectionable we consider Connally to have been a czar as well despite occupying a Senate-confirmed cabinet position.

The creation of the CLC and its czars raises transparency concerns as well. In particular, the CLC Executive Director Rumsfeld also served as counselor to the president, a position he used as justification to decline to appear before Congress.[43] On at least two occasions Rumsfeld refused to testify before a congressional committee in his role as executive director because his "confidential relationship" with Nixon precluded it.[44] Rep. William S. Moorhead (D-PA), the chair of the Subcommittee of the Committee on Government Operations, argued that all Rumsfeld had done was inappropriately dodge legislative oversight by "donning his hat as an adviser to the President."[45] The risks of White House advisers evading Congress by doing just that are great, which is why Senate confirmation should be required when they become more than mere advisers to the president. In the early 1970s, Lyndon B. Johnson's former White House press secretary, George E. Reedy, stated:

> I think from a standpoint of ... access of information ... one of the principal
> problems that has to be faced is the fact that new agencies are being created in the

White House, agencies where information is gathered, collected, and used in a manner that formerly characterized agencies like the Defense Department, State Department, Labor Department, et cetera. . . . Somewhere along the line, we have to take a very careful look at this fundamental problem of the new forms of organizations that are arising, of the new White House staffs that are really no longer personal advisers to the President and who, from a realistic standpoint, should not be considered in that category, but who are housed within the White House confines and therefore are fairly invulnerable to the press.[46]

As the Rumsfeld example highlights, presidents not only attempt to make White House aides "fairly invulnerable to the press" but also to Congress. That is a real problem when program authority is unilaterally centralized in the White House without the traditional balance of power that democratic controls ensure.

By the end of 1971, Congress began modifying the president's economic authority by enacting greater checks. For example, lawmakers provided a more detailed definition of the president's stabilization powers along with requiring Senate confirmation of the Pay Board and Price Commission chairs.[47] Still not every member of Congress was satisfied with the results. Senator William Proxmire (D-WI) stated that the Nixon administration overreached "in its request for unlimited Executive Power" and that Congress "properly modified those powers so that they are more in accord with our traditional constitutional and legal system." However, he said that the bill "still gives the President dictatorial powers to decide whom he will control, how much to control them, and what groups are to be exempt. There are neither standards nor constraints in the legislation."[48] Proxmire was correct. Even the confirmation requirements for the Pay Board and Price Commission only applied to new appointees and not the existing officeholders.

Eventually Nixon issued an executive order abolishing the Pay Board and Price Commission and placing all economic stabilization authority with the executive director of the Cost of Living Council.[49] At that point the Senate Committee on Banking, Housing and Urban Affairs reported a bill requiring the Senate's advice and consent for the appointment of the CLC executive director.[50] In the limited Senate debate on the measure, Senator John Tower (R-TX) said that in requiring confirmation the director would also "be subject to coming down to us on the Hill and talking with us from time to time if we request his presence."[51] The bill passed with no objections; however, the House did not act.[52] Eventually Congress refused to extend the president's stabilization authority, and by June 1974 the Cost of Living Council had been abolished.[53]

Like other presidents, Nixon sought to reorganize the White House Office and the cabinet so that each became a more effective tool for achieving his policy goals.[54] Nixon tasked Roy Ash with heading the President's Advisory Council on

Executive Organization (Ash Council), which would recommend ways to reorganize along those lines. Using a report issued by Lyndon B. Johnson's Heineman Task Force (see the summary section in chapter 4 for more details), the Ash Council recommended the consolidation of seven existing departments and several independent agencies into four "super-departments" that would be called: Human Resources, Community Development, Natural Resources, and Economic Affairs.[55] Once submitted to Congress, however, Nixon's proposal went nowhere. Administrative law scholar Ronald C. Moe explained that lawmakers were leery of passing such a sweeping piece of legislation that would "have played havoc with the existing congressional committee structure and jurisdictions." In addition, since the Democratic Party controlled both chambers of Congress, there was little incentive for giving a Republican president greater power especially in a presidential election year.[56]

Nixon's defeat at the hands of Congress would not prevent him from moving forward with his "super-secretaries" plan. After his November 1972 landslide reelection, Nixon's strategy for executive branch reorganization dovetailed very closely with the advice of presidential scholar Richard Neustadt, who argued against a focus on the Constitution and laws, instead favoring a focus on personalities and persuasive techniques.[57] "Laws and customs," Neustadt declared, "tell us little about leadership in fact." He thought instead that presidential power could be rightly equated to "the power to persuade."[58] As a result, Nixon began carrying out his reorganization plan on his own without consulting Congress, thereby avoiding the risk of legislative refusal to act.

Before unilaterally implementing his plan, however, Nixon made Treasury Secretary George P. Shultz an assistant to the president for economic affairs. In making the announcement, Press Secretary Ron Ziegler said that Shultz "will be the focal point and the overall coordinator of the entire economic policy decisionmaking process, both domestically and internationally."[59] In his memoirs, Shultz said that Nixon even provided him a "suite of offices on the floor above Henry Kissinger's to give me a White House perspective to bring to my tasks."[60] Most likely this was done to send a signal to others that Shultz now occupied a special place in the executive branch hierarchy. Because of the appointment, news reports began calling him the economic czar.[61] Shultz became the first of four czars or "super-secretaries" who would hold White House appointments along with retaining their cabinet positions. Since he possessed coordination responsibilities that went well beyond what Congress had provided through law, we do consider Shultz to have been a czar. In addition, Shultz's status as a cabinet officer and presidential aide raises checks and balances concerns; such individuals holding dual appointments can invoke executive privilege and block necessary congressional oversight over their policymaking duties within and outside the White House.[62]

The Shultz appointment was just the start of Nixon's unilateral executive branch reorganization effort. On January 5, 1973, three other department heads joined Shultz in receiving White House appointments. Under Nixon's plan, Agriculture Secretary Earl L. Butz; Health, Education, and Welfare Secretary Caspar Weinberger; and Housing and Urban Development Secretary James Lynn became "super-secretaries" who would coordinate broad domestic policy areas of natural resources, human resources, and community development. Each received a title of counselor to the president (Butz: counselor for natural resources; Weinberger: counselor for human resources; and Lynn: counselor for community development) and reported to the Assistant to the President for Domestic Affairs John Ehrlichman.[63] Nixon not only provided Butz, Weinberger, and Lynn with office space in the Executive Office Building but also allowed them to use White House stationery. As Mordecai Lee, author of *Nixon's Super-Secretaries*, explained, this "detail meant that counselors were within the White House Office, part of the inner White House, not in EOP as part of an outer presidential ring." Such a relatively simple thing as office stationery, Lee said, was meant as "a signal that Washington insiders would pick up on."[64]

The super-secretaries plan only lasted five months because the Watergate scandal took much of Nixon's time and political energy away from executive reorganization.[65] Despite the brief period in which these positions existed, Butz, Weinberger, and Lynn were short-term czars since each supervised other cabinet members and presumably had some administrative control over them.[66] In addition, their dual appointments as cabinet heads and White House counselors were constitutionally defective. The supervision duties alone provided each new super-secretary far greater power than Congress had intended to delegate through statute. Only by law or a reorganization plan, not the president acting alone, can department structure and responsibilities be modified. Nixon attempted through executive fiat an administrative reform effort that Congress had refused to accept just a year before.

Dual appointments also increase the risk of White House stonewalling. At the time, Senators Jacob Javits (R-NY) and Charles H. Percy (R-IL) even raised the issue at a White House breakfast with members of Congress that Nixon used to unveil his reorganization plan. Javits and Percy were concerned that Butz, Weinberger, and Lynn, as cabinet heads and White House counselors, would decide to assert executive privilege against congressional committee requests to testify, despite having already been confirmed by the Senate. Nixon gave a rather vague answer that executive privilege would only be invoked when "confidential advice to the president" was at issue and "not about lesser subjects."[67]

An ancillary concern is Ehrlichman's position within the White House during the implementation of Nixon's super-secretaries plan. Although we do not consider Ehrlichman to have been a czar, he presumably acted as an intermediary between super-secretaries and Nixon. That administrative structure violated core tenets of the Brownlow Committee report, which prohibited presidential aides from interposing themselves in such a manner.[68] Ehrlichman also ran the newly created Domestic Council, which Nixon intended to play the same role domestically as the NSC did with foreign affairs. However, that did not occur. Peri Arnold explained: "Far from becoming a mechanism for policy formulation, the Domestic Council became a large staff for presidential errands, admittedly increasing presidential reach, but providing little analytic or formulative impact over policy."[69]

The creation of super-secretaries, like most other czars, represented an attempt by Nixon to concentrate power and circumvent congressional oversight. His unilateral action threatened the way public policy and administrative structure should be formed and implemented. In his memoirs of his time with Nixon, Herbert G. Klein argued that the "super-cabinet" system "had dangers of concentrated power far exceeding those of Watergate." To him, Watergate certainly "spelled great disaster to the nation," but "its immediate effect on general policy or legislation was minute or at least indirect until the final days of the Nixon presidency." On the other hand, the "supercabinet was designed to affect every domestic policy of government and thus the potential abuse of power or even this supreme concentration of power posed a danger far greater than Watergate."[70] We agree. Nixon's super-secretaries plan was indeed an abuse of power that posed a danger to the country. Cooperation among the branches (at least when enacting major policy or administrative changes), along with accountability and the rule of law, should be the guiding principles of government.

While Nixon's super-secretaries plan was winding down, an energy crisis began to sweep the nation. An Arab oil embargo combined with a diminished domestic refining capacity produced long car lines at gas stations.[71] On June 29, 1973, Nixon created an energy czar when he appointed Colorado Governor John A. Love to head the Energy Policy Office, an EOP agency unilaterally established by executive order.[72] Nixon charged Love with "formulating and coordinating energy policies at the Presidential level."[73] In December 1973 the Energy Policy Office would be replaced by the Federal Energy Office, which Nixon also created by executive order.[74] Nixon did not provide a clear reason why he made the change, but he appointed Deputy Secretary of Treasury William E. Simon as the new agency's first administrator.[75] Neither the June nor the December executive order cited a law that provided Nixon with the statutory basis for providing coordination authority to a presidentially established agency. Love and Simon therefore were indeed czars since they operated under no statutory authority to coordinate the nation's energy policy. In addition, Simon's position raised concerns as he remained in his post in the Treasury Department while serving as the administrator of the Federal Energy Office.[76]

Within six months of being named the top energy adviser to the president, Simon lost his czar status when John Sawhill became the administrator of the Federal Energy Administration (FEA). The media, however, mistakenly began calling Sawhill the energy czar.[77] Unlike the Energy Policy Office or Federal Energy Office, the FEA had been set up by Congress "to assure that adequate provision is made to meet the energy needs of the Nation." Congress not only provided statutory backing for the FEA but established it as an independent agency. Sawhill's appointment required Senate confirmation and his delegated powers were mainly limited to advising the president and Congress along with assessing and developing energy plans.[78] Finally, Congress never intended the FEA to be a permanent agency as it set the termination date for June 30, 1976, which would be extended to December 31, 1977.[79] The FEA would finally be abolished with the creation of the Department of Energy on August 4, 1977.[80]

Toward the end of Nixon's presidency, Secretary Shultz stepped down from his twin posts as secretary of treasury and assistant to the president for economic affairs. Nixon reevaluated the decision-making structure used to develop and coordinate economic policy and decided not to name one person to the two positions when he replaced Shultz.[81] Instead, Nixon made Deputy Secretary of State Kenneth Rush assistant to the president for economic affairs and William E. Simon secretary of treasury.[82] Dividing the positions, however, did not prevent the media from referring to Rush as the economic czar.[83] Under Title 3 of the U.S. Code, Rush functioned as a presidential aide within the White House Office and on paper had only advisory duties.[84] However, Nixon also made Rush a member of the Cabinet and National Security Council.[85] Newspaper reports suggested that Nixon had given Rush authority over Treasury Secretary Simon and OMB Director Roy Ash. The *New York Times* concluded that Rush "is a man of considerable power with substantive responsibilities that affect every household and every business in the United States."[86] In his 1975 study on the presidency, George E. Reedy confirmed that Rush "was given unusual authority as a Presidential counselor—coordinator of economic policies throughout the administration."[87]

White House aides such as Rush are even more difficult for outside observers to assess than cabinet heads and agency officials placed within the EOP. Are they White House aides merely advising the president or do they make decisions and control statutory programs that were given to cabinet heads? In the case of Rush it appears that he did not fit the Brownlow Committee description of a White House aide who "would remain in the background, issue no orders, make no decisions, emit no public statements."[88] The development of White House aides with rather ambiguous profiles and responsibilities creates significant checks and balances concerns, especially considering that they were intended to be close presidential advisers and not function as line officers within the U.S. government. In June 1974, Rush refused to appear before the Joint Economic Committee in his role as the president's point person on economic matters, citing separation of powers concerns that prevent congressional "testimony of members of the President's immediate staff."[89] Dumbfounded, Senator William Proxmire (D-WI), chair of the Joint Economic Committee, proclaimed: "For the self-described new 'primary adviser' on economic policy to the President to refuse to account to Congress on some spurious notion of separation of powers is both unacceptable and ridiculous." After making the executive privilege claim, Rush appeared on television to answer economic questions and even spoke at the National Association of Manufacturers. Proxmire stated: "The idea that Mr. Rush should appear before non-elected and unofficial groups but refuse to appear before the elected officials of Congress is not only repugnant to good sense but to the Constitution itself."[90] Eventually Nixon gave in and Rush agreed to testify.[91]

GERALD R. FORD AND JIMMY CARTER

For many observers Nixon's time in the White House represented a presidency run amok. Even before his resignation, Congress attempted to restrain the imperial presidency in passing, over Nixon's vetoes, the War Powers Resolution of 1973 and the Congressional Budget and Impoundment Act of 1974. After Nixon left office Congress persisted as it enacted the Foreign Intelligence Surveillance Act of 1978, the Presidential Records Act of 1978, and the Intelligence Oversight Act of 1980. Andrew Rudalevige, in a detailed study on the imperial presidency, said of these laws: "One after another, then, the assumptions and processes that had extended the president's power, his ability to shape governmental behavior and outcomes, were reformed or removed." He added that with "congressional resurgence, it seemed the 'imperial presidency' was an outdated period piece."[92] Indeed, neither Ford nor Carter would try to unilaterally create czars. Raymond Tatalovich and Thomas S. Engeman maintained that the post-Nixon presidents "represented a repudiation of the 'imperial' presidency thesis."[93] At the dawn of the 1980s, Thomas E. Cronin could optimistically write: "The era of the manipulative and imperial presidency has thankfully passed."[94] Nixon's immediate successors would, for a time, give reason to believe that Cronin was right.

As the first post-Nixon occupant of the White House, Ford sought to restore confidence in government by limiting presidential overreach. There would be no unilateral executive action in the form of czars during his time in office. However, the media continued to use the word *czar* for various executive branch officials

such as the Special Action Office for Drug Abuse Prevention director Robert Du-
Pont and the Federal Energy Administration Administrator John Sawhill.[95] Both
positions had been established by law and were subject to Senate confirmation.
Still the media referred to Sawhill's replacement, Frank G. Zarb, as the energy
czar.[96] Despite the persistent use of the term, the label greatly decreased during the
mid- to late 1970s. Only seven officials in six positions earned the czar moniker
from the media during Ford and Carter's time in office. Like his post-Nixon coun-
terpart, Carter also did not create any actual czars.

Most of Ford's media-labeled czars were the product of the ongoing energy crisis, which had carried over from the Nixon administration and had caused great
concern for the public, Congress, and the White House. Ford issued an executive
order establishing the Energy Resources Council within the EOP "to develop, coordinate, and assure the implementation of Federal energy policy." The council
consisted of the secretaries of Interior, State, Treasury, Defense, Commerce, and
Transportation, and the Attorney General, the assistant to the president for economic affairs, Atomic Energy Commission chair, Office of Management and Budget director, Council of Economic Advisers chair, Federal Energy Administration
administrator, Energy Research and Development Administration administrator, Environmental Protection Agency administrator, Council on Environmental
Quality chair, National Science Foundation director, and the executive director of
the Domestic Council. Ford designated Interior Secretary Rogers C. B. Morton to
be council chair.[97]

At the same time, many media reports erroneously referred to Morton and
FEA administrator Frank G. Zarb as the energy czars.[98] As explained above, the
head of the FEA had clear statutory grounding and received Senate confirmation.[99]
As for Morton, section 108 of the Energy Reorganization Act of 1974 authorized
the creation of the Energy Resources Council. Congress specified the council's
duties, which were to "insure communication and coordination among" federal
agencies responsible for energy policy and to make recommendations to the president and Congress. In addition, Congress stipulated that the council chair "may
not refuse to testify before the Congress or any duly authorized committee thereof
regarding the duties of the Council or other matters concerning interagency coordination of energy policy and activities." Finally, Congress established a termination date at either two years or when a "permanent department responsible for
energy and natural resources" came into existence.[100]

During the Carter presidency media reports referred to some statutorily approved administration officials as czars. As during the Ford administration, there
was a continuation of the drug czar label, but instead of the director of the Special
Action Office for Drug Abuse Prevention being given that title, it was reserved for
the Drug Abuse Policy director, Peter G. Bourne.[101] The position, however, should

not be considered a czar. In 1976, Congress passed the Drug Abuse Office and Treatment Act Amendments, which established the Office of Drug Abuse Policy within the EOP. It also included several democratic controls such as requiring Senate confirmation of the director and stating that the office's placement within the EOP "shall not be construed as affecting" congressional access "to information, documents, and studies" or to its personnel. Congress also limited the duties of the director to making recommendations to the president, reviewing federal department and agency's drug policies, and coordination of federal drug abuse prevention functions. The only regulatory authority the director possessed was to implement a nondiscrimination policy that prevented private and public hospitals that received federal funds from refusing admission or treatment to drug abusers. Finally, the director had to submit an annual report to the president and Congress.[102]

The media also kept on using the energy czar moniker. This time around the designation went to the first secretary of the Energy Department, James Schlesinger.[103] Media reports even referred to Schlesinger's replacement, Charles William Duncan Jr., by the same title.[104] Of course neither man was a czar since Congress authorized the Energy Department's creation when it passed the Department of Energy Organization Act, which requires Senate confirmation of the energy secretary along with ensuring that an annual report is made of the department's activities.[105] Speaking during the Senate debate on the bill, Senator Charles H. Percy (R-IL) said, "No one can say we are creating a czar of energy." He then explained that "there are plenty of checks and balances" within the structure created and that Congress had reserved for itself substantial authority "in this field, which will be handled by the committee which will have oversight."[106]

Carter's remaining media-labeled czars were the result of one of the worst inflationary periods in U.S. history. In April 1978 Carter announced as part of his anti-inflation policy the appointment of his Special Representative for Trade Negotiations, Robert S. Strauss, to the position of White House special counselor on inflation.[107] In his new role, media reports called Strauss the nation's inflation czar.[108] The appointment, however, was window dressing meant to demonstrate to the public that the White House was doing something about the problem of prices. The fact was that Strauss exercised no formal powers. As one commentator noted, Carter appointed Strauss apparently to "talk inflation to death."[109] Although Strauss had to be confirmed by the Senate as special representative, the dual appointment as a White House aide raises constitutional concerns even if we do not consider him to have been a czar.[110] Strauss's elevated status as a White House aide meant that there were real dangers of White House stonewalling and the use of executive privilege if Congress began oversight hearings into the administration's inflationary policies or possibly sought to investigate the duties of the special representative.

By October 1978, Carter replaced Strauss as the head of his anti-inflation efforts with Alfred Kahn, who became adviser to the president and chair of the Council on Wage and Price Stability (COWPS).[111] As with Strauss, media reports called Kahn the inflation czar but, again, the title does not fit.[112] In 1974, Congress authorized the creation of COWPS within the EOP to monitor and assess the federal government's anti-inflationary programs. Congress did not provide COWPS with the authority to issue price controls and expressly prohibited the "reimposition of any mandatory economic controls" on "prices, rents, wages, salaries, corporate dividends, or any similar transfers." Finally, COWPS had to submit a report to the president and Congress "from time to time" concerning its activities, findings, and recommendations on containing inflation.[113]

The Ford and Carter administrations provide a useful overview and study of media-named czars. It appears the term was an easy and helpful way to highlight to the public a designation or creation of an office that was intended to somehow address an important public policy issue of the time. News outlets did this regardless of whether the position had been statutorily created, confirmed by the Senate, or possessed actual authority. Of course it was not the primary objective of the media to provide a uniform definition of a czar. This lack of clarity nonetheless has naturally caused great confusion for politicians, scholars, and the public when trying to assess the history and growth of czars. A cursory glance at the Nixon, Ford, and Carter administrations would show the creation and use of czars during their presidencies. However, under closer examination and with a more precise definition, there are clear differences between many of the media-labeled czars and those executive branch officials who were actually czars.

WHITE HOUSE AUTHORIZATION ACT: CONGRESS'S FEEBLE RESPONSE

The pushback against the imperial presidency included concern over the growth of the White House and Executive Office staff dating from the 1940s. It was during the Nixon administration that various members of Congress attempted to provide greater oversight and control over the president's staff.[114] Not until the fall of 1978 did Congress finally pass legislation in the form of the White House Authorization Act, which attempted to limit the number of personnel in the White House Office, the Vice President's Office, the president's domestic policy staff, and the Office of Administration.[115] The law was the first revamping of Title 3 of the U.S. Code since 1948. Its sponsors, Rep. Patricia Schroeder (D-CO), Rep. Herbert E. Harris II (D-VA), and Morris Udall (D-AZ), argued that Title 3 needed to be changed in order to hold the president accountable. In her introductory remarks,

Rep. Schroeder, who chaired the House subcommittee with responsibility over the bill, explained:

> The central issue before us, in this regard, is whether the Congress should acquiesce in, and by implication, approve of, having Presidents who are unaccountable for their funds and their close staff. To oppose placing limitations upon the President's staff, however strongly we might wish to give him a blank check to get his jobs done, is to ignore the duty and power of Congress under article II, section 2, clause 2 of the Constitution to provide from time to time positions in the executive branch. This provision is one of the tensions which the Founders of our Nation put into the structure of the Federal Government. It must not be compromised by our inaction. It must be conscientiously exercised.[116]

Schroeder correctly stated the need for Congress to provide effective oversight and control over the executive branch. There is no separation of powers concern with lawmakers placing limitations on the president's staff positions since Congress must authorize their creation in the first place and is constitutionally obligated to provide oversight of the other branches.

Similarly, Rep. Harris said that the "fundamental point here is to make sure power is in the hands of accountable people: the Cabinet." He noted that "executive advisers and special assistants to the President have their proper advisory role" and nothing more. Congress did not, Harris argued, "vest in them unlimited powers." What concerned him even more was the fact that White House aides are "unelected" and sometimes made "inaccessible" to Congress presumably through executive privilege claims. "Quite simply," Harris declared, "our Government should not be run by, and our President should not depend on a 'palace guard.'" Finally, he warned that "centralized power in the hands of a few anonymous individuals is contrary to a democracy."[117]

Although both Schroeder and Harris's statements provided a thoughtful overview of the constitutional and governing concerns with White House aides, the final legislative product did not do much to limit presidents or hold them accountable. The bill greatly increased the authorized number of personnel in the White House. There would be no limit to the size of the White House Office, but instead the legislation only restricted the number of executive level II (twenty-five) and III (twenty-five) positions along with some of the supergrade staff (fifty positions at GS-18 and "such number of other employees as" the president "may determine . . . not to exceed the" GS-16 rate of pay). The bill even included a provision that authorized the president "to procure for the White House Office . . . temporary or intermittent services of experts and consultants" not to exceed the executive level II pay rate, so even the initial limits on such positions were greatly weakened. The word *temporary* took on a subjective meaning under the bill, as later on the provision reads: "temporary services of any expert or consultant . . . may be procured for a period in excess of one year if the President determines such procurement is necessary." In addition, the bill authorized the staffing of the domestic policy and office of administration personnel within the White House Office: eleven employees not to exceed executive level III pay; twenty-three employees not to exceed the GS-18 level; such "other employees as [the president] may determine to be appropriate" not to exceed the GS-16 level; and another section permitting the employment of "temporary or intermittent services and consultants" not to exceed the GS-18 level.[118]

Aside from the personnel provisions, the bill included a section that authorized $1 million for "unanticipated needs for the furtherance of the national interest, security, or defense, including personnel needs." That section had a reporting requirement for each fiscal year and limited the individual pay provided to not exceed executive level II. Another section provided the president with the authority to detail executive department and agency employees to the White House. Finally, the bill required a general report on the number of executive branch employees detailed to the White House for more than 180 days along with the number of experts and consultants hired and the total number of days employed along with the costs for their services (aggregate and by office). Only later would a general reporting requirement for full-time White House staff be included in the legislation.[119]

Despite the strong endorsement from Schroeder and Harris there was considerable opposition to the bill that centered on the open-ended authorization of presidential personnel along with the lack of true accountability and reporting requirements. Rep. Benjamin Gilman (R-NY) sought to offer an amendment that would have required that presidents, one year after assuming office, submit to Congress a new authorization request for their staff. He argued that lawmakers were "making a serious mistake if we pass legislation that sets a precedent—for future measures containing similar authorizations that are not annual or biannual or even under some 5-year concept of economic planning but are in themselves self-sustaining." Gilman also wanted to offer a second amendment that required a more detailed report from the president on White House personnel explaining that he wanted "to insure the integrity of the oversight function" of Congress "by having available to us by law on a timely basis the information necessary to carry out our duty." At that time neither measure could be acted upon as the Democratic House majority brought the bill up under a closed rule, which prevented amendments from being offered.[120]

Other concerns over the legislation from lawmakers, such as Rep. Henry Hyde (R-IL), centered on the expansion of presidential staff and increasing the funds available to presidents for "unanticipated needs." Hyde declared that "the bill authorizes a number of unprecedented features which ought to concern those recent converts to the idea of executive accountability." He specifically questioned the need for twice as many White House Office staff as Congress had previously authorized. In addition, Hyde decried the absence of checks on presidents, who can "hire an unlimited number of consultants and 'detailees' from other agencies" under the legislation. Finally, Hyde wondered what was meant by the $1 million appropriation for presidents to spend at their discretion "to meet unanticipated needs for the furtherance of the national interest, security or defense." He asked if this was "for petty cash" or "pocket money?" "We are talking about 1 million tax dollars," he continued, "and we deserve to know a few facts, at the very least."[121]

The House eventually voted on the motion to suspend the rules and pass the bill without amendment, but it failed to secure the two-thirds vote.[122] This outcome resulted in Rep. Gilman being able to offer his amendment requiring a stronger reporting measure, which stipulated that presidents provide the number of full-time White House staff in the aggregate and broken down by office. Rep. James Pickle (D-TX) moved to strengthen Gilman's amendment by adding a requirement that the president also report the names of every person working full-time or detailed to the White House, the amount appropriated for their salary, and general title along with a job description.[123] The House agreed to both measures. Rep. Gilman also offered a sunset amendment to provide for authorization "beginning October 1, 1978, and to each of the following 4 fiscal years."[124] Rep. Schroeder rose in opposition but only because she argued that a sunset provision would also eliminate the strengthened reporting requirements, which would mean "we would go back prior to the law and be where we are now."[125] After several other lawmakers also spoke against the amendment, the House voted to reject it by a 171 to 232 margin with 31 members not voting.[126] The House went on to pass the bill by a 265 to 134 vote with 35 lawmakers not voting.[127]

In the Senate, Senator William V. Roth Jr. (R-DE) offered, and the chamber passed, a sunset amendment that provided for authorization of presidential personnel until September 30, 1983.[128] During the conference committee that Congress established to resolve disagreements over the bill, the conferees stripped Roth's amendment. In the conference report, the conferees justified their action by arguing that "a distinction should be made between general sunset provisions which require reauthorization of programs and, the 'sunset' provision in this amendment which would require reenactment of budget authority for the President to hire staff."[129] That statement is strange and confusing without some more information. Yet the conferees offered no additional comments. Nothing in the Constitution or existing law prevents Congress from requiring a president to request annual authorization for his staff. If lawmakers really wanted to hold the president accountable, they should have required him to justify White House personnel, or at least the addition of new aides, from time to time.

Even the House majority was not convinced that the law established substantial controls on the president. The House report on the bill stated that the proposed law "allows the Congress limited oversight."[130] Members of the Senate—both Democratic and Republican—agreed. Senator Harry F. Byrd (VA), an independent Democrat opposed to the bill, questioned Congress's actions for not setting a limit on White House expenditures. After much back and forth, Democratic Senator Lawton Chiles (FL), a supporter of the legislation, admitted that there "is no direct control here so far as a total figure is concerned."[131] Republican Senator Bob Dole (KS) read the bill's authorization provision, which provides "such sums as may be necessary" and quipped: "Frankly, it does not sound like Congress is exerting much control."[132]

The conference committee went on to strip away even more checks from the bill. Aside from removing the sunset provision the conferees eliminated an annual reporting requirement that mandated the president provide to Congress the name, job title, job description, and salary of every individual employed in the White House. The conferees explained that such a reporting requirement "is contrary to Government-wide rules, developed to conform with both the Freedom of Information Act and the Privacy Act, that are tailored to provide for protection of the privacy of individuals involved." In addition, the conferees modified another reporting requirement for federal workers detailed to the White House. Instead of requiring the number and names of all detailed federal workers, the conferees exempted individuals who had worked at the White House for less than thirty days. Here the conferees said that they had "received assurance from the [Carter] administration that, as in the past, this information will be provided to the Congress upon request."[133]

There are several problems with the conferees' actions. Presidential aides are public officials and employees who should be subject to the same democratic controls as any other federal worker. Many states make available the salaries of their public employees, including college and university personnel. Executive office staff should receive the same level of scrutiny. At the very least Congress could have excluded each employee's name but required the listing of job title, job description, and salary. Congress has the constitutional responsibility to appropriate and that includes specifying the salary of presidential aides. All appropriations, even those going to the president, require congressional oversight and scrutiny. Another issue centers on the number of aides presidents can appoint. Although lawmakers provided a set limit of 100 White House aides at various levels of pay, another provision in the law permitted a president to appoint "such number of other employees as he may determine to be appropriate."[134] This provision blew a hole in the idea that Congress would hold presidents to account by placing limits or any kind of supervisory controls upon their staff. Finally, comity is often the better way to manage inter-branch relations as opposed to discord and turmoil. However, just because Congress receives assurances from one administration that it will freely disclose information does not mean all others will do the same.

To ensure proper accountability and to know where all federal workers are serving at any given time, Congress needs full disclosure of presidential staff. The changes made by the conferees greatly weakened an already watered-down bill. Far from holding presidents to account, Congress expanded the EOP without substantial oversight measures and effectively empowered presidents to govern through the White House. Presidential advocates might object that the very act of accounting for executive office staff and appropriations violates the separation of powers. One constitutional principle (separation of powers), however, does not automatically trump another (checks and balances). Congress, as the sole appropriator of federal funds, has a constitutional obligation to hold presidents to account. Avoiding such a responsibility undermines the structural protections created for a constitutional republic. Presidents and their aides cannot wall themselves off from legislative oversight and review with repeated assertions that somehow separation of powers protects them completely. The fact is that the modern age has ushered in a governing system where the presidential staff has taken on increased responsibilities that have normally been carried out by departments and agencies. More vigorous legislative oversight of the White House Office and EOP therefore is required.

SUMMARY

The decade of the 1970s witnessed the height of the alarm over the "imperial presidency." Many saw Nixon's scandals as a hallmark of a presidency run amok. And they also believed that his resignation and the emergence of chief executives with more modest views of their powers would usher in a new era of genuinely balanced constitutional powers. The future would not be so bright for supporters of a return to such a system of government.

Studies of the Nixon presidency understandably focus on the U.S. war in Vietnam, the Watergate scandal, or various disputes with Congress over war powers and impoundment. Although less well known to students of the Nixon era, the president's plan for super-secretaries and his use of czars represent another aspect of the ongoing centralization tendency for modern presidents. The eventual unpopular war in Southeast Asia as well as the scandal leading to Nixon's resignation had the effect of temporarily bottling up the modern trend toward increased independent presidential powers and vastly expanded authority for chief executives. Thus, Presidents Ford and Carter scaled back the presidency in many arenas, including the lack of executive branch czars in their administrations. But again, that was merely a temporary retreat in light of the excesses of the Nixon administration and the resurgence of a strong presidency after the Ford and Carter era—particularly in the last decade under both George W. Bush and Barack Obama.

Even in the aftermath of Watergate there was no effective attempt by Congress to provide oversight and control of executive branch czars. The only legislation passed to limit the centralization tendencies of the modern presidency actually did more to promote the use of czars than hold them at bay. The failure of the redesigned Title 3 to achieve any of the congressional objectives claimed by lawmakers in 1978 should have been a wakeup call for Congress to do more, but it was not.

The reasons are clear why Congress did not seriously attempt to limit the presidency or the use of czars. Since the 1930s the federal government has become all things to all people. It helps clothe and feed the poor, take care of the elderly, educate the young, clean the environment, alleviate discrimination, ensure stable prices of goods, build roads, promote democracy around the world, and much more. As the federal government has taken on more responsibility to act not only on national problems but also on issues of concern to particular groups and individuals, the system of government that has evolved is one in which Congress has delegated its authority with few limits, or presidents have assumed that they have power to act on their own.[135] In the latter cases this situation has resulted in the creation of executive branch czars who often decide rules for industries or coordinate broad policy areas. Lawmakers, particularly of the president's party, have been all too willing to stand by and permit executive governance to continue unchecked as congressional polarization has increased. The situation becomes a fait accompli when the president and czars are no longer constrained by the Constitution or laws.

By the time Obama became president, neither Congress nor the public was interested in Title 3 reforms or how the White House operated. Most members of Congress looked, naturally, to the president for solutions and answers to major problems facing the nation such as the war on terrorism and the economic crisis. In a system of government that relies on executive power, czars become a sought-after tool for implementing public policy, not only by presidents, but even by legislators and the public. As a result, no one should have been shocked that czars continued to exist after Nixon's presidency.

6. Ronald Reagan–Bill Clinton: The Reemergence of Czars

We have traced to this point the origins, evolution, and the temporary decline of executive branch czars. After a brief period during the mid- to late 1970s, when Presidents Gerald R. Ford and Jimmy Carter had not employed czars, fears over the "imperial presidency" began to dissipate. It would logically follow that starting with Ronald Reagan and the reassertion of the strong presidency, there would be a return to the ongoing use of executive branch czars.

But that did not happen. Presidents Reagan, George H. W. Bush, and Bill Clinton did not aggressively use czars. The 1980s–1990s period demonstrates that the mass creation of executive branch czars is not a necessary outcome of an administration that seeks to strengthen presidential powers. Certainly all three of these presidents believed in the notion of a strong presidency possessing substantial independent powers. But czars are only one among many tools that presidents might employ in an attempt to act independently or to wall themselves off from traditional democratic controls. Some presidents have chosen to limit their use of czars or refused to create them at all while exercising presidential powers in various other ways.

At the start of the 1980s, Reagan came into the White House seeking to return the executive branch to what he believed was its proper place in the governing system.[1] But generally he believed that the use of presidential power during his tenure meant the reduction of the federal government in the domestic sphere, not the expansion of it. Reagan's agenda of tax cuts, fewer regulations, and a strong national defense did not need to rely on the creation of many new executive branch positions or czars.[2]

Instead Reagan and many of his allies believed that government was the cause of the country's social and economic troubles. Certainly Reagan sought to increase various presidential powers, but not in ways that necessarily entailed creating czars. Reagan chose to employ other types of unilateral executive action that included the use of appointments, executive orders, signing statements, and the attempted reinvigoration of executive privilege claims.[3] The lack of czars in his administration therefore did not signify a belief in a weak or subservient presidency. Reagan just chose to assert the powers of his office in various other ways.

President George H. W. Bush entered the presidency with a less ambitious and more moderate agenda than that of his predecessor.[4] Bush of course had campaigned in 1988 on the pledge to continue the Reagan legacy. But as president he did so by placing emphasis on fostering a strong and often independent cabinet. As scholar Shirley Anne Warshaw explained: "The departments, not the White House, were shaping the agenda."[5] Thus, the use of czars does not seem at all compatible with Bush's approach to governing. Like his predecessor, Bush did not shy away from using independent powers where possible. But he did so through mechanisms other than appointing czars.

Bill Clinton came into the presidency holding more moderate views than many in his own political party as a "New Democrat" and the former chair of the Democratic Leadership Council.[6] This outlook naturally produced a somewhat less ambitious agenda than some of the past presidents Clinton admired. Even when Clinton pressed policy initiatives such as health-care reform, he tried to do so through legislative enactments, not by unilateral executive action. Various scandals, including the one that led to his 1998 impeachment, distracted the president from his policy agenda for much of his second term.

To be sure, the backlash to the imperial presidency was dissipating for all these presidents, but in some respects it still posed a lingering constraint on their actions.[7] That may also explain in part the relatively few czars during this time.

RONALD REAGAN

President Reagan advocated and pushed for greater presidential powers than his immediate predecessors, but doing so in his case did not include the use of czars. In many ways czars signify a belief in an activist and expansive federal government. A president who wants to reduce, not expand, government may be disinclined to create czars to oversee or manage his policy initiatives. Reagan thus represented an assertive president, but one who wanted to limit government.

Reagan, though, was not completely without officials exercising czar powers. These positions came about not by design, but as a result of the egregious breakdown of presidential control of the national security process within the National Security Council (NSC).[8] We argue throughout this book that czars represent a deviation from democratic controls and constitutional order. One of the most telling examples of the dangers of executive branch czars comes from the Reagan era. The Iran-Contra scandal, as it came to be known, demonstrated that many White House aides could undertake—on their own or with presidential approval—policymaking and even operational roles without the Congress or the public knowing.

The full extent of the use of czars did not become known until the fall of 1986 when the Reagan administration was rocked by the discovery of information that implicated top-level White House officials in a scheme where weapons were sold to Iran in the hopes of securing the release of U.S. hostages. In addition, the money made on the weapons sales went to aiding the Contras—a rebel group that opposed and sought the overthrow of the Nicaraguan government. Congress had prohibited that action by the Boland Amendment. NSC Advisers Robert McFarlane and John Poindexter, along with Lieutenant Colonel Oliver North, deputy director of political-military affairs for the NSC, all were eventually held responsible for putting the entire scheme into operation.[9]

Although never officially designated as such, these individuals exercised czar-like powers in carrying out their illicit weapons and hostages dealings. They directly controlled the selling of arms, negotiating of hostages, and the funneling of money to the Contras.[10] Regardless of whether the president authorized these men to exercise such powers, their actions and lack of accountability highlight the troubles of czars. The concentration of power within the White House that began decades before this scandal resulted in a governing system where the traditional responsibilities of the Defense and State Departments could be, and were, exercised by NSC staff.

The concentration of power does not necessarily result in operational control over policy areas. Reagan's White House staff—like many presidents past and future—did, however, focus on the planning and development of policy. At the start of his presidency Reagan reorganized the Domestic Council into the Office of Policy Development (OPD), led by Assistant to the President for Policy Development Martin Anderson, and also set up small groups consisting of department heads called cabinet councils.[11]

Although we do not consider any official who became part of this new structure to be a czar, the Reagan era practices highlight some of the difficulties with making such a determination. In her book *The Domestic Presidency*, Shirley Anne Warshaw describes how the OPD communicated to the departments "the themes of the Reagan administration and the goals articulated by" Reagan.[12] Anderson and the OPD staff functioned as guides who consistently pressed department heads to remain faithful to the president's agenda.[13] Far from implementing, or even developing, new policy on their own, Anderson and the OPD staff became cheerleaders for Reagan's stated policy preferences.[14] During Anderson's tenure he refused to testify before a House appropriations subcommittee about the OPD's budget request, claiming executive privilege. Such incidents are especially troubling as presidential staffers have increasingly been involved not only in policy development but also in implementation. This particular executive privilege claim is particularly puzzling in that the committee merely wanted information concerning the OPD budget, not Anderson's conversations with Reagan. Although the House reacted by slashing the OPD's budget request, later the funding was restored as part of a continuing resolution.[15] Congress might very well consider creating statutory reporting mechanisms for heads of offices within the White House along with mandatory appearances before oversight committees.

The placement of White House staff between the president and cabinet heads continued to be a troubling development in the Reagan White House. Counselor to the president Edwin Meese continually stymied Secretary of State Alexander Haig. John P. Burke reports that Haig "found that he did not enjoy direct access to the president but had to go through" Meese.[16] In his memoirs, Haig noted that Meese had no constitutional or legal authority over foreign affairs and that it came as a shock to him that a White House staffer would purport to supervise a cabinet officer.[17] As explained in chapter 5, White House advisers have certainly achieved prominence in the area of foreign affairs: McGeorge Bundy under Presidents John F. Kennedy and Lyndon B. Johnson; Henry Kissinger with President Richard M. Nixon; and Zbigniew Brzezinski while serving President Jimmy Carter. Unlike those officials, however, Meese was not the national security adviser. Regardless of the position, White House aides who merely advise but do not implement foreign policy are not czars. We do acknowledge the difficulty of making such a determination when the advising and implementing functions come close to being muddled, which is why we offer a number of reforms to provide better oversight and legislative checks on the White House structure in the conclusions chapter.

The only other known czars during Reagan's presidency were the product of a legislative effort to address the homelessness problem facing the nation. In 1987 Congress passed the Stewart B. McKinney Homeless Assistance Act, which established the Interagency Council on the Homeless (ICH) for a three-year period.[18] Set up as "an independent establishment" within the executive branch, the ICH membership included the heads of sixteen federal departments and agencies. Congress empowered it to review, evaluate, assist, and coordinate the federal government's homelessness efforts with state and local governments.[19] Although headed by a chair selected from its members, an executive director—appointed by the council—oversaw the operations of the ICH.[20] Presidentially (or in this case, council-) appointed executive branch officials who coordinate public policies across departments and agencies can only do so by interfering in the statutory operations of cabinet and agency heads and other officers who do receive Senate confirmation. There is an inherent conflict in allowing such a command structure to exist.

For coordinating officials to effectively do their jobs they need not only statutory backing but also equal status with the very heads of departments and agencies with which they are dealing. That is why we consider officials who do possess coordination functions to be czars. The ICH remains in operation today. We not only place the czar moniker on Cassandra Moore and James Stimpson, who were the ICH executive directors under Reagan, but also on all subsequent officeholders in the George H. W. Bush, George W. Bush, and Barack Obama presidencies.[21]

Like his predecessors, Reagan could not escape the media's mistaken use of the czar label to describe various executive branch officials. For example, at least one *New York Times* reporter inaccurately called Assistant Secretary of Energy for Defense Programs Herman E. Roser the nuclear arms czar.[22] Roser's position had been created by Congress when it established the Department of Energy in 1977. Congress authorized the creation of eight assistant secretaries, who would be nominated by the president and confirmed by the Senate. Congress also specified that the energy secretary had the authority to assign functions to the assistant secretaries.[23]

One of the most well known media czars to have emerged out of the Reagan era was not even created or championed by the president. In fact, it was Congress that wanted to establish a new office or position that would finally take charge of the nation's drug enforcement policies. At the end of 1982 Congress passed, over the protests of Reagan and various administration officials, the Violent Crime and Drug Enforcement Improvements Act, which created a Senate-confirmed director of National and International Drug Operations and Policy within the EOP.[24] In a message accompanying a pocket veto of the bill, Reagan explained that the "creation of another layer of bureaucracy within the Executive Branch would produce friction, disrupt effective law enforcement, and could threaten the integrity of criminal investigations and prosecutions—the very opposite of what its proponents apparently intend." He concluded that the "so-called 'drug Czar' provision was enacted hastily without thoughtful debate and without benefit of any hearings. Although its aim—with which I am in full agreement—is to promote coordination, this can be and is being achieved through existing administrative structures."[25]

Reagan's veto had little to do with opposing the creation of another executive branch official and more to do with Congress imposing on his administration a new structure to dilute executive power. In 1984, Congress created, with Reagan's approval, the Drug Enforcement Policy Board, headed by the attorney general, to coordinate the enforcement of the nation's drug laws.[26] However, throughout the rest of his administration Reagan fought against Congress setting up a new drug enforcement position, arguing that the attorney general should coordinate and manage the federal government's drug control efforts.[27] Only in the last year of his presidency did Reagan agree to such a position, most likely because the public ranked drug control as one of its top concerns during a presidential election year where Vice President George H. W. Bush was the Republican Party's nominee.[28]

By the mid-1980s, Reagan began receiving a large number of complaints and widespread criticism from Congress and the media for the Defense Department's acquisition process for weapons and supplies. One particular scandal had the navy purchasing aircraft ashtrays for $659 apiece. Another story had defense contractors billing the Pentagon for the boarding of a service executive's dog.[29] These were not isolated incidents.[30] As other allegations of overcharging mounted, there were calls to form a commission to look into the procurement issue.[31] The Reagan administration initially resisted such efforts and instead attempted to internally manage the controversy. In January 1985, Defense Secretary Caspar Weinberger announced a Pentagon reorganization plan that placed all responsibility for military procurement in an assistant secretary who would report directly to him.[32] It took Weinberger six months, however, to name James Paul Wade Jr. to the new position. After the appointment the media began improperly referring to Wade as the procurement czar.[33] Congress had authorized the appointment of up to eleven assistant secretary positions.[34] Wade had previously been confirmed by the Senate, and under section 136 of Title 10 of the U.S. Code, the assistant secretaries were to "perform such duties and exercise such powers as the Secretary of Defense may prescribe."[35] Weinberger was well within his authority to reconfigure the duties of the Defense Department personnel and give Wade additional responsibilities.

As Weinberger was carrying out the Defense Department reforms, President Reagan established the President's Blue Ribbon Commission on Defense Management in a response to the criticism over military procurement.[36] Chaired by David L. Packard, founder of Hewlett-Packard and a former deputy secretary of defense under Nixon, the Packard Commission, as it was called, recommended the centralization of the Defense Department's procurement duties within a new undersecretary of defense for acquisition position.[37] On April 1, 1986, Reagan approved the commission's recommendation in National Security Decision Directive 219.[38] In "anticipation of the enactment of legislation establishing" the undersecretary for acquisition, Reagan ordered Defense Secretary Weinberger to outline the position's "roles, functions, and responsibilities." Seven months later, Congress passed the Defense Acquisition Improvement Act of 1986, which provided authorization for the creation of the undersecretary for acquisition position within the Defense Department.[39]

Reagan nominated Richard P. Godwin, who had been the president of Bechtel—one of the nation's largest engineering companies—as the first acquisition undersecretary.[40] On September 25, 1986, the Senate confirmed Godwin to the new position.[41] Within a year, Godwin would resign and be replaced by Robert B. Costello, a former executive director for General Motors.[42] Media accounts inaccurately referred to both men as the procurement or weapons czar.[43] Besides the position of undersecretary of defense for acquisition having been statutorily established, Congress also required Senate confirmation. In addition, any nominee needed to have "extensive management background in the private sector." Finally, Congress had specified the position's responsibilities, which included supervising acquisition within the Defense Department and issuing orders to the secretaries of the armed services for purposes of carrying out the new law.[44] In short, adequate democratic controls were put in place to ensure neither was a czar.

GEORGE H. W. BUSH

Having won the presidency as Reagan's sitting vice president, Bush intended to maintain an agenda of limited government. For the most part this intention did not mean the unilateral creation of czars. The exception was Bush's appointment of Vice President Dan Quayle to head the President's Council on Competitiveness (known as the Quayle Council). Bush announced the establishment of the Quayle Council in April 1989 for purposes of reviewing "regulatory issues and such other matters as may be referred by the President and bear on competitiveness of the United States economy."[45] Aside from that announcement Bush did not issue an executive order and Congress did not pass any measure that could have given the administration authority to establish the council. Only the June 13, 1990, "Memorandum for the Cabinet and Agency Heads" issued by the cabinet secretariat Ede Holiday attempted to somewhat outline the structure and duties of the Quayle Council.[46] However, even that document failed to fully clarify the council's legal authority or the extent of its powers. Former general counsel to the House of Representatives Charles Tiefer remarked that this "vagueness in the council's mandate served the administration strategy well. From the outset of its active phase, the Quayle Council lacked the kind of charter for which there can be a public accounting about the extent of its power and its obedience to limits."[47]

Because of its ability to guide and shape the regulatory process throughout the federal bureaucracy, the Quayle Council in many ways supplanted the authority of cabinet secretaries and agency heads, all the while operating out of public view and using claims of executive privilege to evade accountability.[48] Bush even went so far as to appoint White House Counsel C. Boyden Gray to the Quayle Council, giving him a dual White House role and a claimed basis for refusing to testify before Congress about his part in council deliberations. In a sense, the president did not need a team of czars to make significant policy and regulatory decisions; he had the vice president, with the assistance of the staff of the Quayle Council, to effect all of the desired changes. In his book *The Semi-Sovereign Presidency*, Tiefer detailed a variety of substantive changes in major regulations that took place outside of public view, while various committees in Congress continually requested information about the council only to be stonewalled by an administration seeking to hide as much as it could.[49] A long investigative report by the *Washington Post* did the same and revealed the enormously large policy and regulatory reach of the council, all of which concealed the White House's actual role in the process.[50]

Since Quayle led what should be considered a nonstatutory regulatory review agency, we therefore consider him to have been a czar. By the fall of 1991, a bill was introduced in the Senate to set up a legally based framework for publicly disclosing the regulatory review process of all federal agencies, but it failed to secure passage.[51] The next year, the House voted to eliminate funding for staff salaries on the Quayle Council as a way to force the administration to create a more open review process. Rep. David E. Skaggs (D-CO), sponsor of the appropriations-stripping provision, provided a succinct explanation for the congressional pushback: "The heart of this problem is that the Council operates in secret, not letting the American people or Congress learn even the most basic facts about its activities. . . . The Council refuses to testify before Congress. The Council refuses to provide Congress with requested information on its activities."[52] A veto threat by President Bush, however, convinced the Senate to restore the funds.[53]

In a similar situation as Reagan, Bush faced news stories that maintained various administration officials were czars. For instance, the media continued to call the undersecretary of defense for acquisition the procurement czar.[54] The position, however, remained one that had been established by Congress through the Defense Acquisition Improvement Act of 1986.[55] Therefore the undersecretary did not operate as a czar. William J. Bennett became the second media-labeled czar of the Bush era, having been named by the president to the newly created position of director of the Office of National Drug Control Policy (ONDCP).[56] Yet neither Bennett nor his successor, Bob Martinez, was a czar.[57] Congress had established the ONDCP within the EOP at the end of Reagan's presidency when it passed the Anti-Drug Abuse Act of 1988. In so doing Congress required the ONDCP director to be confirmed by the Senate. The director would establish policies for implementing a National Drug Control Program, coordinate anti-drug efforts with various federal law enforcement agencies, and consult and assist state and local governments. Finally, in two sections of the law Congress included language that required the ONDCP director and agency personnel to be accessible to Congress and its committees. Specifically, one section said that placement of the ONDCP within the EOP "shall not be construed as affecting access by the Congress or committees of either House" to the personnel or information, documents, and studies of the new agency. The other section required the director to "appear before duly constituted committees and subcommittees of the House of Representatives and of the Senate to represent the drug policies of the executive branch."[58]

The last media-labeled czar during Bush's presidency resulted from the late 1980s savings and loan crisis where hundreds of savings and loan associations around the country began defaulting on their obligations. Congress responded by passing the Financial Institutions Reform, Recovery, and Enforcement Act of 1989, which, among other things, created the Office of Thrift Supervision (OTS) within the Treasury Department to improve regulation of the savings and loan associations.[59] Although many news reports referred to the first director of the OTS, T. Timothy Ryan Jr., as the savings and loan czar (sometimes called the thrift czar), the position cannot be considered one for a number of reasons.[60] First, Congress statutorily established the new agency, thus placing it on firm legal footing. Second, the new director would be nominated by the president to a five-year term and be subject to Senate confirmation. Third, Congress required the director to submit an annual report of the activities of the OTS along with making available all records to the General Accounting Office (now the Government Accountability Office) for purposes of an audit. Finally, the director's regulatory powers were guided by various principles set by Congress. For example, in allowing for the regulation of accounting practices, Congress specified that the director must adhere to the standards provided for in Title 12 of the Code of Federal Regulations.[61]

BILL CLINTON

Coming into the presidency after twelve years of Republican rule, many observers expected Clinton to act boldly on a number of domestic policy fronts. However, as a "New Democrat" whose natural instincts were to the political center, Clinton's presidency failed to produce a large number of czars. As explained at the beginning of this chapter, Clinton did not come into the presidency with a New Deal or Great Society type of agenda; he sought instead to work through Congress to accomplish health-care reform.

This outlook did not mean Clinton had no czars during his presidency. The first Clinton-era czar resulted from election-year politics in 1996 as the president attempted to get out in front of voters' concerns over illegal immigration and border crime. In fact Attorney General Janet Reno suggested to the president that she make U.S. Attorney for Southern California Alan D. Bersin—a longtime Clinton friend from Oxford University and Yale Law School—the point person on border security issues.[62] Clinton approved the idea and on October 14, 1995, Reno designated Bersin her special representative for the southwest border. Right away the media called him the border czar.[63] The title was fitting since Reno gave Bersin additional responsibilities and powers that were not provided by law. She directed that Bersin coordinate border enforcement projects with various federal agencies from the Federal Bureau of Investigations to the Drug Enforcement Administration. In addition, Reno placed him in charge of Operation Gatekeeper—a large-scale federal effort to prevent the flow of illegal immigration at the Mexican-U.S. border near San Diego, California. Finally, Bersin became Reno's representative for the purpose of negotiating immigration, drug, and border security issues with the Mexican government.[64]

For the most part Clinton was occupied by never-ending scandals during his second term, including an impeachment battle with Congress, which resulted in a much less focused policy agenda. During his last few years as president Clinton would have only one additional czar whose position grew out of a looming technological problem that could have potentially shut down all of the federal government's computers as the new millennium approached. The major concern centered on a programming issue where older computers had been designed to record years in two digits instead of four. For example, computers would recognize the year 1999 as 99. With the start of a new century some computers might identify the year 2000 as 1900 or some other century and possibly cause chaos for various federal departments and agencies. On February 4, 1998, Clinton issued an executive order that created the President's Council on Year 2000 Conversion (Y2K Council) with John A. Koskinen, a former deputy director of the Office of Management and Budget, as chair.[65] Representatives from each department and various agencies would be members of the Y2K Council. Clinton charged the chair with rather cryptic responsibilities to "oversee the activities of agencies to assure that their systems operate smoothly through the year 2000" along with providing "policy coordination of executive branch activities with State, local, and tribal governments on the Y2K problem, and promote appropriate Federal roles with respect to private sector activities in this area."[66] Quickly Koskinen became known as the Y2K czar.[67]

The Y2K Council functioned as a coordination agency within the federal government and eventually branched out to ensure that the private sector would be ready for the new millennium.[68] Although Koskinen had no statutory authority to order departments, agencies, or the private sector to act, his proximity to the president gave him the perception of power. Many times he would meet with various cabinet officers with Vice President Al Gore at his side "to hammer out a consensus that Y2K repairs would be" completed. In addition, he eventually established more than twenty-five task forces to oversee Y2K compliance with the private sector, United Nations, and the international community.[69] Like many White House aides, the czar moniker is difficult to assess in situations such as this one. Ultimately we consider Koskinen to have been a czar since he planned and coordinated a particular policy area. In assessing the role of the Y2K Council, presidential scholar Bradley H. Patterson Jr. remarked that there "was no way that any one department or agency could handle both the initiative-taking and the coordinating responsibilities: Y2K was a White House task."[70] We disagree. The renovation of the federal government computer systems could have been undertaken by any number of departments or agencies. What should have occurred was a much more detailed and serious response to the pending Y2K problem from Congress. Instead, lawmakers largely remained silent and chose to permit the president to act alone.

Like his predecessors, Clinton could not escape the czar label placed on some of the officials in his administration. Most scholars and interested observers of his presidency are well aware of the great effort Clinton put into health-care reform. Somewhat less well known are the czars titles given to key participants in this reform effort. However, Clinton created no actual czars to pursue his policy goal. The planning for the overhaul of the nation's health-care system began with the President's Task Force on National Health Care Reform. Clinton named his wife, Hillary Clinton, to chair the task force and charged her with preparing a health-care reform bill to submit to Congress within 100 days of his inauguration.[71] To provide additional policy and administrative support, Clinton made his Senior Adviser for Policy Development, Ira Magaziner, the primary White House staffer assigned to the task force.[72] Although numerous media quickly began calling Hillary Clinton and Magaziner health-care czars, we disagree.[73] To be sure, the closed-door nature of the bill-making process made both the First Lady and Magaziner many enemies in Congress, the press, and the public.[74] Those transparency concerns, however, do not make one a czar. Neither had any operational control over health-care policy, which meant their functions remained essentially advisory in nature. In the end they were charged with helping the president design a health-care reform bill. Regardless of the manner they chose to accomplish their tasks, they were not czars.

Even after Clinton submitted his health-care reform proposal to Congress, the media continued to use the czar title. Because of his administration's struggles with convincing lawmakers to support the health-care plan, Clinton decided to appoint Harold M. Ickes as White House deputy chief of staff and charged him with lobbying Congress. In this new role Ickes was referred to as the health-care czar by various news outlets.[75] In denying his "czar" status, Ickes explained that the Clinton White House would be "entering a new phase in health care which is primarily legislation and mobilizing people." Passing the health-care bill would not be a one-person project, Ickes explained. Instead, he would "be working with a team on that."[76] Upon Ickes's arrival at the White House, Clinton quickly reassigned him to work on containing the political fallout from a number of controversies, including

Whitewater.[77] In the end we do not believe Ickes was a czar since Clinton did not empower his new aide with rule making or any other type of operational authority over health-care policy.

Those associated with the health-care reform initiative, however, were not the only ones given the czar moniker by the media. The procurement czar label persisted in Clinton's administration with the undersecretaries of defense for acquisition John M. Deutch (1993–1994), Paul G. Kaminski (1994–1997), and Jacques Gansler (1997–2001) being given that title.[78] Another position that also received the czar designation was the director of the Office of National Drug Control Policy, with Lee P. Brown (1993–1995) and Barry McCaffrey (1996–2001) each referred to by the press as the nation's drug czar.[79] As we previously explained, neither position should be considered a czar as both were statutorily established by Congress with various democratic controls.[80] In the fall of 1993 Congress renamed the Pentagon's chief procurement officer the Under Secretary of Defense for Acquisition and Technology.[81]

One of Clinton's campaign promises was to appoint an "AIDS czar," who would coordinate the federal government's fight against the disease.[82] By June 1993, Clinton announced the creation of the Office of National AIDS Policy Coordinator (ONAPC) within the EOP and appointed Kristine M. Gebbie to the new position.[83] News stories referred to Gebbie as the AIDS czar, but the title overstated her powers.[84] Gebbie had a White House position with close contact with the president, but she could not issue any orders or regulations and had no authority over a budget or personnel. Even the word "Coordinator" in her title was misleading. In fact, Gebbie had to gain the approval of the Health and Human Services Secretary Donna E. Shalala and the White House Domestic Policy Council to advance any new AIDS policy changes.[85] One newspaper even quipped: "Ivan the Terrible, the first Russian czar, had complete power. Kristine Gebbie, America's first AIDS czar, had virtually none."[86] As a result, Gebbie was not a czar. Within fourteen months Gebbie resigned her position, noting that people's expectations of her as a czar were too high.[87]

In August 1994 Clinton named Patricia S. Fleming as the interim coordinator of the ONAPC, and three months later he made her director of that office, now retitled the Office of National AIDS Policy (ONAP).[88] The change in title from coordinator to director appears to have been made by Clinton to appease AIDS activists and homosexual rights groups demands of him to select "a prominent, high-profile czar" who would also be a cabinet officer. Although Clinton did not make the ONAP director a cabinet officer, he did specify that Fleming would have direct access to him and play an "important role" in budget and policy development.[89] Like Gebbie, various news accounts called Fleming, along with her successor, Sandra L. Thurman, the AIDS czar.[90] The problem was that neither

Fleming nor Thurman was a czar as they had no power. According to one account, "Fleming was at the helm of a meek outfit. . . . It did play a role, but by and large, the White House considered the office primarily a liaison with the AIDS community—almost a public relations arm."[91] A clear indicator of Fleming's lack of authority came from Steve Michael, a Washington, D.C., AIDS activist, who said: "I don't see her office as imparting a whole lot. . . . We don't even bother protesting her events, because she has no power."[92] Since the reconfigured office possessed no power and functioned, at best, as an advisory unit to the president, these two individuals were not czars.

Interest group pressure and political calculations also played into Clinton's decision to create the White House Office for Women's Initiatives and Outreach.[93] The new White House unit primarily functioned as an outreach center for women's groups and as a way to show that the role of women was being strengthened in the administration. Clinton picked associate deputy administrator for entrepreneurial development in the U.S. Small Business Administration Betsy Myers to be the first director and gave her the rank of deputy assistant to the president, which brought with it the right to sit in on senior staff meetings.[94] Myers's position, however, lacked the ability to issue orders or regulations and had no budgetary authority.[95] As a result, Myers was not a czar since she had no actual powers. Myers would be succeeded by Audrey Tayse Haynes (1997–1998) and Jennifer Luray (1998–2001).

Clinton also created within the White House the Office of the President's Initiative for One America (One America office). Led by Director Ben Johnson, who also served as assistant to the president, Clinton charged him with promoting "a coordinated strategy to close the opportunity gaps that exist for minorities and the underserved in this country" along with educating the public about race and identifying policies that would foster those goals.[96] Scholar Gary L. Gregg maintained that Clinton had created in Johnson the civil rights outreach czar.[97] We disagree with the designation as Johnson had no budgetary authority or ability to issue orders or produce regulations. A consultant on Clinton's earlier race commission said of the One America office: "I can't see that they've done anything useful. All I hear about is outreach-style meetings that probably contribute to getting the president's constituency business done, but certainly don't contribute in any broader way to advancing the president's substantive goals or vision."[98]

Surprisingly many in the media began calling one of Clinton's cabinet officers a czar. At various times during his tenure as Housing and Urban Development Secretary, Henry Cisneros would be referred to as the czar of housing.[99] In March 1993, after Hurricane Andrew, one newspaper even branded Cisneros the U.S. hurricane-relief czar.[100] Of course the problem with placing the czar label on Cisneros is that the HUD secretary is a cabinet-level position subject to Senate confirmation and routine testimony before Congress. In fact, at the time of Cisneros's appointment the Housing and Urban Development Department had been statutorily established by Congress for nearly thirty years.[101] Cisneros therefore was not a czar.

In the fall of 1995 Clinton created an interagency task force to develop a plan for managing electronic commerce (popularly referred to as "e-commerce") led by his senior policy adviser Ira Magaziner. Over the next year and a half, Magaziner worked on the e-commerce project, with the task force finally issuing a report on July 1, 1997, entitled, "A Framework for Global Electronic Commerce." The task force recommended that the federal government take a hands-off approach to the internet and instead permit more self-regulation by e-commerce businesses.[102] Because of his central role in internet policy development, media accounts labeled Magaziner the internet czar.[103] Although Magaziner clearly had a primary role in the development of a policy plan, he had no authority or control over the internet and therefore should not have been called a czar. In fact, unlike the healthcare reform effort, in which Magaziner played a significant role. Meetings and discussions were held with many parties and done openly instead of behind closed doors. Several drafts of the task force's report were even posted on the internet for public discussion.[104]

By the late 1990s climate change had become such a pressing issue domestically and for the international community that Clinton placed his assistant for special projects, Todd D. Stern, in charge of the issue.[105] Stern helped provide preparatory work for the 1997 White House Conference on Climate Change and the international climate conferences in Kyoto and Buenos Aires. In addition, he chaired two interagency groups—one for domestic issues and another for diplomatic matters—which were charged with formulating environmental policy for the president to consider.[106] Various media outlets said Stern was the administration's climate czar, but we disagree with that label.[107] Although environmental policy development would be greatly centralized within the White House through the use of interagency groups, Clinton did not bestow on Stern any responsibilities to implement environmental policy. Regardless of his perceived status in the Clinton White House, Stern's role was that of a presidential adviser.

Clinton's remaining media-labeled czars resulted from various terrorist threats the nation faced. The first czar originated out of a recommendation made by the President's Commission on Critical Infrastructure Protection (PCCIP)—an advisory unit created after the Oklahoma City bombing—that a White House policy-making office be formed.[108] In response to the PCCIP's report, Clinton created the Critical Infrastructure Coordination Group (CICG) chaired by the National Coordinator for Security, Infrastructure Protection and Counter-Terrorism (National Coordinator), who would be appointed by and report to the president through the national security adviser.[109] Shortly after Clinton's appointment of Richard A. Clarke to the national coordinator position, Clarke became known as the terrorism czar.[110] The label, however, did not fit the functions of the position. Clarke explained that "the notion that there was a Terrorism Czar was misleading." Instead of a powerful new policymaking center within the White House, the various department heads responsible for national security affairs lobbied the president to greatly weaken the new position. The directive creating the national coordinator position, Clarke tells, clearly maintained that it "was just a White House staff job." The coordinator further "could not order law enforcement agents, troops, or spies to do anything, only their agencies could. Some czar." There would be no office with a staff, budget, or ability to make decisions. The national coordinator would have "the appearance of responsibility for counterterrorism, but none of the tools or authority to get the job done."[111]

Finally, at the end of Clinton's presidency, the head of the National Nuclear Security Administration (NNSA), John Gordon, earned the title of nuclear security czar from the media.[112] The NNSA, however, had been established by Congress as a result of two government reports that criticized the Energy Department's longstanding management problems at several national research laboratories that had apparently led to China acquiring U.S. nuclear weapons technology.[113] The resulting political fallout caused Congress to pass the National Nuclear Security Administration Act, which statutorily created the NNSA, to be run by a presidentially nominated and Senate-confirmed undersecretary for nuclear security.[114] As head of the NNSA, Gordon had general authority over all programs and activities relating to nuclear security, but his decisions could be vetoed by the energy secretary.[115] Therefore, we do not consider Gordon to have been a czar since Congress created the NNSA and his position along with providing for a number of checks.

SUMMARY

Ronald Reagan, George H. W. Bush, and Bill Clinton did not completely revive the pre-Watergate presidential use of czars. As Andrew Rudalevige noted regarding presidential powers more generally during this period: "certainly the [president's] office had rebounded since Watergate and Vietnam. But that process had further to go."[116] Reagan's administration preferred to maintain central control of the executive branch; Bush's favored a return to cabinet governance; and Clinton's worked through the legislative process and undoubtedly was constrained by the distraction of scandals and impeachment.

This period did not represent the expanded use of executive branch czars that some might have expected, but it did provide evidence that the practice had not fallen into disuse after Watergate and, perhaps, was being reinvigorated. A complete revival only needed a president truly committed to the notion of unconstrained executive powers and willing to act outside normal legislative and constitutional constraints. With such a person in the White House the possibilities of unilateral action by czars are limitless. There is no stronger proof of that fact than the presidencies of George W. Bush and Barack Obama.

7. George W. Bush, Barack Obama, and the Vast Proliferation of Czars

We have traced to this point the growth and evolution of the position of executive branch czar. When presidents named people to positions known as drug czars, energy czars, terrorism czars, even AIDS czars, there was not substantial public protest. In large part, many perceived the appointments of these positions as evidence of presidents attaching special emphasis to issues that had attracted widespread public concern or interest group lobbying. Yet the failure of Congress to limit or even eliminate the use of executive branch czars led to perhaps the inevitable result that in time presidents would see greater benefit and begin to expand the number of these positions to use as managers of a variety of issues both large and small. The political benefit presidents gain from appointing czars is too tempting. Doing so enables presidents to give something tangible to a constituency with a specific issue concern. The governing payoff is also substantial in that czars enable presidents to do an end run around the normal constraints built into a system of separated powers.

Presidents George W. Bush and Barack Obama took advantage of the acceptance, or at least acquiescence by Congress and the public, of czars as an ongoing feature of the executive branch. Indeed, presidents have pushed the limits of the use of such positions to the degree that there finally has begun to be a serious examination of the propriety of having executive branch czars. Critics of the Bush presidency had expressed alarm at what they perceived as the president's vast overreaches in the exercises of various independent presidential powers. The president's creation and use of various czar positions became a part of the overall critique of presidential powers in the Bush era. Barack Obama, despite many promises to reverse the growing use of independent presidential powers, instead found utility in many Bush-era practices and continued and then expanded them. Indeed, by the early Obama administration, there was a backlash against the expansive use of czars, including legislative proposals to eliminate the practice altogether. One such proposal was successful, but then negated by a controversial presidential signing statement—another unilateral power of the modern presidency.

As is so often the case, criticism of the use of czars in this era usually tracked almost perfectly along partisan lines. Democratic and progressive critics of Bush leveled strong accusations of improper power grabs by the president when he appointed numerous czars. Republican and conservative commentators railed even more fervently against Obama's use of czars. We find much to criticize in both the Bush and Obama extensive uses of executive branch czars.

GEORGE W. BUSH: CZARS UNDER THE UNITARY EXECUTIVE

A key element of the George W. Bush legacy will be his administration's varied attempts to vastly expand the powers of the presidency. Under the "unitary executive" theory that espouses the inherent authority of the president to act unilaterally in a number of areas, the president adopted broad-reaching and in some cases unprecedented efforts to increase the powers of the Oval Office. One of the many ways in which the president did so was to expand the use of executive branch czars. Bush unilaterally appointed a number of new czars with duties overlapping those of cabinet secretaries and other confirmed officials. He also garnered legislative approval in the post-9/11 environment for a number of new positions that were commonly referred to as czars.

On January 29, 2001, President Bush announced a proposal to create a new White House office that would be responsible for allocating federal funds for the needy through faith-based organizations. Entitled the White House Office of Faith-Based and Community Initiatives (WHOFBCI), the office was headed by a director who became widely known as the "faith-based czar."[1] Bush created this new office by executive order and appointed political science professor John Dilulio as its first director.[2]

Congress took up the charge of developing the scope and parameters of the new faith-based initiative. But in the face of considerable political opposition, legislative proposals repeatedly failed. So in December 2002, after nearly two years of legislative wrangling, the president issued an executive order to allow federal tax dollars to be given to religion-based charities. In their book on the faith-based office, here is how scholars Jo Renee Formicola, Mary C. Segers, and Paul Weber described the office's creation: "It took at least a year for the Bush White House to clarify what it meant by its 'faith-based initiative.' The proposal floundered in Congress. The initiative fared better in the executive branch, where the president could invoke executive powers to create agencies and order them to implement existing laws. By the end of his second year in office, the president had done just that—operationalized a controversial office through executive fiat."[3]

Amy E. Black, Douglas L. Koopman, and David K. Ryden, the authors of another book on the faith-based office, in describing the shift from failure to approve the office's powers legislatively to a presidential executive order settling the whole matter, phrased it rather bluntly: "Because the president had power to act unilaterally in the executive branch, the policy fared better there."[4] In creating the new office, Bush also established five faith-based cabinet centers (later increased to seven) for the purpose of implementing such programs and regulations throughout the government. In their detailed account of the faith-based initiative, Black, Koopman, and Ryden tellingly explain that while the whole proposal stalled in Congress, WHOFBCI and cabinet center staff already "were quietly beginning to change regulations, earmark money for faith-based organizations, and generally transform the relationship between the executive branch and religious groups."[5]

It offends constitutional principles when a president creates new units and makes new policies and regulations through executive fiat, especially when he does so after having failed to achieve some of the same goals legislatively. Bush created the new office by executive order, but he had initially waited on Congress to give legislative sanction and substance to the office's core functions. When that did not work, he simply issued another executive order and took Congress out of the equation. By the accounts of the two leading scholarly books on the topic, the president had wanted and expected a legislative victory here to strengthen his hand. The effectiveness of the political opposition to creating a faith-based initiative, which had had a part of its origins in a Clinton-era program and had been supported by both major party presidential nominees in 2000, took the president and his staff by surprise.

The Bush faith-based czar, a non-Senate-confirmed presidential appointee, had authority over policy and regulatory matters, although the office admittedly spent more time on outreach to faith organizations and enabling them to compete for federal grants to carry out social services. Many critics of the office nonetheless complained that the existence of a faith-office and czar violated principles of church-state separation. Yet Dilulio expressed displeasure that the Bush White House actually had given too little policy authority to his office and had cut him out of the circle of key policy advisers to the president. More importantly though, the creation of the new office and czar established a precedent. Bush's successor could have decided that the faith-based initiative violated church-state separation or that it was not an appropriate role for the White House and canceled the office and czar position. Instead, he significantly expanded the roles of each (discussed below).

On September 20, 2001, nine days after the terrorist attacks on the United States, President Bush addressed a joint session of Congress and announced, among other initiatives, the creation of a new cabinet-level Office of Homeland Security (OHS) with a director who reported directly to him.[6] Bush named Pennsylvania governor Tom Ridge to this new post.[7] Only weeks later did the president issue an executive order that set forth the duties of the OHS director, who widely became known as the homeland security czar.[8] A major role of the new czar was to coordinate communications and policy responses among multiple federal agencies and different levels of government.

Ridge thus was a new presidentially appointed officer holding cabinet-level status without Senate confirmation. The president used this arrangement to wall off Ridge from dealing openly with Congress. When Senators Robert C. Byrd (D-WV) and Ted Stevens (R-AK) invited Ridge to testify before the Appropriations Committee, the White House refused to allow such an appearance because Ridge held status as a presidential adviser and not as a full cabinet officer.[9] In a letter to Bush, Byrd and Stevens objected that Ridge was far more than a mere adviser to the president and that the homeland security czar was "the single Executive Branch official with the responsibility to integrate the many complex functions of the various Federal agencies in the formulation and execution of Homeland security programs."[10] The president continued to refuse to allow Ridge to testify.

Ridge relates in his memoirs that he was himself extremely uncomfortable with this arrangement. "Our influence on new spending became a point of contention with Congress. Committees on the Hill called upon me to testify, and I would have been happy to go." Ridge added that he thought it was important to cooperate with Congress given the substantial changes in government structure being introduced by the creation of his office and its activities. "But that kind of partnership seemed out of bounds." The president's chief of staff, Andrew Card, exclaimed to Ridge: "You're working for one person and one person only!" Ridge then adds the key point about the constitutional troubles with his new office: "Indeed, the president prohibited my testimony, holding to the tenet that Oval Office advisers are not subject to congressional subpoena power under the theory of executive privilege." As Ridge reports, when asked by reporters about this arrangement, the president retorted: "He's a part of my staff, and that's part of the prerogative of the executive branch of government, and we hold that very dear."[11]

As a substitute for open testimony, the president instructed Ridge to pay private visits to members of Congress and also to give informal briefings to two House committees. Numerous lawmakers of both parties objected to this arrangement. Ridge recounts one telling episode in which he visited Senator Byrd, who proceeded to pull out a well-worn copy of the Constitution to show the homeland security czar that it is Congress that possesses the power of the purse. As Ridge explains, Byrd objected to the private briefing arrangement and said he would insist on public testimony: "I am unaware of any instance in which a private briefing has been used as a substitute for responding to a Senate Appropriations Committee request for testimony concerning a funding need." Ridge makes it clear that he actually agreed with Byrd and other congressional critics of the Bush administration's approach of concealing the Homeland Security czar from testifying. "I was caught in a highly visible pickle."[12]

He should not have been. Ridge was heading a new government unit that was coordinating and making policy, restructuring entire federal departments and their interactions, and spending large sums of public money. This arrangement especially required legislative involvement. Congress responded appropriately by pushing for the establishment of a Department of Homeland Security (DHS) that would be accountable. As Louis Fisher explained, such a law "would override the president's executive order and neutralize White House arguments about Ridge functioning as a presidential adviser."[13]

Bush initially opposed the idea, but over time he came around to supporting it for practical reasons. Lacking strong support throughout the government, Ridge's office was ineffectual at coordinating the activities of multiple agencies. Congress deemed it necessary to put forward a more coherent reorganization plan for federal departments and agencies involved in aspects of homeland security.[14] Also, the president was left with little choice, as Congress was determined to pass a reorganization plan creating the DHS. As Richard A. Clarke, the person commonly called the terrorism czar and also cyber security czar, wrote in his own memoir, Bush had the choice of eventually signing a bill "named after the man whom the majority of voters had wanted to be Vice President just twenty months earlier" (Senator Joseph Lieberman, D-CT), or he could champion the idea and name it the "Homeland Security Act."[15]

The newly created Department of Homeland Security was headed by a presidentially appointed and Senate-confirmed director. Ridge retained the moniker of czar, although he and his successor, Michael Chertoff, were then more often referred to as Homeland Security Secretary. The czar title indeed was inapt once Congress created the new Department and the Senate confirmed its director.

Because of the 9/11 attacks and the perception of continuing threats to the country, terrorism and security issues were at the forefront of the Bush years. The president had retained the Clinton-appointed, so-called terrorism czar, Richard A. Clarke, although his cabinet-level access had been taken away in the new administration. Clarke's position could not be characterized as a true czar in either the Clinton or the Bush administrations. Clarke retained this position only during the first year of the Bush administration. President Bush nonetheless created new responsibilities for him after the 9/11 attacks by issuing an executive order in October 2001 that established the President's Critical Infrastructure Protection Board, chaired by Clarke.[16] Bush also made Clarke Special Advisor to the President for Cyberspace Security.[17] Clarke's positions were advisory still; he did not make policy or budgetary decisions. Despite the czar moniker, his duties did not merit the title.

In April 2004 Bush issued an executive order creating within the Department of Health and Human Services (HHS) the national health information technology coordinator, a position that became known as the health IT czar. Bush's order gave the HHS secretary the authority to make the appointment "in consultation with the President or his designee."[18] As established, the position was not Senate confirmed, although it operated with an annual budget of about $60 million and set up advisory commissions and awarded contracts to providers of health-care information technology. HHS Secretary Tommy Thompson appointed David J. Brailer to the post in May 2004. Brailer served for two years, and his principal responsibility was to direct a planned long-term, federal-led effort to create a national database of electronic medical records using common standards. After Brailer's resignation, his position was held for one year by an interim director, Robert Kolodner, who eventually was appointed to the full director position by Thompson. The health IT czar position has been continued under the Obama administration with a new director and a larger budget and broader scope of authority (see discussion below).

The creation of czar positions has proven at times to be an invitation to cronyism. Presidents Bush and Obama received a lot of criticism for a number of czar appointees who appeared to critics to be unqualified or underqualified to undertake certain tasks. For example, in 2004, in reaction to fears of bioterrorism and epidemics, the Health and Human Services Department created a new position of assistant secretary for public health emergency preparedness that variably was called the bioterrorism czar and the bird flu czar. The choice of attorney Stewart Simonson elicited howls of protest given his lack of expertise or of any real background at all in the fields of bioterrorism, medical research, or health crisis management.[19] He had been a protégé of HHS Secretary Thompson and corporate counsel to Amtrak prior to his presidentially appointed czar post. Simonson also was an example of a dual appointee—he had status as a Senate-confirmed assistant secretary in HHS[20] and simultaneously held a White House adviser position.[21] In 2006, Congress passed the Pandemic and All-Hazards Preparedness Act establishing the assistant secretary for preparedness and response position and subjecting it to Senate confirmation.[22]

Amidst a food scare in the country in 2007, brought about by *E. coli* and salmonella outbreaks and reports of pet food tainted with poisons, the president created a new position that became known as the "food safety czar." On May 1 of that year the Food and Drug Administration (FDA) commissioner formally announced the appointment of FDA medical officer David W. K. Acheson to the position of Assistant Commissioner for Food Protection.[23] In that post Acheson had mostly advisory authority, although he was also tasked with communicating to the public about food safety and suggesting coordinated responses to food safety issues among various departments and agencies.[24] There is no evidence that he directly made policy or allocated resources. Acheson reported to an FDA deputy commissioner.

This appointment highlights the challenges in defining executive branch czars, especially with the establishment of new positions that overlap the duties of existing confirmed officials. To be sure, President Bush had acted in response to numerous troubling reports about the safety of the supply of foods in the country. Creating a new position enabled the president to showcase that he recognized the gravity of the problem and that he was doing something about it. But why create a new office that is not legislatively authorized when there were plenty of existing officials within the FDA or even the Department of Agriculture who could undertake the same tasks?

By creating this position President Bush had established a precedent for having a national food safety officer. Acheson continued in his job through the first six months of the Obama administration. But most important to our analysis, Obama proceeded to vastly expand the authority of the position, leaving no doubt that it had become an executive branch czar. Whereas Bush had given primarily advisory, along with coordination, powers to the so-called food safety czar, Obama invested the position with wide-ranging policy, regulatory, and budgetary powers (see below).

As we write this analysis, there is an ongoing and, we find at times, fruitless, partisan debate over whether Bush or Obama appointed more czars. The Democratic National Committee actually has even created a video for YouTube—humorously entitled "Dancing with the Czars"—that purports to prove that Bush, not Obama, had the most czars.[25] Obviously the issue has become sensitive to the defenders of these presidents. But as the position of food safety czar illustrates, the counts are not as important as the contexts. Other than the common czar moniker, there is not much to compare when discussing the Bush and Obama food safety officials. One had substantially much more independent authority than the other even though we consider both to be czars.

During the Bush era there were a substantial number of positions labeled czars that were merely advisory (see Table 11 in the Appendix for a listing of media-labeled czars). One was the director of a newly created President's Council on Bioethics, Leon Kass, who was commonly known as the bioethics czar. Yet the czar label overstated his actual role. Bush formed the commission in response to a national debate over the utility and especially the ethics and morality of stem-cell research. The commission was empowered to study the issue and report to the president, not to make policy, issue regulations, or allocate resources. Bush created the bioethics commission and director post by executive order in November 2001.[26] He did not reveal the names of the other commission members until the eve of its first meeting several months later.[27] There is much to object to in the practice of creating a new commission without any statutory basis and then concealing the names of its members until the group meets and it is too late for any outside input. Once the White House released the names of the commissioners, there were criticisms that the group was heavily stacked with persons who had already publicly taken stands against stem-cell research.[28] But given the lack of policy, regulatory, and spending powers, it seems a stretch to put the bioethics czar in the same category as other genuine executive branch czars.

The same goes for the official commonly called Bush's reading czar. The president designated G. Reid Lyon as an ex-officio member of the President's Commission on Excellence in Special Education and chief advocate for promoting reading education in the country. Created by executive order, the president tasked the commission with studying special education needs and recommending policy approaches for improving educational results for special needs students.[29] Lyon was somewhat controversial given his past work promoting phonics, and critics decried him as a policy czar who would use his position to advance the use of phonics nationally.[30] The fact is that Lyon's so-called czar post was merely advisory in nature.

Some of the commonly labeled czar positions were actually presidentially appointed and Senate confirmed and should not have been given the czar moniker. Among these were the Office of Management and Budget Director (who was known as the budget czar), the Under Secretary for Nuclear Security (the nuclear security czar), the Assistant Secretary for Environmental Management (the cleanup czar), the Director of the Office of Information and Regulatory Affairs (the regulation czar), the Director of the Office of National Drug Control Policy (the drug czar), and the Director of the Office of Science and Technology (the science czar), among others (see Table 11). Even Karl Rove, the deputy chief of staff who had an advisory role as a presidential appointee, sometimes was called the political and also the domestic policy czar. In these cases, the czar label was convenient shorthand, used mostly by the popular press, especially in cases of persons with long titles and a lot of responsibilities.

In some cases, presidents may continue but yet significantly change or even downgrade certain positions created by their predecessors. A good example is the so-called AIDS czar, a position that originated in the Clinton administration but received far less emphasis in the Bush years and saw its core functions altered. Bush did not exactly seem eager to get the AIDS czar office off to a running start. As reported by National Public Radio: "For the first few months of the Bush administration, there was a White House Office of National AIDS Policy, but no one seemed to be working there. Public health officials and AIDS activists were concerned there would be no Bush AIDS policy."[31] In April 2001, the president indeed appointed an AIDS czar, Scott Evertz, who would become the first of three such persons to hold that position during the Bush presidency. The frequent rotation of the office signified to some the administration's lack of serious commitment to combat

AIDS. Evertz himself left dissatisfied with the administration's efforts and wrote a report in which he claimed that religious conservative group pressures exerted too much influence over Bush's policies in this area and thus the office's functions had been severely downgraded. Yet, in 2003 the Bush administration and Congress did elevate the international role of this office in making the AIDS czar the overseer of anti-AIDS initiatives both domestically and in U.S. foreign policy.[32]

What is very troubling to those of us who are critical of the rise of executive branch czars is that not only are presidents using these positions to consolidate their powers, but in some cases interest-group pressures generate the push to create a new czar position. Even when existing governmental units have the authority to deal with a crisis, many people demand the creation of a new entity that operates outside the normal governmental structure. Such was the case after the Hurricane Katrina disaster that devastated the coastal areas of the Gulf States. President Bush initially did not appoint a Katrina disaster czar. He didn't think it was necessary to do so. But most Americans were highly critical of the president for what they perceived as his tepid response to the crisis. The incompetent responses of the Federal Emergency Management Agency (FEMA) and its director, Michael Brown, became a topic of widespread national derision.[33] Pressure built for Bush to appoint a czar in the aftermath of the disaster. Americans had lost faith in the ability of FEMA to do its job—and with good reason.

On November 1, 2005, the president issued an executive order that created the position of Coordinator of Federal Support for the Recovery and Rebuilding of the Gulf Coast Region.[34] He appointed the former chairman of the Federal Deposit Insurance Corporation (FDIC), Donald E. Powell, to the position that commonly became known as the Gulf Coast reconstruction czar. A profile story in the *Washington Post* described Powell's duties as "to set goals and policies for everything from restarting the New Orleans economy to rebuilding infrastructure."[35] Powell had a staff of twelve, and he made a number of policy and spending decisions that affected the Gulf region recovery. From a *New York Times* report about his departure from the czar post in March 2008: "Louisiana officials credited him with freeing up federal money at critical points."[36]

There is no disputing that the enormity of the Katrina disaster required a major federal response. Federal institutions exist for the purpose of responding to natural disasters. It makes little sense that if an existing entity performs poorly that the corrective is to have a new presidentially created unit that lacks normal democratic control measures. In this case, an executive branch czar was making policy and grant-funding decisions that could have been handled by statutory officers with clear authority to act.

As we have explained throughout this book, members of Congress should especially be wary of presidents appointing czars. Time and again, czars have become vehicles for cutting Congress out of the policy and budgetary processes. But again, political pressures to respond to crises and troubling situations create the impetuses for elected officials to resort to calling for new czars. In response to the perceived failings of federal, state, and local governments to respond adequately to the health impacts on workers who responded to the 9/11 attacks and those who worked the massive cleanup of the World Trade Center site, some members of Congress lobbied the Bush administration to appoint a 9/11 health czar.[37]

In February 2006 the president appointed the Director of the National Institutes for Occupational Safety and Health, John Howard, to the additional position of federal coordinator of the government's response to Ground Zero health impacts.[38] The former position is Senate confirmed, the latter is not. He became known as the 9/11 health czar.[39] He exercised considerable authority over the coordinating of government responses among multiple federal agencies and also among different levels of government. In this role Howard actually became a strong advocate for the 9/11 workers in ways that put him at odds with the Bush White House. Consequently, Bush did not continue Howard's position when it was up for renewal in July 2008. In 2009 President Barack Obama reappointed Howard to the 9/11 health-care czar position.[40]

BARACK OBAMA: "MORE CZARS THAN THE ROMANOVS"?

Controversy over the use of executive branch czars reached a fever pitch during the Barack Obama administration. The reasons are straightforward: First, President Obama has appointed more czars than any president since Franklin D. Roosevelt, and a good many of them have exercised some of the most formidable powers of any officials in the executive branch. Second, certain high-profile critics of the president—such as cable talk show host Glenn Beck, who effectively drove one czar from office—made the czars controversy a focal point for their attacks against what they considered a dangerous concentration of power in the executive during the Obama administration. Substantial media coverage of the controversy as well as congressional hearings followed. The presence of czars became a fixture in national debates about modern executive branch powers.

The actual number of czars also became a significant debate topic during the early Obama administration. The president's 2008 opponent, Senator John McCain (R-AZ), quipped that "Obama has more czars than the Romanovs."[41] Credible sources report that Obama has exceeded the quantities of his predecessors in appointing czars, although a number of the president's defenders have retorted that, by their own counts, George W. Bush actually had more czars than Obama.

In the past, Americans had come to know about drug czars and energy czars, among other notable ones. More recently there are czars for clean energy, green jobs, nonproliferation, urban affairs, the Troubled Asset Relief Program, and the auto recovery. There is a Great Lakes czar, a California water czar, and a Chesapeake Bay czar. The proliferation of czars in the early Obama administration has been staggering. We wonder if one day there may even be a czar to coordinate czars. And there is even one person, Kenneth Feinberg, who holds two czar positions—"claims czar" and "pay czar." The constitutional problem with Obama's czars is not simply that there are too many of them; it is the extent to which, like Feinberg, many of these officials are acting outside the normal system of checks and balances and democratic accountability. In relying so heavily on czars, Obama has contradicted a strongly worded promise he had made in his 2008 presidential campaign when he stated: "I take the Constitution very seriously. The biggest problems that we're facing right now have to do with George Bush trying to bring more and more power into the executive branch and not go through Congress at all. And that's what I intend to reverse when I'm president of the United States."[42]

We now take up the number of White House czars during the Obama administration and describe the various czar positions. As with past administrations, some of the Obama czars have vast and largely unchecked powers, whereas some labeled as czars are actually statutorily created and accountable and thus should not be in the same category. We therefore also examine the scope of authority exercised by many of these officers and then address the constitutional debates surrounding Obama's czars.

How Many Czars? and Who Are They?

Some czars such as Feinberg are public figures who hold very substantial positions of authority. Some, such as the Chesapeake Bay czar, are very obscure and possess relatively few powers. The media use the czar moniker very loosely at times. And in the Obama administration, some czar positions have been short-lived. It is therefore challenging to establish completely reliable counts of czars. To illustrate the nature of the problem, as we write this analysis there is an ongoing debate over the actual number of czars in the Obama administration. Much of the debate has become quite heated and partisan. No one can seem to agree on the existing number of such positions.

As the czars issue heated up in mid-2009, some conservative opinion leaders charged the Obama administration with having an unprecedented number of czars.[43] A partisan debate ensued over who had more czars—Obama or Bush?

The White House communications director noted that some of Obama's so-called czars were in Senate-confirmed positions.[44]

Although many anti-Obama commentators brought public attention to the existence of so many czars, and highlighted some of the constitutional issues at stake, some took sharp aim at particular czars mostly over ideological or political differences of opinion. A good example is the "diversity czar," Mark Lloyd, whose newly created position resides within the Federal Communications Commission and gives him authority to oversee federal efforts and direct resources to encourage diversity in media ownership.[45] It is one thing to attack Lloyd's powers given that he is an actual czar. But since his appointment Lloyd has been subject to attacks from conservative commentators for some of his past statements and writings.[46] Questioning the legitimacy of having a certain czar position can thus become a mask for trying to undermine a person that certain critics do not like or with whom they simply disagree on politics and policy. Much of the contemporary czars debate gets obscured by that kind of partisan rancor.

Another difficulty is that some of the positions commonly labeled as czars are misnamed. For example, in June 2009 President Obama appointed Lynn Rosenthal as a White House adviser to address issues of domestic violence. Commonly referred to as the "domestic violence czar,"[47] her duties were merely advisory and thus do not pose any problems associated with czars who exercise direct policy and government funding authority. The same analysis applies to the so-called cyber security czar. In 2009 Obama created the new position of the White House Cyber Security Coordinator, a position that reports to the National Security Council (NSC) and also the National Economic Council (NEC). The position is merely advisory and it lacks any policymaking or budgetary decision power.[48] Obama's "border czar," Alan Bersin, transitioned from a non-Senate-confirmed, newly created office where he had substantial policy and regulatory powers, to a recess appointment position that exercises many of the same duties and requires eventual Senate confirmation.[49]

Finally, some officials frequently labeled as czars belonged to new, presidentially created positions but did not fully exercise policymaking, budgetary, or regulatory powers. For example, in January 2009 Obama appointed Lawrence Summers to the position of Chair of the National Economic Council (NEC).[50] Although the council was not statutorily created and the chair not Senate confirmed, Summers's label as the economic czar is arguable given that his role was established as an advisory one. We, however, do not consider Summers to have been a czar since he only helped develop policy during his short stint (until December 2010) as the NEC chair. Another telling example was President Obama's January 2009 appointment of Paul Volcker as the chair of the newly created Economic Recovery Advisory Council.[51] Commonly called the economic czar II, Volcker directed the

new unit that the president's executive order tasked with making recommendations to the president but had no real substantive power. Criticism of the president
over this position sometimes emphasized the creation of a czar position, but other
times actually focused on the president having allegedly underutilized the former
Federal Reserve chair.[52]

The circumstances that Obama inherited when he took office—two wars
abroad, and at home an economic crisis with its possible collapse of the auto industry and meltdown of the banking sector and housing market—generated expectations that the president would take resolute action. With strong partisan
majorities in Congress in 2009 and the traditional leeway in public opinion during
the "honeymoon" period, Obama had an unusual combination of circumstances
to enable him to act boldly on a number of policy fronts. There was little sentiment in the country of the need to constrain the president's domestic powers.
More so, there was an expectation that the president would take the lead in trying
to rescue the country while it was in crisis. To that end, Obama had unusual flex-
ibility to appoint czars to coordinate responses to various crises and even more
routine policy problems. He did not waste any time in doing so.

To deal with the effects of the automobile industry financial crisis, in March
2009 the president appointed an auto recovery czar, Ed Montgomery. The formal
title for Montgomery was the Director of Recovery for Auto Communities and
Workers. A former Clinton administration Labor Department deputy secretary,
Montgomery was tasked with directing federal funds to communities most affected by the near collapse of the auto industry. In a period of just one year, the
automotive industry had eliminated about 400,000 jobs, mostly in midwestern
states such as Michigan, Ohio, and Indiana. Obama thus gave wide discretion to
the auto recovery czar to determine the distribution of billions of dollars from
the $787 billion economic stimulus package that Congress had approved in 2008.
In making the appointment, Obama described the vast duties that Montgomery
would exercise: "[Montgomery] will direct a comprehensive effort that will help
lift up the hardest-hit areas by using the unprecedented levels of funding available
in our Recovery Act and throughout our government to create new manufacturing jobs and new businesses where they're needed most."[53]

On June 23, 2009, Obama issued an executive order that created a new White
House Council on Automotive Communities and Workers, with the auto recovery
czar directing and coordinating its activities. The council consisted of eleven cabinet secretaries, the attorney general, and numerous other high-level government
officials—whose activities in the auto recovery area would thus all be under the
direction of Montgomery. Obama created the council as a temporary entity, set to
expire in two years, in response to the economic dislocations caused by the severe
auto industry decline. The executive order specified that the council would have a

variety of policy and budgetary powers, including coordinating economic recovery assistance at all levels of the federal system.[54]

In June 2010 Montgomery announced he was leaving his position as auto recovery czar in order to accept a position as an academic dean at Georgetown University. Rather than appoint a new czar, though, Obama directed two officials to assume Montgomery's authority: Department of Labor Secretary Hilda Solis and the National Economic Council director Larry Summers, who had already been designated an economic recovery czar.[55]

This czar position highlights some of the reasons that we are troubled with such an arrangement. The president appointed an official not subject to confirmation, to lead a newly created executive branch entity that had no statutory basis, and provided him with responsibility for determining the distribution of large sums of public funds and coordinating policy among multiple departments and agencies. When Montgomery resigned, the president replaced him with two officials—one being a Senate-confirmed secretary of another department and the second a presidential aide. These arrangements came about not due to any constitutionally based understanding, but merely because the president unilaterally decided.

With so many czars in this administration, there is also the problem of seemingly overlapping duties, or at least very blurred lines of responsibilities. In addition to an auto recovery czar, Obama created a car czar position, initially held by Steven Rattner. Formally identified as the Chief Adviser to the Treasury Department on the Automobile Industry, Rattner had the responsibility to decide whether to distribute billions of federal dollars to General Motors, Chrysler, and GMAC, to rescue those companies from financial collapse. He headed a fourteen-member President's Task Force on the Automotive Industry and reported to the Treasury Secretary Tim Geithner. As the two auto companies emerged from bankruptcy in July 2009, Rattner resigned while he was also embroiled in a finance scheme scandal. But for the mere six months that he held the car czar post, Rattner exercised enormous power over the auto industry. As described by a lengthy profile in *New York* magazine, Rattner had "rewrit[ten] the understanding between the car companies and the unions while bending the companies' financiers—his friends and peers—to his will. With what seemed a cool, almost arrogant confidence—his casual dismissal of GM CEO Rick Wagoner reflected this quality—he had played a large role in restructuring the American car industry."[56]

Rattner's position and the auto bailouts were based on questionable legal authority. The Troubled Asset Relief Program (TARP), created by Congress when it passed the Emergency Economic Stabilization Act (EESA), ostensibly gave Rattner the authority to manage the auto bailout. However, Congress created TARP to bail out financial institutions, not the automobile companies. Even the Congressional Oversight Panel created specifically to provide oversight of TARP issued a report noting that the EESA "does not explicitly state that TARP is available to provide assistance to the automotive industry."[57] It appears that the "crisis atmosphere" permitted the rather liberal interpretation of the law to take hold.[58] The lack of clear legislative consent seemed to permit Rattner to act without much or any congressional oversight. In his own account of the auto bailout, Rattner proudly wrote: "The auto rescue succeeded in no small part because we did not have to deal with Congress." He went on to say that "if the task force had not been able to operate under the aegis of TARP, we would have been subject to endless congressional posturing, deliberating, bickering, and micromanagement, in the midst of which one or more of the troubled companies under our care would have gone bankrupt."[59] It is not surprising that a former czar would disparage democratic controls in order to promote a view that unlimited and quick actions by executive officials should win out. If such a view prevails, then executive action, not the protection of liberty, becomes the ultimate purpose of government.

New York Attorney General Andrew Cuomo later prosecuted Rattner for kickbacks to the New York pension fund. As part of a settlement deal, Rattner agreed to pay $10 million and not appear "in any capacity before a public pension fund" for a period of five years. In a separate settlement with the Securities and Exchange Commission, Rattner paid $6 million and agreed to a two-year ban from working in the securities field.[60] These penalties stemmed from illegal actions by Rattner prior to his selection by Obama as an executive branch czar. What were his special talents and training for holding a czar post? He started off as a reporter and got into the merger and acquisition business. Along the way, he gave millions of dollars to a number of Democratic Party candidates for office such as Hillary Clinton and Barack Obama. And here's the key point: would someone such as Rattner have been nominated, much less confirmed, had he been required to face FBI and Senate scrutiny? No matter, because the president decided unilaterally that this wealthy contributor should be appointed. There is no guarantee that a normal vetting process would have revealed Rattner's misdeeds before he assumed a major government position; but most likely it would have.

Although Rattner's work largely seemed finished, the car czar position continued for several more months in the Obama administration. The president soon appointed a replacement czar, Ron Bloom, who had served as Rattner's deputy. Geithner described that, under Bloom, the car czar position would function with a different mandate as "government transitions its role away from day-to-day restructuring to monitoring this vital industry and protecting the substantial investment the American taxpayers have made in GM, Chrysler, and GMAC."[61] In January 2011, Obama promoted Bloom to the position of White House senior counselor for manufacturing policy. He had previously held the title of Chief Adviser to the Treasury Department on the Auto Recovery from July 2009 to January 2011.[62]

One of the most controversial czar appointments was that of Carol Browner as the energy and climate czar. Obama tasked Browner, a former Environmental Protection Agency (EPA) Administrator during the Clinton administration, with duties that far exceeded the role of his own EPA head. She was the main force in the administration in pushing climate change initiatives. Browner played a key role in brokering a deal with automakers and the states to reduce greenhouse gas emissions. Her appointment thus elevated a White House czar above the role of an actual Senate-confirmed Cabinet secretary. Indeed, during her tenure in the czar position, Browner's profile and policy influence so vastly exceeded that of EPA Administrator Lisa Jackson, that very few people outside Washington politics could even recognize the latter's name. There is perhaps no more conspicuous an example of a czar whose authority so completely overshadowed that of a cabinet head directly in the same policy area. Because of her lack of appointment and refusal to testify on the Hill, in the first two years of the administration, congressional Republicans expressed significant opposition to Browner's expansive policy role and promised to challenge her authority if they were to achieve majority status. Very soon after the GOP took control of the House in January 2011, Browner resigned from her position as an administration czar.[63]

Making czar appointments is useful for presidents to showcase their commitments to certain causes. President Obama had campaigned in 2008 on promises of environmental restoration, and certainly many of his supporters wanted to see some substantial efforts to fulfill this goal. In addition to a climate czar, Obama has multiple czars to direct and coordinate policies affecting large bodies of water: a Great Lakes czar, a Chesapeake Bay czar, and a California water czar. There is also an Asian Carp czar empowered to coordinate federal and other governmental-level efforts to keep the invasive species out of the Great Lakes.

One of Obama's specific promises in 2008 was to create a new executive branch position with authority to oversee a multi-agency effort to clean up the Great Lakes. He said he would commit about $5 billion to the effort. In June 2009, EPA Administrator Jackson appointed Cameron Davis, the president of the Alliance for the Great Lakes, to the position of Great Lakes czar.[64] The position gave Davis power to coordinate efforts by federal agencies to implement the Great Lakes Project restoration plan.[65] Jackson also appointed a former Clinton administration assistant administrator for water policy, J. Charles Fox, to the position of Chesapeake Bay czar, a position he held until he resigned in December 2010.[66] Fox had authority to coordinate policy responses among multiple agencies affecting the bay.[67] Both Davis and Fox operated as czars, given their appointments to newly created positions of authority that had decision-making and budgetary power and that lacked confirmation.

In June 2009 Interior Secretary Ken Salazar announced the appointment of David J. Hayes as the deputy interior secretary, a position that the media would refer to as the California water czar. Salazar said that Hayes would "bring all of the key federal agencies to the table" to coordinate government responses to California's water shortages.[68] In addition, Hayes had the power to direct about $160 million toward the state's water problems. Some defenders of Obama's use of czars actually protested the use of the czar label for officials such as Hayes who had initially come to the administration in Senate-confirmed positions.[69] Unlike some of the other executive branch officials we consider czars, Hayes received Senate confirmation to the second-highest-ranked position within the Interior Department and had statutory authority over water resources controlled by the federal government.[70]

On September 8, 2010, the president's Council on Environmental Quality (CEQ) announced the appointment of John Goss as the Asian Carp Director.[71] The appointment came in response to alarms about the invasive fish working its way to the Great Lakes, where it could severely threaten native species. The appointment gave Goss authority over government spending that amounted to about $80 million per year on the Asian carp program.[72] It also has caused some confusion about lines of authority between a Great Lakes czar and yet another czar to keep a certain species out of the Great Lakes.

President Obama generated some of the most controversy over czar appointments on September 17, 2010, when he tapped Harvard University Law School professor Elizabeth Warren to direct a newly created Bureau of Consumer Financial Protection. The president circumvented the normal process of appointment and confirmation when he selected Warren as a temporary director, thus causing an outpouring of protest. Given her controversial views on some consumer issues, the president's opponents alleged that he purposely circumvented the legislative vetting process in order to avoid contentious confirmation hearings and to ensure her placement as head of the new executive branch bureau. Even though the Democrats controlled the Senate at the time, they could not secure the sixty votes required to overcome a GOP-led filibuster. The president therefore skirted normal confirmation procedures by giving Warren the title of assistant to the president and special adviser to the Secretary of the Treasury on the Consumer Financial Protection Bureau. In effect, Treasury Secretary Timothy Geithner would delegate certain of his powers to Warren to enable her to carry out duties as a bureau director.

A massive federal regulatory bill signed into law by Obama on July 21, 2010, created the new bureau.[73] Although it was slated initially to be under the Department of the Treasury, the statute gave the bureau wide-ranging authority to coordinate personnel and decision making among a number of executive branch departments. Various accounts have estimated the bureau's budget at as much as a half billion dollars. Thus, having a new czar with control over such an enormous entity and vast sums of public money also caused many to protest the nature of Warren's appointment. The arrangement for Warren to hold the post was that she would have a "temporary" position in that role for ten months. The authorizing legislation for the new bureau was slated to put its functions fully into effect on the one-year anniversary of the passing of the legislation, thus ensuring Warren ten months' tenure prior to possibly seeking actual Senate confirmation.

Soon after the president announced the appointment, two key House Republicans, Rep. Darrell Issa (CA) and Rep. Spencer Bachus (AL), wrote a strong letter of objection to the White House Counsel Robert Bauer. Issa was the ranking member of the House Committee on Oversight and Government Reform and Bachus the ranking member of the Financial Services Committee. They objected to what they called the "unusual arrangement" of Warren's appointment without confirmation, and they requested details regarding her range of authority and compensation. Lawmakers accused the president of "undermining congressional oversight" authority with this unconfirmed appointment. Perhaps the most damning statement of the "unusual arrangement" was actually intended as an expression of support, when Rep. Barney Frank (D-MA) said, "I congratulate the administration on its creativity."[74] Criticism of the nature of the Warren appointment did not track entirely on partisan lines, though, as some Democrats and independent government transparency advocates expressed their disapproval.[75]

One czar appointment created a major embarrassment for the Obama administration. The "green jobs" czar, Van Jones, resigned his position on September 5, 2009, amidst a flurry of reports that he had affiliated with a group that suggested that President George W. Bush had known of the 9/11 attacks in advance and had allowed them to happen and that Jones had belonged to a pro-Communist organization in the 1990s; there also was a video of Jones making an intemperate remark about Republicans. Obama had given Jones the complicated-sounding title of the "Council on Environmental Quality's Special Adviser on Green Jobs."

Conservative critics of the Obama administration scrutinized the past records of the president's czars for any evidence that he had appointed someone who never would have survived a Senate confirmation process. Once they hit pay dirt with Jones, conservative opinion leaders and politicians relentlessly attacked the appointment as evidence that Obama was using czar posts to create a shadow government of unaccountable officials with outside-the-mainstream views. Well-known commentators such as Sean Hannity and Glenn Beck made attacks on Obama for the Jones appointment regular features of their television and radio programs.

Key legislators opposed to the use of executive branch czars weighed in again with their objections. For example, the chair of the House Republican Conference, Rep. Mike Pence (R-ID), a frequent vocal critic of czars, used the occasion of Jones's resignation to call for an end to the practice of appointing such officials: "In the wake of these recent revelations, the president should suspend any further appointments of so-called czars until Congress has an opportunity to examine the background and responsibilities of these individuals and to determine the constitutionality of such appointments."[76] Several Republican senators also wrote to the president to express their opposition to the vast number and expansive duties of czars in the Obama administration.[77]

Although Republicans largely led the anti-czar movement at this time, there were also strong Democratic Party objections. Senator Dianne Feinstein (D-CA) declared it a "problem" that there were unconfirmed czar positions and called for greater congressional oversight of those officers. She said the problem was serious enough that members of Congress were often in the dark about the functions of various czar positions. As she told a reporter, "I don't know what a car czar does, for example." Senator Byron Dorgan (D-ND) added: "My expectation would be that if you have people with line responsibility, you need to have confirmation."[78] Senator Russell Feingold (D-WI) wrote one of the most pointed letters to the president raising various constitutionally based objections to the expansive use of czars. That letter generated a lengthy reply from the White House counsel Gregory Craig, in which he defended the practice of using czars as constitutionally sound and consistent with the actions of past administrations.[79]

Craig's letter is worth some examination here because he directly challenges key arguments against the use of czars. Early in this letter Craig expresses his purpose: to set the record straight that certain allegations of Obama-created czar positions are false because Congress had earlier created some of those posts. He identifies specifically the Director of the Office of Science and Technology Policy (President Gerald Ford), the Administrator of the Office of Information and Regulatory Affairs (President Ronald Reagan), and the Director of National Intelligence (President George W. Bush). Craig does not reference any sources making the allegation that those three positions were Obama-created czars, and indeed he is correct that none of them can properly be labeled a czar. But here Craig has merely rebutted the vague allegation about those three specific offices that were not at the forefront of some of the serious critiques of the practice of using czars.

Craig then explains that certain other czars have offices that reside within federal agencies and that some of these officials have testified before Congress or else some agency staff members have done so. Here the White House counsel's explanation is troublesome because he is attempting to confuse the issue over accountability. Why is it that certain czars who have offices within a federal agency have testified whereas some others have sent a subordinate to do so? How does sending a staff member within an agency to testify get around the problem of a czar with authority to make policy, coordinate agency responses, and spend public funds while refusing to go to Congress? A more egregious dilemma arises with Craig's statement that the green czar position is within the White House Department of Environmental Quality (DEQ) and that DEQ staff and its director sometimes testify before Congress. Again, this response avoids the issue, which is the powers and accountability of the czar, not of the DEQ director or its staff. Craig further suggests that because certain frequently identified czars are White House advisers, these officials have no legal authority to act and are merely assisting the president in making policy. Yet, some of these czars indeed have brokered deals with Congress, coordinated policy responses among departments and agencies, and also, at various levels of the federal system, made decisions on the allocation of public resources and exercised direct policy authority in many areas. Finally, Craig disputes the allegation of czar status for several NSC officials who we also would not define as czars (see chapter 5).

Craig's letter does not present a convincing case to effectively counter the concerns about czars raised by lawmakers. He cherry-picks certain offices to characterize allegations of too many czars as being largely overstated or false. He maneuvers around questions about accountability by saying that staff of departments and agencies can testify, or that maybe certain czars can do so. And he inaccurately labels some figures with substantial policy and spending authority as possessing no more than an advisory role within the White House. At one point, in attempting to dispute the charge that czars exercise independent authority, he actually confirms it. Craig insists that czars are not created to override the roles of longstanding departments and agencies, "but rather to help coordinate their efforts and help devise comprehensive solutions to complex problems."[80]

A several-month-long investigation by the *Washington Post* that relied on candid discussions with many high-level Obama administration officials contradicts Craig's protest that czars did not supplant the roles of cabinet secretaries. The report indeed revealed a cabinet in which numerous secretaries were shut out of White House policy deliberations while czars played regular key roles. One official who had heard complaints directly from cabinet secretaries commented for the news story that "the White House loops people out. The czars keep people from getting in."[81] The White House response to the cabinet criticism was to create a new office, a Cabinet Communications Director, "to better coordinate with and utilize members of the Cabinet."[82] This official statement was a startling admission of the problem of cabinet members being shut out. It also meant the creation of yet another White House aide getting in between the president and his cabinet, something that Louis Brownlow had said never should happen.

Defenders of Obama's use of czars have often pointed to the fact that some of these positions had their origins in previous administrations. The terrorism czar had its origins in the Bill Clinton administration and is more of a presidential adviser than an actual czar. And several positions are carryovers from the George W. Bush administration, including food safety, health IT, and faith-based czars. President Obama has also followed the established practice of some of his predecessors in appointing numerous special envoys, now commonly known as czars (see chapter 2). But what is undeniable is the substantial increase in the number of czars during the early years of the Obama presidency. Many of these positions reflect the changes in the national agenda brought about by such events as the auto industry crisis, but others simply reflect the different priorities of Obama's administration, such as the green jobs and consumer czars.

In some cases, Obama has significantly shifted the priorities of some of the established positions commonly referred to as czars. Perhaps most important was that the president eliminated cabinet-position status for his "drug czar," Gil Kerlikowske. Strictly speaking, ever since Congress created the so-called drug czar office in 1988, that office would not fall under our definition of a czar. Nonetheless, the office retains the established moniker and does possess many czar-like powers, but its officeholders are confirmed by the Senate (see chapter 5).

To highlight the seriousness attached to the federal government's "war on drugs," presidents Bush, Clinton, and Bush II had given cabinet status to this office. Kerlikowske fueled additional speculation of a reduced policy role for the drug czar office when he declared that it was time to banish what had become the common government rhetoric of a U.S. war on drugs. He emphasized a need to shift the national focus more to the public health aspects and treatment of drug abuse rather than fighting a domestic "war" with tough punitive measures.[83] This shift in policy emphasis and the lack of cabinet status nonetheless did not diminish the potential power of his position, as it remained in the Executive Office of the President and retained the ability to effect policy coordination among multiple federal agencies and across levels of government as well. When announcing the nomination of Kerlikowske, Vice President Joe Biden referred to the position as "someone who could lead at the White House level, coordinating all our nation's drug policy."[84] Indeed, one of the disturbing aspects of this position is the extent to which it has been used to trench on state and local government authority. Numerous times when states and localities have pursued anti-drug policies that did not dovetail with federal-level approaches, or when these jurisdictions have proposed medical marijuana legalization or tried to implement it, the so-called drug czar has intervened and threatened loss of federal revenues. That this office was congressionally authorized therefore did not change the reality that it retains some of the major problems associated with actual executive branch czars.

Another carryover from the Bush II era is the faith-based czar. In February 2009, Obama appointed a young Pentecostal Minister, Joshua DuBois, to the position formally known as the Director of the White House Office of Faith-Based and Neighborhood Partnerships, which is housed under the Domestic Policy Council. Under a somewhat different title that office had been created by President Bush in 2001, and it had exercised some policy and regulatory authority, but had largely focused on outreach to faith-based organizations. As with the Bush-era office, DuBois had responsibility for making decisions about directing federal monies to faith-based social service organizations.[85] This function remained controversial among advocates of a more strict separation of religion and state, many of whom object most strongly to the use of federal tax dollars to fund religion-based organizations' activities. Lacking congressional authorization or approval, the faith-based czar is allocating resources for social services that normally should be the purview of legislatively created programs. Accountability for faith-based expenditures is completely absent. A comprehensive study of the Bush and early Obama era faith-based initiatives issued in June 2009 offered the disturbing finding that "the full extent of public funding for faith-based social services is largely unknown."[86]

Another presidentially created White House structure is the Office of Urban Affairs. Obama created this office by executive order in February 2009 and appointed Adolfo Carrion Jr. as its first director.[87] Carrion held the Urban Affairs czar post until March 2010, when Obama named him the Regional Director for HUD's New York and New Jersey Regional Office. The president's executive order specified very broad policymaking and policy coordination responsibilities for the Urban Affairs director. It gave the director power, for example, to "coordinate the development of the policy agenda for urban America across executive departments and agencies" and "to coordinate all aspects of urban policy." It further authorized the director to target federal expenditures and to coordinate responses among different levels of government in the federal system.[88]

In keeping with the administration's emphasis on promoting healthy habits, in July 2009 the president appointed what the media called a food czar.[89] A former Monsanto Company executive, Michael Taylor, became the senior adviser to the commissioner of the Food and Drug Administration (FDA). According to the White House press release that announced this appointment, Obama gave Taylor authority over assessing food programs and "capacity needs," establishing "regulatory priorities," allocating resources, developing the FDA's budget requests, and "implementation of new food safety legislation."[90]

Obama also appointed his twenty-nine-year-old White House chef, Sam Kass, to the position of first the Food Initiative Coordinator and then the Senior Policy Adviser for Healthy Food Initiatives. Kass became known as a second food czar and is sometimes referred to as the healthy foods czar. As a senior adviser, Kass is not subject to Senate confirmation, although his duties entail coordinating policy for a $400 million per year initiative. Because of his dual role as White House cook and senior policy adviser, Kass's salary is listed as part of the residence staff and thus is excluded from the annual report to Congress on White House staff as required under Title 3 of the U.S. Code.[91] Kass's appointments to his dual roles and the concealing of his real salary as a senior policy adviser are violations of the president's promise of governmental transparency. Kass also looks to be a personal friend—the Obama family cook back in Chicago, presidential golfing buddy, elevated to a senior post with authority over large sums of federal expenditures. The derision of some of the president's critics for this arrangement seems justified.

So does the outcry against the president's having appointed a former reporter, Linda Douglass, to what became known as the "disinformation czar" position. Her formal title was the Director of Communications for the Office of Health Reform in the Department of Health and Human Services (HHS).[92] Thus, although in a temporary position, Douglass was tasked with the duty to coordinate communications strategies to promote the president's health-care reform proposal and also to counter misinformation being spread by various sources on the internet and through email, among other venues. As described on the White House blog: "As part of our effort to push back on the misinformation about health insurance reform, we've launched WhiteHouse.gov/realitycheck. It's full of videos and tools you can use to share the facts with your friends and family. Check it out." The post then features a video of Douglass where she "addresses one example that makes it look like the President intends to 'eliminate' private coverage, when the reality couldn't be further from the truth."[93] Saying that her work was completed, Douglass left her position soon after Obama signed the landmark health-care reform bill into law in March 2010. Although we find much to object to in this strange new temporary White House propaganda position, we leave Douglass off the list of real czars given her lack of policy, regulatory, or budgetary authority.

Obama's more than yearlong push for passage of the health-care bill resulted in another new czar: the head of the White House Office of Health Reform and counselor to the president. In March 2009, the president announced the simultaneous appointments of Governor Kathleen Sebelius as Secretary of HHS (Senate confirmed) and Nancy-Ann DeParle as the health reform czar (nonconfirmed). Upon appointment, DeParle immediately began her work, which involved coordinating the administration "policy agenda across executive departments and agencies" as it relates to "high-quality, affordable, and accessible health care." As the first health-care director, DeParle would be the point person for President Obama in all areas of health care and the administration's reform effort, despite the fact that there was already an existing department that had statutory authority over health-care services and initiatives.[94] In January 2011, as part of a White House staff reshuffling, DeParle moved to the positions of assistant to the president and deputy to the White House Chief of Staff. It appears that the Health Reform Office has ceased to be an active component of the White House Office.

The Obama administration also continued the health information technology czar position that was created in the Bush II era. In March 2009, Health and Human Services Secretary Kathleen Sebelius, under the direction of Obama, formally appointed a medical doctor and researcher, David Blumenthal, to the post of head of the Office of the National Coordinator for Health IT within the Department of Health and Human Services. Blumenthal's task was to encourage government promotion of coordinated medical records through creation of a Nationwide Health Information Network. Blumenthal held the post until his resignation in February 2011. What makes this czar position significant is its authority to employ government incentives and penalties to promote the nationalization of health-care records. Although acknowledged by some advocates as a necessary goal to avoid common medical errors, and derided by others as a violation of privacy, the issue of creating a national database of medical records merits a full public and congressional review. As that debate is occurring in the country and in Congress, an executive branch czar is making unilateral decisions that affect whatever options might emerge from the normal policy process.

Presidential creation of new czar positions is often bolstered by support from sources outside government. Advocacy groups promote czars for their policy areas. Sometimes the creation of czars is advocated by independent groups, too. In 2004, the 9/11 Commission—a congressionally chartered bipartisan commission officially titled the National Commission on Terrorist Attacks upon the United States—recommended the creation of a special czar to combat weapons of mass destruction. So did another bipartisan commission established by Congress, called the Commission on the Prevention of Weapons of Mass Destruction, Proliferation and Terrorism (also known as the WMD Commission). President Bush declined to do so, but Obama, in showcasing his commitment to fight terrorism, endorsed the idea in his 2008 presidential campaign.[95] Soon after his inauguration, Obama fulfilled the pledge when he appointed the director of the Council on Foreign Relations, Gary Samore, to the post variably called the nonproliferation czar or the WMD czar.[96] Like many czars, Samore has dual functions as presidential adviser and also as a coordinator of policy responses across departments and agencies. He played key roles in negotiating treaty agreements, such as the president's proposed Strategic Arms Reduction Treaty with Russia.

Although President Obama entered office with enormous challenges to confront, and thus the temptation was great to use czars on many policy fronts, he had pledged in his 2008 campaign to reverse the Bush-era practice of consolidating

**Number of Executive Branch Positions and Officials
Considered Czars, Gerald R. Ford–Barack Obama**

President	Number of	
	Positions	Officials
Gerald R. Ford	0	0
Jimmy Carter	0	0
Ronald Reagan	3	5
George H. W. Bush	2	2
Bill Clinton	2	2
George W. Bush	8	11
Barack Obama	20	22

Source: Appendix Tables 8, 10, 12, and 14.

executive powers in this fashion. He had also pledged an administration charac-terized by transparency and accountability. Yet many of his czars exert substantial independent policy authority, and they reside outside the normal constraints built into our constitutional republic. The absence of a PAS appointment process for the czars who exercise authority that binds others is especially troubling in a system of checks and balances. Presumably, a shared appointment power provides another layer of check against presidents appointing high-end officials who lack proper qualifications or basic credibility to exercise vast governing powers. The need for a congressional vetting process is particularly noteworthy given the Jones appoint-ment and his resignation under fire. If the Senate does not review high-level ap-pointees, there is no guarantee that the White House will do the job. When asked by reporters whether President Obama had knowledge of Jones's controversial past affiliations and use of epithets to describe Republicans, senior White House adviser David Axelrod said that the president had not even been aware of these facts.[97]

SUMMARY

The Bush and Obama administrations represent a substantial escalation in the presidential use of executive branch czars. The table above shows the number of executive branch positions, and occupants, that we consider czars during the post-Watergate era, from Gerald R. Ford to Obama. At this writing, Presidents Bush and Obama combined have used thirty-two czars during their times in office. That compares with only nine czars during the presidencies of Ford, Carter, Ronald Reagan, George H. W. Bush, and Bill Clinton. In particular, President George W.

Bush has been the focus of a vast recent literature on the growth of independent presidential powers and the decline of democratic controls.[98] The expansion of the practice of appointing presidential czars during his time in office fits the pattern of an administration that often showed little regard for the constitutionally based system of balanced powers.

Although President Obama had pledged to reverse such Bush-era practices, when it comes specifically to the use of executive branch czars, he has actually exceeded his predecessor (see Tables 12 and 14 in the Appendix for documentation). Regarding their use of czars, the legacies of these two administrations disturb us greatly. We believe a congressionally led corrective action is needed. In what follows, we present a concluding analysis of what we perceive as the serious constitutional damage committed by the use of czars, and we offer a proposal for reform to reverse the current trend. Indeed, any change in the system has to be directed by the legislative branch, as the history of the modern era has shown so abundantly that presidents do not readily give up new and expanded powers that appear to have some utility.

8. Conclusions: Restoring the Constitutional Balance

Czars are a function of the growing powers of the presidency and the failure of Congress sufficiently to act to protect its own institutional prerogatives. Modern presidents are commonly expected to set the national agenda and to try to solve complex policy problems. Oftentimes, presidents are not willing to wait for legislative action, but rather they will take the initiative in pushing their agendas or bypass Congress and act on public policy, even without clear legal authority to do so.

The constitutional system of checks and balances anticipates congressional pushback when presidents act outside the boundaries of their authority. Instead, throughout much of modern U.S. history, Congress too often has ceded its authority to presidents. Scholar James P. Pfiffner put it correctly when he wrote: "During most of the twentieth century, presidents often acted aggressively to assert their own authority as against Congress. But Congress has only rarely asserted its own constitutional powers as against the president."[1]

Before the rise of the modern presidency and the vast expansion of executive powers, presidents generally understood that they were not free to create positions without the consent of Congress.[2] They did not assume authority to circumvent statutory officers or legislatively enacted programs by unilateral presidential action. Regrettably for our constitutional republic, there has been a gradual erosion of those traditional rules and norms of the presidency. Under pressure to lead on many policy fronts, and given enormous leeway to act due to expanded powers and congressional deference, modern presidents increasingly have turned to the use of czars.

Presidents Woodrow Wilson and Franklin D. Roosevelt were trailblazers in the creation and the use of czars for implementing their policy objectives. Wilson started the practice in an emergency (World War I), and Roosevelt expanded upon it significantly. Both operated under a theory of the presidency first articulated by President Theodore Roosevelt that would have been foreign to most presidents dating back to the founding of the republic.

Theodore Roosevelt championed an aggressive model of the presidency where the chief executive became "a steward of the people bound actively and affirmatively to do all he could do for the people." He explained that the president not only has a right but a "duty to do anything that the needs of the Nation demanded unless such action was forbidden by the Constitution or by the laws."[3] Roosevelt also claimed that the president "is or ought to be peculiarly representative of the people as a whole." As a result, Roosevelt reasoned that "the actions of the executive offers the only means by which the people can get the legislation they demand and ought to have."[4] He suggested that if the legislative branch failed to govern, its power might need to be exercised elsewhere: "as in any nation which amounts to anything, those in the end must govern who are willing actually to do the work of governing; and insofar as the Senate becomes a merely obstructionist body it will run the risk of seeing its power pass into other hands."[5] Although Roosevelt did not elaborate on where the Senate's power would ultimately rest, it is reasonable to assume he meant that the presidency would be the benefactor.

As president, Wilson would hold and apply an equally expansive view of the presidency. Wilson argued that the president is "predominant and the 'center' of national leadership and representation." The Constitution could evolve to "express the changing temper and purposes of the American people from age to age." Wilson also thought that the presidency was the only institution that could provide active political leadership by channeling public opinion "independent of any constitutional grant of authority, or of constitutional constraints." In his book *Constitutional Government*, Wilson described this new governing norm:

> The nation as a whole has chosen him, and is conscious that it has no other political spokesman. His is the only national voice in affairs. Let him once win the admiration and confidence of the country, and no other single force can withstand him, no combination of forces will easily overpower him. His position takes the imagination of the country. He is the representative of no constituency, but of the whole people. When he speaks in his true character, he speaks for no special interest. If he rightly interpret the national thought and boldly insist upon it, he is irresistible.[6]

Wilson placed independence and power of a president above all other considerations. Because the president seemingly represents the "whole people" he should be free to govern with force since the "object of constitutional government is to bring the active, planning will of each part of the government into accord with the prevailing popular thought and need, and thus make it an impartial instrument of symmetrical national development."[7]

Wilson, like Roosevelt before him, believed that the president was the most capable part of government to lead that effort. Upon facing a national emergency in the form of World War I the presidency, as conceptualized in the early twentieth century, was still limited by the rules and norms of constitutional governance. Presidents did not assume that they possessed extra-constitutional authority to create executive branch positions to carry out their policy goals, even in emergencies. What was a president to do who faced a world war? Still acting under the notion of legislative supremacy as it pertained to government structure, Wilson requested statutory authority from Congress to reorganize the executive branch for purposes of war. Although Congress provided Wilson with the requested reorganization authority, he went further than the law permitted and began to unilaterally create new agencies.

Assuming the White House as a result of Herbert Hoover's failed response to the Great Depression, the second Roosevelt also employed an expansive view of the presidency. It was not until World War II that Roosevelt saw the need to create czars, as an overwhelmingly Democratic Congress had provided all the tools he requested for his New Deal program. Like Wilson, Roosevelt received statutory authority to reorganize the federal government but not to create new agencies. Eventually lawmakers again recognized that they, not the president, had legislative primacy to create government structure and attempted to prevent the unilateral creation of agencies by chief executives. However, that was a momentary pushback, and Congress decided to greatly weaken its earlier prohibition. In section 214 of the 1946 Independent Offices Appropriation Act, Congress permitted the creation of government committees, boards, and interagency groups by appropriations from executive departments and agencies, as long as the new entities served the "common interest of such departments and establishments and [are] composed in whole or in part of representatives thereof."[8]

After Roosevelt, presidents increasingly found czars useful even in nonemergency situations. This development partially reflects a presidency that has been saddled with obligations and functions that have often overwhelmed individual occupants of the White House. Writing in 1956, Clinton Rossiter reported that the modern president wore no fewer than eleven "hats": chief of state, chief executive, commander-in-chief, chief diplomat, chief legislator, chief of party, voice of the people, protector of the peace, manager of prosperity, world leader, and President of the West.[9] With such lofty obligations on their shoulders, no wonder modern presidents believed they needed czars.

The shift away from a more limited conception and role of the presidency received support from leading academics, some of whom came from the executive branch and remained loyal to that institution. In 1960, Richard Neustadt, a former Truman administration official, suggested that the office of the chief executive is essentially divorced from the Constitution and that "presidential power is the power to persuade."[10] This viewpoint directly countered what had been the dominant view of such presidential scholars as Edward S. Corwin, who believed that presidents could only exercise powers that were outlined in the Constitution.[11] Neustadt thought that such a narrow view did not adequately explain the many dimensions of actual presidential power. "What is good for the country is good for the President, and vice versa."[12] Such thinking helped eventually to nurture a view of the presidency that has virtually no restrictions.

Neustadt, however, was not alone. In 1965, James MacGregor Burns wrote in his book, *Presidential Government*, that the "stronger we make the Presidency, the more we strengthen democratic procedures and can hope to realize liberal democratic goals."[13] Two years later, Grant McConnell wrote: "To ask what is to become of the presidency is to ask what is to become of the entire American political order."[14] Finally, in 1968 McGeorge Bundy, a former national security adviser to Presidents John F. Kennedy and Lyndon B. Johnson, penned a book calling for more power in the hands of executive branch officials, particularly the president.[15] The fact was that at the end of the 1960s most academics and practitioners worried about the presidency not being strong enough.[16]

By Richard M. Nixon's time in the White House, George E. Reedy, a former press secretary for Lyndon Johnson, could write that "the Presidency had taken on all the regalia of monarchy except ermine robes, a scepter, and a crown."[17] Nixon indeed was no stranger to the use of czars to serve his policy goals. He would employ czars to combat drugs, price inflation, the energy crisis, and the economic recession. Not only that, but he attempted to unilaterally restructure his cabinet and direct public policy goals through four presidential assistants who should also be considered czars. Only a few years later, the post-Watergate backlash to the imperial presidency produced a more assertive Congress and less aggressive chief executives. Neither Presidents Gerald R. Ford nor Jimmy Carter attempted to create czars to achieve their preferred policy outcomes. For some, the more restrained version of the presidency embodied in Ford and Carter was actually a presidency imperiled.[18] Presidents Ronald Reagan, George H. W. Bush, and Bill Clinton began to again use czars, but the full pre-Watergate revival of the practice would have to wait.

Since then, George W. Bush and Barack Obama have not only accepted czars as a governing norm but have greatly expanded their use. There is no evidence that this trend will be curtailed. In President Obama's first two years in office he has already created more czars than were established during George W. Bush's two terms. Part of the explanation for this massive growth of czars is the passage of time and the dissociation of contemporary presidents with the so-called imperial presidency. Shirley Anne Warshaw noted that the imperial presidency posed a "political stigma" for post-Watergate presidents.[19]

By the time of the Bush and Obama presidencies, the reluctance to create czars had dissipated. Both presidents created numerous new czar positions that largely operated with little to no statutory backing. The Bush and Obama czar appointments have highlighted some very important constitutional and legal issues regarding the unilateral establishment of new positions and offices along with other serious appointment and appropriations concerns. Of course, congressional ambivalence and deference to presidents in an increasingly polarized environment greatly aided in this development. Simply put, presidents and lawmakers have viewed the normal legislative process as too slow and the existing bureaucratic structure as too cumbersome to effectively meet the needs of modern society or the most pressing problems of the day. The result has been that the evolution of the White House Office and presidential staffing has been fueled by this vast expanding role of the federal government, the growth of the "cult of the presidency," the concomitant perception that strong presidents unfettered by external controls are good for the system, and the lack of a sufficient challenge by Congress to protect its own institutional powers.[20]

Certainly the belief that the "president needs help" is unarguable. That reality is hardly unique to the modern presidency, as every chief executive since George Washington has been unable to fulfill the duties of the presidency by himself and thus has needed help. But when that need results in presidents' resorting to the appointments of various czar positions that have little to no accountability to Congress, then serious questions of constitutional and legal authority arise.

WHY ARE CZARS A CONCERN?

The primary issue with czars is that they transform a system of government based on accountability to one in which most power rests unchecked in the executive branch. The constitutional design of the president's appointment power calls for a shared responsibility between the legislative and the executive. The Appointments Clause, particularly the principal officers provision, makes it clear that presidents never were intended to have unilateral authority over executive branch staffing. Further, that Congress controls the funding of executive branch staff establishes that the appointments and duties of executive branch officers were intended to be shared responsibilities with ultimately legislative, not executive, control. The founders devised structural protections, through such mechanisms as the officers versus inferior officers distinction. Over time those distinctions helped guarantee that unelected and unaccountable individuals would not be making important policy and regulatory decisions. Czars allow the executive to be shielded from the process of accountability. This produces public policies and government action that Congress has little to no role in developing.

Another danger in the increased use of czars is that they create exaggerated expectations of the presidency. If czars are a governing mechanism for getting things accomplished, then if they fail or implement bad policies, the president is to blame. But advocates for such a system of governance could argue that czars are the only way to execute public policy. Nonetheless, because some device may have some abstract utility does not make it constitutional. The argument that the country needs czars merely because they help presidents to lead must yield to principles of democratic controls. It does not matter even if czars make the federal government more efficient. The purpose of having a separated system of government is not to promote efficiency, but rather to avoid the concentration of power.[21] Certainly other forms of government are more efficient than ours, but that does not mean we should adopt practices that violate express constitutional language or principles.

Furthermore, although we are not persuaded by the utilitarian arguments for merely greater coordination and government efficiency, after conducting a lengthy review of the history of czars, we also are not all that impressed by the record of czars at coordinating the activities of multiple and often overlapping bureaucratic units and at making government more efficient. The record of accomplishments for czars does not appear to be a good one. Take President Woodrow Wilson's creation of the War Industries Board (WIB) during World War I. He charged Bernard Baruch with ramping up wartime production of defense materials. However, industrial production peaked in May 1917, a full year before Wilson set up the WIB. More recently, neither of President Nixon's czars on inflation and the economy succeeded in their primary task. The same is true of the nation's first drug czar. Nearly ten years later, the federal government revived the "War on Drugs," with first lady Nancy Reagan leading the way with her "Just Say No" campaign. Finally, Tom Ridge was largely ineffectual in his role as George W. Bush's homeland security czar.

Another problem posed by czars is that their existence encourages presidents to continually turn inward for advice and analysis, when it would be most beneficial to seek counsel outside of the executive branch for different perspectives. Scholar Richard Pious makes this key point in his book *Why Presidents Fail*. Pious states that the modern institutionalized presidency with its centralized command and control operation within the White House that was "designed to improve presidential performance, has increased rather than reduced the risks of failure."[22] What Pious finds is that executive branch officials, and presidents in particular, are often ill equipped to manage public policy issues alone. The fact is that presidents need Congress. In questioning the role of modern White House staff—some of whom are actually czars—Pious explains, "too many aides meddle in too much departmental business, antagonize too many legislators, and provide fodder for too many reporters looking to add to their collection of White House scalps."[23] Pious believes a better solution than presidents centralizing power and acting unilaterally is for them to adhere "to framework legislation mandating collaborative governance with Congress."[24] We agree. Since most czars have no place in the Constitution or laws, they operate in a system of governance created by the president. Pious's presidential failure thesis holds for czars. These offices need to be subject to traditional constitutional boundaries and democratic controls.

In 2010, Eric A. Posner and Adrian Vermeule wrote that the aggrandizement of presidential power should not matter, as the actions of the occupants of the White House have been constrained by politics and public opinion. "It is pointless to bewail the [shift to executive governance], and futile to argue that Madisonian structures should be reinvigorated," Posner and Vermeule claim. "Instead," they argue, "attention should shift to the political constraints on the president."[25] Even on the most pressing public issues of the day, many presidents have not been constrained by public opinion. Did President Johnson pull out of Vietnam when the public began to oppose that war? How about President Bush in Iraq? On domestic matters, President Obama went ahead on his push for health-care reform during a time when a majority of the public opposed the measure. When the question comes to governing functions that are not so well known to the public, as is the case with czars, then what is to be done? Posner and Vermeule do not answer that question. To be clear, some czars have shown restraint in the exercise of power without legal or public guidance. To paraphrase from Gene Healy: that czars might have shown restraint while in possession of significant unchecked power is, at best, an uneasy source of comfort.[26]

What has evolved over the nation's history seems to us a worst-case scenario outcome: czars have further fueled the concentration of executive power, undermined democratic controls, added more layers of decision making in government, and, for all of that, they have generally not done a good job of making the executive branch bureaucracy more effective and efficient. In the next section we review some of the more recent legislatively based responses to czars and then offer our own suggestions for how the problems outlined can be corrected.

EFFORTS AT LEGISLATIVE CONTROLS

As the czars controversy heated up in the Barack Obama era, some members of Congress tried to devise a legislative solution to the constitutional problems of allowing the president to appoint nonconfirmed and unaccountable executive branch officials with substantial powers. In 2009, Rep. Jack Kingston (R-GA) introduced a bill entitled the Czar Accountability and Reform Act of 2009, also known as the "CZAR Act." The bill had over 100 cosponsors, and it sought to eliminate the use of public funds to pay the salaries of "any task force, council, or similar office which is established by or at the direction of the President and headed by an individual who has been inappropriately appointed to such position (on other than an interim basis), without the advice and consent of the Senate."[27]

In a Democrat-controlled Congress, the bill failed to pass the House, as the controversy over czars had already become a part of a heated partisan debate.

Senate Republicans had also sought information about eighteen positions in the Obama administration that they considered czars and had asked that the president "refrain from creating any new czar-type posts."[28] As with so many constitutionally based issues over the years in the modern Congress—e.g., war powers, impeachment, signing statements, executive agreements—the positions adopted by most members in this case lined up almost perfectly with their partisan affiliations.

And thus the calculation changed in the House of Representatives after the 2010 elections had given the GOP a majority. In early 2011, Rep. Steven Scalise (R-LA) introduced a bill cleverly entitled the Sunset All Czars Act (H.R. 59).[29] The purpose of this bill was to define *czars* and then to defund the salaries and expenses of all of them.[30] In particular Scalise defined *czar* as "a head of any task force, council, policy office within the Executive Office of the President, or similar office established by or at the direction of the President." In addition, the official would have to be appointed without the Senate's advice and consent; be exempt from the "competitive service by reason of such position's confidential, policy-determining, policy-making, or policy-advocating character"; perform or delegate functions that "would be performed or delegated by an individual in" a Senate-confirmed position; and have no removal date for the position to which he or she was appointed.[31] The definition has much going for it since it attempts to cover officials who operate in the White House without legal authority and who have been given delegated functions meant to be reserved for Senate-confirmed appointees. We believe, however, that Scalise's bill too narrowly defines czars and does not address the issue of presidents establishing new government positions and structures without statutory approval. Subsection IV of the bill even permits the continuation of a czar as long as the president, even without the authorization of Congress, sets a removal date for the position.

On February 17, 2011, by a margin of 249–171, the House passed a version of Scalise's bill as an amendment to a federal spending measure. The amendment specifically targeted a number of the president's policy czars, but it only defunded certain czar positions through the end of the fiscal year and thus had a limited reach. After the vote, Scalise declared on behalf of the members who supported the amendment, "We are tired of [Obama] running this shadow government, where they have got these czars that are literally circumventing the accountability and scrutiny that goes with Senate confirmation."[32] Democrats on the Senate Appropriations Committee labeled the House amendment as "an intrusive micromanagement of the President's White House staff via appropriations."[33]

Facing a Democrat-controlled Senate and a presidential veto, the amendment stood little chance to be more than a symbolic slap at the practice of using czars. However, the Republican House did secure passage of an anti-czar provision as part of the 2011 federal budget compromise. Section 2262 prohibited the use of appropriations in the law for the salaries and expenses of the czars of energy, health reform, car/auto, and urban affairs.[34] The budget, including section 2262, was the result of lengthy negotiations between Obama and lawmakers. Yet when the agreed-upon bill went to the White House for the president's signature, Obama attached the following signing statement to it:

> Section 2262 of the Act would prohibit the use of funds for several positions that involve providing advice directly to the President. The President has well-established authority to supervise and oversee the executive branch, and to obtain advice in furtherance of this supervisory authority. The President also has the prerogative to obtain advice that will assist him in carrying out his constitutional responsibilities, and do so not only from executive branch officials and employees outside the White House, but also from advisers within it.
>
> Legislative efforts that significantly impede the President's ability to exercise his supervisory and coordinating authorities or to obtain the views of the appropriate senior advisers violate the separation of powers by undermining the President's ability to exercise his constitutional responsibilities and take care that the laws be faithfully executed. Therefore, the executive branch will construe section 2262 not to abrogate these Presidential prerogatives.[35]

There are several problems with Obama's assessment of section 2262 and of the president's place within our constitutional system of government. First, Obama mentioned that the president "has well-established authority to supervise and oversee the executive branch, and to obtain advice in furtherance of this supervisory authority." Certainly the Take Care Clause of the Constitution authorizes the president to faithfully carry out law that Congress and the president establish. However, that does not somehow limit lawmakers in their ability to shape public policy and the governing structure that implements it. Every executive department and agency owes its existence to Congress. Lawmakers have the authority to reshape any part of the executive branch—even the White House Office and the Executive Office of the President (EOP)—as they see fit (see the Legislative Establishment of Office section in chapter 1). Nothing in the Constitution prevents that.

Second, Obama noted that the president "has the prerogative to obtain advice" from all quarters of the executive branch. That statement is a truism that was not challenged by the anti-czar provision. Of course presidents can seek advice from White House aides, cabinet secretaries, or other officials within the executive branch. A president can even look to members of Congress and private citizens for advice. Abolishing executive branch structure does not change a president's ability to do so. If that were the case then Congress could only create executive branch positions but not eliminate them. What Obama was really claiming here is that Congress cannot invade his "prerogative" to hire and fire White House staff. No such prerogative exists. As explained in chapter 5, Congress by law determines the number of White House staff and their levels of pay. The president has no open-ended authority that is not subject to democratic controls to hire whomever he likes and have the public pay their salaries.

Obama also argued that section 2262 violates the separation of powers principle "by undermining the President's ability to exercise his constitutional responsibilities and take care that the laws be faithfully executed." Certainly when presidents create positions within the White House Office or EOP that mimic the responsibilities and functions of *statutorily authorized* and *Senate-confirmed* cabinet secretaries, then Congress has every right to intervene. Presidents who continually circumvent the statutorily prescribed governing system by creating czar after czar to evade legislative oversight invite these kinds of actions by Congress to correct the imbalance of power. If a president cannot rely on the secretary of health and human services or another cabinet member, then the constitutional and proper course of action is not to create a position with overlapping duties but to go to Congress to find a statutory solution to the nation's problems. What Obama seemed to have done here was to tell Congress he would avoid confirmation hearings by placing people who perform department and agency functions in czar positions within the White House Office and EOP but also take the congressional appropriations used to pay their salary and expenses, even if lawmakers had clearly stated in law that such funds should not be spent. That kind of reasoning represents the height of presidential hubris and shows an utter contempt for Congress as a co-equal branch of government.

Finally, for a presidential candidate who claimed fidelity to the Constitution and said at numerous events during the 2008 campaign that he would not issue any signing statements, Obama's actions here were particularly troubling and disappointing.[36] In a December 2007 response to the *Boston Globe*, Obama made the following telling statement: "I will not use signing statements to nullify or undermine congressional instructions as enacted into law. The problem with [the George W. Bush] administration is that it has attached signing statements to legislation in an effort to change the meaning of the legislation, to avoid enforcing certain provisions of the legislation that the President does not like, and to raise implausible or dubious constitutional objections to the legislation."[37] Yet, in April 2011 he did just that. What Obama and his staff could not block or modify through concessions or veto threats during budget negotiations with members of Congress, he decided to unilaterally strip from a signed bill. In essence, Obama became the ultimate decider on what is constitutional and proper. Few acts by occupants of the White House so completely embody the unchecked and imperial nature of the modern presidency.

In light of such presidential actions, the efforts of lawmakers to challenge the use of executive branch czars are an important endeavor. Even after the signing statement, Republican lawmakers did not give up the fight. In June 2011, the House added language to a financial services spending bill to eliminate funding for the salaries of four executive branch czars.[38] A week later Senator David Vitter (R-LA) offered an amendment to the Presidential Appointment Efficiency and Streamlining Act that would have cut off funding for non-Senate-confirmed presidential aides who were the heads of task forces, councils, and policy offices.[39] The Senate voted down Vitter's amendment by a four-vote margin with forty-seven senators in support and fifty-one against. Senator Charles Schumer (D-NY), who opposed the measure, explained: "It is a poison pill designed to handcuff the president's ability to assemble a team of top-flight advisers and aides."[40] Despite his defeat, Vitter believed he had succeeded in his goal of shedding light on the matter: "These czars have a great deal of power and authority and I'm pleased that we got a vote to prohibit their funding so that Americans can see who in Congress shares their view that czars are outside traditional constitutional authority."[41]

Politically, the challenges come at an awkward time, because as we write our analysis the partisan overtones to the whole debate and the fact that many observers assume that criticisms of the practice of czars are motivated by anti-Obama sentiments could quickly undermine anyone who seeks to curtail executive power. We have no stake in the partisan debates and certainly we would have offered similarly strong objections to the use of czars had we written this analysis during the Bush II era, for example. And although we agree with the sentiments presently represented mostly by Republicans to curtail czars, we do not believe that recent legislative proposals are sufficient to deal with the constitutional issues at hand. Defunding certain czars in one fiscal year, for example, does not address the core problems that we have identified in this study. A more sweeping approach is needed.

Normally, we would not be optimistic about the chances for a legislatively directed major reform effort against a president's powers. When it comes to constraining the powers of the modern presidency, Congress does not have a good record.[42] Congress has been too willing to defer various responsibilities to the president, even in cases of blatant usurpations of authority. And as Pfiffner points out, many members of Congress often take the short-term view in protecting the interests of a president of their own party, regardless of the long-term constitutional implications.[43] We do not doubt the possibility of such an outcome in the current debates over proposals to rein in executive branch czars. Nonetheless, Congress at times has been responsive to outside pressures to reform. The debate over czars, although intensely partisan and overheated of late, has elevated public awareness of this growing phenomenon and its problems and has thus increased the chances for congressional action. Our analysis to this point has provided the history, evolution, and constitutional issues surrounding czars. We now offer what we consider the proper corrective to the current situation.

REFORM PROPOSALS

To overcome the constitutional problems raised in this analysis, existing federal law on presidential aides needs to be revamped to ensure that these persons are all in official positions and are fully accountable for their duties. To do so requires nothing less than overhauling Title 3, section 105 of the U.S. Code, which authorizes the president "to appoint and fix the pay of employees in the White House Office without regard to any other provision of law regulating the employment or compensation of persons in the Government service. Employees so appointed shall perform such official duties as the President may prescribe." Our proposed reform would not hamper the president and department heads from getting the help that they need, but rather would mandate that all positions in the White House Office and EOP more generally be given official titles and be subject to democratic controls.

Existing White House Office and EOP positions should be statutorily limited in number. In addition, each position occupied by a presidential aide should be named (that is, given an official title), with its duties described, and the list of these officials should be placed in Title 3 rather than spread throughout the U.S. Code or not mentioned at all. Further, presidents should not be able to unilaterally create new positions and define their duties. Rather, a president should seek congressional authorization when he wants to expand White House staff or add new offices. The president also should not be able to transfer department staff to the White House without approval or, at a minimum, should be required to report to Congress on who has been transferred and what duties they have performed. The current law only requires presidents to report detailed department or agency employees after they have been working in the White House for 180 days or longer.[44]

Moreover, annual reports of the name, job title, job description, and salary of every individual employed in the White House Office and EOP should be required. Congress originally had placed such a commonsense reform in the White House Authorization Act of 1978, but it was stripped from the bill during the conference committee negotiations (see chapter 5 for more details). Finally, Congress should create mandatory reporting and appearance requirements for the heads of offices, bureaus, groups, or similarly situated units within the White House Office and EOP. There is a history of Congress inserting such measures into law. In 1988, Congress required the director of the Office of National Drug Control Policy to "appear before duly constituted committees and subcommittees of the House of Representatives and of the Senate to represent the drug policies of the executive branch" as stipulated in the Anti-Drug Abuse Act.[45]

Any position that falls within our definition of a czar should be Senate confirmed, and the law should expressly require that such officeholders testify before Congress, along with mandating reporting requirements. The Brownlow Committee was correct to emphasize that no official should be interposed between the president and department or agency heads. And in a system of democratic accountability, it is also necessary that no official should be interposed between the president and Congress. Both situations have become the norm with the modern presidency and certainly with the rise of czars. Presidential scholar John Hart explains:

> Nowadays, senior White House staffers regularly do what Brownlow said they should not do. They quickly become prominent figures in every administration. They do make decisions, issue instructions, and emit public statements. They do interpose themselves between the president and the heads of departments. They do exercise power on their own account, and, on occasions, certain members of the White House staff have not discharged their functions with restraint. In recent years, some have clearly lacked the high competence Brownlow thought essential, and few have displayed much passion for anonymity. The reality of life in the White House is far removed from the Brownlow Report.[46]

Certainly we are not arguing that White House staff or other executive branch officials that we classify as czars should all go back to some idealized conception of administrative management of the 1930s. Neither the modern presidential staff system nor the presidency can revert back into some preconceived notion of early twentieth-century governance. Yet, constitutional checks are not only needed, but required in a governing system with a strong presidency. Czars may be a convenient vehicle for presidents to avoid the normal constraints of separated powers. However, it is hard to deny that they violate the intentions of those who created our system of delicately balanced powers.

To date, Congress has shown an unwillingness or indifference to reviewing and revamping Title 3 of the U.S. Code. Since the creation of the EOP in 1939, Congress has only twice passed legislation overhauling that title. Hart makes a key point in that regard: "The presidential branch draws considerable institutional strength from the attitude adopted by Congress because that allows it to operate beyond the confines of effective accountability and responsibility, at least on a day-to-day basis."[47] Hart's observation suggests that "the attitude adopted by Congress" needs to change for reform to occur. As many of the examples presented in this volume make clear, members of Congress who have objected to the powers of certain czars, or the refusals of others to testify, have done so in a piecemeal fashion trying to undo the consequences of the legislative branch's own failure to rein in a strong presidency. Congress can no longer be passive; the problem is not going away.

We are aware that there may be questions about such reforms violating core separation of powers principles or charges that they unduly micromanage the president's office and staff. Such concerns seem to be makeweight arguments at best. Congress has given life to the White House Office and EOP by providing presidents with staff at various points throughout much of the previous century. When Louis Brownlow famously said that the "president needs help," Franklin D. Roosevelt looked to Congress, not inward.[48] Finally, a claim that separation of powers somehow isolates a president and his staff from the traditional checks that have been provided by Congress cannot be sustained when considering the vital role the White House now plays in nearly every aspect of domestic and foreign policy. The modern presidency requires greater legislative oversight, particularly of the White House Office and EOP. If presidents want to make claims to some vague notion of White House autonomy, then Congress should be willing to strip them of their statutory authority over domestic and foreign affairs.

Aside from the fact that Congress gave life to the White House Office and EOP, there are practical reasons why there is great danger of providing presidents more and more personnel without asking to what end. Consider the following observation by former White House adviser and now Brookings scholar Stephen Hess: "Enlarging the staff beyond a certain point ensures that more problems are drawn to the White House for resolution, limits the number of problems that might be resolved below the White House level, cuts the time that a president can give any one problem, forces him to spend more time on the care and feeding of his staff, and increases the potential for aides to misspeak in his name."[49] Hess is exactly right. But as Pious correctly points out, the problem is that the "conventional wisdom of president and Congress watchers" suggests quite the opposite—that presidents should expand their staff resources to enable them to take on all of the complex policy problems thrust onto the White House. Pious sees virtue, and we agree, in actually decreasing White House staff resources, in having the president "do less and to make do with less," and in providing Congress with a strengthened collaborative role in policymaking.[50]

The Constitution created a system of government that requires the branches to check each other, not to have them exist separated and free to do whatever they choose. Taking reasonable steps to ensure oversight and accountability is a proper course of action. Louis Fisher has pointed out that legislative diligence in carrying out its core functions is not, as some critics allege, "micromanagement" of the executive branch, but rather the constitutionally anticipated role of Congress to ensure a balanced system in which no one entity absorbs too much power.[51] As czars proliferate and run amok, it is time for Congress to step up to the task and assert its institutional roles of oversight and guarding against executive branch power grabs.

We realize that there are politicians and scholars who believe that presidents are the most capable to determine administrative structure, not only in the White House but for all parts of the executive branch. Such views of the presidency confuse the very nature and purpose of democratic controls in our governing system. Author Michael Lind states the point bluntly and correctly: "Presidential democracy is not democracy." Instead, he adds, "Americans must conclude that democracy does not mean voting for this or that elective monarch every four years and then leaving government to the monarch's courtiers. Democracy means continuous negotiation among powerful and relatively autonomous legislators who represent diverse interests in society."[52]

Executive-dominated government promises much but risks more. Energy and efficiency are important values that can sometimes help to develop public policy to benefit the nation. However, unchecked presidential power carries with it the potential to destroy liberty. "It has been asked," Rep. Alexander White said in the First Congress, "whether a person in the elevated station of the President would abuse his trust? I do not presume he will, but I presume he may: to prevent such evils, the constitution has wisely guarded the exercise of every power."[53]

Indeed, the framers established a government based on republican and structural protections. They never wanted political or policy expediency to outstrip the democratic controls they put in place. Instead, they worked against the creation of an executive-dominated government and believed that power should never be placed in the hands of an unrestrained person, no matter how bright or seemingly incorruptible he may appear to be. "Political idolatry of any stripe, including the divine right of kings or waiting for a Great Man, found no support among the framers," writes Louis Fisher. "They did not put their faith in a single person. Fearing concentrated power, they believed in process and structural checks."[54]

Advocates of a more active and powerful chief executive believe that presidents are best suited to not only make judgments about administrative structure but also to efficiently manage complex government affairs. Yet there is little in U.S. history to validate this exalted view of what presidents are capable of achieving.[55] In his book on the managerial presidency, Peri E. Arnold notes that the "plain fact is that no modern president has fully managed the executive branch." He observes that "the managerial conception of the presidency is untenable." Too many obligations and expectations have been placed on the performance of presidents, he warns. As a result, the "managerial presidency then becomes a trap, offering increased capacity and influence to presidents but creating even greater expectations about presidential performance."[56] Adding to this assessment Harold M. Barger correctly observed: "The myth that a president can control the Executive Branch also belies the reality that the American government was never intended to be managed or led by one person."[57] For far too long Congress has remained idle and permitted president after president to create, modify, and attempt to manage the executive branch with little input or oversight. Such inaction does not conform to the framers' understanding of a republican government where the legislative branch plays a vital part of a successful republic because its source of power is based on consent of the people.

This assessment brings us to our next reform proposal, which calls on a legislative-led reorganization effort of the existing departments and agencies to make them more effective tools for the modern age. If the problem in the executive branch is that departments and agencies are not getting the job done, that there is too much overlap and confusion regarding responsibilities, then Congress should statutorily fix those issues, rather than allow presidents to appoint czars to try to pull everything together. Stephen Hess got it right when he wrote that it is necessary to "reorganize the executive branch to reflect a more realistic approach to solving problems and delivering services. Most departments represent a collection of past resolutions of yesterday's most important problems, of demands on elected officials by yesterday's most important special interest groups, and of long-forgotten bureaucratic fights over jurisdiction. Given the difficulty of changing existing arrangements, presidents have continued to create new agencies and to pull new problems into the White House, where their authority is greater."[58]

CONCLUDING REMARKS

We are aware that this analysis runs against the grain of much contemporary scholarship on the presidency. Since the Progressive Era, there has been a steady and growing infatuation with a strong presidency. To many observers, the complex system of separated powers engenders delay and gridlock. A strong presidency for them represents the promise of governmental efficiency. More and more citizens, too, have looked to the national government to act quickly and, specifically, to the president to solve problems. With widespread scholarly and public support, combined with presidential ambition and congressional acquiescence, the modern vast consolidation of executive powers is no surprise.[59] And thus, it is also no surprise that it has taken so many years for the controversy over executive branch czars to have taken hold. For too long, presidents have had a nearly free hand to appoint these officers with little meaningful oversight and accountability.

It is discouraging that the contemporary debate over executive branch czars has become so polarized and primarily a partisan finger-pointing exercise. Democrats took up the charge against George W. Bush's czars, and Republicans have intensified the criticisms of czars in the Barack Obama administration. And playing completely to type, many who said not a word against Bush's czars beat up on Obama's, and many who defend the current president's practices were harsh critics of his predecessor's. There is little consistency in arguing constitutional principles, but plenty of persistence by legislators and party members in upholding whatever positions just happen to dovetail with partisan interests of the moment.

We would hope that even partisans eventually recognize that they all have a common interest in eliminating the use of czars. Confirmed officers have a duty first and foremost to the law, and secondarily to the interests of the person who happens to be president. Czars have no such duty to the law and perceive their obligation first and foremost to be to the political stakes and campaign promises of the president they serve. Conservative commentators who defended Bush's theory of the unitary executive and constant push for greater executive powers lost their credibility to protest when a Democratic president adopted similar positions. Democrats defending President Obama's extensive use of czars have to realize that their actions today provide validation in the future for a Republican president to do the same, or even more.

As we have argued, czars may appear temporarily to have some utility to the executive branch, but that does not make them constitutionally proper or desirable. Time and again throughout U.S. history, when constitutional principles yielded to matters of convenience—take for example war powers, government surveillance, suspension of citizen freedoms—and presidents were allowed to act without checks on their authority, the direct consequences and overall damage to constitutional governance have been profound. Czars offend the constitutionally based principles of separation of powers, checks and balances, and democratic accountability. They have no proper place in our government and should be eliminated.

Appendix: An Index of Czars and Media-Labeled Czars, 1919–2011

ABBREVIATIONS USED IN THESE TABLES

Department of Agriculture	DOA
Department of Defense	DOD
Department of Education	DOE
Department of Energy	DE
Department of Health and Human Services	HHS
Department of Homeland Security	DHS
Department of the Interior	DOI
Department of Justice	DOJ
Department of State	DOS
Department of the Treasury	DT
Environmental Protection Agency	EPA
Executive Office of the President	EOP
Federal Communications Commission	FCC
Food and Drug Administration	FDA
National Economic Council	NEC
National Security Council	NSC
Office of Emergency Management	OEM
Office of Management and Budget	OMB
President Appointed	PA
Presidential Appointment with Senate Confirmation	PAS
White House Office	WHO

Table 1. Media-Labeled Czars during the Woodrow Wilson–Herbert Hoover Administrations

President	Position	Name	Service Dates	Czar Title	PA, PAS, or Other	Statute/Regulation/Order
Woodrow Wilson	Commissioner of Internal Revenue, DT	John F. Kramer[1]	1919–1921	Dry law or liquor czar	PAS	National Prohibition Act of 1919 (Volstead Act)[2]
Warren Harding	Commissioner of Internal Revenue, DT	Roy A. Haynes[3]	1921–1927	Dry law or liquor czar	PAS	National Prohibition Act of 1919 (Volstead Act)[4]
Calvin Coolidge	"Acting" Prohibition Commissioner, DT	"	1927	"	Other[5]	An Act to Create a Bureau of Customs and a Bureau of Prohibition[6]
	Prohibition Commissioner, DT	James M. Doran[7]	1927–1930	"		
	Director, Public Buildings and Grounds of the National Capital	Clarence O. Sherrill[8]	1925	Washington czar	PA	An Act to Consolidate the Office of Public Buildings and Grounds[9]
Herbert Hoover	Director of Prohibition, DOJ	Amos W. Woodcock[10]	1930–1933	Dry law or liquor czar	Other[11]	Prohibition Reorganization Act of 1930[12]

Table 2. Czars during the Woodrow Wilson–Herbert Hoover Administrations

President	Position	Name	Service Dates	PA, PAS, or Other	Statute/Regulation/Order
Woodrow Wilson	Chair, Committee on Public Information	George Creel	1917–1919	PA	Executive Order[1]
	Administrator, Food Administration	Herbert Hoover	1917–1919	PA	None[2]
	Chair, Exports Administrative Board	Vance McCormick	1917	PA	Executive Order[3]
	Administrator, Fuel Administration	Harry A. Garfield	1917–1919	PA	Executive Order[4]
	Chair, War Trade Board	Vance McCormick	1917–1919	PA	Executive Order[5]
	Co-Chairs, National War Labor Board	William H. Taft Frank P. Walsh	1918–1919	PA	Proclamation[6]
	Chair, War Industries Board	Bernard Baruch	1918–1919	PA	Executive Order[7]
	Chair, Price-Fixing Committee, War Industries Board	Robert S. Brookings	1918–1919	PA	None
Warren Harding	No known czars during the Harding administration.				
Calvin Coolidge	Flood Relief Coordinator[8]	Herbert Hoover[9]	1927	Other[10]	None
Herbert Hoover	No known czars during the Hoover administration.				

Table 3. Media-Labeled Czars during the Franklin D. Roosevelt Administration

Position	Name	Service Dates	Czar Title	PA, PAS, or Other	Statute/Regulation/Order
Congressional Delegation of Agricultural Regulatory Authority, DOA[1]	Henry A. Wallace[2]	1933–1940	Agriculture czar	PAS[3]	Agricultural Adjustment Act[4]
Administrator, Agricultural Adjustment Administration[5]	George N. Peek[6]	1933		Other[7]	Agricultural Adjustment Act[8]
Director, National Recovery Administration	Hugh S. Johnson[9]	1933–1934[10]	Industry czar	PA	Executive Order 6173[11]
Chair, Federal Alcohol Control Administration	Joseph H. Choate Jr.[12]	1933–1935[13]	Dry law or liquor czar	PA	Executive Order 6474[14]
Federal Coordinator of Transportation	Joseph B. Eastman[15]	1933–1936[16]	Railroad czar	Other[17]	Emergency Railroad Transportation Act[18]
Office of Price Administration and Civilian Supply, OEM, EOP	Leon Henderson[19]	1941	Price czar	PA	Executive Order 8734[20]
Administrator, Office of Price Administration, OEM, EOP	"	1941–1942	"		Executive Order 8875[21]
	Prentiss Marsh Brown[22]	1942–1943			
	Chester Bowles[23]	1943–1946			
Office of the Petroleum Coordinator for National Defense, DOI[24]	Harold L. Ickes[25]	1941–1942[26]	Oil czar	Other[27]	Presidential Letter[28]
Office of the Petroleum Coordinator for War, DOI	"	1942	"		Presidential Letter[29]
Petroleum Administrator, Petroleum Administration for War, DOI	"	1942–1946	"		Executive Order 9276[30]

(continued)

Table 3 (continued)

Position	Name	Service Dates	Czar Title	PA, PAS, or Other	Statute/Regulation/ Order
Director, Office of Defense Transportation, OEM, EOP	Joseph B. Eastman[33] J. Monroe Johnson[35]	1941–1944 1944–1949	Transportation czar	PA	Executive Order 8989[34]
Director, Office of War Information, OEM, EOP	Elmer Davis[36]	1942–1945	Information czar	PA	Executive Order 9182[37]
Director, War Production Board, OEM, EOP	Donald Nelson[38] Julius Krug[40]	1942–1944 1944–1945	Production czar	PA	Executive Order 9024[39]
Rubber Director, War Production Board, OEM, EOP	Bill Jeffers[41]	1942–1943	Rubber czar	Other[42]	Executive Order 9246[43]
Director, Office of War Utilities, War Production Board, OEM, EOP	Julius Krug[44]	1943	Power czar	Other[45]	None[46]
Administrator, War Shipping Administration, OEM, EOP	Emory S. Land[47]	1942–1946	Shipping czar	PA	Executive Order 9054[48]
Chair, War Manpower Commission, OEM, EOP	Paul V. McNutt[49]	1942–1945	Manpower czar	PA	Executive Order 9139[50]
Director, Office of Economic Stabilization, OEM, EOP	James F. Byrnes[51] Fred M. Vinson[53] William Hammatt Davis	1942–1943 1943–1945 1945–1946[54]	Economic czar	PA	Executive Order 9250[52]
National Food Program Coordinator, DOA[55]	Claude Wickard[56]	1942–1943[57]	Food czar	Other[58]	Executive Order 9280[59]
Administrator, Administration of Food Production and Distribution, DOA	Chester C. Davis[60]	1943			Executive Order 9332[61]
Administrator, War Food Administration, DOA	Marvin Jones[63]	1943–1945			Executive Order 9334[62]

Table 4. Czars during the Franklin D. Roosevelt Administration

Position	Name	PA, PAS, or Other	Service Dates	Statute/Regulation/Order
Director, National Recovery Administration	Hugh S. Johnson	PA	1933–1934[1]	Executive Order 6173[2]
Federal Coordinator of Transportation	Joseph B. Eastman	Other[4]	1933–1936[3]	Emergency Railroad Transportation Act[5]
Director General, Office of Production Management, OEM, EOP	William S. Knudsen	PA	1941–1942[6]	Executive Order 8629[7]
Director, Division of Defense Housing Coordination, OEM, EOP	Charles F. Palmer	PA	1941–1942[8]	Executive Order 8632[9]
Chair, President's Committee on War Relief Agencies, OEM, EOP	Joseph E. Davis	PA	1941–1942	None[10]
Chair, President's War Relief Control Board, OEM, EOP	"	PA	1942–1946[11]	Executive Order 9205[12]
Chair, National Defense Mediation Board, OEM, EOP	Clarence A. Dykstra	PA	1941–1942[13]	Executive Order 8716[14]
Administrator, Office of Price Administration and Civilian Supply, OEM, EOP	Leon Henderson	PA	1941	Executive Order 8734[15]
Administrator, Office of Price Administration, OEM, EOP	"	PA	1941–1942[16]	Executive Order 8875[17]
Division of Defense Aid Reports, OEM, EOP	James H. Burns		1941[18]	Executive Order 8751[19]
Administrator, Office of Lend-Lease Administration, OEM, EOP	Edward R. Stettinius	PA	1941–1943[20]	Executive Order 8926[21]
Director, Office of Civilian Defense, OEM, EOP	Fiorello H. LaGuardia	PA	1941–1942	Executive Order 8757[22]
	James M. Landis		1942–1943	
	John B. Martin		1943–1945[23]	
Director, Office of the Coordinator of Inter-American Affairs, OEM, EOP	Nelson Rockefeller	PA	1941–1944	Executive Order 8840[24]
	Wallace K. Harrison		1944–1946[25]	
Director, Office of Inter-American Affairs, OEM, EOP	"	PA		Executive Order 9532[26]
Chair, Supply Priorities and Allocations Board, OEM, EOP	Henry A. Wallace[27]	Other[29]	1941–1942[28]	Executive Order 8875[30]
Executive Director, Supply Priorities and Allocations Board, OEM, EOP	Donald Nelson	PA		"
Director, Office of Defense Health and Welfare Services, OEM, EOP	Paul V. McNutt[31]	PA	1941–1943[32]	Executive Order 8890[33]
Director, Office of Censorship, OEM, EOP	Bryon Price	PA	1941–1945[34]	Executive Order 8985[35]
Director, Office of Defense Transportation, OEM, EOP	Joseph B. Eastman	PA	1941–1944	Executive Order 8989[36]
	J. Monroe Johnson		1944–1949[37]	

(continued)

Table 4 (continued)

Position	Name	Service Dates	PA, PAS, or ther	Statute/Regulation/ Order
Chair, National War Labor Board, OEM, EOP	William H. Davis	1942–1945[38]	PA	Executive Order 9017[39]
Director, War Production Board, OEM, EOP	Donald Nelson	1942–1944	PA	Executive Order 9024[40]
	Julius Krug	1944–1945[41]		
Director, Office of War Information, OEM, EOP	Elmer Davis	1942–1945[42]	PA	Executive Order 9182[43]
Rubber Director, War Production Board, OEM, EOP	Bill Jeffers	1942–1943	Other[44]	Executive Order 9246[45]
	James F. Clark	1944–1945[46]		
Administrator, War Shipping Administration, OEM, EOP	Emory S. Land	1942–1946[47]	PA	Executive Order 9054[48]
Director, War Relocation Authority, OEM, EOP	Milton S. Eisenhower	1942	PA	Executive Order 9102[49]
	Dillon S. Myer	1942–1946[50]		
Chair, War Manpower Commission, OEM, EOP	Paul V. McNutt[51]	1942–1945[52]	Other[53]	Executive Order 9139[54]
Director, Office of Economic Stabilization, OEM, EOP	James F. Byrnes	1942–1943	PA	Executive Order 9250[55]
	Fred M. Vinson	1943–1945		
	William Hammatt Davis	1945–1946[56]		
Administrator, Petroleum Administration for War, DOI	Harold L. Ickes[57]	1942–1946	Other[58]	Executive Order 9276[59]
	Ralph K. Davies (Acting Administrator)	1942–1946[60]		
National Food Program Coordinator, DOA[61]	Claude Wickard[62]	1942–1943	Other[63]	Executive Order 9280[64]
Administrator, Administration of Food Production and Distribution, DOA	Chester C. Davis	1943	"	Executive Order 9332[65]
Administrator, War Food Administration, DOA	Marvin Jones	1943–1945[67]		Executive Order 9334[66]
Director, Office of War Utilities, War Production Board, OEM, EOP	Julius Krug	1943	Other[68]	None[69]
	Edward Falck	1944–1945[70]	"	
Director, Office of War Mobilization, OEM, EOP	James F. Byrnes	1943–1944[71]	PA	Executive Order 9347[72]
Director, Office of Economic Warfare, OEM, EOP	Leo T. Crowley	1943[73]	PA	Executive Order 9361[74]
Administrator, Foreign Economic Administration, OEM, EOP	Leo T. Crowley	1943–1945[75]	PA	Executive Order 9380[76]
Administrator, Surplus War Property Administration, Office of War Mobilization, OEM, EOP	William L. Clayton	1944[77]	Other[78]	Executive Order 9425[79]

Table 5. Media-Labeled Czars during the Harry S Truman–Lyndon B. Johnson Administrations

President	Position	Name	Service Dates	Czar Title	PA, PAS, or Other	Statute/Regulation/Order
Harry S Truman	Director, Office of War Mobilization and Reconversion	John Snyder[1]	1945–1946	Reconversion czar	PAS	War Mobilization and Reconversion Act of 1944[2]
		John R. Steelman[3]	1946–1947[4]			
	National Food Program Coordinator, DOA[5]	Clinton P. Anderson[6]	1945–1948[7]	Food czar	Other[8]	Executive Order 9577[9]
	Housing Expediter, Office of War Mobilization and Reconversion	Wilson W. Wyatt[10]	1945–1947	Housing czar	PA	Executive Order 9686[11]
	Government Representative, DOA	Gayle C. Armstrong[12]	1946	Meat czar	Other[13]	DOA Regulation[14]
	The Assistant to the President, WHO	John R. Steelman[15]	1949	U.S. project czar	PA	Reorganization Act of 1939[16] and Presidential Memorandum
	Director of Guided Missiles, Office of Secretary of Defense, DOD	K. T. Keller	1950–1953	Missiles czar[17]	Other[18]	National Security Act Amendments of 1949[19]
	Director, Office of Defense Mobilization, EOP	Charles E. Wilson[20]	1950–1952	Mobilization czar	PAS	Executive Order 10193[21]
		John R. Steelman (Acting)[22]	1952			
Dwight D. Eisenhower	Special Assistant for Guided Missiles, DOD	Eger V. Murphree[23]	1956–1957	Military missiles czar	Other[24]	Second Supplemental Appropriation Act, 1951[25]
	Office of Director of Guided Missiles, DOD	William M. Holaday[26]	1957–1958	"		DOD Directive 5105.10[27]
	Special assistant to the president for science and technology, WHO	James Killian[28]	1957–1959	Missile or science czar	PA	White House Authorization Act of 1948[29]
	Director, Advanced Research Projects Agency, DOD	Roy W. Johnson[30]	1958–1959	Defense or military space czar	Other[31]	Department of Defense Directive 5105.15[32]

(continued)

Table 5 (continued)

President	Position	Name	Service Dates	Czar Title	PA, PAS, or Other	Statute/Regulation/Order
John F. Kennedy	Special assistant to the president for science and technology, WHO	Jerome B. Wiesner[33]	1961–1964	Science czar	PA	White House Authorization Act of 1948[34]
	Special assistant to the president on regulatory matters, WHO	James M. Landis[35]	1961	Agency czar	PA	White House Authorization Act of 1948[36]
	Special Representative for Trade Negotiations, EOP	Christian A. Herter[37]	1962	Trade czar	PAS	The Trade Expansion Act of 1962[38]
Lyndon B. Johnson	Assistant Secretary of State for Inter-American Affairs, DOS	Thomas C. Mann[39]	1964–1965	Latin American policy czar	PAS	Department of State Regulations[40]
	Special Assistant for Consumer Affairs, WHO	Esther Peterson[41]	1964–1967	Consumer czar	PA	White House Authorization Act of 1948[42]
	Special assistant of the war on poverty programs, WHO	Sargent Shriver[43]	1964	Anti-poverty czar	PA	White House Authorization Act of 1948[44]
	Director, Office of Economic Opportunity, EOP	"	1964–1969	"	PAS	Economic Opportunity Act of 1964[45]
	Civil Rights Coordinator, Vice-President's Office[46]	Hubert Humphrey[47]	1964–1965[48]	Civil rights czar	Other[49]	Presidential Delegation of Authority[50]
	Chair, President's Council on Equal Opportunity, EOP	"	1965[51]	"		Executive Order 1197[52]

Table 6. Czars during the Harry S Truman–Lyndon B. Johnson Administrations

President	Position	Name	Service Dates	PA, PAS, or Other	Statute/Regulation/Order
Harry S Truman	National Food Program Coordinator, DOA[1]	Clinton P. Anderson[2]	1945–1948	Other[3]	Executive Order 9577[4]
	Assistant to the President, WHO	John R. Steelman	1945–1946	PA	Reorganization Act of 1939[5]
	The Assistant to the President, WHO	"	1946–1953		"
	Administrator, Civilian Production Administration, OEM, EOP	John D. Small	1945–1946[6]	PA	Executive Order 9638[7]
	Housing Expediter, Office of War Mobilization and Reconversion	Wilson W. Wyatt	1945–1946[8]	PA	Executive Order 9686[9]
	Director of Liquidation, OEM, EOP	Robert L. McKeever	1946[10]	PA	Executive Order 9674[11]
	Director, Central Intelligence Group	Sidney W. Sourers	1946	PA	Presidential Directive[12]
		Hoyt S. Vandenberg	1946–1947	"	"
		Roscoe H. Hillenkoetter	1947[13]	"	"
	Administrator, Philippine Alien Property Administration, OEM, EOP	James M. Henderson	1946–1951[14]	PA	Executive Order 9789[15]
Dwight D. Eisenhower	Administrator, Federal Civil Defense Administration, OEM, EOP	Millard Caldwell	1950–1951[16]	PA	Executive Order 10186[17]
	Director, Office of Director of Guided Missiles, DOD	William M. Holaday	1957–1959[18]	Other[19]	DOD Directive 5105.10[20]
	Director, Advanced Research Projects Agency, DOD	Roy W. Johnson	1958–1959	Other[21]	DOD Directive 5105.15[22]
John F. Kennedy	No known czars during the Kennedy administration.				

(continued)

Table 6 (continued)

President	Position	Name	Service Dates	PA, PAS, or Other	Statute/Regulation/Order
Lyndon B. Johnson	Special assistant of the war on poverty programs, WHO	Sargent Shriver	1964	PA	White House Authorization Act of 1948[23]
	Chair, Federal Reconstruction and Development Planning Commission, EOP	Clinton P. Anderson[24]	1964	Other[25]	Executive Order 11150[26]
	Executive Director, Federal Reconstruction and Development Planning Commission, EOP	Dwight Ink[27]	1964	"	Executive Order 11150[28]
	Civil Rights Coordinator, Vice-President's Office[29]	Hubert Humphrey[30]	1964–1965[31]	Other[32]	None
	Chair, President's Council on Equal Opportunity, EOP	"	1965[33]	"	Executive Order 11197[34]

Table 7. Media-Labeled Czars during the Richard M. Nixon–Jimmy Carter Administrations

President	Position	Name	Service Dates	Czar Title	PA, PAS, or Other	Statute/Regulation/Order
Richard M. Nixon	Director of Communications, WHO	Herbert G. Klein[1]	1969–1973	Information czar	PA	White House Authorization Act of 1948[2]
	Director, Special Action Office for Drug Abuse Prevention, EOP	Jerome Jaffe[3]	1971–1973	Drug czar	PA	Executive Order 11599[4]
		Robert DuPont[6]	1973–1977		PAS	Drug Abuse and Treatment Act of 1972[5]
	Director, National Institute on Drug Abuse, National Institute of Mental Health, United States Public Health Service, Department of Health, Education, and Welfare	"	1973–1978	"	Other[7]	Drug Abuse and Treatment Act of 1972[8]
	Chair, Cost of Living Council, EOP	John Connally[9]	1971–1972	Economic or Price czar	Other[10]	Executive Order 11615[11]
	Pay Board, Cost of Living Council, EOP	George H. Boldt[12]	1971–1973[13]	Pay czar	PA	Executive Order 11627[14]
	Chair, Price Commission, Cost of Living Council, EOP	C. Jackson Grayson Jr.[15]	1971–1973	Price czar	PA	Executive Order 11627[16]
	Director, Energy Policy Office, EOP	John A. Love[17]	1973	Energy czar	PA	Executive Order 11726[18]
	Administrator, Federal Energy Office, EOP	William E. Simon[19]	1973–1974	"	PA	Executive Order 11748[20]
	Administrator, Federal Energy Administration	John Sawhill[21]	1974	"	PAS	Federal Energy Administration Act of 1974[22]
	Assistant to the President for Economic Affairs, WHO	George P. Shultz[23]	1972–1974[24]	Economic czar	PA	White House Authorization Act of 1948[25]
	Assistant to the President for Economic Affairs, WHO	Kenneth Rush[26]	1974	"	PA	White House Authorization Act of 1948[27]

(continued)

Table 7 (continued)

President	Position	Name	Service Dates	Czar Title	PA, PAS, or Other	Statute/Regulation/Order
Gerald R. Ford	Director, Special Action Office for Drug Abuse Prevention, EOP	Robert DuPont[28]	1973–1977	Drug czar	PAS	Drug Abuse and Treatment Act of 1972[29]
	Administrator, FEA	John Sawhill[30]	1974	Energy czar	PAS	Federal Energy Administration Act of 1974[31]
		Frank G. Zarb[32]	1975–1977	"		
	Chair, Energy Resources Council, EOP[33]	Rogers C. B. Morton[34]	1974–1975[35]	"	Other[36]	Energy Reorganization Act of 1974[37]
Jimmy Carter	Director, Office of Drug Abuse Policy, EOP	Peter G. Bourne[38]	1977–1978[39]	Drug czar	PAS	Drug Abuse Office and Treatment Act Amendments of 1976[40]
	Secretary, DE	James Schlesinger[41]	1977–1979	Energy czar	PAS	Department of Energy Organization Act of 1977[42]
		Charles William Duncan Jr.[43]	1979–1981			
	Special Representative for Trade Negotiations, EOP	Robert S. Strauss[44]	1978	Inflation czar	PAS	The Trade Act of 1974[45]
	Special Counselor on Inflation, WHO	"	"	"	PA	White House Authorization Act of 1978[46]
	Chair, Council on Wage and Price Stability, EOP	Alfred Kahn[47]	1978–1980		PA	Council on Wage and Price Stability Act[48]
	Advisor to the President, WHO	"	"			White House Authorization Act of 1978[49]

Table 8. Czars during the Richard M. Nixon–Jimmy Carter Administrations

President	Position	Name	Service Dates	PA, PAS, or Other	Statute/Regulation/Order
Richard M. Nixon	Director, OMB, EOP	George P. Shultz	1970–1972	PA	Reorganization Plan No. 2 of 1970[1]
		Casper W. Weinberger	1972–1973		
		Roy L. Ash	1973–1974[2]		
	Director, Special Action Office for Drug Abuse Prevention, EOP	Jerome Jaffe	1971–1973[3]	PA	Executive Order 11599[4]
	Chair, Cost of Living Council, EOP	John Connally[5]	1971–1972	Other[6]	Executive Order 11615[7]
		George P. Shultz[8]	1972–1974		
	Executive Director, Cost of Living Council, EOP	Donald Rumsfeld	1971–1973	PA	Executive Order 11615[9]
		John T. Dunlop	1973–1974[10]		
	Pay Board, Cost of Living Council, EOP	George H. Boldt	1971–1973[11]	PA	Executive Order 11627[12]
	Chair, Price Commission, Cost of Living Council, EOP	C. Jackson Grayson Jr.	1971–1973[13]	PA	Executive Order 11627[14]
	Assistant to the President for Economic Affairs, WHO	George P. Shultz[15]	1972–1974	PA	White House Authorization Act of 1948[16]
	Counselor for Natural Resources, WHO	Earl L. Butz[17]	1973	PA	White House Authorization Act of 1948[18]
	Counselor for Human Resources, WHO	Caspar Weinberger[19]	1973	PA	White House Authorization Act of 1948[20]
	Counselor for Community Development, WHO	James Lynn[21]	1973	PA	White House Authorization Act of 1948[22]
	Director, Energy Policy Office, EOP	John A. Love	1973	PA	Executive Order 11726[23]
	Administrator, Federal Energy Office, EOP	William E. Simon	1973–1974	PA	Executive Order 11748[24]
	Assistant to the President for Economic Affairs, WHO	Kenneth Rush	1974	PA	White House Authorization Act of 1948[25]
Gerald R. Ford	No known czars during the Ford administration.				
Jimmy Carter	No known czars during the Carter administration.				

Table 9. Media-Labeled Czars during the Ronald Reagan–Bill Clinton Administrations

President	Position	Name	Service Dates	Czar Title	PA, PAS, or Other	Statute/Regulation/Order
Ronald Reagan	Assistant Secretary of Energy for Defense Programs, DE	Herman E. Roser[1]	1981–1984	Nuclear arms czar	PAS	Department of Energy Organization Act of 1977[2]
	Assistant Secretary of Defense for Acquisition and Logistics, DOD	James Paul Wade Jr.[3]	1985–1986	Procurement czar	PAS	DOD Authorization Act, 1984[4]
	Under Secretary of Defense for Acquisition, DOD	Richard P. Godwin[5]	1986–1987	"	"	Defense Acquisition Improvement Act of 1986[6]
		Robert B. Costello[7]	1987–1989			
George H. W. Bush	Under Secretary of Defense for Acquisition, DOD	John A. Betti[8]	1989–1991	Procurement czar	PAS	Defense Acquisition Improvement Act of 1986[9]
		Donald J. Yockey[10]	1991–1993			
	Director, Office of National Drug Control Policy, EOP	William J. Bennett[11]	1989–1990	Drug czar	PAS	National Narcotics Leadership Act of 1988[12]
		Bob Martinez[13]	1991–1993			
	Director, Office of Thrift Supervision, DT	T. Timothy Ryan Jr.[14]	1990–1997	Savings and loan or thrift czar	PAS	Financial Institutions Reform, Recovery, and Enforcement Act of 1989[15]
Bill Clinton	Under Secretary of Defense for Acquisition, DOD	John M. Deutch[16]	1993–1994	Procurement czar	PAS	Defense Acquisition Improvement Act of 1986[17]
	Under Secretary of Defense for Acquisition and Technology, DOD	Paul G. Kaminski[18]	1994–1997	"	"	National Defense Authorization Act for Fiscal Year 1994[19]
		Jacques Gansler[20]	1997–2001	"		
	Director, Office of National Drug Control Policy, EOP	Lee P. Brown[21]	1993–1995	Drug czar	PAS	National Narcotics Leadership Act of 1988[22]
		Barry McCaffrey[23]	1996–2001			
	Secretary, Department of Housing and Urban Development	Henry Cisneros[24]	1993–1997	Housing czar	PAS	Department of Housing and Urban Development Act[25]
	Office of the National AIDS Policy Coordinator, EOP	Kristine M. Gebbie[26]	1993–1994	AIDS czar	PA	None[27]
	Director, Office of National AIDS Policy, EOP	Patricia S. Fleming[28]	1994–1997	"	"	
		Sandra L. Thurman[29]	1997–2001	"	"	

Position	Name	Dates	Czar title	Type	Legal authority
Chair, The President's Task Force on National Health Care Reform, EOP	Hillary Clinton[30]	1993	Health-care czar	Other[31]	None[32]
Senior Adviser to the President for Policy Development, WHO	Ira Magaziner[33]	1993	"	PA	White House Authorization Act of 1978[34]
White House Deputy Chief of Staff, WHO	Harold M. Ickes[35]	1994–1996	"	PA	White House Authorization Act of 1978[36]
Senior Adviser to the President for Policy Development, WHO	Ira Magaziner[37]	1995–1998	Internet policy or internet czar	PA	White House Authorization Act of 1978[38]
U.S. Attorney for Southern California, DOJ	Alan D. Bersin[39]	1995–1998[40]	Border czar	PAS	Section 541 of Title 28 of the U.S. Code[41]
Special Representative on Southwest Border issues, DOJ	"	"	"	Other[42]	None
National Coordinator for Security, Infrastructure Protection and Counter-terrorism, NSC	Richard A. Clarke[43]	1998–2001	Terrorism czar	PA	Presidential Decision Directive 63[44]
Assistant to the President and Staff Secretary, WHO	Todd D. Stern[45]	1995–1998[46]	Climate czar	PA	White House Authorization Act of 1978[47]
Assistant to the President for Special Projects (climate change), WHO	"	1998–1999	"		White House Authorization Act of 1978[48]
Chair, The President's Council on Year 2000 Conversion, EOP	John A. Koskinen[49]	1998–2000	Y2K czar	PA	Executive Order 1307350
Assistant to the President, WHO	"	"	"	"	White House Authorization Act of 1978[51]
Under Secretary for Nuclear Security, National Nuclear Security Administration, DE	John Gordon[52]	2000–2002	Nuclear security czar	PAS	National Nuclear Security Administration Act[53]

Table 10. Czars during the Ronald Reagan–Bill Clinton Administrations

President	Position	Name	Service Dates	PA, PAS, or Other	Statute/Regulation/Order
Ronald Reagan	Assistant to the President for National Security Affairs, WHO	Robert McFarlane	1983–1985	PA	White House Authorization Act of 1978[1]
		John Poindexter	1985–1986		
	Deputy Director of Political-Military Affairs, NSC	Oliver North	1983–1986	Other[2]	National Security Act of 1947[3]
	Executive Director, Interagency Council on the Homeless	Cassandra Moore	1987–1988	Other[4]	McKinney–Vento Homeless Assistance Act[5]
		James Stimpson (Acting Director)	1988		
George H. W. Bush	Chair, President's Council on Competitiveness, EOP	Dan Quayle[6]	1989–1993	Other[7]	None[8]
	Executive Director, Interagency Council on the Homeless	Patricia Carlile	1989–1992	Other[9]	McKinney–Vento Homeless Assistance Act[10]
Bill Clinton	U.S. Attorney for Southern California, DOJ	Alan D. Bersin	1995–1998[11]	PAS	Section 541 of Title 28 of the U.S. Code[12]
	Special Representative on Southwest Border issues, DOJ	"	"	Other[13]	None
	Chair, The President's Council on Year 2000 Conversion, EOP	John A. Koskinen	1998–2000	PA	Executive Order 13073[14]
	Assistant to the President, WHO	"	"	"	White House Authorization Act of 1978[15]

Table 11. Media-Labeled Czars during the George W. Bush Administration

Position	Name	Service Dates	Czar Title	PA, PAS, or Other	Statute/Regulation/Order
Under Secretary for Nuclear Security, National Nuclear Security Administration, DE	John Gordon[1] Linton F. Brooks[4] Thomas P. D'Agostino[5]	2000–2002[2] 2003–2007 2007–present	Nuclear security czar	PAS	National Nuclear Security Administration Act[3]
Director, OMB, EOP	Mitch Daniels[6] Joshua Bolten[8] Rob Portman[9] Jim Nussle[10]	2001–2003 2003–2006 2006–2007 2007–2009	Budget czar	PAS	Reorganization Plan No. 2 of 1970[7]
Assistant Secretary for Environmental Management, DE	Jessie Roberson[11] James Rispoli[13]	2001–2004 2005–2008	Cleanup czar	PAS	Department of Energy Organization Act[12]
Assistant to the President for Homeland Security, WHO	Tom Ridge[14]	2001–2002	Homeland security czar	PA	Executive Order 13228[15]
Secretary, DHS	" Michael Chertoff[17]	2003–2004 2005–2009		PAS	Homeland Security Act of 2002[16]
Under Secretary of Defense for Acquisition and Technology, DOD	Edward C. Aldridge[18]	2001–2003	Procurement czar	PAS	National Defense Authorization Act for Fiscal Year 1994[19]
Under Secretary of Defense for Acquisition, Technology, and Logistics, DOD	Michael W. Wynne[20] Kenneth J. Krieg[23] John J. Young Jr.[24]	2003–2005[21] 2005–2007 2007–2009	" " "	" " "	National Defense Authorization Act for Fiscal Year 2000[22]
Director, Office of Information and Regulatory Affairs, OMB, EOP	John D. Graham[25] Susan Dudley[27]	2001–2006 2006–2009	Regulatory czar	PAS	Paperwork Reduction Act of 1980[26]
Director, Office of National Drug Control Policy, EOP	John P. Walters[28]	2001–2009	Drug czar	PAS	National Narcotics Leadership Act of 1988[29]
Chair, The President's Council on Bioethics, EOP	Leon Kass[30]	2001–2005	Bioethics czar	PA	Executive Order 13237[31]

(continued)

Table 11 (continued)

Position	Name	Service Dates	Czar Title	PA, PAS, or Other Statute/Regulation/Order
Ex-officio Member,[32] President's Commission on Excellence in Special Education, EOP	G. Reid Lyon[33]	2001–2005	Reading czar	PA	Executive Order 13227[34]
Director, Office of Science and Technology Policy, EOP	John H. Marburger[35]	2001–2009	Science czar	PAS	National Science and Technology Policy, Organization, and Priorities Act of 1976[36]
Director, Office of National AIDS Policy, EOP	Scott Evertz[37] Joe O'Neill[39] Carol J. Thompson[40]	2001–2002 2002–2003 2004–2006[41]	AIDS czar	PA	White House Authorization Act of 1978[38]
Director, Office of Faith-Based and Community Initiatives, EOP	John Dilulio[42] Jim Towey[44] Jay Hein[45]	2001–2002 2002–2006 2006–2009	Faith-based czar	PA	Executive Order 13199[43]
National Coordinator for Security, Infrastructure Protection and Counter-terrorism, NSC	Richard A. Clarke[46]	2001	Terrorism czar	PA	Presidential Decision Directive 63[47]
National Director and Deputy National Security Advisor for Combating Terrorism, NSC	Wayne Downing[48]	2001–2002	"	PA	White House Authorization Act of 1978[49]
Chair, President's Critical Infrastructure Protection Board, EOP	Richard A. Clarke[50]	2001–2003	Cyber security czar	PA	Executive Order 13231[51]
Special Advisor to the President for Cyberspace Security, WHO	"	"	"	"	White House Authorization Act of 1978[52]
Director, National Cybersecurity Center, DHS	Rod Beckstrom[53]	2008–2009	"	Other[54]	January 2008 Classified Executive Order[55]
Executive Director, United States Interagency Council on Homelessness	Phil Mangano[56]	2002–2009	Homeless czar	PA	McKinney–Vento Homeless Assistance Act[57]

Position	Name	Czar type	Appt.	Dates	Authority
Coordinator of U.S. Government Activities to Combat HIV/AIDS Globally, with the rank of Ambassador	Randall Tobias[58], Mark Dybul[60]	Global AIDS czar	PAS	2003–2006, 2006–2009	United States Leadership against HIV/AIDS, Tuberculosis, and Malaria Act of 2003[59]
Assistant Secretary for Public Health Emergency Preparedness, HHS	Stewart Simonson[61]	Bioterrorism or bird flu czar	PA	2004–2006[62]	HHS Regulations[63]
Advisor to the President for Public Health Emergency Preparedness, WHO	"	"	"	"	White House Authorization Act of 1978[64]
Assistant Secretary of Commerce for Manufacturing and Services, Department of Commerce	Al Frink Jr.[65], William "Woody" Sutton[67]	Manufacturing czar	PAS	2004–2007, 2007–2009	Consolidated Appropriations Act of 2004[66]
Deputy Chief of Staff and Senior Advisor to the President, WHO	Karl Rove[68]	Political or domestic policy czar[69]	PA	2004–2006	White House Authorization Act of 1978[70]
National Health Information Technology Coordinator, HHS[71]	David J. Brailer[72]	Health IT czar	Other[73]	2004–2006	Executive Order 13335[74]
Director of National Intelligence	John Negroponte[75], John Michael McConnell[77]	Intelligence or spy czar	PAS	2005–2007, 2007–2009	Intelligence Reform and Terrorism Prevention Act[76]
Counselor to the President, WHO	Dan Bartlett[78]	Communications czar	PA	2005–2007	White House Authorization Act of 1978[79]
Assistant to the President for Policy and Strategic Planning, WHO	Michael J. Gerson[80]	Policy czar	PA	2005–2006	White House Authorization Act of 1978[81]
Coordinator of Federal Support for the Recovery and Rebuilding of the Gulf Coast Region	Donald E. Powell[82]	Gulf Coast reconstruction czar	PA	2005–2008	Executive Order 13390[83]
Undersecretary of State for Public Diplomacy and Public Affairs, DOS	Karen Hughes[84], James Glassman[86]	Public diplomacy czar	PAS	2005–2007, 2007–2009	Foreign Affairs Reform and Restructuring Act of 1998[85]

(continued)

Table 11 (continued)

Position	Name	Service Dates	Czar Title	PA, PAS, or Other	Statute/Regulation/Order
Principal Deputy Assistant Secretary of State for Near Eastern Affairs, DOS	Elizabeth Cheney[87]	2005–2006	Democracy czar	Other[88]	Department of State Regulations[89]
Co-chair, Iran Syria Policy and Operations Group	"	"	"	"	
Special coordinator to Respond to Health Effects of September 11 Attacks, World Trade Center Medical Monitoring and Treatment Program	John Howard[90]	2006–2008	9/11 health czar	PA	None
Director, National Institute for Occupational Safety and Health, Centers for Disease Control and Prevention, HHS	"	"	"	Other[91]	Occupational Safety and Health Act of 1970[92]
Assistant Secretary of Labor for Mine Safety and Health, Department of Labor	Richard Stickler[93]	2006–2009	Mine safety czar	PAS	Mine Safety and Health Act of 1977[94]
Administrator, US Agency for International Development	Randall Tobias[95]	2006–2007	Foreign aid czar	PAS	Foreign Assistance Act of 1961[96]
Deputy Assistant Secretary of Population Affairs, HHS	Eric Keroack[97]	2006–2007	Family planning or birth control czar	Other[98]	Family Planning Services and Population Research Act of 1970[99]
Assistant Commissioner for Food Protection, FDA	David W. K. Acheson[100]	2007–2009	Food safety czar	Other[101]	New position within FDA[102]
Assistant to the President and Deputy National Security Advisor for Iraq and Afghanistan, NSC	Douglas Lute[103]	2007–present	War czar	PAS	Defense Officer Personnel Management Act[104]
Interim Assistant Secretary of the Treasury for Financial Stability, DT	Neel Kashkari[105]	2008–2009	Bank bailout czar	PAS[106]	Emergency Economic Stabilization Act of 2008[107]

Table 12. Czars during the George W. Bush Administration

Position	Name	Service Dates	PA, PAS, or Other	Statute/Regulation/Order
Assistant to the President for Homeland Security, WHO	Tom Ridge	2001–2002	PA	Executive Order 13228[1]
Director, Office of Faith-Based and Community Initiatives, EOP	John DiIulio Jim Towey Jay Hein	2001–2002 2002–2006 2006–2009	PA	Executive Order 13199[2]
Executive Director, United States Interagency Council on Homelessness[3]	Phil Mangano	2002–2009	Other[4]	McKinney–Vento Homeless Assistance Act[5]
Assistant Secretary for Public Health Emergency Preparedness, HHS	Stewart Simonson	2004–2006[6]	PA	HHS Regulations[7]
Advisor to the President for Public Health Emergency Preparedness, WHO	"	"	"	White House Authorization Act of 1978[8]
National Health Information Technology Coordinator, HHS	David J. Brailer Robert Kolodner	2004–2006 2006–2009	Other[9]	Executive Order 13335[10]
Coordinator of Federal Support for the Recovery and Rebuilding of the Gulf Coast Region	Donald E. Powell	2005–2008	PA	Executive Order 13390[11]
Special coordinator to Respond to Health Effects of September 11 Attacks, World Trade Center Medical Monitoring and Treatment Program	John Howard	2006–2008	PA	None
Director, National Institute for Occupational Safety and Health, Centers for Disease Control and Prevention, HHS	"	"	Other[12]	Occupational Safety and Health Act of 1970[13]
Assistant Commissioner for Food Protection, FDA	David W. K. Acheson 2007–2009		Other[14]	New position within FDA[15]

Table 13. Media-Labeled Czars during the Barack Obama Administration

Position	Name	Service Dates	Czar Title	PA, PAS, or Other	Statute/Regulation/Order
Assistant to the President and Deputy National Security Advisor for Iraq and Afghanistan, NSC	Douglas Lute[1]	2007–present[2]	War czar	PAS	Defense Officer Personnel Management Act[3]
Under Secretary of Defense for Acquisition, Technology, and Logistics, DOD	Ashton B. Carter[4]	2009–present	Procurement or acquisition czar	PAS	National Defense Authorization Act for Fiscal Year 2000[5]
Office of Faith-Based and Neighborhood Partnerships, EOP	Joshua DuBois[6]	2009–present	Faith-based czar	PA	Executive Order 13498[7]
Deputy Secretary, DOI	David J. Hayes[8]	2009–present	California water czar	PAS	Federal Employees Pay Comparability Act of 1990[9]
Associate Administrator, EPA	J. Charles Fox[10] Jeff Corbin	2009–2010 2009–present	Chesapeake Bay or bay czar	Other[11]	Executive Order 13508; 74 FR 63752 (Dec. 4, 2009).
White House Cybersecurity Coordinator, NSC and NEC	Melissa Hathaway[12] Howard A. Schmidt[14]	2009 2009–present	Cyber security czar	PA	White House Authorization Act of 1978[13]
Chair, Recovery Accountability and Transparency Board	Earl Devaney[15]	2009–present[16]	Stimulus accountability czar	PAS[17]	American Recovery and Reinvestment Act of 2009[18]
Special Assistant to the President, WHO	Gary Samore[19]	2009–present	Nonproliferation czar	PA	White House Authorization Act of 1978[20]
White House Coordinator for Arms Control and Weapons of Mass Destruction, Proliferation, and Terrorism, NSC	"	"	"	"	None

Position	Name	Years	Czar	Classification	Legal Authority
Special Master for Compensation, DT	Kenneth Feinberg	2009–present	Pay czar[21]	Other[22]	DT regulation[23]
Commissioner, U.S. Customs and Border Protection, DHS	Alan D. Bersin[24]	2010–present	Border czar	PAS	Homeland Security Act of 2002[25]
Assistant Secretary for International Affairs, DHS	"	2009–2010[26]	"	Other[27]	Homeland Security Act of 2002 and Dept. of Homeland Security Reorganization Plan[28]
Special Representative for Border Affairs, DHS	"	"	"	"	Homeland Security Secretary Designation[29]
Director, Office of Health Reform, EOP	Nancy-Ann DeParle[30]	2009–2011	Health reform czar	PA	Executive Order 13507[31]
Counselor to the President, WHO					White House Authorization Act of 1978[32]
Director, Office of Energy and Climate Change, EOP	Carol Browner[33]	2009–2011	Energy czar	PA	None[34]
Assistant to the President for Energy and Climate Change, WHO					White House Authorization Act of 1978[35]
Director, Office of National AIDS Policy, EOP	Jeffrey Crowley[36]	2009–present	AIDS czar	PA	White House Authorization Act of 1978[37]
Director of National Intelligence	Dennis C. Blair[38]	2009–2010	Intelligence czar	PAS	The Intelligence Reform and Terrorism Prevention Act of 2004[39]
Director, Office of National Drug Control Policy, EOP	Gil Kerlikowske[40]	2009–present	Drug czar	PAS	National Narcotics Leadership Act of 1988[41]
Assistant Secretary for Financial Stability, DT	Herb Allison[42]	2009–present	Bailout or TARP czar	PAS	Emergency Economic Stabilization Act[43]
Director, Office of Information and Regulatory Affairs, OMB, EOP	Cass Sunstein[44]	2009–present	Regulation czar	PAS	Paperwork Reduction Act of 1980[45]

(continued)

Table 13 (continued)

Position	Name	Service Dates	Czar Title	PA, PAS, or Other	Statute/Regulation/Order
Assistant to the President for Homeland Security and Counterterrorism, WHO	John O. Brennan[46]	2009–present	Terrorism czar	PA	Executive Order 13228[47]
Director, Office of Urban Affairs, EOP	Adolfo Carrion Jr.[48]	2009–2010	Urban affairs czar	PA	Executive Order 13503[49]
Federal Chief Information Officer, OMB, EOP	Vivek Kundra[50]	2009–present	Information or infotech czar[51]	PA	E-Government Act of 2002[52]
Special Adviser on Green Jobs, Enterprise and Innovation, White House Council on Environmental Quality, EOP	Anthony "Van" Jones[53]	2009	Green jobs czar	PA	National Environmental Policy Act of 1969[54]
Associate Director, Office of Science and Technology Policy, EOP	Aneesh Chopra[55]	2009–2012	Technology czar	PAS	Presidential Science and Technology Advisory Organization Act of 1976[56]
Chief Technology Officer	"	"	"	PA	None
Director, Office of Science and Technology Policy, EOP	John Holdren[57]	2009–present	Science czar	PAS	Presidential Science and Technology Advisory Organization Act of 1976[58]
Co-Chair, President's Council of Advisers on Science and Technology, EOP	"	"	"	PA	Executive Order 13226[59]
Chief Performance Officer, OMB, EOP	Jeffrey Zients[60]	2009–present	Government performance czar	PA	None
Deputy Director for Management, OMB, EOP	"	"	"	PAS	Chief Financial Officers Act of 1990[61]
Chief Adviser on the Auto Industry, DT	Steven Rattner[62]	2009	Car or auto czar	Other[63]	None
Senior Adviser on the Auto Industry, DT	Ron Bloom[64]	2009–2011	"	PA	None
Member, President's Task Force on the Auto Industry, EOP	"	"	"	PA	None[65]
Counselor to the President for Manufacturing Policy, WHO	"	"	"	PA	White House Authorization Act of 1978[66]

Position	Name	Dates	Czar	Type	Statutory Authority
Special Advisor to the EPA Administrator, Great Lakes National Program Office, EPA	Cameron Davis[67]	2009–present	Great Lakes czar	Other[68]	None
Member, Presidential Task Force on the Auto Industry, EOP	Ed Montgomery[69]	2009–2010	Auto recovery czar	PA	None[70]
Director of Recovery for Auto Communities and Workers, EOP	"	"	"	"	Executive Order 13509[71]
Program Manager, Weatherization and Intergovernmental Program, Office of Energy Efficiency and Renewable Energy, DE	Gilbert P. Sperling[72]	2008–2010[73]	Weatherization czar	Other[74]	The American Recovery and Reinvestment Act of 2009[75]
	Tobias Russell (Acting)	2010–2011			
	LeAnn M. Oliver[76]	2011–present			
Advisor to the President and the Vice President on Domestic Violence and Sexual Assault Issues, WHO and Vice-President's Office	Lynn Rosenthal[77]	2009–present	Domestic violence czar	Other[78]	White House Authorization Act of 1978[79]
Special Envoy for Climate Change, DOS	Todd D. Stern[80]	2009–present	Climate czar	Other[81]	None
Associate General Counsel and Chief Diversity Officer, Office of Communications Business Opportunities, FCC	Mark Lloyd[82]	2009–present	Diversity czar	PA	None
Director of Communications, Office of Health Reform, HHS assigned out indefinitely to the Office of Health Reform, EOP	Linda Douglass[83]	2009–2010	Disinformation czar	Other[84]	Executive Order 13507[85]
Chair, NEC	Larry Summers[86]	2009–present	Economic czar	PA	Executive Order 12835[87]
Chair, Economic Recovery Advisory Board, EOP	Paul Volcker[88]	2009–present	Economic czar II	PA	Executive Order 13501[89]
Secretary, DOE	Arne Duncan[90]	2009–present	Education czar	PAS	Department of Education Organization Act[91]

(continued)

Table 13 (continued)

Position	Name	Service Dates	Czar Title	PA, PAS, or Other	Statute/Regulation/Order
Deputy Commissioner for Foods, Office of Foods, FDA	Michael Taylor[92]	2009–present	Food czar	Other[93]	FDA Regulation[94]
Assistant Secretary of State for Western Hemisphere Affairs, DOS	Arturo Valenzuela[95]	2009–present	Latin American czar	PAS	An Act to Authorize the Appointment of Two Additional Assistant Secretaries of State[96]
Intellectual Property Enforcement Coordinator, EOP	Victoria A. Espinel[97]	2009–present	Copyright czar	PAS	Prioritizing Resources and Organization for Intellectual Property Act of 2008[98]
National Coordinator for Health Information Technology, HHS	David Blumenthal[99]	2009–2011	Health IT czar	Other[100]	Executive Order 13335[101]
Assistant Deputy Secretary of the Office of Safe and Drug-Free Schools, DOE	Kevin Jennings[102]	2009–present	Safe schools czar	Other[103]	Safe and Drug-Free Schools and Communities Act[104]
Special Representative for Trade Negotiations, EOP	Ron Kirk[105]	2009–present	Trade czar	PAS	The Trade Act of 1974[106]
Gulf Coast Relief Coordinator[107]	Ray Mabus[108]	2010–present[109]	Gulf czar	Other[110]	None[111]
Head of British Petroleum Claims Fund	Kenneth Feinberg	2010–present	Claims czar[112]	Other[113]	None
Asian Carp Director, Council on Environmental Quality, EOP	John Goss[114]	2010–present	Asian carp czar	PA	White House Authorization Act of 1978[115]
Assistant Chief, White House Residence Senior Policy Adviser for Healthy Food Initiatives, WHO	Sam Kass[116]	2010–present	Healthy foods czar	PA	White House Authorization Act of 1978[117]
Assistant to the president, WHO	Elizabeth Warren[118]	2010–2011	Consumer protection czar	PA	White House Authorization Act of 1978[119]
Special Adviser to the Secretary of the Treasury on the Consumer Financial Protection Bureau, DT	"	"	"	"	None

Table 14. Czars during the Barack Obama Administration

Position	Name	Service Dates	PA, PAS, or Other	Statute/Regulation/Order
Office of Faith-Based and Neighborhood Partnerships, EOP	Joshua DuBois	2009–present	PA	Executive Order 13498[1]
Associate Administrator, EPA	J. Charles Fox	2009–present	Other[2]	Executive Order 13508, 74 FR 63752 (Dec. 4, 2009)
Special Assistant to the President, WHO	Gary Samore	2009–present	PA	White House Authorization Act of 1978[3]
White House Coordinator for Arms Control and Weapons of Mass Destruction, Proliferation, and Terrorism, NSC	"	"	"	None
Special Master for Compensation, DT	Kenneth Feinberg	2009–present	Other[4]	DT Regulation[5]
Director, Office of Health Reform, EOP	Nancy-Ann DeParle	2009–2011	PA	Executive Order 13507[6]
Counselor to the President, WHO	"	"	"	White House Authorization Act of 1978[7]
Director, Office of Energy and Climate Change, EOP	Carol Browner	2009–2011	PA	None[8]
Assistant to the President for Energy and Climate Change, WHO	"	"	"	White House Authorization Act of 1978[9]
Director, Office of Urban Affairs, EOP	Adolfo Carrion Jr.	2009–2010	PA	Executive Order 13503[10]
Special Adviser on Green Jobs, Enterprise and Innovation, White House Council on Environmental Quality, EOP	Anthony "Van" Jones	2009	PA	National Environmental Policy Act of 1969[11]
Executive Director, United States Interagency Council on Homelessness	Peter Dougherty (Acting Director)	2009	Other[12]	McKinney–Vento Homeless Assistance Act[13]
	Barbara Poppe	2009–present		
Chief Adviser on the Auto Industry, DT	Steven Rattner	2009	Other[14]	None

(continued)

Table 14 (continued)

Position	Name	Service Dates	PA, PAS, or Other	Statute/Regulation/Order
Senior Adviser on the Auto Industry, DT	Ron Bloom	2009–2011	PA	None
Member, President's Task Force on the Auto Industry, EOP	"	"	PA	None[15]
Counselor to the President for Manufacturing Policy, WHO	"	"	PA	White House Authorization Act of 1978[16]
Special Advisor to the EPA Administrator, Great Lakes National Program Office, EPA	Cameron Davis	2009–present	Other[17]	None
Member, Presidential Task Force on the Auto Industry, EOP	Ed Montgomery	2009–2010	PA	None[18]
Director of Recovery for Auto Communities and Workers	"	"	"	Executive Order 13509[19]
Associate General Counsel and Chief Diversity Officer, Office of Communications Business Opportunities, FCC	Mark Lloyd	2009–present	PA	None
Deputy Commissioner for Foods, Office of Foods, FDA	Michael Taylor	2009–present	Other[20]	FDA Regulation[21]
National Coordinator for Health Information Technology, HHS	David Blumenthal	2009–2011	Other[22]	Executive Order 13335[23]
Head of British Petroleum Claims Fund	Kenneth Feinberg	2010–present	Other[24]	None
Asian Carp Director, Council on Environmental Quality, EOP	John Goss	2010–present	PA	White House Authorization Act of 1978[25]
Assistant Chief, White House Residence Senior Policy Adviser for Healthy Food Initiatives, WHO	Sam Kass	2010–present	PA	White House Authorization Act of 1978[26]
Assistant to the president, WHO	Elizabeth Warren	2010–present	PA	White House Authorization Act of 1978[27]
Special Adviser to the Secretary of the Treasury on the Consumer Financial Protection Bureau, DT	"	"	"	None

NOTES

PREFACE

1. There are exceptions including, among others: David Adler, Nancy Baker, Phillip J. Cooper, Jeffrey Crouch, Jasmine Farrier, Louis Fisher, Katy Harriger, Nancy Kassop, Kenneth Mayer, James P. Pfiffner, Richard Pious, Christopher Pyle, Robert Spitzer, and William Weaver.

2. Louis Fisher, *Constitutional Conflicts between Congress and the President* (Lawrence: University Press of Kansas, 5th ed., 2007), xi. See also Ada Finifster, ed., *Political Science: The State of the Discipline* (Washington, DC: American Political Science Association, 1993), 2:366; Lucas A. Powe Jr., *The Warren Court and American Politics* (Cambridge, MA: Harvard University Press, 2000), preface.

CHAPTER I. CZARS AND THE U.S. CONSTITUTION

1. Ed O'Keefe, "Obama's 'Pay Czar' to Oversee BP Victims' Fund," *Washington Post*, June 17, 2010, A19.

2. Deborah Solomon, "White House Set to Appoint Pay Czar," *Wall Street Journal*, June 5, 2009, A2.

3. 122 Stat. 3765 (2008); 123 Stat. 115, 516 (2009); 12 USC 5221 (2006).

4. Press Briefing by Deputy Press Secretary Bill Burton, June 21, 2010, http://www.white house.gov/the-press-office/press-briefing-deputy-press-secretary-bill-burton-62110.

5. Press Briefing by Press Secretary Robert Gibbs, June 29, 2010, http://www.whitehouse .gov/the-press-office/press-briefing-press-secretary-robert-gibbs-62910.

6. Press Briefing by Press Secretary Robert Gibbs and National Incident Commander Thad Allen, July 1, 2010, http://www.whitehouse.gov/the-press-office/press-briefing-press-secretary -robert-gibbs-and-national-incident-commander-thad-al.

7. The White House Blog, "A New Process and a New Escrow Account for Gulf Oil Spill Claims from BP," June 17, 2010, http://www.whitehouse.gov/blog/2010/06/17/a-new-process -and-a-new-escrow-account-gulf-oil-spill-claims-bp.

8. Barack Obama, "President Barack Obama Delivers Remarks on Meeting with B.P.," *Congressional Quarterly Transcriptions*, June 15, 2010.

9. *The Federalist* no. 49, in *The Federalist*, Benjamin F. Wright, ed. (New York: MetroBooks, 2002), 348.

10. *The Federalist* no. 9 in ibid., 125. For a detailed account of Hamilton's views on republican government, see Gerald Stourzh, *Alexander Hamilton and the Idea of Republican Government* (Stanford, CA: Stanford University Press, 1970).

11. Brutus, Oct. 18, 1787, in *The Anti-Federalist Papers*, Ralph Ketcham, ed. (New York: Mentor Book, 1986), 276.

12. Speeches of Melancton Smith, June 20–27, 1788, in ibid., 341.

13. *The Federalist* no. 51, in Wright, *Federalist*, 356.

14. *The Federalist* no. 37, in ibid., 268.

15. *The Federalist* no. 77, in ibid., 487–488.

16. Virginia Senator Stevens Thomas Mason, quoted in Larry D. Kramer, *The People Themselves: Popular Constitutionalism and Judicial Review* (New York: Oxford University Press, 2004), 107.

17. *The Federalist* no. 51, in Wright, *Federalist*, 356.

18. The Letters of "Agrippa" in *The Antifederalists*, Cecelia M. Kenyon, ed. (New York: Bobbs-Merrill, 1966), 153.

19. "The Address and Reasons of Dissent of the Minority of the Convention of Pennsylvania to Their Constituents," in Ketcham, *Anti-Federalist Papers*, 251.

20. *The Federalist* no. 51, in Wright, *Federalist*, 356.

21. *Merriam-Webster's Collegiate Dictionary*, 11th ed. (Springfield, MA: Merriam-Webster, 2005), 312.

22. Hans Sperber and Travis Trittschuh, *Dictionary of American Political Terms* (Detroit: Wayne State University Press, 1964), 111.

23. Bradley H. Patterson Jr., *The White House Staff: Inside the West Wing and Beyond* (Washington, DC: Brookings Institution Press, 2000), 264.

24. James P. Pfiffner, "Presidential Use of White House 'Czars,'" Testimony before the Senate Committee on Homeland Security and Governmental Affairs, U.S. Congress, Oct. 22, 2009, 1, http://hsgac.senate.gov/public/index.cfm?FuseAction=Hearings.Hearing&Hearing_ID=5b22 e173-5b74-46a0-b2ab-d300b6381de4.

25. Examples of dual appointments include: Paul V. McNutt, who served as director of the Office of Defense Health and Welfare Services and administrator of the Federal Security Agency (Franklin D. Roosevelt); John Steelman, who served as assistant to the president and director of the Office of War Mobilization and Reconversion (Harry S Truman); Esther Peterson, who served as special assistant for consumer affairs and assistant secretary within the Department of Labor (Lyndon B. Johnson); and John Connally who served as chair of the Cost of Living Council and secretary of treasury (Richard Nixon).

26. For example, all top-level officials within the Department of the Treasury receive Senate confirmation. See 31 U.S.C. § 301 (2006).

27. 64 Stat. 419 (1950); 3 U.S.C. § 301 (2006). For a detailed account of the law, see Glendon A. Schubert Jr., "The Presidential Subdelegation Act of 1950," *Journal of Politics* 13 (Nov. 1951): 647–674.

28. *United States v. Maurice*, 26 Fed. Cas. 1211, 1214 (C.C. Va. 1823).

29. *Buckley v. Valeo*, 424 U.S. 1, 126, footnote 162 (1976).

30. *United States v. Hartwell*, 73 U.S. (6 Wall.) 385, 393 (1867).

31. 99 U.S. 508, 511–512 (1878).

32. 424 U.S. 1, 126 (1976).

33. 20 Op. Att'y Gen. 124, 140 (1996).

34. Ibid., 143.

35. Ibid., 144.

36. Ibid., 144, footnote 57.

37. Ibid., 145, footnote 60.

38. Ibid., 148.

39. Office of Legal Counsel, "Officers of the United States within the Meaning of the Appointments Clause," April 16, 2007, http://www.justice.gov/olc/2007/appointmentsclausev10 .pdf, 4.

40. Ibid., 11–12.

41. Ibid., 12.

42. Ibid., 32.

43. Kevin Scholette, "The American Czars," *Cornell Journal of Law and Public Policy* 20 (Fall 2010): 233.

44. 487 U.S. 654, 671–672 (1988).

45. Nick Bravin, "Is *Morrison v. Olson* Still Good Law? The Court's New Appointments Clause Jurisprudence," *Columbia Law Review* 98 (1998): 1116.

46. 487 U.S. 654, 671 (1988).

47. *Edmond v. United States*, 520 U.S. 651, 661–662 (1997).

48. Ibid., 662–663.

49. John R. Martin, "*Morrison v. Olson* and Executive Power," *Texas Review of Law & Politics* 4 (Spring 2000): 529.

50. Jacqueline M. Weyand, "Presidential Appointment of Czars: Executive Power Play or Administrative Renewal?" *Northwestern Interdisciplinary Law Review* 3 (Spring 2010): 140.

51. Executive Order 8248, 4 FR 3864 (Sept. 8, 1939).

52. 53 Stat. 561 (1939).

53. 92 Stat. 2445 (1978).

54. U.S. Constitution, Art. I, sec. 1.

55. John Locke, *Two Treatises of Government* (New York: Hafner Press, 1947), 194.

56. 276 U.S. 394, 409 (1928).

57. *A.L.A. Schechter Poultry Corporation v. United States*, 295 U.S. 495 (1935); *Panama Refining Co. v. Ryan*, 293 U.S. 388 (1935).

58. 293 U.S. 388, 421 (1935).

59. Ibid.

60. *A.L.A. Schechter Poultry Corporation v. United States*, 295 U.S. 495, 529–530 (1935).

61. Ibid., 541.

62. Ibid., 551.

63. *Industrial Union Department, AFL-CIO v. American Petroleum Institute*, 448 U.S. 607 (1980).

64. Ibid., 685.

65. Ibid., 687.

66. *Whitman v. American Trucking Associations, Inc.*, 531 U.S. 457 (2001).

67. Ibid., 472.

68. Ibid., 475–476.

69. *Mistretta v. United States*, 488 U.S. 361, 415–416 (1989) (Justice Scalia's dissenting opinion).

70. 84 Stat. 799 (1970); Marvin H. Kosters, *Controls and Inflation: The Economic Stabilization Program in Retrospect* (Washington, DC: American Enterprise Institute, 1975), 3–14.

71. Executive Order 11615, 36 FR 15727 (Aug. 15, 1971); Executive Order 11627, 35 FR 11627 (Oct. 15, 1971).

72. 85 Stat. 38 (1971).

73. See Executive Order 11592, 36 FR 8555 (May 6, 1971).

74. 1971 Pub. Papers 1024 (Oct. 7, 1971). See also Kosters, *Controls and Inflation*, 18, and Arnold R. Weber, *In Pursuit of Price Stability: The Wage-Price Freeze of 1971* (Washington, DC: Brookings Institution Press, 1973), 23.

75. Robert M. Pallitto and William G. Weaver, *Presidential Secrecy and the Law* (Baltimore and London: Johns Hopkins University Press, 2007), 115.

76. See generally Mark J. Rozell, *Executive Privilege: Presidential Power, Secrecy, and Accountability*, 3rd ed. (Lawrence: University Press of Kansas, 2010).

77. Executive Order 13507, 74 FR 17071–17073 (April 8, 2009).

78. "Obama Expands Car Czar's Duties," *Washington Post*, Sept. 8, 2009, A13; Neil King Jr., "Auto Czar Quits Post Six Months into the Job," *Wall Street Journal*, July 14, 2009, A1. Bloom held multiple titles: Chief Adviser to the Treasury Department on the Auto Recovery from July 2009 to January 2011; Senior Adviser for the Manufacturing Industry from September 2009 to January 2011; Senior Adviser for the Treasury Department on the Auto Industry (February 2009 to January 2011).

79. David Shepardson, "The Inside Story of the GM, Chrysler Bailouts," *Detroit News*, Nov. 24, 2009, A1.

80. Bill Saporito, "Ron Bloom," Time.com, April 29, 2010, http://www.time.com/time /specials/packages/article/0,28804,1984685_1984864_1985429,00.html.

81. Executive Order 13503, 74 FR 8139 (Feb. 19, 2009).

82. John Cornyn, Statement at Senate Judiciary Committee hearing, "Examining the History and Legality of Executive Branch 'Czars,'" Oct. 6, 2009, 2, http://judiciary.senate.gov/pdf/10 -06-09%20Cornyn%20testimony.pdf.

83. John William Burgess, *Political Science and Comparative Constitutional Law* (Boston and London: Ginn, 1891), 2:206.

84. *The Federalist* no. 69, in Wright, *Federalist*, 449.

85. George Burton Adams, *Constitutional History of England* (New York: Holt, 1921), 78. Alpheus Todd, *On Parliamentary Government in England: Its Origin, Development, and Practical Operation* (London: Longmans, Green, 1867), 2:244.

86. Phillip J. Cooper, *By Order of the President: The Use and Abuse of Executive Direct Action* (Lawrence: University Press of Kansas, 2002), 7.

87. U.S. Constitution, Art. II, sec. 2.

88. *The Federalist* no. 69, in Wright, *Federalist*, 449.

89. 1 Annals of Congress 604 (June 22, 1789).

90. 17 U.S. 316 (1819).

91. *United States v. Maurice,* 26 Fed. Cas. 1211, 1214 (C.C.D. Va. 1823).

92. 5 Op. Att'y Gen. 88 (April 19, 1849).

93. 10 Op. Att'y Gen. 11, 15 (March 5, 1861).

94. 18 Op. Att'y Gen. 171 (May 6, 1885).

95. 272 U.S. 52, 129 (1926).

96. Edward S. Corwin, *The President: Office and Powers, 1787–1957*, 4th ed. (New York: New York University Press, 1957), 70 (emphasis in original).

97. 9 U.S. Op. Off. Legal Counsel 76 (Aug. 23, 1985).

98. Ibid., 77–78.

99. Ibid., 78.

100. John Hart discusses the issue of White House aides not receiving congressional authorization from 1948 through 1978. See Hart, *The Presidential Branch: From Washington to Clinton*, 2nd ed. (Chatham, NJ: Chatham House Publishers, 1995), 172–173.

101. 116 Stat. 2135 (2002).

102. House Rule XXI, clause 2; House Rule XXII, clause 5; and Senate Rule XVI.

103. 317 F. Supp. 715 (E.D.N.Y. 1970). See also Louis Fisher, "Authorization-Appropriation Process in Congress: Formal Rules and Informal Practices," *Catholic University Law Review* 29 (Winter 1979): 83.

104. Fisher, "Authorization-Appropriation Process in Congress," 84.

105. 87 Stat. 555 (1973); Fisher, "Authorization-Appropriation Process in Congress," 84.

106. Letter from Sen. Robert Byrd to President Barack Obama, Feb. 23, 2009, http://www .eenews.net/public/25/9865/features/documents/2009/02/25/document_gw_02.pdf.

107. *In re Sealed Case*, 121 F.3d 729, 752 (D.C. Cir. 1997).

108. Ibid., 746.

109. Mark J. Rozell and Mitchel A. Sollenberger, "Executive Privilege and U.S. Attorneys' Firings," *Presidential Studies Quarterly* 38 (June 2008): 315–328; Thomas E. Mann, Norman J. Ornstein, Mark J. Rozell, and Mitchel A. Sollenberger, Amicus Brief filed in the case of *Committee on the Judiciary v. Harriet Miers, et al.,* Civil no. 1:08-cv-00409 (D.D.C. 2008).

110. Louis Fisher and Harold C. Relyea, "Presidential Staffing—A Brief Overview," July 25, 1978, in U.S. House of Representatives, Subcommittee on Employee Ethics and Utilization of the Committee on Post Office and Civil Service, 95th Cong., 2nd sess., Committee Print no. 95-17, 86.

111. Ibid., 56. For a similar assessment, see Patrick Anderson, *The President's Men: White House Assistants of Franklin D. Roosevelt, Harry S. Truman, Dwight D. Eisenhower, John F. Kennedy, and Lyndon B. Johnson* (Garden City, NY: Doubleday, 1968), 1, 394–395.

112. Hart, *Presidential Branch*, 236.

113. Anderson, *President's Men*, 397.

114. Joe Garofoli, "Obama Adviser on Green Jobs under Attack," *San Francisco Chronicle*, Sept. 5, 2009, A1.

115. "Van Jones to CEQ," March 10, 2009, White House website, http://www.whitehouse.gov /blog/09/03/10/Van-Jones-to-CEQ/; Chadwick Marlin, "Van Jones: The Face of Green Jobs," The Big Money, http://www.thebigmoney.com/articles/mothers-milk/2009/04/19/van-jones -face-green-jobs.

116. On this analogy, we are indebted to Louis Fisher.

117. Solomon, "White House Set to Appoint Pay Czar," A2.

118. 122 Stat. 3765, 3887 (2008); 12 U.S.C. § 5229 (2006).

119. U.S. President's Committee on Administrative Management, *Report of the President's Committee* (Washington, DC: GPO, 1937), 5.

120. Thomas Cronin, *The State of the Presidency* (Boston: Little, Brown, 1975), 118.

121. The only position not included in the tables is the special envoy which is a particular class of czars that we address separately in chapter two.

CHAPTER 2. THE ORIGINS AND GROWTH OF EXECUTIVE BRANCH CZARS

1. Carl Marcy, *Presidential Commissions* (New York: King's Crown Press, 1945), preface.

2. Ibid., 109, footnote 4.

3. U.S. Congress, House of Representatives, "Administration of the Executive Departments," House Report no. 194, March 3, 1837, 8–9. The report by Van Ness and Kendall is listed in the Appendix.

4. Ibid., 288.

5. 11 *Congressional Globe* 482 (May 14, 1842).

6. Ibid., 481; Frank Popper, *The President's Commissions* (New York: Twentieth Century Fund, 1970), 7.

7. David Flitner Jr., *The Politics of Presidential Commissions* (New York: Transnational Publishers, 1986), 8; Robert J. Morgan, *A Whig Embattled: The Presidency under John Tyler* (Lincoln: University of Nebraska Press, 1954), 90.

8. John Tyler to the House of Representatives, Feb. 9, 1842, in *A Compilation of the Messages and Papers of the Presidents*, James D. Richardson, ed. (New York: Bureau of National Literature, 1897), 3:1952.

9. Henry Clay, *The Papers of Henry Clay*, Robert Seager II, ed. (Lexington: University Press of Kentucky, 1988), 9:653.

10. 5 Stat. 523, 533 (1842).

11. 4 Op. Att'y Gen. 106 (Oct. 25, 1842).

12. 4 Op. Att'y Gen. 248 (Sept. 21, 1843).

13. 21 Dec. of the Comp. of the Treasury 443 (Jan. 5, 1915).

14. 5 Dec. of the Comp. Gen. of the U.S. 554 (Jan. 29, 1926).

15. 31 U.S.C. § 1346 (2006).

16. Hugh Davis Graham, "The Ambiguous Legacy of American Presidential Commissions," *Public Historian* 7 (Spring 1985): 10.

17. Popper, *President's Commissions*, 7–8; Graham, "Ambiguous Legacy," 10; Alan L. Dean, "Ad Hoc Commissions for Policy Formulation?" in *The Presidential Advisory System*, Thomas E. Cronin and Sanford D. Greenberg, eds. (New York: Harper & Row, 1969), 103.

18. Flitner, *Politics of Presidential Commissions*, 11–13.

19. 35 Stat. 945, 1027 (1909).

20. Theodore Roosevelt, *Theodore Roosevelt: An Autobiography* (New York: Scribner's Sons, 1913), 417.

21. 44 Cong. Rec. 4615 (July 27, 1909).

22. 31 U.S.C. § 1346 (2006).

23. For a detailed account of one of Taft's commissions, see Louis Fisher, *Presidential Spending Power* (Princeton, NJ: Princeton University Press, 1975), 29–31.

24. There is a third law called the Russell Amendment, discussed in chapter 3, which tried to limit presidents creating agencies without seeking congressional authorization.

25. Marcy, *Presidential Commissions*, 5.

26. The Iran-Contra Affair could be used as an extreme but all too real example of a president, or at least his White House aides, bypassing clear legislative intent not to appropriate funds for an intended purpose but doing so through other sources. For background on the Iran-Contra Affair and an analysis of the dangers of presidents carrying out their policy goals with private and foreign funds, see Louis Fisher, *Constitutional Conflicts between Congress and the President*, 5th ed. (Lawrence: University Press of Kansas, 2007), 214–219.

27. 27 Op. Atty. Gen. 432, 437 (June 26, 1909).

28. Thomas R. Wolanin, *Presidential Advisory Commissions: Truman to Nixon* (Madison: University of Wisconsin Press, 1975), 67.

29. Roosevelt, *Theodore Roosevelt*, 416 (emphasis in original).

30. Fisher, *Presidential Spending Power*, 66–70.

31. 56 Stat. 995 (1942); 69 Stat. 192 (1955); Wolanin, *Presidential Advisory Commissions*, 67–68. For a detailed account of the history of the Special Projects Fund, see John Hart, *The Presidential Branch: From Washington to Clinton*, 2nd ed. (Chatham, NJ: Chatham House Publishers, 1995), 166–167.

32. Dean, "Ad Hoc Commissions for Policy Formulation?" 108.

33. 3 U.S.C. § 108 (2006).

34. U.S. Constitution, Art. I, sec. 6.

35. Edward S. Corwin, *The President: Office and Powers, 1787–1857*, 4th ed. (New York: New York University Press, 1957), 71.

36. Wolanin, *Presidential Advisory Commissions*, 71.

37. E. Wilder Spaulding, *Ambassadors Ordinary and Extraordinary* (Washington, DC: Public Affairs Press, 1961), 6.

38. George Washington to Gouverneur Morris, Oct. 13, 1789, in *The Life of Gouverneur Morris*, Jared Sparks, ed. (Boston: Gray & Bowen, 1832), 2:3–4; Spaulding, *Ambassadors Ordinary and Extraordinary*, 6; Henry M. Wriston, "The Special Envoy," *Foreign Affairs* 38 (1959): 220; Henry M. Wriston, *Executive Agents in American Foreign Relations* (Baltimore: Johns Hopkins University Press, 1929), 157.

39. John Ferling, *The Ascent of George Washington: The Hidden Political Genius of an American Icon* (New York: Bloomsbury Press, 2009), 327; Walter Stahr, *John Jay: Founding Father* (New York: Continuum International Publishing, 2006), 314–315; Quincy Wright, *The Control of American Foreign Relations* (New York: MacMillan, 1922), 326.

40. Elmer Plischke, *Diplomat in Chief: The President at the Summit* (New York: Praeger, 1986), 71.

41. Ibid., 75.

42. Wriston, "Special Envoy," 223–224; Plischke, *Diplomat in Chief*, 97–99.

43. Arthur D. Howden Smith, *Mr. House of Texas* (New York: Funk & Wagnalls, 1940), 139.

44. Wriston, "Special Envoy," 224.

45. David B. Wooner and Richard G. Kurial, *FDR, the Vatican, and the Roman Catholic Church in America, 1933–1945* (New York: Palgrave MacMillan, 2003), 165; George Q. Flynn, "Franklin Roosevelt and the Vatican: The Myron Taylor Appointment," *Catholic Historical Review* 58 (July 1972): 171–194.

46. William H. Standley and Arthur A. Ageton, *Admiral Ambassador to Russia* (Chicago: Regnery, 1955), 252.

47. Plischke, *Diplomat in Chief*, 99.

48. Wriston, "Special Envoy," 221–222, 235.

49. The appropriations used to pay for special envoys largely come from a contingent fund account for foreign relations that dates to a July 1, 1790, act of Congress. See 1 Stat 128; Stephen F. Knott, *Secret and Sanctioned: Covert Operations and the American Presidency* (New York: Oxford University Press, 1996), 49–60; John Mabry Mathews, *The Conduct of American Foreign Relations* (New York: Century, 1922), 72.

50. James Madison to James Monroe, May 6, 1822, *The Writings of James Madison*, Gaillard Hunt, ed. (New York: G. P. Putnam's Sons, 1910), 9:93.

51. 7 Op. Att'y Gen. 186, 193–194 (May 25, 1855).

52. Ibid., 198–199.

53. Ibid., 193.

54. 2 Stat. 608–609 (1810).

55. John Quincy Adams to the Senate, Dec. 26, 1825, in Richardson, *Messages and Papers of the Presidents*, 2:884–886; John Quincy Adams to the House of Representatives and Senate, March 5, 1826, in ibid., 894; 7 Op. Att'y Gen. 186, 206 (May 25, 1855).

56. Thomas Hart Benton, ed., *Abridgment of the Debates of Congress* (New York: Appleton, 1859), 11:232.

57. Ibid., 343. The 1831 appropriations law can be found at 4 Stat. 452.

58. 5 Stat. 624 (1843).

59. Wright, *Control of American Foreign Relations*, 313.

60. William Blackstone, *Commentaries on the Laws of England*, 7th ed. (Oxford: Clarendon Press, 1775), 1:253.

61. U.S. Constitution, Art. II, sec. 2; Morgan, *Whig Embattled*, 122.

62. Steven G. Calabresi and Christopher S. Yoo, *The Unitary Executive: Presidential Power from Washington to Bush* (New Haven, CT: Yale University Press, 2008).

63. Louis Fisher, "Invoking Inherent Powers: A Primer," *Presidential Studies Quarterly* 37 (March 2007): 2; see also Louis Fisher, "The Unitary Executive and Inherent Executive Power," *University of Pennsylvania Journal of Constitutional Law* 12 (February 2010): 569–591.

64. Wright, *Control of American Foreign Relations*, 326; Wriston, *Executive Agents in American Foreign Relations*, 187.

65. Benton, *Abridgment of the Debates of Congress*, 5:85.

66. Ibid., 87.

67. Jessee S. Reeves, *American Diplomacy under Tyler and Polk* (Baltimore: Johns Hopkins University Press, 1907), 327.

68. Diary entry Feb. 28, 1848, in *The Diary of James Polk during His Presidency, 1845 to 1849*, Milo M. Quaife, ed. (Chicago: A. C. McClurg, 1910), 3:364–365.

69. Wriston, *Executive Agents in American Foreign Relations*, 189; Henry S. Wriston, "Presidential Special Agents in American Diplomacy," *American Political Science Review* 10 (August 1916): 498.

70. For an overview of the constitutional and legal concerns pertaining to statutory qualifications, see Mitchel A. Sollenberger, "Statutory Qualifications on Appointments: Congressional and Constitutional Choices," *Public Administration Quarterly* 34 (Summer 2010): 202–237.

71. 10 Stat. 619 (1855).

72. 7 Att'y Gen. Op. 186, 214 (May 25, 1855); Wright, *Control of American Foreign Relations*, 324.

73. 27 Stat. 496, 497 (1893); Wriston, *Executive Agents in American Foreign Relations*, 132.

74. 35 Stat. 672 (1909).

75. U.S. Constitution, Art. I, sec. 6.

76. Elmer Plischke, *United States Diplomats and their Missions: A Profile of American Diplomatic Emissaries since 1778* (Washington, DC: American Enterprise Institute for Public Policy Research, 1975), 115.

77. George F. Hoar, *Autobiography of Seventy Years* (New York: Scribners, 1903), 2:50.

78. Plischke, *Diplomat in Chief*, 110.

79. Michael A. Fletcher and Brady Dennis, "Obama's Many Policy 'Czars' Draw Ire from Conservatives," *Washington Post*, Sept. 16, 2009, A6; Editorial, "Czar Wars," *Richmond Times-Dispatch*, July 20, 2009, A8; French Maclean, "Obama's Embrace of 'Czars' a Bad Thing for Democracy," *Herald & Review* (Decatur, IL), July 31, 2009, A4; Carol Rosenberg, "New Czar's Goal: Find Nations for Detainees," *Miami Herald*, March 13, 2009, A3; Daniel L. Gardner, "It Continues to be about the Economy," *Starkville Daily News*, July 19, 2009, A4.

80. "Nasby in Detroit," *Chicago Tribune*, Sept. 10, 1866, 1; William Safire, "A Czar Is Not a Tsar," *New York Times*, Nov. 13, 1983, SM24; Robert Remini, *Andrew Jackson* (New York: Harper, 1969), 185; Marquis James, *Andrew Jackson: Portrait of a President* (New York: Grosset & Dunlap, 1937), 307; Ben Zimmer, "Czar Wars," *Slate.com*, Dec. 29, 2008, http://www.slate.com /id/2207055.

81. Safire, "Czar Is Not a Tsar," SM24; Hans Sperber and Travis Trittschuh, *Dictionary of American Political Terms* (Detroit: Wayne State University Press, 1964), 111; Zimmer, "Czar Wars."

82. Samuel Walker McCall, *Thomas B. Reed* (Boston and New York: Houghton Mifflin, 1914), 169; "At the Nation's Capitol: New 'Czar' in Cannon," *Los Angeles Times*, March 6, 1906, 4; "Says He Is No Czar," *Washington Post*, Dec. 10, 1908, 2.

83. 3 Stat. 266, 269–270 (1816).

84. "Czar Is Set in His Plans," *Los Angeles Times*, Dec. 6, 1922, 1; N. W. Baxter, "Joint League Session Shows Landis Is Czar," *Washington Post*, Dec. 13, 1923, 17; Zimmer, "Czar Wars."

85. "Western Film Czar Defends Industry," *Los Angeles Times*, Dec. 12, 1922, 28; "Will Hays, Czar of Movies, 'Doing Nicely' at Hospital," *Chicago Daily Tribune*, May 8, 1941, 16.

86. Football czar: Bill Roper, "Frowns on Grid Czar," *Los Angeles Times*, Nov. 21, 1922, 2. Restaurant czar: "Restaurateurs Seek Czar," *New York Times*, July 30, 1922, 20. Radio czar: "Recommends a Radio 'Czar,'" *New York Times*, May 10, 1926, 20. Building czar: "Wants a Building Czar," *New York Times*, Dec. 5, 1926, 1. Cleaners' czar: "Glatzmayer Won't Be Cleaners' 'Czar,'" *New York Times*, Sept. 21, 1928, 56. Cleaning czar: "Mayor Walker Has New Job," *Los Angeles Times*, Feb. 26, 1928, 8. Beauty czar: "Beauty 'Czar' Assured to Rule the Industry," *New York Times*, Oct. 2, 1930, 13. Concert czar: "Milton Diamond Appointed 'Concert Czar' by America's Principal Booking Agencies," *New York Times*, Oct. 10, 1930, 25. Oil czar: "California's Oil Industry Would Make Reeser Czar," *Wall Street Journal*, Oct. 24, 1931, 1.

87. "Drys Split over Law," *Los Angeles Times*, June 19, 1921, 1; Arthur Sears Henning, "Andrews Made Dry Law Czar by President," *Chicago Daily Tribune*, July 25, 1925, 1; "Dry Chiefs Win Fight," *Los Angeles Times*, March 24, 1927, 1.

88. 41 Stat. 305, 308 (1919).

89. "From Sick Bed Slams Haynes as Modern Czar," *Chicago Daily Tribune*, Feb. 10, 1922, 3.

90. At that time wiretaps were not considered as searches under the Fourth Amendment. See *Olmstead v. United States*, 277 U.S. 438 (1928).

91. 44 Stat. 1381 (1927).

92. David Cannadine, *Mellon: An American Life* (New York: Random House, 2008), 291, 397.

93. 46 Stat. 427 (1930).

94. For a useful discussion on this point, see David K. Nichols, *The Myth of the Modern Presidency* (University Park: Pennsylvania State University Press, 1994), 171.

95. Herbert Croly, *The Promise of American Life* (New York: MacMillan, 1914), 69.

96. Richard Hofstadter, *The Age of Reform: From Bryan to F.D.R.* (New York: Knopf, 1955), 265.

97. Ibid.

98. Raymond Tatalovich and Thomas S. Engeman, *The Presidency and Political Science: Two Hundred Years of Constitutional Debate* (Baltimore: Johns Hopkins University Press, 2003), 85.

99. Ronald J. Pestritto and William J. Atto, *American Progressivism* (Lanham, MD: Lexington Books, 2008), 19.

100. 39 Stat. 619, 649–650 (1916).

101. Bernard Baruch, *Baruch: The Public Years* (New York: Holt, Rinehart and Winston, 1960), 43; Carter Field, *Bernard Baruch: Park Bench Statesman* (New York: McGraw-Hill, 1944), 149.

102. James Miller Leake, "The Conflict over Coordination," *American Political Science Review* 12 (Aug. 1918): 378; Charles G. Fenwick, *Political Systems in Transition: War-Time and After* (New York: Century, 1920), 193, 194.

103. Leake, "Conflict over Coordination," 379–380.

104. 56 Cong. Rec. 4506 (April 3, 1918).

105. Ibid., 4946 (April 11, 1918).

106. Ibid., 4951.

107. 40 Stat. 556 (1918).

108. Ibid., 557.

109. "Executive Order [Establishment of War Industries Board]," May 28, 1918, in Richardson, *Messages and Papers of the Presidents*, 18:8518–8519.

110. House of Representatives, Committee on the Judiciary, "Administration of the So-called Overman Act," House Doc. no. 1841, 65th Cong., 3rd sess., March 3, 1919, 29.

111. Curtice N. Hitchcock, "The War Industries Board: Its Development, Organization, and Functions," *Journal of Political Economy* 26 (June 1918): 547.

112. Theodore Roosevelt, *Theodore Roosevelt: An Autobiography* (New York: Macmillan, 1913), 388–389.

113. Ibid., 306.

114. Theodore Roosevelt, Letter to John St. Loe Strachey, Feb. 12, 1906, in *The Letters of Theodore Roosevelt*, Elting E. Morison, ed. (Cambridge, MA: Harvard University Press, 1952), 5:151.

115. Woodrow Wilson, *Constitutional Government in the United States* (New York: Columbia University Press, 1917), 68.

116. Ibid., 14.

117. See generally James Grant, *Bernard M. Baruch: The Adventures of a Wall Street Legend* (New York: Simon & Schuster, 1983), 177–178; Baruch, *Baruch: The Public Years*, 58–69; Margaret L. Coit, *Mr. Baruch* (Boston: Houghton Mifflin, 1957), 185–194.

118. Grant, *Bernard M. Baruch*, 172. See also Baruch, *Baruch: The Public Years*, 79.

119. Field, *Bernard Baruch*, 155.

120. Clarence Arthur Berdahl, *War Powers of the Executive in the United States* (Urbana: University of Illinois Press, 1921), 174; Bruce D. Porter, *War and the Rise of the State* (New York: The Free Press, 1994), 271.

121. Baruch, *Baruch: The Public Years*, 72–73; William White, *Bernard Baruch: Portrait of a Citizen* (New York: Harcourt, Brace, 1950), 52.

122. Field, *Bernard Baruch*, 178.

123. Grant, *Bernard M. Baruch*, 176.

124. Executive Order 2594 (April 13, 1917), in Richardson, *Messages and Papers of the Presidents*, 17:8247.

125. Allan M. Winkler, *The Politics of Propaganda: The Office of War Information, 1942–1945* (New Haven, CT: Yale University Press, 1978), 2.

126. 40 Stat. 217 (1917).

127. James R. Mock and Cedric Larson, *Words That Won the War: The Story of the Committee on Public Information, 1917–1919* (New York: Russell & Russell, 1968), 42.

128. 40 Stat. 553 (1918).

129. Mock and Larson, *Words That Won the War*, 19.

130. Winkler, *Politics of Propaganda*, 3.

131. Alan Axelrod, *Selling the Great War: The Making of American Propaganda* (New York: Palgrave MacMillan, 2009), 218–219.

132. 41 Stat. 327 (1919). See also Axelrod, *Selling the Great War*, 216, 217–218; Mock and Larson, *Words That Won the War*, 60–61.

133. "Statement [Food Control Program]," May 19, 1917, in Richardson, *Messages and Papers of the Presidents*, 17:8262–8264.

134. 40 Stat. 276 (1917).

135. Robert Higgs, *Crisis and Leviathan: Critical Episodes in the Growth of American Government* (New York: Oxford University Press, 1987), 136.

136. "Executive Order [Appointing Fuel Administrator]," Aug. 23, 1917, in Richardson, *Messages and Papers of the Presidents*, 17:8330.

137. "Statement [Food Control Program]," May 19, 1917, in ibid., 17:8263.

138. Four days after signing the Lever Act, Wilson issued an executive order creating the Food Administration Grain Corporation and appointed Hoover as its director without Senate confirmation. Wilson's action effectively delegated to the Food Administration the formal

powers Congress had recently authorized. "Executive Orders [Creating Food Administration Grain Corporation]," Aug. 14, 1917, in ibid., 8324–8326. See also Higgs, *Crisis and Leviathan*, 136.

139. Higgs, *Crisis and Leviathan*, 138.

140. Ibid., 137.

141. 40 Stat. 217, 219–226 (1917). The executive order was not published. It is referenced in EO "Vesting Power and Authority in Designated Officers and Making Rules and Regulations under Trading with the Enemy Act and Title VII of the Act, Approved June 15, 1917," Oct. 12, 1917, in Richardson, *Messages and Papers of the Presidents*, 17:8368.

142. Ralph M. Goldman, *The National Party Chairmen and Committees* (New York: M. E. Sharpe, 1990), xvii.

143. EO "Vesting Power and Authority in Designated Officers," in Richardson, *Messages and Papers of the Presidents*, 17:8368.

144. William Franklin Willoughby, *Government Organization in War Time and After* (New York: D. Appleton, 1919), 132.

145. The idea for such an agency resulted from a meeting of the National Labor Conference Board set up by Labor Secretary William B. Wilson at the suggestion of the CND.

146. U.S. Department of Labor, *National War Labor Board* (Washington, DC: GPO, 1922), 10.

147. Wilson's proclamation creating the NWLB can be found in ibid., 34.

148. Richard B. Gregg, "The National War Labor Board," *Harvard Law Review* 33 (Nov. 1919): 40.

149. Valerie Jean Conner, *The National War Labor Board: Stability, Social Justice, and the Voluntary State in World War I* (Chapel Hill: University of North Carolina Press, 1983), 133.

150. U.S. Department of Labor, *National War Labor Board*, 36.

151. Robert D. Cuff, *The War Industries Board: Business-Government Relations during World War I* (Baltimore: Johns Hopkins University Press, 1973), 222–223; Simon Litman, *Prices and Price Control in Great Britain and the United States during the World War* (New York: Oxford University Press, 1920), 205.

152. Coit, *Mr. Baruch*, 202.

153. Cuff, *War Industries Board*, 224.

154. Ibid., 224.

155. Robert K. Murray, *The Harding Era: Warren G. Harding and His Administration* (Minneapolis: University of Minnesota Press, 1969), 73.

156. David Greenberg, *Calvin Coolidge* (New York: Times Books, 2006), 12; Sidney M. Milkis and Michael Nelson, *The American Presidency: Origins and Development, 1776–1998* (Washington, DC: CQ Press, 1999), 242; Patrick M. Garry, *Liberalism and American Identity* (Kent, OH: Kent State University Press, 1992), 63.

157. *Official Report of the Proceedings of the Seventeenth Republican National Convention*, George L. Hart, ed. (New York: Tenny Press, 1920), 258–259.

158. Calvin Coolidge, *The Autobiography of Calvin Coolidge* (Plymouth, VT: The Calvin Coolidge Memorial Foundation, 1989), 232.

159. "Calls Sherrill Czar of Washington," *New York Times*, July 19, 1925, 1; "False Rumors Mislead Blanton, Says Sherrill," *Washington Post*, July 19, 1925, 2; L. C. Speers, "Col. Sherrill— New Washington 'Czar,'" *New York Times*, Aug. 9, 1925, 8.

160. 67 Cong. Rec. 3553 (Feb. 8, 1926).

161. 43 Stat. 983 (1925).

162. House of Representatives, Committee on Public Buildings and Grounds, Hearings on

H.R. 5764, May 6, 1921 (Washington, DC: GPO, 1921); "Madden Telegram Vetoes Reopening of Bathing Beach," *Washington Post*, June 15, 1925, 2.

163. Kevin R. Kosar, "Disaster Response and Appointment of a Recovery Czar: The Executive Branch's Response to the Flood of 1927," *CRS Report*, Oct. 25, 2005; Ben F. Johnson, *Arkansas in Modern America, 1930–1999* (Fayetteville: University of Arkansas Press, 2000), 10.

164. Robert Sobel, *Coolidge: An American Enigma* (Washington, DC: Regnery Publishing, 1998), 315.

165. Kosar, "Disaster Response and Appointment of a Recovery Czar," 10.

166. Ibid., 8.

167. Nathan Grundstein, *Presidential Delegation of Authority in Wartime* (Pittsburgh: University of Pittsburgh Press, 1961), 16.

168. Kendrick A. Clements, *Woodrow Wilson: World Statesman* (Boston: Twayne, 1987), 183.

169. Clinton Rossiter, *Constitutional Dictatorship: Crisis Government in the Modern Democracies* (Princeton, NJ: Princeton University Press, 1948), 249.

170. David M. Kennedy, *Over Here: The First World War and American Society* (New York: Oxford University Press, 2004), 125.

171. Charles Seymour, *Woodrow Wilson and the World War: A Chronicle of Our Times* (New Haven, CT: Yale University Press, 1921), 189.

172. Niall A. Palmer, *The Twenties in America: Politics and History* (Edinburgh, UK: Edinburgh University Press, 2006).

CHAPTER 3. FRANKLIN D. ROOSEVELT: CZARS IN THE MODERN PRESIDENCY

1. Brink Lindsey, *Against the Dead Hand: The Uncertain Struggle for Global Capitalism* (New York: John Wiley and Sons, 2002), 77–78.

2. William E. Leuchtenburg, "The New Deal and the Analogue of War," in *Change and Continuity in Twentieth Century America*, John Braeman, Robert H. Bremner, and Everett Walters, eds. (Columbia: Ohio State University Press, 1964), 109.

3. Mario R. Di Nunzio, *Franklin D. Roosevelt and the Third American Revolution* (Santa Barbara, CA: ABC-CLIO, 2011), 27; Emily S. Rosenberg, "Progressive Internationalism and Reformed Capitalism: New Freedom to New Deal," in *Reconsidering Woodrow Wilson*, John Milton Cooper Jr., ed. (Washington, DC: Woodrow Wilson Center Press, 2008), 253–277; Michael McGerr, *A Fierce Discontent: The Rise and Fall of the Progressive Movement in America, 1870–1920* (New York: Oxford University Press, 2005), 316; Rexford G. Tugwell, "The Progressive Orthodoxy of Franklin D. Roosevelt," *Ethics* 64 (Oct. 1953): 1–23; Rexford G. Tugwell, "The New Deal: The Progressive Tradition," *Western Political Quarterly* 3 (Sept. 1950): 390–427.

4. Frank Freidel, *Franklin D. Roosevelt: The Apprenticeship* (Boston: Little, Brown, 1952), 135.

5. McGerr, *A Fierce Discontent*, 316. See also John Morton Blum, *The Progressive Presidents: Roosevelt, Wilson, Roosevelt, Johnson* (New York: W. W. Norton, 1980); Ernest K. Lindley, *Franklin D. Roosevelt: A Career in Progressive Democracy* (New York: Blue Ribbon Books, 1931), 322–335.

6. William E. Leuchtenburg, *The FDR Years: On Roosevelt and His Legacy* (New York: Columbia University Press, 1995), 30.

7. Edward S. Corwin, *The President: Office and Powers, 1787–1857*, 4th ed. (New York: New York University Press, 1957), 252.

8. Harold J. Berman, *Law and Revolution, II: The Impact of the Protestant Reformations on the Western Legal Tradition* (Cambridge, MA: Harvard University Press, 2006), 226; Christopher N. May, "Presidential Defiance of 'Unconstitutional' Laws: Reviving the Royal Prerogative," *Hastings Constitutional Law Quarterly* 21 (Summer 1994): 872.

9. U.S. Constitution, Art. II, sec. 3.

10. Herbert Emmerich, *Federal Organization and Administrative Management* (Birmingham: University of Alabama Press, 1971), 63.

11. "A Czar for Agriculture," *Washington Post*, March 17, 1933, 6; "An Unwilling Czar," *Washington Post*, April 16, 1933, 6.

12. 48 Stat. 31 (1933).

13. "From a Senator's Diary," *Washington Post*, June 25, 1933, 7. See also Jordan A. Schwarz, *The Speculator: Bernard M. Baruch in Washington, 1917-1965* (Chapel Hill: University of North Carolina Press, 1981), 280; Bernard Sternsher, *Rexford Tugwell and the New Deal* (New Brunswick, NJ: Rutgers University Press, 1964), 192.

14. Edwin G. Nourse, Joseph S. Davis, and John D. Black, *Three Years of the Agricultural Adjustment Administration* (Washington, DC: Brookings Institution Press, 1937), 277.

15. Dean Albertson, *Roosevelt's Farmer: Claude R. Wickard in the New Deal* (New York: Columbia University Press, 1961), 75.

16. 297 U.S. 1 (1936).

17. 52 Stat. 31 (1938).

18. Executive Order 6173, June 16, 1933, in *The Public Papers and Addresses of Franklin D. Roosevelt*, Samuel I. Rosenman, ed. (New York: Random House, 1938), 2:247.

19. 48 Stat. 195 (1933).

20. Bernard Bellush, *The Failure of the NRA* (New York: W. W. Norton, 1975), 36.

21. John Kennedy Ohl, *Hugh S. Johnson and the New Deal* (Dekalb, IL: Northern Illinois University Press, 1985), 113-137.

22. 295 U.S. 495, 531 (1935).

23. Ibid., 542.

24. 48 Stat. 211 (1933).

25. "A Message on Emergency Railroad Legislation," May 4, 1933, in Rosenman, *Public Papers and Addresses*, 2:155.

26. "Bill Sets Up Rail Czar," *Los Angeles Times*, April 28, 1933, 1; "A Railroad Czar," *Los Angeles Times*, April 29, 1933, A4; "Eastman Declares He Is Not a 'Czar,'" *New York Times*, June 17, 1933, 3; "Not Czar, Says Eastman," *Wall Street Journal*, June 19, 1933, 5.

27. Claude Moore Fuess, *Joseph B. Eastman: Servant of the People* (New York: Columbia University Press, 1952), 211.

28. Earl Latham, *The Politics of Railroad Coordination, 1933-1936* (Cambridge, MA: Harvard University Press, 1959), 86-101.

29. Ibid., 96.

30. Carl Brent Swisher, "Joseph B. Eastman—Public Servant," *Public Administration Review* 5 (Winter 1945): 46.

31. Fuess, *Joseph B. Eastman*, 205.

32. Executive Order 6474, Dec. 4, 1933, in Rosenman, *Public Papers and Addresses*, 2:508-509.

33. "Choate Made 'Czar' to Control Liquor," *New York Times*, Nov. 30, 1933, 24; "U.S. May Use Club on High Liquor Prices," *Washington Post*, Dec. 7, 1933, 1; "Canada Helped Keep U.S. Dry; To Be Rewarded," *Chicago Daily Tribune*, Dec. 15, 1933, 10.

34. Kenneth J. Meier, *The Politics of Sin: Drugs, Alcohol, and Public Policy* (New York: M. E. Sharpe, 1994), 156.

35. "White House Statement on Conference with Legislative Leaders after Supreme Court Decision on N.R.A.," June 4, 1935, in Rosenman, *Public Papers and Addresses*, 4:225.

36. 49 Stat. 977 (1935).

37. Ibid., 978.

38. Terry M. Moe and William G. Howell, "The Presidential Power of Unilateral Action," *Journal of Law, Economics, and Organization* 15 (April 1999): 158.

39. "White House Statement on the Appointment of a Committee to Formulate a Plan for the Reorganization of the Executive Branch of the Government," March 22, 1936, in Rosenman, *Public Papers and Addresses*, 5:144–146; and Leuchtenburg, *The FDR Years*, 169.

40. Frederick C. Mosher, ed., *"The President Needs Help"* (Lanham, MD: University Press of America, 1988), 4; Louis Brownlow, *The Autobiography of Louis Brownlow: Passion for Anonymity* (Chicago: University of Chicago Press, 1958), 2:355.

41. U.S. President's Committee on Administrative Management, *Report of the President's Committee* (Washington, DC: GPO, 1937), 5.

42. For a detailed account of the initial rejection of Roosevelt's reorganization plan, see Richard Polenberg, *Reorganizing Roosevelt's Government: The Controversy over Executive Reorganization, 1936–1939* (Cambridge, MA: Harvard University Press, 1966).

43. 53 Stat. 561 (1939).

44. 53 Stat. 813 (1939).

45. Executive Order 8248, 4 FR 3864 (Sept. 8, 1939).

46. Andrew H. Bartels, "The Office of Price Administration and the Legacy of the New Deal, 1939–1946," *Public Historian* 5 (Summer 1983): 5–6.

47. In 1940 Roosevelt revived the National Defense Advisory Commission, which had statutory backing dating to the World War I era. See 39 Stat. 649 (1916); Matthew J. Dickinson, *Bitter Harvest: FDR, Presidential Power and the Growth of the Presidential Branch* (New York: Cambridge University Press, 1999), 124.

48. William L. Langer and S. Everett Gleason, *The Challenge to Isolation, 1937–1940* (New York: Harper & Brothers, 1952), 675.

49. Charles A. Beard, *President Roosevelt and the Coming of the War, 1941: A Study in Appearances and Realities* (New Haven, CT: Yale University Press, 1948), 13.

50. Marc Landy and Sidney M. Milkis, *Presidential Greatness* (Lawrence: University Press of Kansas, 2000), 188; Dickinson, *Bitter Harvest*, 117; Robert A. Divine, *The Reluctant Belligerent: American Entry into World War II*, 2nd ed. (New York: John Wiley & Sons, 1979), 7–9. See generally Langer and Gleason, *Challenge to Isolation*; Beard, *President Roosevelt and the Coming of the War*.

51. See constitutional scholar Edward S. Corwin's criticism of Roosevelt's actions in *President*, 243. See also Charles E. Walcott and Karen M. Hult, *Governing the White House: From Hoover through LBJ* (Lawrence: University Press of Kansas, 1995), 163; Dickinson, *Bitter Harvest*, 125; Emmerich, *Federal Organization and Administrative Management*, 71.

52. Harold C. Relyea, "Exigency and Emergency," in *The Executive Office of the President: A Historical, Biographical, and Bibliographical Guide* (Westport, CT: Greenwood Press, 1997), 278.

53. Melvyn Dubofsky, *The State and Labor in Modern America* (Chapel Hill: University of North Carolina Press, 1994), 178.

54. Executive Order 8629, 6 FR 191 (Jan. 7, 1941).

55. For a useful overview of Knudsen's reluctance to force the private sector to change its

production, see Nelson Lichtenstein, *Labor's War at Home: The CIO in World War II* (Philadelphia: Temple University Press, 1982), 40.

56. Emmerich, *Federal Organization and Administrative Management*, 72.

57. Executive Order 9040, 7 FR 527 (Jan. 24, 1942); A. J. Wann, *The President as Chief Administrator: A Study of Franklin D. Roosevelt* (Washington, DC: Public Affairs Press, 1968), 157.

58. Executive Order 8632, 6 FR 295 (Jan. 14, 1941).

59. In February 1942, Roosevelt created the National Housing Agency to replace the DDHC along with other agencies. However, we do not consider its head to be a czar since Senate confirmation was required of the position. See Executive Order 9070, 7 FR 1529 (Feb. 24, 1942).

60. 1941 Pub. Papers 57 (March 13, 1941).

61. Robert H. Bremner, *American Philanthropy*, 2nd ed. (Chicago: University of Chicago Press, 1988), 159.

62. Executive Order 9205, 7 FR 5803 (July 25, 1942); James J. Cooke, *Chewing Gum, Candy Bars, and Beer: The Army PX in World War II* (Columbia: University of Missouri Press, 2009), 33.

63. Executive Order 8716, 6 FR 1532 (March 19, 1941); Relyea, "Exigency and Emergency," 272.

64. Executive Order 9017, 7 FR 237 (Jan. 12, 1942). For an overview of both agencies, see Currin V. Shields, "The Authority of the War Labor Board," *Wisconsin Law Review* 1943 (May 1943): 378–401; Rufus G. Poole, "The National War Labor Board," *American Bar Association Journal* 28 (June 1942): 395–441; Rufus G. Poole, "The National War Labor Board," *American Bar Association Journal* 28 (July 1942): 466–506.

65. Shields, "Authority of the War Labor Board," 396–401.

66. Executive Order 8734, 6 FR 1917 (April 11, 1941).

67. The media also referred to Henderson as the price czar. See Walter Trohan, "Fire Price Czar Henderson, Dies Asks F.D.R.," *Chicago Daily Tribune*, Sept. 8, 1941, 1; "Price Czar Henderson Quits as Member of SEC," *Chicago Daily Tribune*, Dec. 18, 1942, 1.

68. Bartels, "Office of Price Administration," 9.

69. Ibid.

70. Executive Order 8875, 6 FR 4483 (Aug. 28, 1941).

71. Bartels, "Office of Price Administration," 10.

72. Ibid., 11, 12.

73. 56 Stat. 23, 29 (1942).

74. Ibid., 27.

75. Ibid., 24–25.

76. Ibid., 25, 31–32.

77. *Yakus v. United States*, 321 U.S. 414, 426 (1944).

78. Kenneth R. Mayer, *With the Stroke of a Pen: Executive Orders and Presidential Power* (Princeton, NJ: Princeton University Press, 2001), 74; Arthur M. Schlesinger Jr., *The Imperial Presidency* (Boston: Houghton Mifflin, 1973), 377.

79. 55 Stat. 31, 33 (1941).

80. Executive Order 8751, 6 FR 2301 (May 2, 1941); Relyea, "Exigency and Emergency," 271; Dickinson, *Bitter Harvest*, 176.

81. Executive Order 8926, 6 FR 5519 (Oct. 29, 1941); Relyea, "Exigency and Emergency," 277.

82. 6 FR 2760 (May 28, 1941). For Ickes's firsthand account, see Harold L. Ickes, *The Autobiography of a Curmudgeon* (New York: Reynal & Hitchcock, 1943), chapter 16.

83. Frank L. Kluckhorn, "Roosevelt Names Ickes as Oil Czar," *Washington Post*, June 1, 1941, 1;

Cecil B. Dickson, "Ickes Is Now Czar of U.S. Power Sources," *Washington Post*, June 22, 1941, 11; Dickinson, *Bitter Harvest*, 134.

84. Gerald D. Nash, *United States Oil Policy, 1890–1964* (Pittsburgh, PA: University of Pittsburgh Press, 1968), 160.

85. 7 FR 3668 (May 16, 1942); Nash, *United States Oil Policy*, 160–166.

86. Executive Order 8757, 6 FR 2517 (May 20, 1941); Laura McEnaney, *Civil Defense Begins at Home: Militarization Meets Everyday Life in the Fifties* (Princeton, NJ: Princeton University Press, 2000), 17.

87. Executive Order 8840, 6 FR 3857 (July 30, 1941); Darlene Rivas, *Missionary Capitalist: Nelson Rockefeller in Venezuela* (Chapel Hill: University of North Carolina Press, 2002), 42–43.

88. Executive Order 9532, 10 FR 3173 (March 23, 1945).

89. Executive Order 8990, 6 FR 4625 (Sept. 3, 1941); Relyea, "Exigency and Emergency," 274–275.

90. Noel F. Busch, "Nelson A. Rockefeller," *Life*, April 27, 1942, 80.

91. Donald H. Riddle, *The Truman Committee: A Study in Congressional Responsibility* (New Brunswick, NJ: Rutgers University Press, 1964).

92. Dickinson, *Bitter Harvest*, 137.

93. Executive Order 8839, 6 FR 3823 (July 30, 1941); Mark L. Kleinman, *A World of Hope, a World of Fear: Henry A. Wallace, Reinhold Niebuhr, and American Liberalism* (Columbus: Ohio State University Press, 2000), 145.

94. In July 1943, Roosevelt replaced the board with the Office of Economic Warfare (OEW) and appointed Leo T. Crowley to be the director of the new agency, which exercised the same responsibilities as its predecessor. However, we believe Crowley should be considered a czar since Roosevelt chose to augment the powers of the OEW by transferring the functions and responsibilities of the U.S. Commercial Company, the Rubber Development Corporation, the Petroleum Reserve Corporation, and the Export-Import Bank of Washington to the new agency. See Executive Order 9361, 8 FR 9861 (July 15, 1943); Relyea, "Exigency and Emergency," 276.

95. Executive Order 8875, 6 FR 4483 (Aug. 28, 1941); Dickinson, *Bitter Harvest*, 138.

96. Executive Order 8985, 6 FR 6625 (Dec. 19, 1941). See also Michael S. Sweeney, *Secrets of Victory: The Office of Censorship and the American Press and Radio in World War II* (Chapel Hill: University of North Carolina Press, 2001), 36.

97. 55 Stat. 838, 840–841 (1941).

98. The media also referred to Price as the censorship czar. See Walter Trohan, "Wickard Shorn of Food Powers: Czar Appointed," *Chicago Daily Tribune*, March 26, 1943, 19; "Food: The Tenth Czar," *Time*, April 5, 1943, http://www.time.com/time/magazine/article/0,9171,790873,00.html.

99. 1941 Pub. Papers 574 (Dec. 19, 1941).

100. Executive Order 8985, 6 FR 6625 (Dec. 19, 1941).

101. Sweeney, *Secrets of Victory*, 40–70; Jeffery A. Smith, *War and Press Freedom* (New York: Oxford University Press, 1999), 151.

102. 55 Stat. 838 (1941).

103. Corwin, *President*, 243. See also Edward S. Corwin, *Presidential Power and the Constitution* (Ithaca, NY: Cornell University Press, 1976), 165.

104. Albert L. Sturm, "Emergencies and the Presidency," *Journal of Politics* 11 (Feb. 1949): 135.

105. Executive Order 9182, 7 FR 4468, 4469 (June 13, 1942).

106. The media also referred to Davis as the information czar. See Patricia Grady, "Visiting

King Negotiates Crowded Social Schedule," *Washington Post*, June 26, 1942, 18; Drew Pearson, "Merry-Go-Round," *Palm Beach Post* (Florida), July 31, 1942, 4.

107. Winkler, *Politics of Propaganda*, 67–71.

108. Executive Order 8989, 6 FR 6725 (Dec. 18, 1941).

109. The media called Eastman the transportation czar. See "F.D.R. Names Czar of All U.S. Transportation," *Chicago Daily Tribune*, Dec. 24, 1941, 1; Jerry Kluttz, "The Federal Diary," *Washington Post*, June 2, 1942, 17.

110. Fuess, *Joseph B. Eastman*, 274, 275, 295.

111. Executive Order 9024, 7 FR 329, 330 (Jan. 16, 1942).

112. Alfred Friendly, "Nelson Gets Full Power over War Production," *Washington Post*, Jan. 17, 1942, 1; Chesly Manly, "Choice of Nelson as Arms 'Czar' Pleases Capital," *Chicago Daily Tribune*, Jan. 15, 1942, 9. See also Donald M. Nelson, *Arsenal of Democracy: The Story of American War Production* (New York: Harcourt, Brace, 1946), 194.

113. For a good overview of the extent of Nelson's power, see Nelson, *Arsenal of Democracy*.

114. Doris Kearns Goodwin, *No Ordinary Time: Franklin and Eleanor Roosevelt: The Home Front in World War II* (New York: Simon & Schuster, 1994), 315.

115. James Q. Wilson, *Bureaucracy: What Government Agencies Do and Why They Do It* (New York: Basic Books, 2000), 271. See also Wann, *President as Chief Administrator*, 158–159.

116. Executive Order 9246, 7 FR 7379 (Sept. 17, 1942).

117. Robert De Vore, "Jeffers, Union Pacific Head, Is Rubber Czar," *Washington Post*, Sept. 16, 1942, 1; William J. Enright, "'Czars' Will Rule on Industry Needs," *New York Times*, Dec. 15, 1942, 37; Nelson, *Arsenal of Democracy*, 305.

118. Luther Gulick, *Administrative Reflections from World War II* (Birmingham: University of Alabama Press, 1948). 99.

119. 8 FR 2007 (Feb. 16, 1943). See also 8 FR 2147 (Feb. 18, 1943).

120. Ben W. Gilbert, "Krug Selection as Power Czar Portends Fuel Supply Conflict," *Washington Post*, Jan. 23, 1943, 1; Martha Rhyne, "Office of War Utilities Quietly Goes About Tremendous War Job," *Washington Post*, April 24, 1943, B4; Felix Belair Jr., "Truman Names Krug Secretary of the Interior," *New York Times*, Feb. 27, 1946, 1. See also Nelson, *Arsenal of Democracy*, 365.

121. Executive Order 9054, 7 FR 837–839 (Feb. 7, 1942).

122. The media also called Land the shipping czar. See James G. Simonds, "Land Made Czar of War Shipping," *Washington Post*, Feb. 10, 1942, 7; "The President's Day," *Washington Post*, Feb. 10, 1942, 5; Michael Chinigo, "8-Million-Ton Shipping Goal in Sight, Land Tells President," *Washington Post*, Sept. 26, 1942, 1.

123. Executive Order 9102, 7 FR 2165 (March 18, 1942).

124. 323 U.S. 214 (1944).

125. I. George Blake, *Paul V. McNutt: Portrait of a Hoosier Statesman* (Indianapolis, IN: Central Publishing, 1966), 303–304.

126. Executive Order 9139, 7 FR 2919 (April 18, 1942). See also Blake, *Paul V. McNutt*, 304.

127. "Manpower Policy," *Washington Post*, Dec. 5, 1942, 8; Ben W. Gilbert, "McNutt Gets Full Control over All U.S. Manpower," *Washington Post*, Dec. 6, 1942, 1; "Manpower Czar," *Washington Post*, Dec. 7, 1942, 14; Jerry Kluttz, "The Federal Diary," *Washington Post*, Jan. 25, 1943, B1.

128. Blake, *Paul V. McNutt*, 305.

129. Robert De Vore, "Economic Czar 'Jimmy' Byrnes Is Popular Administrator," *Washington Post*, Oct. 11, 1942, B5; "Wages Frozen at Sept. 15 Level; Salaries Limited," *Chicago Daily Tribune*, Oct. 4, 1942, 12.

130. Executive Order 9250, 7 FR 7871 (Oct. 3, 1942). See also Edward H. Hobbs, *Behind the*

President: The Study of Executive Office Agencies (Washington, DC: Public Affairs Press, 1954), 187; Wann, *President as Chief Administrator*, 161–162.

131. 56 Stat. 765 (1942).

132. James F. Byrnes, *Speaking Frankly* (New York: Harper & Brothers, 1947), 17.

133. Dickinson, *Bitter Harvest*, 148–149.

134. Executive Order 9276, 7 FR 10091 (Dec. 4, 1942). In 1943, Roosevelt created a parallel entity to the PAW within the Interior Department called the Solid Fuels Administration for War (SFAW). We apply the same legal analysis to the SFAW. Executive Order 9332, 8 FR 5355 (April 19, 1943).

135. John W. Frey and H. Chandler Ide, *A History of the Petroleum Administration for War* (Washington, DC: GPO, 1946), 26.

136. Executive Order 9280, 7 FR 10179 (Dec. 5, 1942). See Albertson, *Roosevelt's Farmer*, 310–311.

137. Walter Trohan, "Wickard Shorn of Food Powers," *Chicago Daily Tribune*, March 26, 1943, 19; "Roosevelt Outlines Food Czar Order," *Los Angeles Times*, Dec. 7, 1942, 18; Albertson, *Roosevelt's Farmer*, 332.

138. Executive Order 9280, 7 FR 10179 (Dec. 5, 1942).

139. Roosevelt could have merely restated powers already delegated to the agriculture secretary by Congress. However, unlike the president's 1941 letter to the interior secretary in regards to making him Petroleum Coordinator for National Defense, the agriculture secretary did not have the same authority to regulate the agricultural industry. As a result, the two cabinet-level positions should be treated differently for purposes of classifying them as czars.

140. Albertson, *Roosevelt's Farmer*, 370–371, 377–378.

141. Executive Order 9322, 8 FR 3807 (March 30, 1943) and Executive Order 9334, 8 FR 5423 (April 27, 1943).

142. "Choice of Davis as Czar Lauded by Food Groups," *Chicago Daily Tribune*, March 27, 1943, 2; Ernest K. Lindley, "Food Czar Davis," *Washington Post*, March 29, 1943, 9; "Food Czar," *Washington Post*, April 1, 1943, 12; "Food Czar Acts to Curb Black Market," *Los Angeles Times*, April 11, 1943, 1; "Food Czar Asks Stable Price to Aid Production," *Chicago Daily Tribune*, Aug. 19, 1943, 11; "Food Czar Jones Urges Extension on Life of CCC," *The Evening Independent* (St. Petersburg, FL), Sept. 29, 1943, 1; Drew Pearson, "Merry-Go-Round," *Washington Post*, Feb. 7, 1944, 10.

143. Executive Order 9322, 8 FR 3807 (March 30, 1943).

144. Herman Miles Somers, *Presidential Agency: The Office of War Mobilization and Reconversion* (New York: Greenwood Press, 1969), 49. See also Wann, *President as Chief Administrator*, 164–165.

145. Somers, *Presidential Agency*, 51. See also Keith E. Eiler, *Mobilizing America: Robert P. Patterson and the War Effort, 1940–1945* (Ithaca, NY: Cornell University Press, 1997), 367.

146. Somers, *Presidential Agency*, 52.

147. Executive Order 9347, 8 FR 7207 (May 27, 1943).

148. Senate Judiciary Committee, "Senate Confirmation of Officers and Employees of the United States," Report no. 180, 78th Cong., 1st sess., April 14, 1943, 5.

149. Ibid., 6.

150. Sidney M. Shalett, "President Opposes Congress Control over Federal Jobs," *New York Times*, Feb. 21, 1943, 1; 89 Cong. Rec. 5825 (June 14, 1943).

151. 89 Cong. Rec. 5933 (June 15, 1943); Joseph P. Harris, *The Advice and Consent of the Senate* (Berkeley and Los Angeles: University of California Press, 1953), 374.

152. The FEA replaced the Office of Economic Warfare (created in July 1943 by Roosevelt) which Crowley had also led.

153. Executive Order 9380, 8 FR 13081 (Sept. 25, 1943).

154. Executive Order 9425, 9 FR 2071 (Feb. 19, 1944).

155. 58 Stat. 765, 768 (1944).

156. "The President's Statement on Signing the Surplus Property Act of 1944," Oct. 3, 1944, in Rosenman, *Public Papers and Addresses*, 5:300.

157. 58 Stat. 361, 387 (1944).

158. 90 Cong. Rec. 1963 (Feb. 23, 1944).

159. Ibid., 3059 (March 24, 1944).

160. Ibid., 3063.

161. William G. Howell, *Power without Persuasion: The Politics of Direct Presidential Action* (Princeton, NJ: Princeton University Press, 2003), 132.

162. Ibid., 133.

163. Dickinson, *Bitter Harvest*, 157.

164. 90 Cong. Rec. 6790 (Aug. 8, 1944).

165. 58 Stat. 785.

166. Specifically, the law authorized the director "to delegate to the appropriate agencies and provide for the redelegation of the powers and duties vested in him, except the power to issue orders and regulations to other executive agencies." Ibid., 786.

167. Corwin, *President*, 243.

168. Mayer, *With the Stroke of a Pen*, 71; Wann, *President as Chief Administrator*, 182.

169. Editorial, "Food Czar," *Washington Post*, Dec. 8, 1942, 12.

170. Landy and Milkis, *Presidential Greatness*, 192.

171. Stephen Hess, *Organizing the Presidency*, 3rd ed. (Washington, DC: Brookings Institution Press, 2002), 34.

172. 59 Stat. 106, 134 (1945).

173. Howell, *Power without Persuasion*, 133.

174. 31 U.S.C. § 1346-1347 (2006).

175. Probably the most well known advocate of the Rooseveltian model of the presidency is Richard E. Neustadt. See Richard E. Neustadt, *Presidential Power and the Modern Presidents: The Politics of Leadership from Roosevelt to Reagan* (New York: Free Press, 1990). James MacGregor Burns also played an important role in advancing the Rooseveltian model. See James MacGregor Burns, *Presidential Government: The Crucible of Leadership* (Boston: Houghton Mifflin, 1973), 116.

CHAPTER 4. HARRY S. TRUMAN – LYNDON B. JOHNSON: CONSOLIDATING THE USE OF CZARS

1. For a general overview of this point, see Stephen Hess, *Organizing the Presidency*, 3rd ed. (Washington, DC: Brookings Institution Press, 2002), 36–48; Louis Fisher, *Constitutional Conflicts between Congress and the President* (Lawrence: University Press of Kansas, 2007), 266–267.

2. Drew Pearson, "Merry-Go-Round," *Washington Post*, Oct. 12, 1945, 9; "Reconversion Ruler," *Wall Street Journal*, July 21, 1945, 1; Herman Miles Somers, *Presidential Agency: The Office of War Mobilization and Reconversion* (New York: Greenwood Press, 1969), 87.

3. Executive Order 9577, 10 FR 8087 (July 3, 1945).

4. 1945 Pub. Papers 414 (Oct. 25, 1945).

5. Ken Hechler, *Working with Truman: A Personal Memoir of the White House Years* (Columbia: University of Missouri Press, 1986), 45; Alfred Dick Sander, *A Staff for the President: The Executive Office, 1921-1952* (Westport: Greenwood Press, 1989), 79; David McCullough, *Truman* (New York: Simon & Schuster, 1992), 592; Robert H. Ferrell, *Harry S. Truman: A Life* (Columbia: University of Missouri Press, 1996) 189; Hess, *Organizing the Presidency*, 38.

6. Colin J. Davis, *Waterfront Revolts: New York and London Dockworkers, 1946-61* (Urbana: University of Illinois Press, 2003), 88.

7. Hechler, *Working with Truman*, 46; John R. Steelman and H. Dewayne Kreager, "The Executive Office as Administrative Coordinator," *Law and Contemporary Problems* (1956): 688; Matthew J. Dickinson, *Bitter Harvest: FDR, Presidential Power and the Growth of the Presidential Branch* (New York: Cambridge University Press, 1999), 158; Somers, *Presidential Agency*, 72, 95; Patrick Anderson, *The President's Men: White House Assistants of Franklin D. Roosevelt, Harry S Truman, Dwight D. Eisenhower, John F. Kennedy and Lyndon B. Johnson* (Garden City, NY: Doubleday, 1968), 92.

8. 92 Cong. Rec. 7314 (June 21, 1946).

9. Alfred Dick Sander, *Eisenhower's Executive Office* (Westport, CT: Greenwood Press, 1999), 3.

10. Hechler, *Working with Truman*, 46; Somers, *Presidential Agency*, 96.

11. 1946 Pub. Papers 356 (July 25, 1946).

12. Executive Order 9791, 11 FR 12277 (Oct. 17, 1946); Charles E. Walcott and Karen M. Hult, *Governing the White House: From Hoover through LBJ* (Lawrence: University Press of Kansas, 1995), 197; Somers, *Presidential Agency*, 80, 99; Sander, *Staff for the President*, 100.

13. Executive Order 9809, 11 FR 14281 (Dec. 12, 1946); Somers, *Presidential Agency*, 100-101.

14. 58 Stat. 785, 792 (1944).

15. 1946 Pub. Papers 493 (Dec. 12, 1946); Sander, *Staff for the President*, 100.

16. Anderson, *President's Men*, 92.

17. 1946 Pub. Papers 491 (Dec. 12, 1946); Somers, *Presidential Agency*, 98.

18. Francis H. Heller, ed., *The Truman White House: The Administration of the President, 1945-1953* (Lawrence: The Regents Press of Kansas, 1980), 66.

19. 1948 Pub. Papers 963 (Dec. 10, 1948); Steelman and Kreager, "Executive Office as Administrative Coordinator," 688; Michael J. Hogan, *A Cross of Iron: Harry S. Truman and the Origins of the National Security State, 1945-1954* (New York: Cambridge University Press, 2000), 217.

20. "Memorandum to Agency Heads on the Channeling of Federal Procurement, etc., Programs to Areas of Economic Distress," 1949 Pub. Papers 380-381 (July 14, 1949). Steelman's responsibilities over federal agencies and programs, however, date to at least 1946. Harry S. Truman, *Memoirs by Harry S. Truman* (Garden City, NY: Doubleday, 1956), 2:26; 1946 Pub. Papers 491 (Dec. 12, 1946).

21. "Truman Appoints U.S. Project Czar," *Los Angeles Times*, July 15, 1949, 1; "Washington Calling," *Pittsburg Press*, July 17, 1949, 1.

22. Steelman and Kreager, "Executive Office as Administrative Coordinator," 688.

23. Anderson, *President's Men*, 93.

24. Subcommittee on Constitutional Rights, Committee on the Judiciary, "Executive Privilege," 86th Cong., 1st sess., March 13, 1959, 205; Herbert Brownell Jr., "Memorandum on Separation of Powers," *Federal Bar Journal* 14 (1954): 85. For a detailed account of the difficulty of

serving the subpoenas, see Special Subcommittee, Committee on Education and Labor, "Investigation of GSI Strike," 80th Cong., 2nd sess., Jan. 20, 26, 28; Feb. 2, 3, 10, 11, 28; March 6, 8, and 9, 1948, 347–353.

25. House Report no. 1595, "Make Available Certain Information," 80th Cong., 2nd sess., March 22, 1948, 3.

26. Executive Order 9638, 10 FR 12591 (Oct. 4, 1945).

27. "WPB Folds; CPA Tells Future Plans," *The Billboard*, Oct. 20, 1945, 73.

28. Executive Order 9674, 11 FR 333 (Jan. 4, 1946). See also Harold C. Relyea, "Exigency and Emergency," in *The Executive Office of the President: A Historical, Biographical, and Bibliographical Guide*, Harold C. Relyea, ed. (Westport, CT: Greenwood Press, 1997), 279; "Truman Appoints R. L. McKeever to Direct Liquidation of Temporary War Agencies," *New York Times*, Jan. 6, 1946, 9; John F. Gerrity, "McKeever to Direct Liquidation Program for Wartime Agencies," *Washington Post*, Jan. 6, 1946, M1.

29. Executive Order 9789, 11 FR 11981 (Oct. 14, 1946).

30. 40 Stat. 411, 415 (1917).

31. 60 Stat. 418 (1946).

32. Laura McEnaney, *Civil Defense Begins at Home: Militarization Meets Everyday Life in the Fifties* (Princeton, NJ: Princeton University Press, 2000), 15.

33. Executive Order 10186, 15 FR 8557 (Dec. 1, 1950).

34. 64 Stat. 1245 (1951).

35. 1945 Pub. Papers 539 (Dec. 12, 1945).

36. Executive Order 9686, 11 FR 1033 (Jan. 26, 1946).

37. Even the media called Wyatt a czar. "Mayor Who Streamlined Louisville Will Test His Mettle in Nation's Toughest Job—Housing Czar," *Wall Street Journal*, Dec. 13, 1945, 5; Drew Pearson, "Merry-Go-Round," *Washington Post*, Dec. 15, 1945, 12.

38. Andrew J. Huebner, *The Warrior Image: Soldiers in American Culture from the Second World War to the Vietnam Era* (Chapel Hill: University of North Carolina Press, 2008), 61; Allan D. Wallis, *Wheel Estate: The Rise and Decline of Mobile Homes* (New York: Oxford University Press, 1991), 104.

39. Huebner, *The Warrior Image*, 62; 60 Stat. 207 (1946).

40. 60 Stat. 207, 208–210 (1946).

41. W. C. Bryant, "Whither Wyatt?" *Wall Street Journal*, Nov. 8, 1946, 1.

42. 60 Stat. 207, 208, 210, 211–212 (1946).

43. L. Britt Snider, *The Agency and the Hill: CIA's Relationship with Congress, 1946–2004* (Washington, DC: Center for the Study of Intelligence, 2008), 3; John Ranelagh, *The Agency: The Rise and Decline of the CIA* (New York: Simon & Schuster, 1986), 103.

44. The January 22, 1946, directive is reprinted in William M. Leary, ed., *The Central Intelligence Agency: History and Documents* (Birmingham: University of Alabama Press, 1984), 126–127. See also David F. Rudgers, *Creating the Secret State: The Origins of the Central Intelligence Agency, 1943–1947* (Lawrence: University Press of Kansas, 2000), 90; Ranelagh, *The Agency*, 102.

45. Snider, *Agency and the Hill*, 3. See also David M. Barrett, *The CIA and Congress: The Untold Story from Truman to Kennedy* (Lawrence: University Press of Kansas, 2005), 10.

46. Arthur Darling, *The Central Intelligence Agency: An Instrument of Government to 1950* (University Park: Pennsylvania State University Press, 1990), 169.

47. Kenneth R. Mayer, *With the Stroke of a Pen: Executive Orders and Presidential Power* (Princeton, NJ: Princeton University Press, 2001), 166; Darling, *Central Intelligence Agency*, 71.

48. 58 Stat. 361, 387 (1944).

49. Rudgers, *Creating the Secret State*, 130.

50. Snider, *The Agency and the Hill*, 5.

51. 61 Stat. 495 (1947).

52. Robert J. Donovan, *Conflict and Crisis: The Presidency of Harry S. Truman, 1945–1948* (Columbia: University of Missouri Press, 1996), 235; McCullough, *Truman*, 577.

53. Executive Order 9685, 11 FR 989 (Jan. 24, 1946). A week later Truman issued another executive order further expanding the government takeover of the meat packing industry. Executive Order 9690, 11 FR 13337 (Feb. 2, 1946).

54. 57 Stat. 163, 164 (1943).

55. Ibid., 168.

56. Proclamation 2714, 1946 Pub. Papers 514 (Dec. 31, 1946).

57. 11 FR 1003 (Jan. 25, 1946); "U.S. Czar Named for Meat Plants," *Los Angeles Times*, Jan. 25, 1946, 1; George Hartman, "Steel Strike Is Cause; Meat Seizure Ordered," *Chicago Daily Tribune*, Jan. 25, 1946, 1.

58. Preparedness Investigating Subcommittee of the Senate Armed Services Committee, "Inquiry into Satellite and Missile Programs," 85th Cong., 1st and 2nd sess., Nov. 25, 26, 27, Dec. 13, 14, 16, and 17, 1957, Jan. 10, 13, 15, 16, 17, 20, 21, and 23, 1958, Part 1, 302; James M. Gavin, "The Tragic Mistakes and Bickering That Undermine Preparedness," *Life*, Aug. 4, 1958, 78; Peter Galison and Bruce William Hevly, *Big Science: The Growth of Large-Scale Research* (Stanford, CA: Stanford University Press, 1992), 321; Stephen I. Schwartz, *Atomic Audit: The Costs and Consequences of U.S. Nuclear Weapons since 1940* (Washington, DC: Brookings Institution Press, 1998), 128.

59. Committee on Government Operations, "Organization and Management of Missile Programs," 86th Cong., 1st sess., House Report no. 1121, 9; Committee on Science and Astronautics, "Space, Missiles, and the Nation," 86th Cong., 2d sess., House Report no. 2092, 5.

60. Preparedness Investigating Subcommittee, "Inquiry into Satellite and Missile Programs," 302.

61. 63 Stat. 578, 581 (1949).

62. Committee on Government Operations, "Organization and Management of Missile Programs," 9.

63. Edward H. Hobbs, *Behind the President: A Study of Executive Office Agencies* (Washington, DC: Public Affairs Press, 1954), 192.

64. Executive Order 10161, 15 FR 6105 (Sept. 9, 1950).

65. 64 Stat. 798 (1950).

66. 61 Stat. 495, 499 (1947).

67. 66 Stat. 296, 300.

68. 1950 Pub. Papers 746–747 (Dec. 16, 1950).

69. Executive Order 10193, 15 FR 9031 (Dec. 16, 1950). For a discussion of the relationship of the ODM, ESA, director of price stabilization, and WSB, see Robert J. Donovan, *Tumultuous Years: The Presidency of Harry S. Truman, 1949–1953* (Columbia: University of Missouri Press, 1996), 325; Richard E. Neustadt, *Presidential Power and the Modern Presidents: The Politics of Leadership from Roosevelt to Reagan* (New York: Free Press, 1990), 13–15.

70. 1950 Pub. Papers 744 (Dec. 15, 1950).

71. "Wilson Gets Blank Check as Czar of Mobilization," *Evening Independent* (St. Petersburg, FL), Dec. 16, 1950, 1; Jerry Kluttz, "The Federal Diary," *Washington Post*, Jan. 3, 1951, B1; "Wilson Tells Plans," *Wall Street Journal*, Feb. 9, 1951, 5.

72. Sander, *Staff for the President*, 351. See also Hobbs, *Behind the President*, 193.

73. Sander, *Staff for the President*, 351; Hobbs, *Behind the President*, 194.

74. Executive Order 10200, 16 FR 61 (Jan. 3, 1951). For a discussion of the replacement of the NSRB by the DMB, see Sander, *Staff for the President*, 357; Hobbs, *Behind the President*, 197.

75. Hess, *Organizing the Presidency*, 53.

76. Ibid., 64.

77. Three years before Wilson had abolished the director of guided missiles position created under Truman. See Committee on Government Operations, "Organization and Management of Missile Programs," 9–10, 14; Committee on Science and Astronautics, "Space, Missiles, and the Nation," 5–6; Robert A. Divine, *The Sputnik Challenge* (New York: Oxford University Press, 1993), 29.

78. Anthony Leviero, "'Czar' Appointed to Speed Output in Missiles Race," *New York Times*, March 28, 1956, 1; Drew Pearson, "New Missile Czar Figured in Quiz," *Washington Post*, April 2, 1956, 35; Marquis Childs, "New Missile 'Czar' Faces Rough Task," *Washington Post*, April 3, 1956, 20.

79. Divine, *Sputnik Challenge*, 29; Preparedness Investigating Subcommittee, "Inquiry into Satellite and Missile Programs," 302; Committee on Government Operations, "Organization and Management of Missile Programs," 15; Drew Pearson and John F. Anderson, *U.S.A.—Second-Class Power?* (New York: Simon & Schuster, 1958), 176.

80. 64 Stat. 1223, 1235 (1951). See also 102 Cong. Rec. 11615 (July 2, 1956).

81. 1957 Pub. Papers 796 (Nov. 7, 1957); James R. Killian Jr., *Sputnik, Scientists, and Eisenhower: A Memoir of the First Special Assistant to the President for Science and Technology* (Cambridge, MA: MIT Press, 1977), 26; Edward J. Burger Jr., *Science at the White House: A Political Liability* (Baltimore and London: Johns Hopkins University Press, 1980), 7–8; James R. Killian Jr., *The Education of a College President: A Memoir* (Cambridge, MA: MIT Press, 1985), 267; Roger Pielke Jr. and Roberta Klein, "The Rise and Fall of the President's Science Advisor," in *Presidential Science Advisors: Perspectives and Reflections on Science, Policy, and Politics*, Roger Pielke Jr. and Roberta A. Klein, eds. (New York: Springer, 2010), 151.

82. Don Shannon, "U.S. Missile Czar Appointed by Ike," *Los Angeles Times*, Nov. 8, 1957, 1; Walter Trohan, "Ike's Program for U.S.," *Chicago Daily Tribune*, Nov. 8, 1957, 1.

83. George Dixon, "Washington Scene....," *Washington Post*, Dec. 2, 1957, A11.

84. Killian, *Sputnik, Scientists, and Eisenhower*, 31.

85. David Z. Robinson, "Politics in the Science Advising Process," in *Science Advice to the President*, 2nd ed., William T. Golden, ed. (Washington, DC: AAAS Press, 1993), 222; John Hart, *The Presidential Branch: From Washington to Clinton*, 2nd ed. (Chatham, NJ: Chatham House Publishers, 1995), 96.

86. Letter from Eisenhower to Killian in Killian, *Sputnik, Scientists, and Eisenhower*, 35–36. See also Killian, *Education of a College President*, 267; Bradley H. Patterson, Jr., *The Ring of Power: The White House Staff and Its Expanding Role in Government* (New York: Basic Books, 1988), 274–275; Divine, *Sputnik Challenge*, 50.

87. Killian, *Sputnik, Scientists, and Eisenhower*, 60–67; Benjamin P. Greene, *Eisenhower, Science Advice, and the Nuclear Test-Ban Debate, 1945–1963* (Stanford, CA: Stanford University, 2007), 37.

88. 1957 Pub. Papers 867.

89. Walcott and Hult, *Governing the White House*, 198.

90. Executive Order 10807, 24 FR 1897 (March 13, 1959); Walcott and Hult, *Governing the White House*, 198; Patterson, *Ring of Power*, 275.

91. 1957 Pub. Papers 797 (Nov. 7, 1957).

92. DoD Directive 5105.10, Nov. 15, 1957, reproduced in Preparedness Investigating Subcommittee, "Inquiry into Satellite and Missile Programs," 451–452. See also Divine, *Sputnik Challenge*, 50.

93. "New Czar for Missiles," *New York Times*, May 14, 1957, 16; "Rocket Adviser Holaday Shuns Role of 'Czar,'" *Los Angeles Times*, Jan. 1, 1958, 25; Drew Pearson, "Holaday to Quit as Missile Czar," *Washington Post*, Jan. 9, 1958, B11.

94. Committee on Government Operations, "Organization and Management of Missile Programs," 17.

95. 63 Stat. 578, 581 (1949).

96. 67 Stat. 638, 639 (1953).

97. 5 U.S.C. § 171d (1952).

98. Preparedness Investigating Subcommittee, "Inquiry into Satellite and Missile Programs," 346–347.

99. Ibid., 348.

100. The order occurred on April 8, 1959. See 105 Cong. Rec. 17277 (Aug. 28, 1959).

101. DoD Directive 5105.15, "Department of Defense Advanced Research Projects Agency," Feb. 7, 1958, http://www.darpa.mil/WorkArea/DownloadAsset.aspx?id=2473.

102. Robert Hartmann, "Air Force May Handle Man-in-Space Flight," *Los Angeles Times*, Feb. 8, 1958, 1; Bem Price, "U.S. Space 'Czar' Little Known in Washington," *Los Angeles Times*, Aug. 3, 1958, 26; Jack Anderson, "Too Many Czars in Space Work," *Washington Post*, Jan. 3, 1959, D7.

103. Katie Hafner and Matthew Lyon, *Where Wizards Stay Up Late: The Origins of the Internet* (New York: Touchstone, 1998), 20.

104. DoD Directive 5105.15. See also Committee on Government Operations, "Organization and Management of Missile Programs," 17; Committee on Science and Astronautics, "Space, Missiles, and the Nation," 7.

105. 72 Stat. 11, 13–14 (1958).

106. Roger E. Bilstein, *Stages of Saturn: A Technological History of the Apollo/Saturn Launch Vehicles* (Washington, DC: NASA History Office, 1996), 27.

107. 72 Stat. 514, 520 (1958); 105 Cong. Rec. 17279 (Aug. 28, 1959); Committee on Government Operations, "Organization and Management of Missile Programs," 19; Gregg Herken, *Cardinal Choices: Presidential Science Advising from the Atomic Bomb to SDI* (Stanford, CA: Stanford University Press, 2000), 117.

108. ARPA still had a significant array of research as it would go on to help in the creation of the Internet. See Paul N. Edwards, *The Closed World: Computers and the Politics of Discourse in Cold War America* (Cambridge, MA: MIT Press, 1997), 260.

109. Hess, *Organizing the Presidency*, 66.

110. John Lear, "Kennedy Aide Ties Science to Arms Curb," *Washington Post*, March 5, 1961, E7; Robert C. Toth, "Adviser to President Called 'Science Czar,'" *Los Angeles Times*, Nov. 20, 1963, 6; "Science Chief for Kennedy Assails Critics," *Los Angeles Times*, Nov. 22, 1963, 3.

111. Walcott and Hult, *Governing the White House*, 199–200.

112. Killian, *Sputnik, Scientists, and Eisenhower*, 25–26.

113. Ibid., 26; 27 FR 5419 (June 7, 1962); Burger, *Science at the White House*, 8.

114. "Wiesner Confirmed to Head New Science Office," *Science*, July 27, 1962, 270.

115. 63 Stat. 203 (1949).

116. Ibid., 207.

117. U.S. Constitution, Art. I, sec. 7.

118. Thomas K. McCraw, *Prophets of Regulation: Charles Francis Adams, Louis D. Brandeis, James M. Landis, Alfred E. Kahn* (Cambridge, MA: Harvard University Press, 1984), 207; Donald A. Ritchie, *James M. Landis: Dean of the Regulators* (Cambridge, MA: Harvard University Press, 1980), 179–180; "No 'Czar,' Landis Says," *New York Times*, Feb. 1, 1961, 28; "'Courage, Imagination' Urged by Landis for Agency Members," *Washington Post*, Feb. 1, 1961, A7.

119. Julius Duscha, "'Czar' Is Urged for Agencies," *Washington Post*, Dec. 27, 1960, A1; Max Freedman, "More Power for President?" *Guardian* (UK), Dec. 28, 1960, 9.

120. "Senate Unit to Oppose Agency 'Czar,'" *Washington Post*, March 26, 1961, A2; "Senate Group Protest Federal Agency 'Czar,'" *Los Angeles Times*, March 26, 1961, C1. Kennedy's recommendations were also rejected by the Administrative Conference of the United States, a temporary agency established to study federal administrative procedures. "Single 'Czar' Plan for Agencies Rejected in Report to Kennedy," *Washington Post*, Jan. 6, 1963, A6.

121. Laurence Burd, "Kennedy Asks Overhaul for U.S. Agencies," *Chicago Daily Tribune*, April 14, 1961, 5.

122. Ritchie, *James M. Landis*, 181.

123. McCraw, *Prophets of Regulation*, 207.

124. "Name Herter U.S. Trade Czar," *Chicago Daily Tribune*, Nov. 16, 1962, 6; "Herter Picked by Kennedy for Foreign Trade Post," *Wall Street Journal*, Nov. 16, 1962, 3.

125. 76 Stat. 872, 878 (1962).

126. Hess, *Organizing the Presidency*, 38.

127. Quoted in Joseph A. Califano Jr., *Inside: A Public and Private Life* (New York: Public Affairs, 2004), 155.

128. Hess, *Organizing the Presidency*, 82.

129. Ibid., 85–86.

130. See, for example, Califano's remarks on his more important duties as Johnson's domestic aide. Califano, *Inside: A Public and Private Life*, 155–161.

131. 1963–1964 (Book I) Pub. Papers 255 (Feb. 1, 1964); Scott Stossel, *Sarge: The Life and Times of Sargent Shriver* (Washington, DC: Smithsonian Books, 2004), 333; Emmette S. Redford and Marlan Blissett, *Organizing the Executive Branch: The Johnson Presidency* (Chicago: University of Chicago Press, 1981), 83; Mark I. Gelfand, "The War on Poverty," in *Exploring the Johnson Years*, Robert A. Divine, ed. (Austin: University of Texas Press, 1981), 131.

132. 1963–1964 (Book I) Pub. Papers 291 (Feb. 12, 1964).

133. Jerry Doolittle, "Scrabble Replaces Low Numbers Game," *Washington Post*, Jan. 13, 1964, B1; Charles Mohr, "Shriver Confers on Poverty Here," *New York Times*, April 1, 1964, 17; Robert S. Allen and Paul Scott, "'Poverty Czar' Power to Be Issue," *Los Angeles Times*, July 7, 1964, A5.

134. 1963–1964 (Book I) Pub. Papers 366–367 (March 15, 1964).

135. 1963–1964 (Book I) Pub. Papers 379 (March 16, 1964).

136. Sar A. Levitan, *The Great Society's Poor Law: A New Approach to Poverty* (Baltimore: Johns Hopkins University Press, 1969), 42. See also Robert J. Spitzer, "Resources Development," in Relyea, *Executive Office of the President*, 322.

137. 78 Stat. 508 (1964).

138. Ibid., 518, 528, 532. For a detailed account of the OEO's operation, see Levitan, *Great Society's Poor Law.*

139. Stephen Haycox, *Alaska: An American Colony* (Seattle: University of Washington Press, 2006), 277. See also Clinton P. Anderson, *Outsider in The Senate: Senator Clinton Anderson's Memoirs* (New York and Cleveland: World Publishing, 1970), 249.

140. Dwight A. Ink, "After Disaster: Recovering from the 1964 Alaskan Earthquake," in *Mismanaging Mayhem: How Washington Responds to Crisis*, James Jay Carafano and Richard Weitz, eds. (Westport, CT: Greenwood Press, 2008), 69.

141. Don Irwin, "Naming of 'Czar' for Alaska Relief Studied," *Los Angeles Times*, April 1, 1964, 12.

142. Executive Order 11150, 29 FR 4789 (April 2, 1964).

143. Ibid.

144. Anderson, *Outsider in the Senate*, 252.

145. Patterson, *Ring of Power*, 276.

146. Ibid., 277.

147. 59 Stat. 106, 134 (1945).

148. Anderson, *Outsider in the Senate*, 252–261.

149. Senator Anderson even tried turning down the appointment by noting: "I did not feel up to accepting such a burden on top of my normal Senate duties." Ibid., 249.

150. Ibid., 252. See also Richard Allan Baker, *Conservation Politics: The Senate Career of Clinton P. Anderson* (Albuquerque: University of New Mexico Press, 1985), 213.

151. Harold C. Fleming and Virginia Fleming, *The Potomac Chronicle: Public Policy and Civil Rights from Kennedy to Reagan* (Athens: University of Georgia Press, 2010), 130–131; Timothy Nel Thurber, *The Politics of Equality: Hubert H. Humphrey and the African American Freedom Struggle* (New York: Columbia University Press, 1999), 171.

152. Thurber, *Politics of Equality*, 171; "Johnson Names Humphrey as 'Czar' of Civil Rights," *Wall Street Journal*, Dec. 11, 1964, 5.

153. Executive Order 11197, 30 FR 1721 (Feb. 5, 1965); Thurber, *Politics of Equality*, 171; Timothy Walch, *At the President's Side: The Vice Presidency in the Twentieth Century* (Columbia: University of Missouri Press, 1997), 110; Redford and Blissett, *Organizing the Executive Branch*, 123.

154. Executive Order 11247, 30 FR 12327 (Sept. 24, 1965); Allen J. Matusow, *The Unraveling of America: A History of Liberalism in the 1960s* (Athens: University of Georgia Press, 2009), 211; Steven F. Lawson, *Civil Rights Crossroads: Nation, Community, and the Black Freedom Struggle* (Lexington: University Press of Kentucky, 2006), 50; Stephen Skowronek, *The Politics Presidents Make: Leadership from John Adams to Bill Clinton* (Cambridge, MA: Harvard University Press, 1997), 352.

155. Executive Order 11246, 30 FR 12319 (Sept. 24, 1965); Executive Order 11247, 30 FR 12327 (Sept. 24, 1965). See also Steven F. Lawson, "Civil Rights," in Divine, *Exploring the Johnson Years*, 113.

156. Carl Solberg, *Hubert Humphrey: A Biography* (St. Paul: Minnesota Historical Society Press, 2003), 277.

157. Walter LaFeber, "Latin American Policy," in Divine, *Exploring the Johnson Years*, 63–64.

158. Philip Potter, "Johnson, Erhard Will Seek To Improve East-West Ties," *The Sun* (Baltimore), Dec. 28, 1963, 1; Henry Gemmill, "Inflation Eats Away at Brazil's Economy, Undermines Other Latin American Lands," *Wall Street Journal*, Jan. 16, 1964, 8; Rowland Evans and Robert Novak, "Washington Sharpens Its Knives for Mann," *Los Angeles Times*, April 3, 1964, A5.

159. 58 Stat. 798 (1944).

160. U.S. Department of State, Office of the Historian website, "Assistant Secretaries of State for Western Hemisphere Affairs," http://history.state.gov/departmenthistory/people /principalofficers/assistant-secretary-for-western-hemisphere.

161. 18 Stat. 85, 90 (1874).

162. 22 U.S.C. § 2664 (2006).

163. LaFeber, "Latin American Policy," 64.

164. Jack Anderson, "The Washington Merry-Go-Round," *Washington Post*, March 9, 1964, B23; Drew Pearson, "The Major 'Meets' the Senator," *Los Angeles Times*, March 9, 1964; Jack Anderson, "Viet War Follows Mao's Pattern," *Washington Post*, March 12, 1964, D15.

165. 1963–1964 (Book I) Pub. Papers 108; Executive Order 11136, 29 FR 129 (Jan. 3, 1964); Esther Peterson, *Restless: The Memoirs of Labor and Consumer Activist Esther Peterson* (Washington, DC: Caring Publishing, 1995), 120.

166. Janet M. Martin, *The Presidency and Women: Promise, Performance and Illusion* (College Station: Texas A&M Press, 2003), 101–102. See also Paul Y. Hammond, *LBJ and the Presidential Management of Foreign Relations* (Austin: University of Texas Press, 1992), 207–208.

167. David M. Welborn, *Regulation of the White House: The Johnson Presidency* (Austin: University of Texas Press, 1993), 206–207; Martin, *Presidency and Women*, 101–102.

168. See generally Shirley Anne Warshaw, *Powersharing: White House-Cabinet Relations in the Modern Presidency* (Albany: State University of New York Press, 1996).

169. Frederick Mosher, ed., *"The President Needs Help"* (Lanham, MD: University Press of America, 1988), 17, cited in John P. Burke, *The Institutional Presidency: Organizing and Managing the White House from FDR to Clinton*, 2nd ed. (Baltimore: Johns Hopkins University Press, 2000), 37.

170. Hess, *Organizing the Presidency*, 86.

171. Doris Kearns, "Lyndon Johnson's Political Personality," in *The Presidency Reappraised*, Thomas E. Cronin and Rexford G. Tugwell, eds. (New York: Praeger, 1977), 128.

172. Peri E. Arnold, *Making the Managerial Presidency: Comprehensive Reorganization Planning, 1905–1980* (Princeton, NJ: Princeton University Press, 1986), 239.

173. "Report of the President's Task Force on Government Reorganization," Nov. 6, 1964, container 1, Task Force Reports (Lyndon Baines Johnson Library), ii.

174. Arnold, *Making the Managerial Presidency*, 242–243.

175. "Report of the President's Task Force on Government Reorganization," 13–18.

176. Ibid., 21.

177. On this point, see F. G. Hutchins, "Presidential Autocracy in America," in Cronin and Tugwell, *Presidency Reappraised*, 141.

178. Redford and Blissett, *Organizing the Executive Branch*, 189.

179. Ronald C. Moe, *Administrative Renewal: Reorganization Commissions in the 20th Century* (Lanham, MD: University Press of America, 2003), 84.

180. Larry Berman, "The Office of Management and Budget That Almost Wasn't," *Political Science Quarterly* 92 (Summer 1977): 291.

181. Redford and Blissett, *Organizing the Executive Branch*, 199.

182. Arnold, *Making the Managerial Presidency*, 258.

183. Redford and Blissett, *Organizing the Executive Branch*, 200. See also Berman, "The Office of Management and Budget," 292.

184. Redford and Blissett, *Organizing the Executive Branch*, 203–204; Arnold, *Making the Managerial Presidency*, 260.

185. Colin Campbell, *Managing the Presidency: Carter, Reagan, and the Search for Executive Harmony* (Pittsburgh, PA: University of Pittsburgh Press, 1996), 36.

186. Moe, *Administrative Renewal*, 85.

187. Peri E. Arnold, "Executive Reorganization and the Executive Office of the President,"

in Relyea, *Executive Office of the President*, 429; Redford and Blissett, *Organizing the Executive Branch*, 209; Arnold, *Making the Managerial Presidency*, 263.

188. Arnold, "Executive Reorganization and the Executive Office of the President," 429.

CHAPTER 5. RICHARD M. NIXON–JIMMY CARTER: CONGRESS'S FEEBLE RESPONSE

1. Stephen Hess, *Organizing the Presidency*, 3rd ed. (Washington, DC: Brookings Institution Press, 2002), 92.

2. Arthur M. Schlesinger Jr., *The Imperial Presidency* (Boston: Houghton Mifflin, 1973), 377.

3. Hess, *Organizing the Presidency*, 93.

4. John Anthony Maltese, *Spin Control: The White House Office of Communications and the Management of Presidential News* (Chapel Hill: University of North Carolina Press, 1992), 27. For a firsthand account of the appointment, see Herbert G. Klein, *Making It Perfectly Clear* (Garden City, NY: Doubleday, 1980), 32–45. For media references to Klein as czar, see R. W. Apple Jr., "Nixon's Soft Voice," *New York Times*, Nov. 26, 1968, 35; "Information Post Draws Criticism," *St. Petersburg Independent*, Nov. 28, 1968, 14A; "Rep. Moss Assails Klein's New Post," *New York Times*, Nov. 29, 1968, 58; Jack Anderson, "Ad Men Polishing President's Image," *Washington Post*, Dec. 1, 1969, B11.

5. Maltese, *Spin Control*, 28. See also Hess, *Organizing the Presidency*, 106–107; R. Gordon Hoxie, ed., *The White House: Organization and Operations* (New York: Center for the Study of the Presidency, 1971), 37.

6. R. W. Apple Jr., "Kissinger Named a Key Nixon Aide in Defense Policy," *New York Times*, Dec. 3, 1968, 1.

7. 61 Stat. 495, 496 (1947).

8. Joseph G. Bock, *The White House Staff and the National Security Assistant: Friendship and Friction at the Water's Edge* (Westport, CT: Greenwood Press, 1987), 2. For additional discussion of the executive secretary's role, see Amy B. Zegart, *Flawed by Design: The Evolution of the CIA, JCS, and NSC* (Stanford, CA: Stanford University Press, 1999), 78.

9. John P. Burke, *Honest Broker? The National Security Advisor and Presidential Decision Making* (College Station: Texas A&M University Press, 2009), 119.

10. Ivo H. Daalder and I. M. Destler, *In the Shadow of the Oval Office: Profiles of the National Security Advisers and the Presidents They Served—From JFK to George W. Bush* (New York: Simon & Schuster, 2009), 60.

11. Burke, *Honest Broker*, 119; Jean A. Garrison, *Games Advisors Play: Foreign Policy in the Nixon and Carter Administrations* (College Station: Texas A&M University Press, 1999), 35. Aside from the talks with the Soviet Union, Rogers's exclusion reached to the Nixon administration's discussions concerning normalized relations with China. See Edward S. Mihalkanin, *American Statesmen: Secretaries of State from John Jay to Colin Powell* (Westport, CT: Greenwood Press, 2004), 427.

12. Robert Dallek, *Nixon and Kissinger: Partners in Power* (New York: HarperCollins, 2007), 505; Jussi M. Hanhimaki, *The Flawed Architect: Henry Kissinger and American Foreign Policy* (New York: Oxford University Press, 2004), 427; Hess, *Organizing the Presidency*, 111; Joan Hoff, *Nixon Reconsidered* (New York: Basic Books, 1995), 148.

13. Burke, *Honest Broker*, 12, 56–104; Zegart, *Flawed by Design*, 84.

14. Anna Kasten Nelson, *The Policy Makers: Shaping American Foreign Policy from 1947 to the Present* (Lanham, MD: Rowman & Littlefield, 2009), 70.

15. Burke, *Honest Broker*, 337; Bock, *White House Staff*, 144. For a good overview of the differences and similarities between Kissinger and Brzezinski, see Gerry Argyris Andrianopoulos, *Kissinger and Brzezinski: The NSC and the Struggle for Control of US National Security Policy* (New York: St. Martin's Press, 1991).

16. Louis Fisher, *Presidential Spending Power* (Princeton, NJ: Princeton University Press, 1975), 47–48.

17. Ibid., 50.

18. Shelley L. Tomkin, *Inside OMB: Politics and Process in the President's Budget Office* (New York: M. E. Sharpe, 1998), 49.

19. Fisher, *Presidential Spending Power*, 51; Larry Berman, *The Office of Management and Budget and the Presidency, 1921–1979* (Princeton, NJ: Princeton University Press, 1979), 112.

20. Fisher, *Presidential Spending Power*, 51–52; Tomkin, *Inside OMB*, 50.

21. See Executive Order 11592, 36 FR 8555 (May 6, 1971).

22. 64 Stat. 419 (1950); 3 U.S.C. § 301 (1970).

23. Fisher, *Presidential Spending Power*, 51.

24. U.S. Congress, Senate, "Senate Confirmation of Director and Deputy Director of the Office of Management and Budget," Report no. 93-7, 93rd Cong., 1st sess., Jan. 29, 1973, 3. Cited in Fisher, *Presidential Spending Power*, 52.

25. U.S. Congress, House of Representatives, "Requiring Confirmation of Future Appointments of the Director and Deputy Director of the Office of Management and Budget, Report no. 93-697, 93rd Cong., 1st sess., Dec. 5, 1973, 6.

26. 88 Stat. 11 (1974); Fisher, *Presidential Spending Power*, 54–55; Berman, *Office of Management and Budget*, 124.

27. 1971 Pub. Papers 738 (June 17, 1971); Michael Flamm, "Politics and Pragmatism: The Nixon Administration and Crime Control," in *White House Studies Compendium*, Anthony J. Eksterowicz and Glenn P. Hastedt, eds. (New York: Nova Science Publishers, 2008), 6:132–133.

28. Executive Order 11599, 36 FR 11793 (June 17, 1971). The media also referred to the position as a czar. See Dana Adams Schmidt, "New Drug Abuse Chief Is Told He Doesn't Have Enough Power," *New York Times*, June 29, 1971, 14; M. A. Farber, "Veterans Still Fight Vietnam Drug Habits," *New York Times*, June 2, 1974, 1.

29. 1971 Pub. Papers 739, 743 (June 17, 1971).

30. 86 Stat. 65, 85 (1972).

31. Marvin H. Kosters, *Controls and Inflation: The Economic Stabilization Program in Retrospect* (Washington, DC: American Enterprise Institute, 1975), 3–14.

32. Executive Order 11615, 36 FR 15727 (Aug. 15, 1971).

33. Bradley Graham, *By His Own Rules: The Ambitions, Successes, and Ultimate Failures of Donald Rumsfeld* (New York: PublicAffairs, 2009), 98; Rowan Scarborough, *Rumsfeld's War: The Untold Story of America's Anti-Terrorist Commander* (Washington, DC: Regnery, 2004), 74; Richard Murray, "The Lawyer's Washington: The Challenges of Phase III," *ABA Journal* 59 (March 1973): 301.

34. Executive Order 11627, 35 FR 11627 (Oct. 15, 1971). See also C. Jackson Grayson Jr., *Confessions of a Price Controller* (Homewood, IL: Dow Jones-Irwin, Inc., 1974), 5.

35. William Chapman, "Connally Cast as Nixon's Strong Man," *Washington Post*, Aug. 22, 1971, 1; Louis Dombrowski, "Stans First to Opt for Controls," *Chicago Tribune*, Aug. 27, 1971, C7; Murray Seeger, "Connally, a Texas Democrat, Now President's Strongman," *Los Angeles Times*, Oct. 10, 1971, 1; Victor Riesel, "Nixon-Meany Cold War Rises To White Heat," *The Portsmouth Times*, Nov. 13, 1971, 6; John P. Mackenzie, "His Conduct in Phoenix: 'Reprehensible,'" *St.*

Petersburg Times, Nov. 15, 1971, 19A; Philip Shabecoff, "Senate Panel Approves Boldt and Grayson as Pay and Price Chiefs," *New York Times*, Jan. 28, 1972, 15; Ronald L. Soble, "Ex-Price Czar Warns Nation May Soon Return to Controls," *Los Angeles Times*, Oct. 24, 1974, F13.

36. 84 Stat. 799 (1970).

37. 64 Stat. 419 (1950); 3 U.S.C. § 301 (2006).

38. *Hampton v. United States*, 276 U.S. 394, 409 (1928).

39. 85 Stat. 38 (1971).

40. *Amalgamated Meat Cutters v. Connally*, 337 F.Supp. 737, 747–753 (D.D.C. 1971).

41. Ibid., 758.

42. Ibid., 759.

43. 1971 Pub. Papers 1024 (Oct. 7, 1971). See also Kosters, *Controls and Inflation*, 18, and Arnold R. Weber, *In Pursuit of Price Stability: The Wage-Price Freeze of 1971* (Washington, DC: Brookings Institution Press, 1973), 23.

44. Robert M. Pallitto and William G. Weaver, *Presidential Secrecy and the Law* (Baltimore and London: Johns Hopkins University Press, 2007), 115.

45. U.S. House of Representatives, Subcommittee of the Committee on Government Operations, "U.S. Government Information Policies and Practices—Problems of Congress in Obtaining Information from the Executive Branch, Part 8," 92nd cong., 2nd sess., May 12, 15, 16, 23, 24, 31; and June 1, 1972 (Washington, DC: GPO, 1972), 2996.

46. U.S. House of Representatives, Subcommittee of the Committee on Government Operations, "U.S. Government Information Policies and Practices—Problems of Congress in Obtaining Information from the Executive Branch, Part 4," 92nd Cong., 2nd sess., March 6, 7, 10, 14, and 17, 1972 (Washington, DC: GPO, 1972), 1013–1014. See also Herbert I. Schiller, *The Mind Managers* (Boston: Beacon Press, 1973), 53.

47. 85 Stat. 743, 746 (1971).

48. 117 Cong. Rec. 43258 (Nov. 29, 1971).

49. Executive Order 11695, 38 FR 1473, 1477 (Jan. 11, 1973).

50. Senate Committee on Banking, Housing and Urban Affairs, "Amendment to the Economic Stabilization Act," 93rd Cong., 1st sess., S. Report 93-1, Jan. 18, 1973.

51. 119 Cong. Rec. 1950–1951 (Jan. 23, 1973).

52. Ibid., 1951.

53. 87 Stat. 27, 29 (1973); George P. Shultz and Kenneth W. Dam, *Economic Policy: Beyond the Headlines* (New York: W. W. Norton, 1977), 75. Nixon's Executive Order 11788 abolished the Cost of Living Council. See 39 FR 22113 (June 20, 1974).

54. Ronald C. Moe, *Administrative Renewal: Reorganization Commissions in the 20th Century* (Lanham, MD: University Press of America, 2003), 86–87.

55. Ibid., 91–92; Mordecai Lee, *Nixon's Super-Secretaries: The Last Grand Presidential Reorganization Effort* (College Station: Texas A&M University Press, 2010), 2.

56. Moe, *Administrative Renewal*, 93. See also Lee, *Nixon's Super-Secretaries*, 3–4.

57. Moe, *Administrative Renewal*, 93–94.

58. Richard E. Neustadt, *Presidential Power: The Politics of Leadership* (New York: John Wiley and Sons, 1960), 7, 11.

59. 1972 Pub. Papers Appendix E-5 (Dec. 1, 1972). See also Lee, *Nixon's Super-Secretaries*, 40–41; Richard P. Nathan, *The Plot That Failed: Nixon and the Administrative Presidency* (New York: John Wiley & Sons, 1975), 67.

60. George P. Shultz, *Turmoil and Triumph: My Years as Secretary of State* (New York: Charles Scribner's Sons, 1993), 300.

61. Linda Charlton, "Nixon Designates Shultz to Guide Economic Policy," *New York Times*, Dec. 2, 1972, 1; Courtney R. Sheldon, "Shultz: The Money Czar in New Nixon Cabinet," *Christian Science Monitor*, Dec. 2, 1972, 1; Tom Wicker, "Shultz: Cabinet's New Czar," *Palm Beach Post*, Dec. 5, 1972, A10; Rowland Evans and Robert Novak, "From George Shultz, a Whiff of Protectionism," *Washington Post*, Feb. 11, 1973, D7.

62. Andrew Rudalevige, *The New Imperial Presidency: Renewing Presidential Power after Watergate* (Ann Arbor: University of Michigan Press, 2005), 62.

63. 1973 Pub. Papers 2, 4 (Jan. 5, 1973). See also Nathan, *Plot That Failed*, 68.

64. Lee, *Nixon's Super-Secretaries*, 43.

65. Ibid., 5–6, 180–195.

66. Nathan, *Plot That Failed*, 69.

67. Lee, *Nixon's Super-Secretaries*, 56.

68. U.S. President's Committee on Administrative Management, *Report of the President's Committee* (Washington, DC: GPO, 1937), 5.

69. Peri E. Arnold, *Making the Managerial Presidency: Comprehensive Reorganization Planning, 1905–1980* (Princeton, NJ: Princeton University Press, 1986), 298. Cited in John P. Burke, *The Institutional Presidency: Organizing and Managing the White House from FDR to Clinton*, 2nd ed. (Baltimore and London: Johns Hopkins University Press, 2000), 19.

70. Klein, *Making It Perfectly Clear*, 368.

71. Robert J. Spitzer, "Resources Development," in *The Executive Office of the President: A Historical, Biographical, and Bibliographical Guide*, Harold C. Relyea, ed. (Westport, CT: Greenwood Press, 1997), 333.

72. Executive Order 11726, 38 FR 17711 (June 29, 1973). The media also referred to Love as an energy czar. See "Energy 'Czar' Choice," *New York Times*, June 23, 1973, 1; "Nixon Appoints Gov. Love as 'Energy Czar,'" *Los Angeles Times*, June 29, 1973, 2; Carroll Kilpatrick, "Gov. Love Is Named U.S. Energy Czar," *Washington Post*, June 30, 1973, A1.

73. 1973 Pub. Papers 623 (June 29, 1973).

74. Executive Order 11748, 38 FR 33575 (Dec. 4, 1973). In order to allow for an orderly transition, Nixon did not abolish the Energy Policy Office until the following year. Executive Order 11775, 39 FR 11415 (March 26, 1974).

75. Like Love, the media also referred to Simon as a czar. See Edwin L. Dale Jr., "William Simon: The First Real Energy Czar," *New York Times*, Dec. 9, 1973, 26; "Changing of the Czars," *Wall Street Journal*, Dec. 4, 1973, 26; "New Energy Czar To Rule by Jan. 1 on Fuel Rationing," *Wall Street Journal*, Dec. 5, 1973, 2; "Nixon picks Wall Street Millionaire as Power Czar," *Chicago Tribune*, Dec. 5, 1973, B13. See also William E. Simon, *A Time for Reflection: An Autobiography* (Washington, DC: Regnery, 2004), 92.

76. Hobart Rowen, "The Future of the Energy Czar," *Washington Post*, Feb. 14, 1974, A23.

77. Rowland Evans and Robert Novak, "Energy Czar Sawhill's Common Cause," *Washington Post*, April 28, 1974, C7; "Fuel for a Trip to Absurdity," *Los Angeles Times*, Aug. 28, 1974, C6; Leonard F. Perkins, "Favors Higher Gas Tax," *Chicago Tribune*, Sept. 19, 1974, A2; "Energy Czar Denies Pressure to Resign," *Los Angeles Times*, Oct. 22, 1974, 2.

78. 88 Stat. 96, 99 (1974).

79. Ibid., 115; 90 Stat. 1125, 1132 (1976).

80. 91 Stat. 565, 577 (1977).

81. Roger B. Porter, *Presidential Decision Making: The Economic Policy Board* (New York: Cambridge University Press, 1982), 31.

82. 1974 (Book I) Pub. Papers. 462 (May 29, 1974); Porter, *Presidential Decision Making*, 31.

83. Bill Anderson, "Demand for Economic Czar Rises," *Chicago Tribune*, May 23, 1974, 18; Bill Neikirk, "Rush Is Likely Economy Czar Choice," *Chicago Tribune*, May 24, 1974, 7; Hobart Rowen, "Rush Chosen as Coordinator of Nixon Economic Advisers," *Washington Post*, May 25, 1974, A1.

84. 3 U.S.C. § 106 (1970). See also 62 Stat. 672 (1948).

85. 1974 (Book I) Pub. Papers 462 (May 29, 1974).

86. "Unaccountable Power," *New York Times*, June 19, 1974, 44. See also Rowland Evans and Robert Novak, "Executive Privilege: A Needless Confrontation," *Washington Post*, July 4, 1974, A15.

87. George E. Reedy, *The Presidency* (New York: Arno Press, 1975), 152. See also Stephen E. Ambrose, *Nixon: Ruin and Recovery, 1973–1990* (New York: Simon & Schuster, 1991), 387.

88. U.S. President's Committee on Administrative Management, *Report of the President's Committee* (Washington, DC: GPO, 1937), 5.

89. Partial transcript of letter from Kenneth Rush to William Proxmire, June 13, 1974, cited in "Nixon's Economic Adviser Won't Testify," *New York Times*, June 14, 1974, 15.

90. "Rush Bars Testimony on Hill," *Washington Post*, June 15, 1974, A2.

91. Douglas W. Cray, "Rush Will Testify to Congress," *New York Times*, July 17, 1974, 47; "Nixon Economic Aide Reverses Stand, Agrees Now to Testify," *Los Angeles Times*, July 17, 1974, 2.

92. Rudalevige, *New Imperial Presidency*, 7.

93. Raymond Tatalovich and Thomas S. Engeman, *The Presidency and Political Science: Two Hundred Years of Constitutional Debate* (Baltimore: Johns Hopkins University Press, 2003), 160.

94. Thomas E. Cronin, *The State of the Presidency*, 3rd ed. (Boston, MA: Little, Brown, 1980), 210.

95. George W. Liebmann, *The Gallows in the Grove: Civil Society in American Law* (Westport, CT: Praeger, 1997), 217; M. A. Farber, "Veterans Still Fight Vietnam Drug Habits," *New York Times*, June 2, 1974, 1; "Fuel for a Trip to Absurdity," *Los Angeles Times*, Aug. 28, 1974, C6; Leonard F. Perkins, "Favors Higher Gas Tax," *Chicago Tribune*, Sept. 19, 1974, A2; "Energy Czar Denies Pressure to Resign," *Los Angeles Times*, Oct. 22, 1974, 2.

96. Rowland Evans and Robert Novak, "Ford's Energy Showdown," *Washington Post*, June 29, 1975, C7; Rowland Evans and Robert Novak, "Zarb Makes His Mark on the Hill," *Washington Post*, April 12, 1975, A11; Jack Anderson and Les Whitten, "Zarb Weighs Bid to Break Up Big Oil," *Washington Post*, Dec. 2, 1975, D14.

97. Executive Order 11814, 39 FR 36955 (Oct. 16, 1974).

98. "Oil-Swap Plan Wins Backing of Ford Panel," *Wall Street Journal*, Oct. 25, 1974, 2; Rowland Evans and Robert Novak, "Confusion on the New Energy Council," *Washington Post*, Nov. 2, 1974, A15; George C. Wilson, "Public-Interest Groups Criticize Energy Team," *Washington Post*, Nov. 5, 1974, A3; Casey Bukro, "Morton Predicts Economic Upturn," *Chicago Tribune*, Feb. 6, 1975, 7.

99. 88 Stat. 96, 99 (1974).

100. 88 Stat. 1233, 1241–1242 (1974).

101. "Carter Drug Unit Nominee Opposed," *Washington Post*, March 2, 1977, A9; Alexander Cockburn and James Ridgeway, "Bourne: Is the Case Closed?" *Village Voice*, Aug. 21, 1978, 15.

102. 90 Stat. 241 (1976).

103. Thomas O'Toole, "A Man without Airs," *Washington Post*, Dec. 24, 1976, A7; "Energy Czar," *Los Angeles Times*, May 26, 1979, A1; "Cabinet Members' Resignations and Carter's Replies," *New York Times*, July 21, 1979, 8.

104. Stephen E. Nordlinger, "Shift from Schlesinger to Duncan Puts a Businessman at Energy Helm," *The Sun* (Baltimore, MD), July 21, 1979, A5; Richard Halloran, "Carter's Choice for Energy Czar," *New York Times*, July 29, 1979, F1; Rowland Evans and Robert Novak, "Jordan Purges Tito Funeral List," *The Victoria Advocate* (Victoria, TX), May 11, 1980, 3.

105. 91 Stat. 565 (1977).

106. 123 Cong. Rec. 15308 (May 18, 1977).

107. 1978 (Book I) Pub. Papers 726 (April 11, 1978).

108. Art Pine and James L. Rowe Jr., "Strauss Urges 'Toughest' Program on Wages, Prices," *Washington Post*, Sept. 20, 1978, A2; Rowland Evans and Robert Novak, "The Anti-Inflation 'Czar,'" *Washington Post*, April 14, 1978, A17; Hobart Rowen and Art Pine, "Strauss Dons Inflation Warrior's Helmet," *Washington Post*, April 15, 1978, A8.

109. Clayton Frichey, "That War on Inflation," *Washington Post*, Oct. 14, 1978, A17.

110. 88 Stat. 1978, 1999 (1975).

111. 1978 (Book II) Pub. Papers 1849 (Oct. 25, 1978).

112. Bill Neikirk, "Carter Names Kahn as His New Price Czar," *Chicago Tribune*, Oct. 26, 1978, 1; James L. Rowe Jr., "Kahn to Roam throughout the Economy," *Washington Post*, Nov. 10, 1978, D1; "Inflation Czar? Kahn's Powers Are a Bit Less Than Royal," *Milwaukee Journal*, Nov. 13, 1978, 10; Carole Shifrin, "Kahn: He's the Top Banana in Administration," *Washington Post*, Dec. 6, 1978, E5.

113. 88 Stat. 750 (1974).

114. John Hart, *The Presidential Branch: From Washington to Clinton*, 2nd ed. (Chatham, NJ: Chatham House Publishers, 1995), 172–173.

115. 92 Stat. 2445 (1978).

116. 124 Cong. Rec. 8632 (April 4, 1978).

117. Ibid., 8633–8634.

118. Ibid., 8629–8630.

119. Ibid., 8630–8631.

120. Ibid., 8635.

121. Ibid., 8636.

122. Ibid., 8647.

123. Ibid., 10121 (April 13, 1978).

124. Ibid., 10122.

125. Ibid., 10123.

126. Ibid., 10124.

127. Ibid., 10126.

128. Ibid., 20904 (July 14, 1978).

129. U.S. Senate, "White House Personnel Authorization," Conference Report no. 95-1258, 95th Cong., 2nd sess., Sept. 28, 1978, 3–4.

130. U.S. House of Representatives, "White House Personnel Authorization," Report no. 95-979, 95th Cong., 2nd sess., March 16, 1978, 8.

131. 124 Cong. Rec. 20898 (April 14, 1978).

132. Ibid., 20901.

133. U.S. Senate, "White House Personnel Authorization," 3.

134. 92 Stat. 2445 (1978).

135. On this point, see Harold M. Barger, *The Impossible Presidency: Illusions and Realities of Executive Power* (Glenview, IL: Scott, Foresman, 1984), chapter 1.

CHAPTER 6. RONALD REAGAN–BILL CLINTON: THE REEMERGENCE OF CZARS

1. See generally Morton Rosenberg, "Congress's Prerogative over Agencies and Agency Decisionmakers: The Rise and Demise of the Reagan Administration's Theory of the Unitary Executive," *George Washington Law Review* 57 (Jan. 1989): 627–703.

2. Stephen Hess, *Organizing the Presidency*, 3rd ed. (Washington, DC: Brookings Institution Press, 2002), 123.

3. Andrew Rudalevige, *The New Imperial Presidency: Renewing Presidential Power after Watergate* (Ann Arbor: University of Michigan Press, 2005), 168–183.

4. Shirley Anne Warshaw, *Powersharing: White House–Cabinet Relations in the Modern Presidency* (Albany: State University of New York Press, 1996), 168.

5. Ibid., 189.

6. See generally Alex Waddan, *Clinton's Legacy? A New Democrat in Governance* (New York: Palgrave, 2002); James MacGregor Burns and Georgia Jones Sorenson, *Dead Center: Clinton-Gore Leadership and the Perils of Moderation* (New York: Simon & Schuster, 1999).

7. Warshaw, *Powersharing*, 132.

8. Richard M. Pious, *Why Presidents Fail* (Lanham, MD: Rowman & Littlefield, 2008), 115.

9. John P. Burke, *The Institutional Presidency: Organizing and Managing the White House from FDR to Clinton* (Baltimore and London: Johns Hopkins University Press, 2000), 38, 154.

10. Pious, *Why Presidents Fail*, 115–148. See generally Lawrence E. Walsh, *Firewall: The Iran-Contra Conspiracy and Cover-Up* (New York: Norton, 1998).

11. Warshaw, *Powersharing*, 151; Burke, *Institutional Presidency*, 141.

12. Shirley Anne Warshaw, *The Domestic Presidency: Policy Making in the White House* (Boston, MA: Allyn and Bacon, 1997), 128.

13. Shirley Anne Warshaw, "Staffing Patterns in the Modern White House," in *Presidential Policymaking: An End-of-Century Assessment*, Steven A. Shull, ed. (Armonk, NY: M. E. Sharpe, 1999), 143; Shirley Anne Warshaw, *The Keys to Power: Managing the Presidency* (New York: Longman, 2000), 159.

14. Martin Anderson, *Revolution* (San Diego, CA: Harcourt Brace Jovanovich, 1988), 231; Andrew Rudalevige, *Managing the President's Program: Presidential Leadership and Legislative Policy Formulation* (Princeton, NJ: Princeton University Press, 2002), 59.

15. John Hart, *The Presidential Branch: From Washington to Clinton*, 2nd ed. (Chatham, NJ: Chatham House Publishing, 1995), 160–161.

16. Burke, *Institutional Presidency*, 38.

17. Alexander M. Haig Jr., *Caveat: Realism, Reagan, and Foreign Policy* (New York: Macmillan, 1984), 76.

18. In 2004, Congress changed the title of the council from "Interagency Council on the Homeless" to "United States Interagency Council on Homelessness." 118 Stat. 394 (2004).

19. 101 Stat. 482, 486–487 (1987). Congress subsequently renamed the law the McKinney-Vento Homeless Assistance Act after Rep. Bruce Vento, a chief sponsor of the original bill, died.

20. We are not prepared to name the ICH chair as a czar since the Housing and Urban Development secretary, a Senate-confirmed cabinet officer who already exercised statutory authority over homelessness issues, normally chaired the committee. However, we acknowledge that a strong case can be made for doing so.

21. Congress did not provide for reauthorization of the ICH in 1993 and the council remained inactive as an independent agency throughout Bill Clinton's presidency (Clinton, however, did establish the ICH as a working group within the White House Domestic Policy Council,

but we are not willing to call the reconstituted homelessness unit head a czar). Not until 2001 did Congress again authorize the ICH as an independent agency.

22. D. Hershey Jr., "The Czar in Charge of Nuclear Arms," *New York Times*, Dec. 12, 1981, 20.

23. 91 Stat. 565, 570 (1977).

24. The text of the act can be found at 128 Cong. Rec. 32767–32779 (Dec. 20, 1982).

25. 1983 (Book I) Pub. Papers 49 (Jan. 14, 1983).

26. 98 Stat. 2168–2169 (1984).

27. "Reagan to Unify Effort on Drugs," *New York Times*, Feb. 4, 1987, D24.

28. Howard Abadinsky, *Drug Use and Abuse: A Comprehensive Introduction*, 6th ed. (Belmont, CA: Thomson, 2008), 68; Mark C. Donovan, *Taking Aim: Target Populations and the Wars on AIDS and Drugs* (Washington, DC: Georgetown University Press, 2001), 39; "Reagan and Bush Place New Stress on the Drug Issue," *New York Times*, May 19, 1988, A1.

29. "Defense Reformer Is a Team Player," *Milwaukee Journal*, July 18, 1985, 14.

30. James R. Locher III, *Victory on the Potomac: The Goldwater-Nichols Act Unifies the Pentagon* (College Station: Texas A&M University Press, 2002), 280; Wayne Biddle, "'Horror Stories' and Pentagon's Budget," *New York Times*, May 24, 1985, A13.

31. Locher, *Victory on the Potomac*, 292.

32. Karen Tumulty and James Gerstenzang, "Pentagon Freeze Backed in Senate," *Los Angeles Times*, Jan. 30, 1985, B1; George C. Wilson, "Defense Dept. May Reassign Top Prober," *Washington Post*, May 18, 1985, A3; Robert S. Greenberger, "New Defense Aide Warns Contractors on Excessive Costs," *Wall Street Journal*, July 17, 1985, 12.

33. Michael Weisskopf, "Defense 'Procurement Czar' Named," *Washington Post*, July 6, 1985, A7; Michael Weisskopf, "At Work: Pentagon's New Troubleshooter," *Washington Post*, July 16, 1985, A13; Michael Weisskopf, "'Procurement Czar' Loses Mandate," *Washington Post*, Dec. 6, 1985, A8.

34. 97 Stat. 614, 686 (1983).

35. 10 U.S.C. § 136 (1982).

36. Locher, *Victory on the Potomac*, 296; William H. Gregory, *The Defense Procurement Mess* (Lexington, MA: Lexington Books, 1989), 8.

37. J. S. Przemieniecki, *Acquisition of Defense Systems* (Washington, DC: American Institute of Aeronautics and Astronautics, 1993), 16.

38. Ronald Reagan, "Implementation of the Recommendations of the President's Commission on Defense Management," National Security Decision Directive 219, April 1, 1986, http://www.fas.org/irp/offdocs/nsdd/nsdd-219.htm.

39. 100 Stat. 1783-130 (1986).

40. 1986 (Book II) Pub. Papers 1032 (Aug. 1, 1986); Gregory, *Defense Procurement Mess*, 28.

41. 132 Cong. Rec. 26189 (Sept. 25, 1986).

42. 1987 (Book II) Pub. Papers 1068 (Sept. 23, 1987); 133 Cong. Rec. 36066 (Dec. 17, 1987); Gregory, *Defense Procurement Mess*, 28.

43. Marjorie Williams, "Insult and Injury As 'Weapons Czar' Assumes New Post," *Washington Post*, Oct. 6, 1986, A13; Clarence A. Robinson Jr., "Will the Bloated B-1B Be a Drag on the Stealth Bomber?" *Los Angeles Times*, Dec. 1, 1986, B5; John H. Cushman Jr., "Pentagon Tightens Its Buying Rules," *New York Times*, Dec. 28, 1986, E4; Tim Carrington, "Meanwhile, Back at the Pentagon, Nominee to Top Weapons Job Sets Sights," *Wall Street Journal*, Sept. 25, 1987, 31; John H. Cushman Jr., "Pentagon Nominee Stresses Efficiency," *New York Times*, Sept. 28, 1987, D2; Malcolm Gladwell, "Are Defense Contracts Worth Cheating For?" *Washington Post*, July 10, 1988, 21; "The New Regime," *Washington Post*, June 19, 1989, A7.

44. 100 Stat. 1783-130 (1986).

45. Charles Tiefer, *The Semi-Sovereign Presidency: The Bush Administration's Strategy for Governing without Congress* (Boulder, CO: Westview Press, 1994), 65.

46. Ibid., 66.

47. Ibid., 67.

48. Bradley H. Patterson Jr., *The White House Staff: Inside the West Wing and Beyond* (Washington, DC: Brookings Institution Press, 2000), 302; Christopher S. Kelley, "The Unitary Executive and the Clinton Administration," in *The Unitary Executive and the Modern Presidency*, Ryan J. Barilleaux and Christopher S. Kelley, eds. (College Station: Texas A&M University Press, 2010), 110; Mark J. Rozell, *Executive Privilege: Presidential Power, Secrecy, and Accountability*, 3rd ed. (Lawrence: University Press of Kansas, 2010), 117–119.

49. Tiefer, *Semi-Sovereign Presidency*, 61–88. See also Peter Shane, *Madison's Nightmare: How Executive Power Threatens American Democracy* (Chicago: University of Chicago Press, 2009), 152–153; Barry D. Friedman, *Regulation in the Reagan-Bush Era: The Eruption of Presidential Influence* (Pittsburgh, PA: University of Pittsburgh Press, 1995), 165.

50. Bob Woodward and David Broder, "Quayle's Quest: Curb Rules, Leave 'No Fingerprints,'" *Washington Post*, Jan. 9, 1992, A1.

51. Louis Fisher, *The Politics of Shared Power: Congress and the Executive* (College Station: Texas A&M University Press, 1998), 39.

52. Tiefer, *Semi-Sovereign Presidency*, 86.

53. Ibid., 87.

54. Joel Glenn Brenner, "Ford Motor Executive Seen as Favorite for Defense Job," *Washington Post*, June 24, 1989, C1; Steven Pearlstein, "Incoming at Pentagon: A 'Czar,'" *Washington Post*, May 22, 1991, A19; "Yockey to Act as USD/A until Replacement Confirmed," *Defense News*, Dec. 14, 1990, 1; "The Contest for the 2nd Seawolf," *Daily Press* (Newport News, VA), June 23, 1991, A4.

55. 100 Stat. 1783-130 (1986).

56. 1989 (Book I) Pub. Papers 224 (March 13, 1989). Philip Shenon, "Nominee for 'Drug Czar' Has Tough-Talking Past," *New York Times*, Jan. 13, 1989, D17; Michael Isikoff, "'Drug Czar' Won't Be a Cabinet Member," *Washington Post*, Jan. 25, 1989, A19. See also William J. Bennett, John J. Dilulio Jr., and John P. Walters, *Body Count: Moral Poverty . . . And How to Win America's War against Crime and Drugs* (New York: Simon & Schuster, 1996), 149.

57. Paul M. Barrett, "Bob Martinez, Bush's Proposed New Drug Czar, Is Criticized as Lacking Some Key Qualifications," *Wall Street Journal*, Feb. 25, 1991, A10; Bill McAllister, "Questions for Drug Policy Nominee," *Washington Post*, Feb. 27, 1991, A23.

58. 102 Stat. 4181–4183 (1988).

59. 103 Stat. 183, 278 (1989).

60. "Ryan in Wings as Savings & Loan Czar," *Los Angeles Times*, March 9, 1990, D2; "Thrift Czar Earns Respect after Rocky Start," *Pittsburgh Post-Gazette*, July 8, 1991, B6; Tim W. Ferguson, "Hopes Born in Korea Snag on U.S. Thrift Law," *Wall Street Journal*, Oct. 27, 1992, A17.

61. 103 Stat. 183, 278–280 (1989).

62. Neil Morgan, "That's White House Clout along the Border," *San Diego Union-Tribune*, Jan. 14, 1996, A2. See also Doug J. Swanson, "Federal Czars Find Real Power Often Ends Up Limited," *Dallas Morning News*, Jan. 15, 1996, 10A; Valarie Alvod, "Clinton's Czar Puts His Mark on Border: U.S. Attorney Seizes Immigration Issue," *San Diego Union-Tribune*, Aug. 14, 1996, A1.

63. Valerie Alvord, "Bersin Is Expected to Become 'Border Czar,'" *San Diego Union-Tribune*, Oct. 14, 1995, A19; Anthony Depalma, "Mexico and U.S. to Patrol Border Trouble Spots," *New*

York Times, Oct. 27, 1995, A14; Steve Fainaru, "Mexican Drug Lords Thrive at Sand Diego's Doorstep," *Boston Globe*, Sept. 1, 1996, A1.

64. Ken Ellingwood, *Hard Line: Life and Death on the U.S.-Mexico Border* (New York: Vintage Books, 2005), 39; "Reno Names Prosecutor as 'Border Czar,'" *Los Angeles Times*, Oct. 14, 1995, 7A. For a detailed account of Operation Gatekeeper, see Joseph Nevins, *Operation Gatekeeper and Beyond: The War on "Illegals" and the Remaking of the U.S.-Mexico Boundary*, 2nd ed. (New York: Routledge, 2010).

65. Patterson Jr., *White House Staff*, 273.

66. Executive Order 13073, 63 FR 6467 (Feb. 4, 1998).

67. Matthew L. Wald, "Few Answers on Monster of All Cyberbugs," *New York Times*, March 19, 1998, A19; Jim Landers, "John Koskinen," *Dallas Morning News*, Nov. 29, 1998, J1; Philip Shenon, "Washington's Man in the Middle of Millennium Madness," *New York Times*, Dec. 13, 1999, A16; John Simons, "For Clinton's Y2K, No Bubbly, No Panic Either," *Wall Street Journal*, Dec. 30, 1999, A14; Marc Fisher, "Something to Celebrate: A Return to Normalcy," *Washington Post*, Jan. 2, 2000, A9.

68. Stephen Goldsmith and William D. Eggers, *Governing by Network: The New Shape of the Public Sector* (Washington, DC: Brookings Institution Press, 2004), 68.

69. David M. Abshire, *Triumphs and Tragedies of the Modern Presidency: Seventy-Six Case Studies in Presidential Leadership* (Westport, CT: Greenwood Press, 2001), 272.

70. Patterson Jr., *White House Staff*, 273.

71. 1993 (Book I) Pub. Papers 13 (Jan. 25, 1993).

72. Bill Clinton, *My Life* (New York: Alfred A. Knopf, 2004), 482.

73. Martha Sherrill, "The Health Czar, at Her Other Job," *Washington Post*, Jan. 27, 1993, D1; Grady Sandy, "A Cure for America's Hillary Jitters," *Atlanta Journal Constitution*, Jan. 27, 1993, A11; Abigail Traford, "Public Perceptions and Expert Opinions," *Washington Post*, Feb. 16, 1993, Z6; Maureen Dowd, "Hillary Clinton Says She Once Tried to Be Marine," *New York Times*, June 15, 1994, B8; Blair S. Walker, "Healthcare Compare Loses Favor," *USA Today*, April 1, 1993, B3; Michael K. Frisby, "Dueling Initiatives: NAFTA vs. Health Care," *Wall Street Journal*, Sept. 3, 1993, A10; Carolyn Lochhead, "Health Czar Sees Plan's 'Land Mines,'" *San Francisco Chronicle*, Dec. 14, 1993, A6; Editorial, "Slouching toward Ira," *Wall Street Journal*, May 22, 1996, A22; Tony Snow, "Clinton's 'Kids First' Hatched 4 Years Ago," *USA Today*, March 5, 1997, A13.

74. Haynes Johnson and David S. Broder, *The System: The American Way of Politics at the Breaking Point* (Boston and New York: Little, Brown, 1997), 140–143.

75. Lisa Hoffman, "Clinton Passes over Celeste for Health Care Reform Czar," *Cincinnati Post*, Dec. 23, 1993, 5A; Robin Toner, "Washington at Work; New Health Care Czar Preparing for Long Leap," *New York Times*, Jan. 24, 1994, A12; "Health Czar's Mission," *New York Times*, Jan. 24, 1994, A1; Mike Royko, "Health Czar Doesn't Need to Know Health Care," *The Sun* (Baltimore, MD), Jan. 28, 1994, 2A; "Ickes Enters Legislative Fray," *Rocky Mountain News* (CO), June 12, 1994, 85A.

76. "Harold Ickes to Coordinate Strategy on Health Reform," *Orlando Sentinel*, Dec. 23, 1993, A14.

77. David Blumenthal and James A. Morone, *The Heart of Power: Health and Politics in the Oval Office* (Berkeley and Los Angeles: University of California Press, 2009), 375; Clinton, *My Life*, 584.

78. Otto Kreisher, "Company Anxious about C-17 Fate: Stakes Are High for McDonnell Douglas," *San Diego Union-Tribune*, Aug. 5, 1993, C1; Tim Weiner, "Man in the News: John Mark Deutch; Reluctant Helmsman for a Troubled Agency," *New York Times*, March 11, 1995,

A8; Eric Schmitt, "Pentagon Divided by Radar Jammer," *New York Times*, July 6, 1995, A1; Thomas E. Ricks, "Deal Would Test Pentagon Policies about Competition," *Wall Street Journal*, Dec. 17, 1996, A3; Tim Smart, "Fighting for Foreign Sales," *Washington Post*, Feb. 17, 1999, E1; Anne Marie Squeo and Thomas E. Ricks, "Pentagon Seeks to Manage Competition," *Wall Street Journal*, Nov. 30, 1999, A3.

79. Joseph B. Treaster, "Ex-Commissioner of New York Named Drug 'Czar,'" *New York Times*, April 28, 1993, A15; Whitman Knapp, "Dethrone the Drug Czar," *New York Times*, May 9, 1993, E15; "Lee Brown Becomes Drug Czar," *New York Times*, July 2, 1993, A11; Christopher S. Wren, "New Drug Czar Is Seeking Ways to Bolster His Hand," *New York Times*, March 17, 1996, 18; Christopher S. Wren, "Scouting Trip Brings Drug Czar No Easy Answers," *New York Times*, April 29, 1996, A18.

80. 100 Stat. 1783-130 (1986); 102 Stat. 4181 (1988).

81. 107 Stat. 1547, 1728 (1993).

82. Patterson, *White House Staff*, 265; Richard L. Berke, "Clinton Delays Naming AIDS Czar," *New York Times*, Feb. 28, 1993, 24; Al Kamen, "AIDS Post Has Potential Czar, Needs a Home," *Washington Post*, March 31, 1993, A17.

83. 1993 (Book I) Pub. Papers 932 (June 25, 1993); 1993 (Book II) Pub. Papers 1641 (Sept. 30, 1993).

84. Adam Nagourney, "Clinton to Name AIDS Czar Today," *USA Today*, June 25, 1993, A2; David Tuller, "AIDS Czar Named after Long Delay," *San Francisco Chronicle*, June 25, 1993, A2; Christopher H. Foreman Jr., "What the AIDS Czar Can't Do," *New York Times*, July 14, 1993, A19.

85. Spencer Rich, "Clinton Names Health Ex-Official First AIDS Policy Coordinator," *Washington Post*, June 26, 1993, A2.

86. Doug J. Swanson, "Federal Czars Find Real Power Often Ends Up Limited," *Dallas Morning News*, Jan. 15, 1996, 10A.

87. Philip J. Hilts, "Clinton Picks New Director of AIDS Policy," *New York Times*, Nov. 11, 1994, A20.

88. 1994 (Book II) Pub. Papers 2060 (Nov. 10, 1994).

89. Ibid., 2061.

90. Joyce Price, "New AIDS Czar Claims Power to Achieve Results," *Washington Times*, Nov. 11, 1994, A4; "Clinton Appoints New AIDS Czar," *San Francisco Chronicle*, Nov. 11, 1994, A3; Paul Bedard, "Clinton to Name New Czar for AIDS," *Washington Times*, April 7, 1997, A1; Susan Okie, "AIDS Policy Director Puts Stress on Science," *Washington Post*, April 22, 1997, A17.

91. Greg Behrman, *The Invisible People: How the U.S. Has Slept through the Global AIDS Pandemic* (New York: Simon & Schuster, 2004), 103.

92. J. Jennings Moss, "The Czar Trip," *The Advocate*, Dec. 12, 1995, 26.

93. Bill Clinton's White House website, "White House Office for Women's Initiatives and Outreach," http://clinton2.nara.gov/WH/EOP/Women/OWIO/index.html; Noelle Norton and Barbara Morris, "Feminist Organizational Structure in the White House: The Office of Women's Initiatives and Outreach," *Political Research Quarterly* 56 (Dec. 2003): 481–482.

94. Patterson, *White House Staff*, 179.

95. Norton and Morris, "Feminist Organizational Structure in the White House," 482.

96. Bill Clinton White House website, "About the White House Office for the President's Initiative for One America," at http://clinton4.nara.gov/Initiatives/OneAmerica/about_the_office.html; Bill Clinton White House Website, "Biography of the Director: Ben Johnson," at

http://clinton3.nara.gov/Initiatives/OneAmerica/bio-rbj.html; Patterson, *White House Staff*, 275; Ann Scales, "Office to Spearhead Clinton Race Efforts," *Boston Globe*, Feb. 5, 1999, A20.

97. Gary L. Gregg, *Thinking about the Presidency: Documents and Essays from the Founding to the Present* (Lanham, MD: Rowman & Littlefield, 2005), 96.

98. Francine Kiefer, "Leading a One-Man Charge for Diversity—Clinton's Point-Man on Race Takes on Racial Profiling, Corporate America, and Hollywood," *Christian Science Monitor*, March 2, 2000, 3.

99. Samuel Francis, "The Radical Ambitions of Our New Housing Czar," *Washington Times*, March 1, 1994, A17; Eric Siegel and JoAnna Daemmrich, "Schmoke Stands Behind Henson, Despite HUD Audit," *The Sun* (Baltimore, MD), Sept. 23, 1994, B1; Jeff Dickerson, "Why Rebuild a Center for Crime and Poverty?" *Atlanta Journal Constitution*, June 4, 1996, A8.

100. Richard Wallace and Fran Brennan, "A New Alarm about Andrew Storm Czar Urges More Aid," *Miami Herald*, March 4, 1993, 1A; Editorial, "Cisneros Is on Target," *Miami Herald*, March 6, 1993, 24A; John Donnelly, "HUD Chief: Be Patient in Hurricane Recovery," *Miami Herald*, March 25, 1993, 1B.

101. 79 Stat. 667 (1965).

102. Milton Mueller, *Ruling the Root: Internet Governance and the Taming of Cyberspace* (Cambridge, MA: MIT Press, 2004), 156; Ira C. Magaziner, "Creating a Framework for Global Electronic Commerce," July 1999, http://www.pff.org/issues-pubs/futureinsights /fi6.1globaleconomiccommerce.html; Joe Klein, *The Natural: The Misunderstood Presidency of Bill Clinton* (New York: Broadway Books, 2003), 186–187; Martin Gay, *Recent Advances and Issues in Computers* (Westport, CT: Greenwood Press, 2000), 89; Patrick J. DeSouza, *Economic Strategy and National Security: A Generation Approach* (Boulder, CO: Westview Press, 2000), 238.

103. Thomas W. Haines, "Magaziner Sees Net Revolution," *Seattle Times*, Oct. 17, 1997, E1; Eric Sorensen, "Forum Focuses on Net Regulation," *Seattle Times*, Jan. 8, 1998, A8; Max Schulz, "Coveted Internet Cash Cow," *Washington Times*, Jan. 30, 1998, A19; Jon Swartz, "A Web of Conspiracy Theories," *San Francisco Chronicle*, Nov. 16, 1998, B1.

104. John M. Broder, "Ira Magaziner Argues for Minimal Internet Regulation," *New York Times*, June 30, 1997, D1; Warren P. Stobel, "Magaziner's Former Critics Not Unhappy with Him Now," *Washington Times*, June 30, 1997, A3.

105. Patterson, *White House Staff*, 271; 1998 (Book I) Pub. Papers 1112 (March 11, 1998); U.S. Government Manual (1998), 91; John H. Cushman Jr., "Clinton Hones Sales Pitch on Global Warming Pact," *New York Times*, Oct. 4, 1997, A10.

106. Patterson, *White House Staff*, 271.

107. Cushman, "Clinton Hones Sales Pitch," A10.

108. Executive Order 13010, 61 FR 37347 (July 15, 1996); Michael A. Vatis, "Cyber Attacks: Protecting America's Security against Digital Threats," in *Countering Terrorism: Dimensions of Preparedness*, Arnold M. Howitt and Robyn L. Pangi, eds. (Cambridge, MA: MIT Press, 2003), 238–239. See also Leigh Armistead, *Information Operations: Warfare and the Hard Reality of Soft Power* (Dulles, VA: Brassey's, 2004), 107–108.

109. Bill Clinton, Presidential Decision Directive 63, May 1998, http://clinton2.nara.gov /WH/EOP/NSC/html/documents/NSCDoc3.html.

110. Judith Miller and William J. Broad, "Exercise Finds U.S. Unable to Handle Germ War Threat," *New York Times*, April 26, 1998, A1; M. J. Zuckerman, "Anti-Terror 'Czar' to Coordinate $7B Effort," *USA Today*, May 4, 1998, A1; Joseph Perkins, "Feel Like You're Being Watched?" *Washington Times*, Sept. 15, 1999, A18.

111. Richard A. Clarke, *Against All Enemies: Inside America's War on Terror* (New York: Simon & Schuster, 2004), 170.

112. Jonathan S. Landay, "Senate Oks New Security Chief for Nation's Nuclear Arsenal," *The State* (Columbia, SC), June 15, 2000, A12; John Diamond, "Missing Nuclear Lab Secrets Spark Call to Tighten Classification Rules," *Chicago Tribune*, June 15, 2000, 8; Stacey Zolt, "Energy Pick Is Likely to Be Grilled about Lack of Nuclear Experience," *Albuquerque Tribune*, Jan. 4, 2001, A6.

113. Thomas Alfred Johnson, *National Security Issues in Science, Law, and Technology* (Boca Raton, FL: CRC Press, 2007), 466; Harold C. Relyea and Thomas P. Carr, *The Executive Branch: Creation and Reorganization* (Hauppauge, NY: Nova Publishers, 2003), 7.

114. 113 Stat. 953 (1999).

115. Ibid., 958.

116. Rudalevige, *New Imperial Presidency*, 209–210.

CHAPTER 7. GEORGE W. BUSH, BARACK OBAMA, AND THE VAST PROLIFERATION OF CZARS

1. Stephen Hess, *Organizing the Presidency*, 3rd ed. (Washington, DC: Brookings Institution Press, 2002), 170; Larry Lipman, "Faith-Based Initiatives Czar Has History of Helping," *Palm Beach Post*, Feb. 9, 2002, 4A; Joseph Curl, "Faith-Initiative Chief to Leave Post in June," *Washington Times*, April 19, 2006, A6.

2. Executive Order 13199, 66 FR 8499 (Jan. 29, 2001). Dilulio had committed to serve for merely six months and indeed he resigned in August 2001. David Kuo assumed the director duties temporarily until the president tapped Jim Towey for the job. Towey left in 2006 and was replaced by Jay Hein.

3. Jo Renee Formicola, Mary C. Segers, and Paul Weber, *Faith-Based Initiatives and the Bush Administration* (Lanham, MD: Rowman & Littlefield, 2003), 2.

4. Amy E. Black, Douglas L. Koopman, and David K. Ryden, *Of Little Faith: The Politics of George W. Bush's Faith-Based Initiatives* (Washington, DC: Georgetown University Press, 2004), 6.

5. Ibid., 22.

6. George W. Bush, "Address to a Joint Session of Congress and the American People" (Washington, DC: Executive Office of the President), Sept. 20, 2001.

7. Eric Pianin and Bradley Graham, "Ridge Is Tapped to Head Homeland Security Office," *Washington Post*, Sept. 21, 2001, A1.

8. Executive Order 13228, 66 FR 51812 (Oct. 8, 2001).

9. "Letter to Ridge Is Latest Jab in Fight over Balance of Powers," *New York Times*, March 5, 2002, A8.

10. Letter from Senators Robert C. Byrd and Ted Stevens to President George W. Bush, March 15, 2002. Cited in Louis Fisher, *The Politics of Executive Privilege* (Durham, NC: Carolina Academic Press, 2004), 225.

11. Tom Ridge, *The Test of Our Times* (New York: St. Martin's Press, 2009), 91–92.

12. Ibid., 92. In his book *Losing America*, Senator Byrd recounts in detail his frustrations with trying to get Ridge to testify. See Robert C. Byrd, *Losing America: Confronting a Reckless and Arrogant Presidency* (New York: Norton, 2004), 100–101.

13. Fisher, *Politics of Executive Privilege*, 226.

14. See Charles E. Walcott and Karen M. Hult, "The Bush Staff and Cabinet System," in

Testing the Limits: George W. Bush and the Imperial Presidency, Mark J. Rozell and Gleaves Whitney, eds., (Lanham, MD: Rowman & Littlefield, 2009), 35.

15. Richard A. Clarke, *Against All Enemies: Inside America's War on Terror* (New York: Simon & Schuster, 2004), 250; 116 Stat. 2135 (2002). See also 6 U.S.C. § 111 (2006).

16. Executive Order 13231, 66 FR 53063 (Oct. 16, 2001).

17. "New Counter-Terrorism and CyberSpace Security Positions Announced," Oct. 9, 2001, http://georgewbush-whitehouse.archives.gov/news/releases/2001/10/20011009-4.html;   Ariana Eunjung Cha, "For Clarke, a Career of Expecting the Worst—Newly Appointed Cyberspace Security Czar Aims to Prevent 'Digital Pearl Harbor,'" *Washington Post*, Nov. 4, 2001, A10; Ross Kerber, "Cyber-Structure Still At Risk—Effort To Prevent 'An Electronic Pearl Harbor' Is Lagging," *Boston Globe*, June 25, 2002, D1; Sherwood Boehlert, "An Electronic Maginot Line," *Washington Times*, Dec. 3, 2002, A19.

18. Executive Order 13335, 69 FR 24059 (April 27, 2004); Michael Romano, "Of Capital Importance," *Modern Healthcare* 35 (Aug. 22, 2005): 6; Jonathan D. Epstein, "Test Set for Electronic Health Insurance Payment Plan," *Buffalo News*, Sept. 4, 2006, B7; Gilbert Chan, "CalPERS Out to Tame Health Fees," *Sacramento Bee*, June 5, 2007, D1.

19. Molly Ivins, "An Administration of Cronies," *Buffalo News*, Nov. 18, 2005, A13; see also the many critical comments of leading public health officials in Jeremy Scahill, "Germ Boys and Yes Men," *The Nation*, Nov. 9, 2005, http://www.thenation.com/article/germ-boys-and-yes-men; and Erika Lovley, "Czar (n): An Insult, a Problem Solver," *Politico*, Oct. 21, 2008, http://www.politico.com/news/stories/1008/14751.html.

20. 67 FR 48903 (July 26, 2002); 67 FR 71568 (Dec. 2, 2002). See also 42 U.S.C. § 3501(a) (2000).

21. His two titles thus were: Assistant Secretary for Public Health Emergency Preparedness, Department of Health and Human Services (HHS) and Advisor to the President for Public Health Emergency Preparedness.

22. 120 Stat. 2831, 2833-2834 (2006).

23. FDA Commissioner Announces New Food Protection Position, http://www.fda.gov/NewsEvents/Newsroom/PressAnnouncements/2007/ucm108903.htm.

24. Rick Weiss, "Meet David Acheson: Your Stomach's Best Friend," *Washington Post*, July 4, 2007, A13.

25. "Dancing with the Czars," DemRapidResponse, posted Sept. 16, 2009, http://www.youtube.com/watch?v=ZXy-vPN_i7A. At the time of our viewing of the video, it had already been watched over 100,000 times and there were more than 1,100 comments posted about it on the YouTube site.

26. Executive Order 13237, 66 FR 59851–59854 (Nov. 28, 2001).

27. Rick Weiss, "Bush Unveils Bioethics Council," *Washington Post*, Jan. 17, 2002, A21.

28. Ibid.

29. Executive Order 13227, 66 FR 51287 (Oct. 2, 2001).

30. Bob Davis, "NIH Researcher Makes Phonics Focus of Bush Reading Initiative," *Wall Street Journal*, April 23, 2001.

31. NPR, *All Things Considered*, April 9, 2001.

32. 117 Stat. 711, 721 (2003); 22 U.S.C. § 2651a (2006).

33. Matt Stearns and Seth Borenstein, "FEMA Leader Has Unlikely Background," *Miami Herald*, Sept. 4, 2005, 23A; Spencer S. Hsu and Susan B. Glasser, "FEMA Director Singled Out by Response Critics," *Washington Post*, Sept. 6, 2005, A1; Andrew Zajac and Andrew Martin, "Top FEMA Leaders Short on Experience," *Chicago Tribune*, Sept. 7, 2005, 4.

34. Executive Order 13390, 70 FR 67327 (Nov. 1, 2005).

35. Spencer Hsu and Terence O'Hara, "A Bush Loyalist Tackles Katrina Recovery," *Washington Post*, Nov. 21, 2005, A8.

36. Matthew L. Wald, "Bush's Czar to Rebuild Gulf Coast Is Resigning," *New York Times*, March 1, 2008, A14.

37. Carolyn Maloney, "Members of Congress Joined by Sick and Injured 9/11 Workers, Health Professionals and Union Leaders at Ground Zero Event," Press Release, http://maloney.house.gov/index.php?Itemid=61&id=1049&option=com_content&task=view.

38. His formal title truly is a mouthful: Special Coordinator to Respond to Health Effects of September 11 Attacks, World Trade Center (WTC) Medical Monitoring and Treatment Program.

39. Michael McAuliff, "WTC Medical Czar Gets Swift Kick," *New York Daily News*, Sept. 8, 2006, 7; Nicole Bode, "Hill Warns 9-11 Health Budget Losing Its Life," *New York Daily News*, Dec. 19, 2006, 45; Heidi J. Shrager, "Sick 9/11 Heroes Face Cut-off of Treatment," *Staten Island Advance* (NY), Dec. 19, 2006, A1.

40. Associated Press, "Obama Administration Rehires 9/11 Health Czar," *Seattle Times*, Sept. 3, 2009, http://seattletimes.nwsource.com/html/nationworld/2009802109_apusattackshealth.html.

41. Senator John McCain, twitter account, May 30, 2009, http://twitter.com/SenJohnMcCain/status/1972425520.

42. Barack Obama, "Remarks at a Campaign Event," *Congressional Quarterly Transcriptions*, March 31, 2008.

43. Kay Bailey Hutchison, "Czarist Washington," *Washington Post*, Sept. 13, 2009, A25. See also Michael A. Fletcher and Brady Dennis, "Obama's Many Policy 'Czars' Draw Ire from Conservatives," *Washington Post*, Sept. 16, 2009, A6.

44. Anita Dunn, "The Truth about 'Czars,'" White House website, Sept. 16, 2009, http://www.whitehouse.gov/blog/the-truth-about-czars/. Without a clear definition the counting indeed gets confusing. For example, there are some Senate-confirmed officials who have been given czar duties that are outside the normal purview of their confirmed posts (e.g., California water czar). And then there are other officials in the Obama administration who were Senate confirmed to statutorily created positions (e.g., science czar, drug czar, intelligence czar, stimulus czar, TARP czar, copyright czar, trade czar) and yet are still regularly labeled czars. Like Dunn and many of the president's other defenders, we do not consider those officials to be true czars.

45. Lloyd's formal title is Associate General Counsel and Chief Diversity Officer, Office of Communications Business Opportunities at the Federal Communications Commission. See http://www.fcc.gov/ogc/lloyd.html.

46. See, for example, Thomas Mitchell, "A Czar for Every Harm—Including Media Bias," *Las Vegas Review-Journal*, Sept. 20, 2009, D2; Amanda Carpenter, "Diversity Czar Takes Heat over Remarks," *Washington Times*, Sept. 23, 2009, A1.

47. Bonnie Erbe, "Obama's Endless Czar List Now Includes Domestic Violence Aide," June 9, 2009, http://www.usnews.com/opinion/blogs/erbe/2009/06/29/obamas-endless-czar-list-now-includes-a-domestic-violence-aide.

48. Associated Press, "Obama Picks New Cyber Czar," Dec. 22, 2009, http://www.msnbc.msn.com/id/34517252/ns/politics-more_politics/. The first Obama appointee to this position was Melissa Hathaway, who left the administration and was replaced by Howard Schmidt.

49. "Secretary Napolitano Highlights Illegal Immigration Enforcement, Appoints Alan Bersin as Assistant Secretary for International Affairs and Special Representative for Border Affairs,"

April 15, 2009, http://www.dhs.gov/ynews/releases/pr_1239820176123.shtm. Bersin's initial position in the Obama administration was named the Department of Homeland Security Assistant Secretary for International Affairs and Special Representative for Border Affairs. In March 2010 the president gave a recess appointment to Bersin as the Commissioner of U.S. Customs and Border Protection. He retained the moniker of czar throughout both positions. See Mike Dorning, "Loosely Defined, but Czars on the Rise," *Chicago Tribune*, June 14, 2009, 3; Michael A. Fletcher and Brady Dennis, "Obama's Many Policy 'Czars' Draw Ire from Conservatives," *Washington Post*, Sept. 16, 2009, A6.

50. This position originated with Clinton's Executive Order 12835, 58 FR 6189 (Jan. 25, 1993).

51. Executive Order 13501, 74 FR 6983 (Feb. 6, 2009).

52. Tom Hamburger and Christi Parsons, "White House Czars' Power Stirs Criticism," *Chicago Tribune*, March 5, 2009, 10; Dale McFeatters, "Czarist Washington," *Deseret News* (Salt Lake City, UT), Sept. 17, 2009, A16; Yalman Onaran and Hans Nichols, "Volcker Sidelined as Obama Reshapes Advisory Panel," Jan. 6, 2011, http://www.bloomberg.com/news/2011-01-06/volcker -sidelined-as-obama-reshapes-economic-panel-for-business-outreach.html.

53. Tami Luhby, "Obama Taps Czar to Help Autoworkers," *CNN Money*, March 30, 2009, http://money.cnn.com/2009/03/30/news/economy/recovery_director/index.htm.

54. Executive Order 13509 74 FR 30903 (June 23, 2009).

55. Paul A. Eisenstein, "Auto Recovery Czar Stepping Down," *The Detroit Bureau*, June 14, 2010, http://www.thedetroitbureau.com/2010/06/auto-recovery-czar-stepping-down/.

56. Steve Fishman, "Exit the Czar," *New York*, Aug. 2, 2009, http://nymag.com/news /features/58193/. For additional background on the firing of Wagoner, see Steven Rattner, *Overhaul: An Insider's Account of the Obama Administration's Emergency Rescue of the Auto Industry* (Boston, MA: Houghton Mifflin Harcourt, 2010), 111, 134.

57. Congressional Oversight Panel, "The Use of TARP Funds in the Support and Reorganization of the Domestic Automotive Industry," Sept. 9, 2009, 71, http://cop.senate.govdocuments /cop-090909-report.pdf.

58. Rattner, *Overhaul*, 57, 152.

59. Ibid., 301.

60. Peter Lattman, "Rattner Settles Pension Inquiry for $10 Million," *New York Times*, Dec. 31, 2010, A3.

61. Ron Bloom biography, WhoRunsGov website, http://www.whorunsgov.com/Profiles /Ron_Bloom.

62. Ibid.

63. Gabriel Nelson, "Energy and Climate Czar Browner's Resignation Seen as the End of an Era," *New York Times*, Jan. 25, 2011, http://www.nytimes.com/gwire/2011/01/25/25greenwire -energy-and-climate-czar-browners-resignation-s-34804.html.

64. Davis's official title was Special Advisor to the EPA Administrator, Great Lakes National Program Office (GLNP).

65. John Flesher, "Obama Appoints Czar for Great Lakes Cleanup," *USA Today*, June 5, 2009, http://www.usatoday.com/tech/science/environment/2009-06-05-great-lakes_N.htm.

66. Fox's formal title was Associate Administrator of the EPA.

67. Karl Blankenship, "Chuck Fox to Head New International Oceans Organization," *Chesapeake Bay Journal*, Jan. 2011, http://www.bayjournal.com/article.cfm?article=4014.

68. Tracie Cone, "Feds Assign 'California Water Czar,'" *Business Journal*, June 28, 2009, http://www.thebusinessjournal.com/agriculture/889-feds-assign-california-water-czar.

69. See Anita Dunn, "The Truth about 'Czars,'" *White House Blog*, Sept. 16, 2009, http://www.whitehouse.gov/blog/The-Truth-About-Czars/.

70. See generally, 43 U.S.C. § 1451–1457 (2006).

71. "Council on Environmental Quality Appoints John Goss as Asian Carp Director," White House website, Sept. 8, 2010, http://www.whitehouse.gov/administration/eop/ceq/Press_Releases/September_8_2010.

72. Daniel Fromson, "All Hail the Asian Carp Czar," *The Atlantic*, Sept. 9, 2010, http://www.theatlantic.com/food/archive/2010/09/all-hail-the-asian-carp-czar/62724/; David Gura, "White House 'Asian Carp Czar' Outlines His Strategy for Eradicating Species," *NPR's The Two-Way*, Oct. 7, 2010, http://www.npr.org/blogs/thetwo-way/2010/10/07/130404545/asian-carp-czar-john-goss; Joel Hood, "White House Picks Asian Carp Czar," *Chicago Tribune*, Sept. 8, 2010, 16.

73. 124 Stat. 1376 (2010).

74. Quoted in Sewell Chan, "Interim Plan for Warren Raises Even Supporters' Eyebrows," *New York Times*, Sept. 17, 2010, B2.

75. Ibid.

76. Lisa Lerer, "GOP Czar Revolt Scores Its First Win as Van Jones Resigns," *Politico*, Sept. 7, 2009, http://www.politico.com/news/stories/0909/26781.html.

77. Letters from Lamar Alexander, Robert F. Bennett, Christopher S. Bond, Susan Collins, Mike Crapo, and Pat Roberts to Barack Obama, Sept. 14, 2009 (on file with authors).

78. Manu Raju, "Democrats Join Czar Wars," *Politico*, Sept. 17, 2009, http://news.yahoo.com/s/politico/20090917/pl_politico/27265.

79. Letter from Gregory B. Craig to Russell D. Feingold, Oct. 5, 2009 (on file with author).

80. Ibid.

81. Anne E. Kornblut, "White House Moving to Repair Troubled Relationship with Cabinet," *Washington Post*, March 9, 2011, A4.

82. Quoted in ibid.

83. Gary Fields, "White House Czar Calls for End to 'War on Drugs,'" *Wall Street Journal*, May 14, 2009, A3.

84. Bob Curley, "It's Official: Kerlikowske to Head ONDCP, But Won't Serve in Obama's Cabinet," *Join Together*, March 11, 2009, http://www.jointogether.org/news/features/2009/its-official-kerlikowske-to-html.

85. Office of Faith-Based and Neighborhood Partnerships, White House website, http://www.whitehouse.gov/administration/eop/ofbnp.

86. David J. Wright, "Taking Stock: The Bush Faith-Based Initiative and What Lies Ahead," The Roundtable on Religion and Social Welfare Policy, June 11, 2009, http://www.religionandsocialpolicy.org/final_report/full_report_060809.pdf, 85.

87. Executive Order 13503, 74 FR 8139 (Feb. 19, 2009).

88. Office of Urban Affairs, White House website, http://www.whitehouse.gov/the_press_office/Executive-Order-Establishment-of-the-White-House-Office-of-Urban-Affairs/.

89. Tracey Planinz, "Will Obama's New Food Czar End Organic Farming?" Examiner.com, Aug. 10, 2009, http://www.examiner.com/x-11401-Orlando-Alternative-Medicine-Examiner~y2009m8d10-Will-Obamas-new-Food-Czar-end-organic-farming; "Cash for Clunkers Wastes Usable Cars," *Herald-Journal* (Spartanburg, SC), Aug. 14, 2009, A6.

90. 74 FR 41713 (Aug. 18, 2009); 75 FR 7490 (Feb 19, 2010). See also "Office of Foods: Overview and Mission," http://www.fda.gov/AboutFDA/CentersOffices/OC/OfficeofFoods/ucm196720.htm.

91. Editorial, "A Food Czar? Really?" *Investors Business Daily*, July 16, 2010, A16; "Obama

Family Cook Named Policy Adviser," *Corruption Chronicles*, July 14, 2010, http://www.judicial watch.org/blog/2010/jul/obama-family-cook-named-policy-adviser.

92. Executive Order 13507, 74 FR 17071 (April 8, 2009). See also "Secretary Sebelius Announces HHS Office of Health Reform Personnel," May 11, 2009, http://www.hhs.gov/news/press/2009pres/05/20090511a.html.

93. "Facts Are Stubborn Things", The White House Blog, Aug. 4, 2009, http://www.whitehouse.gov/blog/Facts-Are-Stubborn-Things/.

94. EO 13507, 74 FR 17071 (April 8, 2009).

95. Judith Miller, "Gary Samore Tapped as Weapons of Mass Destruction 'Czar,'" Jan. 29, 2009, http://www.foxnews.com/politics/2009/01/29/gary-samore-tapped-weapons-mass-destruction -czar/.

96. Samore's formal title is Special Assistant to the President and White House Coordinator for Arms Control and Weapons of Mass Destruction, Proliferation, and Terrorism at the National Security Council (NSC).

97. "White House 'Green Jobs Czar' Van Jones Resigns," *Washington Times*, Sept. 6, 2009, http://www.washingtontimes.com/news/2009/sep/06/green-jobs-czar-van-jones-resigns /?page=1.

98. See John Dean, *Worse Than Watergate: The Secret Presidency of George W. Bush* (New York: Little, Brown, 2004); Frederick A. O. Schwarz and Aziz Z. Huq, *Unchecked and Unbalanced: Presidential Power in a Time of Terror* (New York: New Press, 2007); Matthew A. Crenson and Benjamin Ginsberg, *Presidential Power: Unchecked and Unbalanced* (New York: W.W. Norton, 2007); Joseph Margulies, *Guantanamo and the Abuse of Presidential Power* (New York: Simon & Schuster, 2007); Charlie Savage, *Takeover: The Return of the Imperial Presidency and the Subversion of Democracy* (New York: Little, Brown, 2007); James P. Pfiffner, *Power Play: The Bush Presidency and the Constitution* (Washington, DC: Brookings Institution Press, 2008); Alasdair Roberts, *The Collapse of Fortress Bush: The Crisis of Authority in American Government* (New York: New York University Press, 2008); Mark J. Rozell and Gleaves Whitney, *Testing the Limits: George W. Bush and the Imperial Presidency* (Lanham, MD: Rowman & Littlefield, 2009); Peter M. Shane, *Madison's Nightmare: How Executive Power Threatens American Democracy* (Chicago: University of Chicago Press, 2009); Christopher H. Pyle, *Getting Away with Torture: Secret Government, War Crimes, and the Rule of Law* (Washington, DC: Potomac Books, 2009); Julian E. Zelizer, ed., *The Presidency of George W. Bush: A First Historical Assessment* (Princeton, NJ: Princeton University Press, 2010).

CHAPTER 8. CONCLUSIONS: RESTORING THE CONSTITUTIONAL BALANCE

1. James P. Pfiffner, *Power Play: The Bush Presidency and the Constitution* (Washington, DC: Brookings Institution Press, 2008), 240.

2. The exception, as described in chapter 2, is the special envoy position.

3. Theodore Roosevelt, *Theodore Roosevelt: An Autobiography* (New York: Macmillan, 1913), 388–389.

4. Ibid., 306.

5. Theodore Roosevelt, Letter to John St. Loe Strachey, Feb. 12, 1906, in *The Letters of Theodore Roosevelt*, Elting E. Morison, ed. (Cambridge, MA: Harvard University Press, 1952), 5:151.

6. Woodrow Wilson, *Constitutional Government in the United States* (New York: Columbia University Press, 1917), 68.

7. Ibid., 14.

8. 59 Stat. 106, 134 (1945).

9. Clinton Rossiter, *The American Presidency* (New York: Harcourt, Brace, 1956). See also Godfrey Hodgson, *All Things To All Men: The False Promise of the Modern American Presidency* (New York: Simon & Schuster, 1981), 70.

10. Richard E. Neustadt, *Presidential Power: The Politics of Leadership* (New York: Wiley, 1960), 10.

11. Edward S. Corwin, *The Presidency: Office and Powers*, 4th ed. (New York: New York University Press, 1957).

12. Neustadt, *Presidential Power*, 185.

13. James MacGregor Burns, *Presidential Government: The Crucible of Leadership* (Boston: Houghton Mifflin, 1965), 330.

14. Grant McConnell, *The Modern Presidency* (New York: St. Martin's Press, 1967), 87.

15. McGeorge Bundy, *The Strength of Government* (Cambridge, MA: Harvard University Press, 1968).

16. See Norton E. Long, "Reflections on Presidential Power," *Public Administration Review* 29 (Sept./Oct. 1969): 442–450.

17. George E. Reedy, *The Twilight of the Presidency* (New York: World Publishing, 1970), 9.

18. Michael A. Genovese, *The Presidential Dilemma: Revisiting Democratic Leadership in the American System*, 3rd ed. (New Brunswick, NJ: Transaction Publishers, 2010), 29.

19. Shirley Anne Warshaw, *Powersharing: White House-Cabinet Relations in the Modern Presidency* (Albany: State University of New York Press, 1996), 132.

20. See Gene Healy, *The Cult of the Presidency: America's Dangerous Devotion to Executive Power* (Washington, DC: Cato Institute, 2008).

21. On this key point, see the analysis of Peter M. Shane, *Madison's Nightmare: How Executive Power Threatens American Democracy* (Chicago: University of Chicago Press, 2009), especially chapters 1–2. There is a significant debate among scholars over whether politicization and the institutionalized presidency are necessary modern responses to the growing demands and expectations of our chief executives. See Terry Moe, "The Politicized Presidency," in *New Directions in American Politics* John E. Chubb and Paul E. Peterson, eds., (Washington, DC: Brookings Institution Press, 1985), 269.

22. Richard M. Pious, *Why Presidents Fail: White House Decision Making from Eisenhower to Bush II* (Lanham, MD: Rowman & Littlefield, 2008), 280.

23. Ibid., 285.

24. Ibid., 292.

25. Eric A. Posner and Adrian Vermeule, *The Executive Unbound: After the Madisonian Republic* (New York: Oxford University Press, 2010), 209.

26. Healy, *Cult of the Presidency*, 97.

27. H.R. 3226, "The Czar Accountability and Reform Act of 2009," 111th Cong., 1st sess., http://www.opencongress.org/bill/111-h3226/text.

28. Lisa Lerer, "GOP Senators Seek End to Czars," *Politico*, Sept. 16, 2009, http://www.politico.com/news/stories/0909/27214.html.

29. H.R. 59, "Sunset All Czars Act," 112th Congress, 1st sess., http://www.opencongress.org/bill/112-h59/show.

30. See Mark J. Rozell and Mitchel A. Sollenberger, "Congress Should Deal with Unchecked Czars," *Roll Call*, Feb. 1, 2011, http://www.rollcall.com/issues/56_75/-202978-1.html; Mark J. Rozell and Mitchel A. Sollenberger, "Beware of the Collapse of the 'Open Presidency,'" *Roll Call*, Oct. 29, 2009, http://www.rollcall.com/issues/55_49/-40008-1.html.

31. H.R. 59, "Sunset All Czars Act," 112th Congress, 1st sess., http://www.opencongress.org/bill/112-h59/show.

32. Andrew Restuccia, "GOP Votes to Dethrone Obama's Policy Czars," *The Hill*, Feb. 17, 2011, http://thehill.com/blogs/e2-wire/677-e2-wire/144961-house-republicans-vote-to-defund-obamas-policy-czars.

33. Quoted in Robin Bravender, "Senate Democrats: Save the Czars!" *Politico*, March 4, 2011, http://www.politico.com/news/stories/0311/50684.html.

34. H.R. 1473, "Department of Defense and Full-Year Continuing Appropriations Act, 2011." See also Robin Bravender, "President Obama to Ignore 'Czar' Ban," *Politico*, April 17, 2011, http://www.politico.com/news/stories/0411/53342.html; James Risen, "Obama Takes On Congress over Policy Czar Positions," *New York Times*, April 17, 2011, A17.

35. Barack Obama, "Statement by the President on H.R. 1473," April 15, 2011, http://www.whitehouse.gov/the-press-office/2011/04/15/statement-president-hr-1473.

36. For video evidence of Obama saying on the campaign trail that he will not issue any signing statements, see, "Obama on Presidential Signing Statements," http://www.youtube.com/watch?v=seAR1S1Mjkc&feature=player_embedded.

37. Charlie Savage, "Barack Obama's Q&A," *Boston Globe*, Dec. 20, 2007, http://www.boston.com/news/politics/2008/specials/CandidateQA/ObamaQA/.

38. Robin Bravender, "House GOP Continues Czar War," *Politico*, June 14, 2011, http://www.politico.com/news/stories/0611/56992.html.

39. S. Amdt. 499, 112th Cong., 1st sess.

40. Josiah Ryan, "Senate Kills Measure to Defund Policy 'Czars,'" *The Hill*, June 23, 2011, http://thehill.com/homenews/senate/168119-senate-kills-amendment-to-end-czars-.

41. Staff, "Sen. David Vitter Goes after President Barack Obama's 'Czars,'" *Times-Picayune*, June 25, 2011, http://www.nola.com/politics/index.ssf/2011/06/sen_david_vitter_goes_after_pr.html.

42. Louis Fisher, *On Appreciating Congress: The People's Branch* (Boulder, CO: Paradigm, 2010), 13: Since the New Deal era, Fisher observes, Congress "has in large part allowed its powers to decline, partly for refusing to fight off encroachments and in some cases by taking the initiative to surrender power." See also Louis Fisher, *Congressional Abdication on War and Spending* (College Park: Texas A&M Press, 2000); Jasmine Farrier, *Congressional Ambivalence: The Political Burdens of Constitutional Authority* (Lexington: University Press of Kentucky, 2010).

43. Pfiffner, *Power Play*, 240.

44. 3 U.S.C. § 112 (2006).

45. 102 Stat. 4181–4183 (1988).

46. John Hart, *The Presidential Branch: From Washington to Clinton*, 2nd ed. (Chatham, NJ: Chatham House Publishers, 1995), 111.

47. Ibid., 238.

48. U.S. President's Committee on Administrative Management, *Report of the President's Committee* (Washington, DC: Government Printing Office, 1937), 5.

49. Stephen Hess, *Organizing the Presidency*, 3rd ed. (Washington, DC: Brookings Institution Press, 2002), 178.

50. Pious, *Why Presidents Fail*, 285.

51. Louis Fisher, "Micromanagement by Congress: Reality and Mythology," in *The Fettered Presidency: Legal Constraints on the Executive Branch*, L. Gordon Crovitz and Jeremy A. Rabkin, eds. (Washington, DC: American Enterprise Institute for Public Policy Research, 1989), 139.

52. Michael Lind, "The Out-of-Control Presidency," *New Republic*, Aug. 15, 1995, 18–23. See also on this point Michael A. Genovese, "Is the Presidency Dangerous to Democracy?" in *The*

Presidency and the Challenge of Democracy, Michael A. Genovese and Lori Cox Han, eds. (New York: Palgrave Macmillan, 2006), 19.

53. 1 *Annals* 393 (May 19, 1789).

54. Louis Fisher, *On Appreciating Congress*, 41–42.

55. For additional information on this point, see Harold M. Barger, *The Impossible Presidency: Illusions and Realities of Executive Power* (Glenview, IL: Scott, Foresman, 1984), chapter 5.

56. Peri E. Arnold, *Making the Managerial Presidency* (Princeton, NJ: Princeton University Press, 1986), 361–362. See also Hess, *Organizing the Presidency*, 204; and Raymond Tatalovich and Thomas S. Engeman, *The Presidency and Political Science: Two Hundred Years of Constitutional Debate* (Baltimore, MD: Johns Hopkins University Press, 2003), 205.

57. Barger, *The Impossible Presidency*, 146.

58. Hess, *Organizing the Presidency*, 201.

59. See generally Posner and Vermeule, *Executive Unbound*.

APPENDIX: AN INDEX OF CZARS AND MEDIA-LABELED CZARS, 1919–2011

Table 1

1. "Power of Czar to Prohibition Commissioner: Nicholas Did Not Possess the Authority of Kramer the House Is Told Today," *Miami News* (FL), June 18, 1921, 1; "Prohibition Forces Split Over New Law," *The Sun* (Baltimore, MD), June 19, 1921, 2; "U.S. Dry Agents Face Shakeup from New Czar," *Chicago Daily Tribune*, July 31, 1927, 1.

2. 41 Stat. 305, 308 (1919).

3. "Drys Split over Law," *Los Angeles Times*, June 19, 1921, 11; "From Sick Bed Slams Haynes as Modern Czar," *Chicago Daily Tribune*, Feb. 10, 1922, 3; "Haynes Now Slated for Prohibition Chief," *Washington Post*, March 24, 1927, 1; "Dry Chiefs Win Fight: Haynes Slated to Be New Czar," *Los Angeles Times*, 1.

4. 41 Stat. 305, 308 (1919).

5. Treasury Secretary appointed.

6. 44 Stat. 1381 (1927).

7. "Mellon Upholds Shoot to Kill Orders to Drys," *Chicago Daily Tribune*, July 2, 1929, 4.

8. "Calls Sherrill Czar of Washington," *New York Times*, July 19, 1925, 1; "False Rumors Mislead Blanton, Says Sherrill," *Washington Post*, July 19, 1925, 2; L. C. Speers, "Col. Sherrill—New Washington 'Czar,'" *New York Times*, Aug. 9, 1925, 8; "Victors over 'Gang' to Rule Cincinnati," *New York Times*, Dec. 31, 1925, 17.

9. 43 Stat. 983 (1925).

10. "Hoover Names Personal Dry as 'Dry Czar,'" *Chicago Daily Tribune*, Nov. 2, 1929, 2; "New Dry Chief Faces a Difficult Task," *New York Times*, June 29, 1930, 50; "Woodcock Chosen Dry Bureau's Head," *Washington Post*, June 24, 1930, 2; Laurence M. Benedict, "Dry Czar's Plans Laid," *Los Angeles Times*, July 29, 1930, 1.

11. Attorney General appointed.

12. 46 Stat. 427 (1930).

Table 2

1. EO "Creating Committee on Public Information," April 13, 1917, in *The Compilation of the Messages and Papers of the Presidents*, James D. Richardson, ed. (New York: Bureau of National Literature, 1921), 17:8247.

2. Wilson created the agency in May 1917. Not until August of that year did Congress provide statutory authority. See "Statement [Food Control Program]," May 19, 1917, in Richardson, *Compilation of the Messages and Papers*, 8262–8264; 40 Stat. 276 (1917).

3. The executive order was not published. It is referenced in EO "Vesting Power and Authority in Designated Officers and Making Rules and Regulations under Trading with the Enemy Act and Title VII of the Act, Approved June 15, 1917," Oct. 12, 1917, in ibid., 8368.

4. EO "[Appointing Fuel Administrator]," Aug. 23, 1917, in ibid., 8330. See also EO "[Creating Food Administration Grain Corporation]," Aug. 14, 1917, in ibid., 8324–8326.

5. EO "Vesting Power and Authority in Designated Officers," in ibid., 8366.

6. Presidential Proclamation, "National War Labor Board," April 8, 1918, in *1919 Supplement to the United States Compiled Statutes Annotated* (St. Paul, MN: West Publishing, 1920), 1:641–644.

7. EO "[Establishment of War Industries Board]," May 28, 1918, in Richardson, *Compilation of the Messages and Papers*, 18:8518–8519.

8. Not an official title. Coolidge never provided a title for Hoover.

9. Hoover also served as secretary of commerce during this time.

10. Presidential designation.

Table 3

1. Not an official title.

2. "A Czar for Agriculture," *Washington Post*, March 17, 1933, 6; "An Unwilling Czar," *Washington Post*, April 16, 1933, 6.

3. Wallace served as agriculture secretary during this time.

4. 48 Stat. 31, 37 (1933).

5. In 1942 the AAA would be consolidated into the Agricultural Conservation and Adjustment Administration by EO 9069. See 7 FR 1409 (Feb. 23, 1942).

6. Jordan A. Schwarz, *The Speculator: Bernard M. Baruch in Washington, 1917–1965* (Chapel Hill: University of North Carolina Press, 1981), 280; Bernard Sternsher, *Rexford Tugwell and the New Deal* (New Brunswick, NJ: Rutgers University Press, 1964), 192; "From a Senator's Diary," *Washington Post*, June 25, 1933, 7.

7. Agriculture Secretary appointed.

8. 48 Stat. 31, 37 (1933).

9. "Industry Czar Tells Plans to Help Workers," *Chicago Daily Tribune*, June 21, 1933, 1; W. B. Francis, "Industry Czar Faces Hurdles," *Los Angeles Times*, June 23, 1933, 8; John Boettiger, "Johnson, Czar of Industry, Is Man in a Hurry," *Chicago Daily Tribune*, July 3, 1933, 1.

10. In 1935, the Supreme Court declared the NRA to be unconstitutional. *Schechter Poultry Corp. v. United States*, 295 U.S. 495, 531 (1935).

11. EO 6173, 1933 Pub. Papers 247 (June 16, 1933). See also 48 Stat. 195 (1933).

12. "Choate Made 'Czar' to Control Liquor," *New York Times*, Nov. 30, 1933, 24; "Canada Helped Keep U.S. Dry; to Be Rewarded," *Chicago Daily Tribune*, Dec. 15, 1933, 10; "Choate To Quit As Liquor Czar," *Miami News*, June 20, 1935, 2.

13. Abolished in 1935 by an act of Congress. See 49 Stat. 977 (1935).

14. EO 6474, 1933 Pub. Papers 508 (Dec. 4, 1933).

15. "Bill Sets Up Rail Czar," *Los Angeles Times*, April 28, 1933, 1; "A Railroad Czar," *Los Angeles Times*, April 29, 1933, A4; "Eastman Declares He Is Not A 'Czar,'" *New York Times*, June 17, 1933, 3; "Not Czar, Says Eastman," *Wall Street Journal*, June 19, 1933, 5.

16. Law expired in 1936. See 49 Stat. 376 (1935).

17. Law stipulated that the Federal Coordinator of Transportation "shall be appointed by the President, by and with the advice and consent of the Senate, or be designated by the President from the membership of the" Interstate Commerce Commission. As an ICC member, Eastman was designated by President Roosevelt to the position.

18. 48 Stat. 211 (1933).

19. "President Sets Up New Agency to Rule Prices," *Chicago Daily Tribune*, April 12, 1941, 6; "U.S. Price Czar Asserts He Can Enforce Fixing," *Chicago Daily Tribune*, May 28, 1941, 29; "Price Czar Henderson Puts On Exciting Show," *Washington Post*, Aug. 29, 1941, B4.

20. EO 8734, 6 FR 1917 (April 15, 1941).

21. EO 8875, 6 FR 4483 (Aug. 28, 1941).

22. Ed Ainsworth, "As You Might Say," *Los Angeles Times*, March 27, 1943, A4; Drew Pearson, "Merry-Go-Round," *Washington Post*, May 29, 1943, 9.

23. "OPA Closes Gasoline Station of Mother Aiding Service Son," *Chicago Daily Tribune*, April 22, 1944, 1; "Price-Wage Czar," *Wall Street Journal*, Feb. 12, 1946, 1; "Hold Your Hats—Here We Go," *Chicago Daily Tribune,* Feb. 16, 1946, 10.

24. Ickes appointed Ralph K. Davies, vice president of Standard Oil of California, "Acting Petroleum Coordinator for National Defense" from 1941 to early 1942 and then named him Deputy Petroleum Coordinator/Administrator from 1942–1946. See 6 FR 5016 (Oct. 6, 1941); 7 FR 404 (Jan. 20, 1942); Dudley J. Hughes, *Oil in the Deep South* (Jackson: University Press of Mississippi, 1993), 182.

25. Frank L. Kluckhorn, "Roosevelt Names Ickes as Oil Czar," *Washington Post*, June 1, 1941, 1; Cecil B. Dickson, "Ickes Is Now Czar of U.S. Power Sources," *Washington Post*, June 22, 1941, 11.

26. During this time Ickes served as Interior Secretary.

27. Presidential designation.

28. 6 FR 2760 (May 28, 1941).

29. 7 FR 3668 (April 20, 1942).

30. EO 9276, 7 FR 10091 (Dec. 2, 1942).

31. Walter Trohan, "Wickard Shorn of Food Powers: Czar Appointed," *Chicago Daily Tribune*, March 26, 1943, 19; "Food: The Tenth Czar," *Time*, April 5, 1943, http://www.time.com /time/magazine/article/0,9171,790873,00.html.

32. EO 8985, 6 FR 6625 (Dec. 23, 1941).

33. "F.D.R. Names Czar of All U.S. Transportation," *Chicago Daily Tribune*, Dec. 24, 1941, 1; Jerry Kluttz, "The Federal Diary," *Washington Post*, June 2, 1942, 17.

34. EO 8989, 6 FR 6725–6727 (Dec. 25, 1941).

35. Jerry Kluttz, "The Federal Diary," *Washington Post*, July 3, 1944, 3.

36. "Food: The Tenth Czar," *Time*, April 5, 1943, http://www.time.com/time/magazine /article/0,9171,790873,00.html; Patricia Grady, "Visiting King Negotiates Crowded Social Schedule," *Washington Post*, June 26, 1942, 18; "Rebuff for Mr. Davis," *Washington Post*, July 11, 1942, 8; Drew Pearson, "Merry-Go-Round," *Palm Beach Post* (Florida), July 31, 1942, 4.

37. EO 9182, 7 FR 4468 (June 16, 1942).

38. Alfred Friendly, "Nelson Gets Full Power over War Production," *Washington Post,* Jan. 17, 1942, 1; "President Gives Nelson Full Power of Czar," *Los Angeles Times*, Jan. 17, 1942, 1; Chesly Manly, "Choice of Nelson as Arms 'Czar' Pleases Capital," *Chicago Daily Tribune*, Jan. 15, 1942, 9.

39. EO 9024, 7 FR 329 (Jan. 17, 1942).

40. "Head of W.P.B. Here to Bolster Man Power Drive," *Los Angeles Times*, Dec. 12, 1944, 1; "Fresh Reshuffles," *Washington Post*, Dec. 21, 1944, 4.

41. Robert De Vore, "Jeffers, Union Pacific Head, Is Rubber Czar," *Washington Post*, Sept. 16, 1942, 1; William J. Enright, "'Czars' Will Rule on Industry Needs," *New York Times*, Dec. 15, 1942, 37.

42. Director of the War Production Board appointed.

43. EO 9246, 7 FR 7379 (Sept. 19, 1942).

44. Ben W. Gilbert, "Krug Selection as Power Czar Portends Fuel Supply Conflict," *Washington Post*, Jan. 23, 1943, 1; Martha Rhyne, "Office of War Utilities Quietly Goes about Tremendous War Job," *Washington Post*, April 24, 1943, B4; Felix Belair Jr., "Truman Names Krug Secretary of the Interior," *New York Times*, Feb. 27, 1946, 1.

45. Director of the War Production Board appointed.

46. Created by regulations of the War Production Board. See 8 FR 2007 (Feb. 16, 1943); 8 FR 2147 (Feb. 18, 1943).

47. James G. Simonds, "Land Made Czar of War Shipping," *Washington Post*, Feb. 10, 1942, 7; "The President's Day," *Washington Post*, Feb. 10, 1942, 5; Michael Chinigo, "8-Million-Ton Shipping Goal in Sight, Land Tells President," *Washington Post*, Sept. 26, 1942, 1.

48. EO 9054, 7 FR 837 (Feb. 10, 1942).

49. "Manpower Policy," *Washington Post*, Dec. 5, 1942, 8; Ben W. Gilbert, "McNutt Gets Full Control over All U.S. Manpower," *Washington Post*, Dec. 6, 1942, 1; "Manpower Czar," *Washington Post*, Dec. 7, 1942, 14; Jerry Kluttz, "The Federal Diary," *Washington Post*, Jan. 25, 1943, B1.

50. EO 9139, 7 FR 2919 (April 21, 1942).

51. Robert De Vore, "Economic Czar 'Jimmy' Byrnes Is Popular Administrator," *Washington Post*, Oct. 11, 1942, B5; "Wages Frozen at Sept. 15 Level; Salaries Limited," *Chicago Daily Tribune*, Oct. 4, 1942, 12.

52. EO 9250, 7 FR 7871 (Oct. 6, 1942).

53. Drew Pearson, "Merry-Go-Round," *Washington Post*, Nov. 1, 1943, 6; Drew Pearson, "Merry-Go-Round," *Washington Post*, Nov. 6, 1943, B6; "A.F.L. Will Ask President to Oust Vinson as Stabilizer," *Los Angeles Times*, Jan. 18, 1944, A1; Drew Pearson, "Hannegan Is Acting to Bolster Democrats," *Washington Post*, Feb. 20, 1944, B5.

54. Abolished by EO 9762, 11 FR 8073 (July 25, 1946).

55. Not an official title. Roosevelt never provided a title for Wickard.

56. Walter Trohan, "Wickard Shorn of Food Powers," *Chicago Daily Tribune*, March 26, 1943, 19; "Food Czar," *Washington Post*, Dec. 8, 1942, 12; "Roosevelt Outlines Food Czar Order," *Los Angeles Times*, Dec. 7, 1942, 18.

57. During this time Wickard also served as Agriculture Secretary.

58. Presidential designation and delegation of power.

59. EO 9280, 7 FR 10179 (Dec. 8, 1942).

60. "Choice of Davis as Czar Lauded by Food Groups," *Chicago Daily Tribune*, March 27, 1943, 2; Ernest K. Lindley, "Food Czar Davis," *Washington Post*, March 29, 1943, 9; "Food Czar," *Washington Post*, April 1, 1943, 12; "Food Czar Acts to Curb Black Market," *Los Angeles Times*, April 11, 1943, 1.

61. EO 9322, 8 FR 3807 (March 30, 1943).

62. EO 9334, 8 FR 5423 (April 27, 1943).

63. "Food Czar Asks Stable Price to Aid Production," *Chicago Daily Tribune*, Aug. 19, 1943, 11; "Food Czar Jones Urges Extension on Life of CCC," *The Evening Independent* (St. Petersburg, FL), Sept. 29, 1943, 1; Drew Pearson, "Merry-Go-Round," *Washington Post*, Feb. 7, 1944, 10.

Table 4

1. In 1935, the Supreme Court declared the NRA to be unconstitutional. *Schechter Poultry Corp. v. United States,* 295 U.S. 495, 531 (1935).

2. EO 6173, 1933 Pub. Papers 247 (June 16, 1933). See also 48 Stat. 195 (1933).

3. Law expired in 1936. See 49 Stat. 376 (1935).

4. Law stipulated that the Federal Coordinator of Transportation "shall be appointed by the President, by and with the advice and consent of the Senate, or be designated by the President from the membership of the" Interstate Commerce Commission. As an ICC member, Eastman was designated by President Roosevelt to the position.

5. 48 Stat. 211 (1933).

6. Roosevelt abolished the agency in 1942. See EO 9040, 7 FR 527 (Jan. 24, 1942).

7. EO 8629, 6 FR 191 (Jan. 7, 1941).

8. Abolished by EO 9070, 7 FR 1529 (Feb. 24, 1942).

9. EO 8632, 6 FR 295 (Jan. 11, 1941).

10. Roosevelt did issue a presidential letter. See 1941 Pub. Papers 57 (March 13, 1941).

11. Abolished by EO 9723, 11 FR 5345 (May 14, 1946).

12. EO 9205, 7 FR 5803 (July 25, 1942).

13. Abolished by EO 9017, 7 FR 237 (Jan. 12, 1942).

14. EO 8716, 6 FR 1532 (March 19, 1941).

15. EO 8734, 6 FR 1917 (April 15, 1941).

16. Once the Emergency Price Control Act of 1942 became law, the agency head ceased to be a czar. 56 Stat. 23, 29 (1942).

17. EO 8875, 6 FR 4483 (Aug. 28, 1941).

18. Abolished by EO 8926, 6 FR 5519 (Oct. 28, 1941).

19. EO 8751, 6 FR 2301 (May 2, 1941).

20. Abolished by EO 9380, 8 FR 13081 (Sept. 25, 1943).

21. EO 8926, 6 FR 5519 (Oct. 29, 1941).

22. EO 8757, 6 FR 2517 (May 20, 1941).

23. Abolished by EO 9562, 10 FR 6639 (June 4, 1945).

24. EO 8840, 6 FR 3857 (July 30, 1941).

25. Abolished by 9710, 11 FR 3941 (April 10, 1946).

26. EO 9532, 10 FR 3173 (March 23, 1945).

27. Served as vice president at the time.

28. Abolished by EO 9024, 7 FR 329 (Jan. 16, 1942).

29. Presidential designation.

30. EO 8875, 6 FR 4483 (Aug. 28, 1941).

31. McNutt served as the Federal Security Administrator.

32. Abolished by EO 9338, 8 FR 5659 (April 29, 1943).

33. EO 8990, 6 FR 4625 (Sept. 3, 1941).

34. Abolished by EO 9631, 10 FR 12304 (Sept. 28, 1945).

35. EO 8985, 6 FR 6625 (Dec. 23, 1941).

36. EO 8989, 6 FR 6725 (Dec. 25, 1941).

37. Abolished by EO 10065, 14 FR 3719 (July 6, 1949).

38. Abolished by EO 9672, 11 FR 221 (Dec. 31, 1945).

39. EO 9017, 7 FR 237 (Jan. 12, 1942).

40. EO 9024, 7 FR 329 (Jan. 17, 1942).

41. Abolished by EO 9638, 10 FR 12591 (Oct. 4, 1945).

42. Abolished by EO 9608, 10 FR 11223 (Aug. 31, 1945).

43. EO 9182, 7 FR 4468 (June 16, 1942).

44. Director of the War Production Board appointed.

45. EO 9246, 7 FR 7379 (Sept. 19, 1942).

46. Abolished along with the War Production Board.

47. Abolished by 60 Stat. 501 (1946).

48. EO 9054, 7 FR 837 (Feb. 10, 1942).

49. EO 9102, 7 FR 2165 (March 18, 1942).

50. Abolished by EO 9742, 11 FR 7125 (June 25, 1946).

51. McNutt served as the Federal Security Administrator.

52. Abolished by EO 9617, 10 FR 11929 (Sept. 19, 1945).

53. Presidential designation.

54. EO 9139, 7 FR 2919 (April 21, 1942).

55. EO 9250, 7 FR 7871 (Oct. 6, 1942).

56. Abolished by EO 9620, 10 FR 12033 (Sept. 20, 1945) and then reestablished by EO 9699, 11 FR 1929 (Feb. 21, 1946). Abolished by EO 9809, 11 FR 14281 (Dec. 12, 1946).

57. Ickes served as Secretary of Interior.

58. Presidential designation.

59. EO 9276, 7 FR 10091 (Dec. 4, 1942).

60. EO 9718, 11 FR 4965 (May 3, 1946).

61. Not an official title. Roosevelt never provided a title for Wickard.

62. During this time Wickard also served as Agriculture Secretary.

63. Presidential designation and delegation of power.

64. EO 9280, 7 FR 10179 (Dec. 5, 1942).

65. EO 9322, 8 FR 3807 (March 30, 1943).

66. EO 9334, 8 FR 5423 (April 27, 1943).

67. Abolished by EO 9577, 10 FR 8087 (June 29, 1945).

68. Director of the War Production Board appointed.

69. Created by regulations of the War Production Board. See 8 FR 2007 (Feb. 16, 1943); 8 FR 2147 (Feb. 18, 1943).

70. Abolished along with the War Production Board.

71. With the passage of the War Mobilization and Reconversion Act in 1944 the agency director ceased to be a czar. See 58 Stat. 785 (1944).

72. EO 9347, 8 FR 7207 (May 27, 1943).

73. Abolished by EO 9380, 8 FR 13081 (Sept. 25, 1943).

74. EO 9361, 8 FR 9861 (July 15, 1943).

75. Abolished by 9630, 10 FR 12245 (Sept. 27, 1945).

76. EO 9380, 8 FR 13081 (Sept. 25, 1943).

77. Abolished with the establishment of the Surplus Property Board. See 58 Stat. 768 (1944).

78. The War Mobilization director appointed.

79. EO 9425, 9 FR 2071 (Feb. 19, 1944).

Table 5

1. Drew Pearson, "Merry-Go-Round," *Washington Post*, Oct. 12, 1945, 9; "Washington Wire," *Wall Street Journal*, Sept. 21, 1945, 1; "Reconversion Ruler," *Wall Street Journal*, July 21, 1945, 1.

2. 58 Stat. 785 (1944).

3. Drew Pearson, "Merry-Go-Round," *Palm Beach Post* (Florida), July 4, 1946, 4; Drew Pearson, "Merry-Go-Round," *Indian Valley Record* (Greenville, CA), Aug. 1, 1946, 2.

4. Law expired.

5. Not an official title. Like Roosevelt, Truman never provided a title for the delegation of authority.

6. "Raymond Moley—The Food Czar," *Los Angeles Times*, May 31, 1945, A4; S. H. Scheibla, "Food Czar's Ukase," *Wall Street Journal*, June 1, 1945, 1; "Bitter Path Ahead, Says Food Czar," *Washington Post*, June 13, 1945, 4.

7. Anderson served as Agriculture Secretary during this time.

8. Presidential designation.

9. EO 9577, 10 FR 8087 (July 3, 1945).

10. "Mayor Who Streamlined Louisville Will Test His Mettle in Nation's Toughest Job—Housing Czar," *Wall Street Journal*, Dec. 13, 1945, 5; Drew Pearson, "Merry-Go-Round," *Washington Post*, Dec. 15, 1945, 12; Venice T. Spraggs, "Truman Stand, New Legislation May Break Negro Housing Bottleneck," *Chicago Defender*, Dec. 22, 1945, 10; Drew Pearson, "Merry-Go-Round," *Washington Post*, April 13, 1946, 7.

11. EO 9686, 11 FR 1033 (Jan. 26, 1946). See also 60 Stat. 207 (1946); "Letter to Wilson Wyatt Appointing Him Housing Expediter," 1945 Pub. Papers 539 (Dec. 12, 1945).

12. "U.S. Czar Named for Meat Plants," *Los Angeles Times*, Jan. 25, 1946, 1; George Hartman, "Steel Strike Is Cause; Meat Seizure Ordered," *Chicago Daily Tribune*, Jan. 25, 1946, 1; "Plant Seizure Is 'Double-Cross' by Truman, Claim," *The Citizen-Advertiser* (Auburn, NY), Jan. 26, 1946, 1; "Top Men: Unionist Clark, Armstrong the Rancher," *Milwaukee Journal*, Jan. 26, 1946, 1.

13. Agriculture Secretary appointed.

14. "Designation of Government Representative and Delegation of Authority with Respect to Possession and Operation of Plants and Facilities," 11 FR 1003 (Jan. 25, 1946). Regulation based on President Truman's Executive Order 9685, "Authorizing the Secretary of Agriculture to Take Possession of and Operate Certain Plants and Facilities Used in the Production, Processing, Transportation, Sale and Distribution of Livestock, Meat, Meat Products and By-Products," 11 FR 989 (Jan. 24, 1946).

15. "Truman Appoints U.S. Project Czar," *Los Angeles Times*, July 15, 1949, 1; "Washington Calling," *Pittsburg Press*, July 17, 1949, 1.

16. 53 Stat. 561 (1939). See "Memorandum to Agency Heads on the Channeling of Federal Procurement, Etc., Programs to Areas of Economic Distress," 1949 Pub. Papers 380–381 (July 14, 1949).

17. Preparedness Investigating Subcommittee of the Senate Armed Services Committee, "Inquiry into Satellite and Missile Programs," 85th Cong., 1st and 2nd sess., Nov. 25, 26, 27, Dec. 13, 14, 16, and 17, 1957, Jan. 10, 13, 15, 16, 17, 20, 21, and 23, 1958, Part 1, 302; James M. Gavin, "The Tragic Mistakes and Bickering That Undermine Preparedness," *Life*, Aug. 4, 1958, 78; Peter Galison and Bruce William Hevly, *Big Science: The Growth of Large-Scale Research* (Stanford, CA: Stanford University Press, 1992), 321; Stephen I. Schwartz, *Atomic Audit: The Costs and Consequences of U.S. Nuclear Weapons since 1940* (Washington, DC: Brookings Institution Press, 1998), 128.

18. Defense secretary appointed.

19. The law authorized the secretary of defense "to appoint and fix the compensation of such civilian personnel as may be necessary for the performance of the functions of the Department of Defense other than those of the Departments of the Army, Navy, and Air Force." 63 Stat. 578, 581 (1949).

20. "White House Statement Concerning a Meeting with the Congressional Leaders to

Discuss the National Emergency," Dec. 13, 1950, in 1950 Pub. Papers 744; Jerry Kluttz, "The Federal Diary," *Washington Post*, Jan. 3, 1951, B1; Jerry Kluttz, "The Federal Diary," *Washington Post*, Jan. 5, 1951, B1; "Wilson Tells Plans," *Wall Street Journal*, Feb. 9, 1951, 5.

21. EO 10193, 15 FR 9031 (Dec. 16, 1950).

22. "Crisis in Steel," *New York Times*, April 6, 1952, E1.

23. Anthony Leviero, "'Czar' Appointed to Speed Output in Missiles Race," *New York Times*, March 28, 1956, 1; Drew Pearson, "New Missile Czar Figured in Quiz," *Washington Post*, April 2, 1956, 35; Marquis Childs, "New Missile 'Czar' Faces Rough Task," *Washington Post*, April 3, 1956, 20.

24. Defense secretary appointed.

25. 64 Stat. 1223, 1235 (1951).

26. "New Czar for Missiles," *New York Times*, May 14, 1957, 16; "Rocket Adviser Holaday Shuns Role of 'Czar,'" *Los Angeles Times*, Jan. 1, 1958, 25; Drew Pearson, "Holaday to Quit as Missile Czar," *Washington Post*, Jan. 9, 1958, B11.

27. DoD Directive 5105.10, Nov. 15, 1957, reproduced in Preparedness Investigating Subcommittee of the Senate Armed Services Committee, "Inquiry into Satellite and Missile Programs," 85th Cong., 1st and 2nd sess., Nov. 25, 26, 27, Dec. 13, 14, 16, and 17, 1957, Jan. 10, 13, 15, 16, 17, 20, 21, and 23, 1958, Part 1, 451–452.

28. Don Shannon, "U.S. Missile Czar Appointed by Ike," *Los Angeles Times*, Nov. 8, 1957, 1; "Missile Czar Pledges Fast Mobilization," *Los Angeles Times*, Nov. 8, 1957, 1; Walter Trohan, "Ike's Program for U.S.," *Chicago Daily Tribune*, Nov. 8, 1957, 1; "Budget Power Proposed for Missile Czar," *Chicago Daily Tribune*, Dec. 1, 1957, 5.

29. 62 Stat. 672 (1948); 3 U.S.C. § 106 (1952). See also "Radio and Television Address to the American People on Science in National Security," 1957 Pub. Papers 796 (Nov. 7, 1957); "Special Message to the Congress Transmitting Reorganization Plan 2 of 1962," 1962 Pub. Papers 280 (March 29, 1962).

30. Robert Hartmann, "Air Force May Handle Man-in-Space Flight," *Los Angeles Times*, Feb. 8, 1958, 1; Bem Price, "U.S. Space 'Czar' Little Known in Washington," *Los Angeles Times*, Aug. 3, 1958, 26; Jack Anderson, "Too Many Czars in Space Work," *Washington Post*, Jan. 3, 1959, D7.

31. Defense secretary appointed.

32. DoD Directive 5105.15, Feb. 7, 1958, http://www.darpa.mil/Docs/DARPA_Original _Directive_1958_200807180942212.pdf. See also 72 Stat. 11, 13–14 (1958).

33. John Lear, "Kennedy Aide Ties Science to Arms Curb," *Washington Post*, March 5, 1961, E7; Robert C. Toth, "Adviser to President Called 'Science Czar,'" *Los Angeles Times*, Nov. 20, 1963, 6; "Science Chief for Kennedy Assails Critics," *Los Angeles Times*, Nov. 22, 1963, 3.

34. 62 Stat. 672 (1948); 3 U.S.C. § 106 (1958). See also "Radio and Television Address to the American People on Science in National Security," 1957 Pub. Papers 796 (Nov. 7, 1957); "Special Message to the Congress Transmitting Reorganization Plan 2 of 1962," 1962 Pub. Papers 280 (March 29, 1962).

35. "No 'Czar' Landis Says," *New York Times*, Feb. 1, 1961, 28; "'Courage, Imagination' Urged by Landis for Agency Members," *Washington Post*, Feb. 1, 1961, A7; "Kenney Lauds Ad Men's Drive to Explain Their Economic Role," *New York Times*, Feb. 2, 1961, 37.

36. 62 Stat. 672 (1948); 3 U.S.C. § 106 (1958).

37. 1962 Pub. Papers 827 (Nov. 15, 1962); "Name Herter U.S. Trade Czar," *Chicago Daily Tribune*, Nov. 16, 1962, 6; "Herter Picked by Kennedy for Foreign Trade Post," *Wall Street Journal*, Nov. 16, 1962, 3.

38. 76 Stat. 872, 878 (1962).

39. Philip Potter, "Johnson, Erhard Will Seek to Improve East-West Ties," *The Sun* (Baltimore, MD), Dec. 28, 1963, 1; Henry Gemmill, "Inflation Eats Away at Brazil's Economy, Undermines Other Latin American Lands," *Wall Street Journal*, Jan. 16, 1964, 8; Rowland Evans and Robert Novak, "Washington Sharpens Its Knives for Mann," *Los Angeles Times*, April 3, 1964, A5.

40. The State Department first created the "Assistant Secretary of State for American Republic Affairs" in 1944 and renamed it the "Assistant Secretary for Inter-American Affairs" on Oct. 3, 1949. See the history for "Assistant Secretaries of State for Western Hemisphere Affairs" at the U.S. Department of State, Office of the Historian website, http://history.state.gov/departmenthistory/people/principalofficers/assistant-secretary-for-western-hemisphere. The Secretary of State has general authority to "prescribe duties for the Assistant Secretaries and the clerks of bureaus, as well as for all the other employees in the department" under 22 U.S.C. § 2664 (2006); 18 Stat. 85, 90 (1874).

41. Jack Anderson, "The Washington Merry-Go-Round," *Washington Post*, March 9, 1964, B23; Drew Pearson, "The Major 'Meets' the Senator," *Los Angeles Times*, March 9, 1964; Jack Anderson, "Viet War Follows Mao's Pattern," *Washington Post*, March 12, 1964, D15.

42. 62 Stat. 672 (1948); 3 U.S.C. § 106 (1964).

43. "Remarks at the Swearing In of Sargent Shriver as Director, Office of Economic Opportunity," 1963–1964 Pub. Papers 1360 (Oct. 16, 1964); Jerry Doolittle, "Scrabble Replaces Low Numbers Game," *Washington Post*, Jan. 13, 1964, B1; Charles Mohr, "Shriver Confers on Poverty Here," *New York Times*, April 1, 1964, 17; Robert S. Allen and Paul Scott, "'Poverty Czar' Power to Be Issue," *Los Angeles Times*, July 7, 1964, A5.

44. 62 Stat. 672 (1948); 3 U.S.C. § 106 (1964).

45. 78 Stat. 508 (1964).

46. Not an official title. Johnson never provided a title for Humphrey when delegating civil rights authority to his vice president.

47. Timothy Nel Thurber, *The Politics of Equality: Hubert H. Humphrey and the African American Freedom Struggle* (New York: Columbia University Press, 1999), 171; "Johnson Names Humphrey as 'Czar' of Civil Rights," *Wall Street Journal*, Dec. 11, 1964, 5.

48. In Sept. 1965, Johnson confirmed that the responsibilities for civil rights enforcement and coordination belong to the DOJ and other departments and agencies. See EO 11246, 30 FR 12319 (Sept. 24, 1965).

49. Presidential designation.

50. Harold C. Fleming and Virginia Fleming, *The Potomac Chronicle: Public Policy and Civil Rights from Kennedy to Reagan* (Athens: University of Georgia Press, 2010), 130–131; Thurber, *Politics of Equality*, 171.

51. Abolished by EO 11247, 30 FR 12327 (Sept. 24, 1965).

52. EO 11197, 30 FR 1721 (Feb. 5, 1965).

Table 6

1. Not an official title. Like Roosevelt, Truman never provided a title for the delegation of authority.

2. Anderson served as Agriculture Secretary during this time.

3. Presidential designation.

4. EO 9577, 10 FR 8087 (July 3, 1945).

5. 53 Stat. 561 (1939); 3 U.S.C. § 45a (1940).

6. Abolished by EO 9809, 11 FR 14281 (Dec. 12, 1946).

7. EO 9638, 10 FR 12591 (Oct. 4, 1945).

8. The position ceased to be a czar when Congress statutorily established it by passing the Veterans Emergency Housing Act of 1946. See 60 Stat. 207 (1946).

9. EO 9686, 11 FR 1033 (Jan. 26, 1946). See also Veterans Emergency Housing Act of 1946, 60 Stat. 207 (1946); "Letter to Wilson Wyatt Appointing Him Housing Expediter," 1945 Pub. Papers 539 (Dec. 12, 1945).

10. Abolished by EO 9744, 11 FR 7255 (June 27, 1946).

11. EO 9674, 11 FR 333 (Jan. 4, 1946).

12. The Jan. 22, 1946, Directive is reprinted in William M. Leary, ed., *The Central Intelligence Agency: History and Documents* (Birmingham: University of Alabama Press, 1984), 126–127.

13. The agency director ceased to be a czar once the National Security Act of 1947 became law. See 61 Stat. 495 (1947).

14. Abolished by EO 10254, 16 FR 5829 (June 15, 1951). Congress specified that the agency "shall cease to exist after June 30, 1951." See 64 Stat. 699 (1950).

15. EO 9789, 11 FR 11981 (Oct. 14, 1946).

16. On Jan. 12, 1951, Congress provided statutory backing to the FCDA and its administrator when Truman signed the Federal Civil Defense Act of 1950 into law. As a result, the FCDA administrator needed to be confirmed by the Senate. See 64 Stat. 1245 (1951).

17. EO 10186, 15 FR 8557 (Dec. 1, 1950).

18. The director position would revert back to special assistant status by order of the Defense secretary on April 8, 1959. See 105 Cong. Rec. 17277 (Aug. 28, 1959).

19. Defense secretary appointed.

20. DoD Directive 5105.10, Nov. 15, 1957, reproduced in Preparedness Investigating Subcommittee of the Senate Armed Services Committee, "Inquiry into Satellite and Missile Programs," 85th Cong., 1st and 2nd sess., Nov. 25, 26, 27, Dec. 13, 14, 16, and 17, 1957, Jan. 10, 13, 15, 16, 17, 20, 21, and 23, 1958, Part 1, 451–452.

21. Defense secretary appointed.

22. DOD Directive 5105.15, Feb. 7, 1958, http://www.darpa.mil/Docs/DARPA_Original_Directive_1958_200807180942212.pdf. See also 72 Stat. 11, 13–14 (1958).

23. 62 Stat. 672 (1948); 3 U.S.C. § 106 (1964).

24. Anderson was a sitting senator from New Mexico.

25. Presidential designation.

26. EO 11150, 29 FR 4789 (April 2, 1964).

27. Ink was the Assistant General Manager of the Atomic Energy Commission.

28. EO 11150, 29 FR 4789 (April 2, 1964).

29. Not an official title. Johnson never provided a title for Humphrey when delegating civil rights authority to his vice president.

30. Timothy Nel Thurber, *The Politics of Equality: Hubert H. Humphrey and the African American Freedom Struggle* (New York: Columbia University Press, 1999), 171; "Johnson Names Humphrey as 'Czar' of Civil Rights," *Wall Street Journal*, Dec. 11, 1964, 5.

31. In Sept. 1965, Johnson confirmed that the responsibilities for civil rights enforcement and coordination belong to the DOJ and other departments and agencies. See EO 11246, 30 FR 12319 (Sept. 24, 1965).

32. Presidential designation.

33. Abolished by EO 11247, 30 FR 12327 (Sept. 24, 1965).

34. EO 11197, 30 FR 1721 (Feb. 5, 1965).

Table 7

1. R. W. Apple Jr., "Nixon's Soft Voice," *New York Times*, Nov. 26, 1968, 35; "Information Post Draws Criticism," *St. Petersburg Independent*, Nov. 28, 1968, 14A; "Rep. Moss Assails Klein's New Post," *New York Times*, Nov. 29, 1968, 58; Jack Anderson, "Ad Men Polishing President's Image," *Washington Post*, Dec. 1, 1969, B11.

2. 62 Stat. 672 (1948); 3 U.S.C. § 106 (1964).

3. Dana Adams Schmidt, "New Drug Abuse Chief Is Told He Doesn't Have Enough Power," *New York Times*, June 29, 1971, 14; M. A. Farber, "Veterans Still Fight Vietnam Drug Habits," *New York Times*, June 2, 1974, 1.

4. EO 11599, 35 FR 11793 (June 17, 1971).

5. 86 Stat. 65, 85 (1972).

6. George W. Liebmann, *The Gallows in the Grove: Civil Society in American Law* (Westport, CT: Praeger, 1997), 217; M. A. Farber, "Veterans Still Fight Vietnam Drug Habits," *New York Times*, June 2, 1974, 1.

7. HEW Secretary appoints.

8. 86 Stat. 65, 85 (1972).

9. Louis Dombrowski, "Stans First to Opt for Controls," *Chicago Tribune*, Aug. 27, 1971, C7; Murray Seeger, "Connally, a Texas Democrat, Now President's Strongman," *Los Angeles Times*, Oct. 10, 1971, 1.

10. Presidential designation.

11. EO 11615, 36 FR 15727 (Aug. 15, 1971).

12. Victor Riesel, "Inside Labor: No-Nonsense Judge Heads New Pay Board," *Beaver County Times*, Nov. 9, 1971, A6; Victor Riesel, "Nixon-Meany Cold War Rises to White Heat," *The Portsmouth Times*, Nov. 13, 1971, 6; Paul Scott, "Price Commission Chairman Is Powerful," *Lewiston Daily Sun*, Dec. 6, 1971, 3.

13. Abolished by EO 11695, 38 FR 1473 (Jan. 11, 1973).

14. EO 11627, 35 FR 11627 (Oct. 15, 1971).

15. 1971 Pub. Papers 1026 (Oct. 7, 1971); Philip Shabecoff, "Senate Panel Approves Boldt and Grayson as Pay and Price Chiefs," *New York Times*, Jan. 28, 1972, 15; Ronald L. Soble, "Ex-Price Czar Warns Nation May Soon Return to Controls," *Los Angeles Times*, Oct. 24, 1974, F13.

16. EO 11627, 35 FR 11627 (Oct. 15, 1971).

17. "Energy 'Czar' Choice," *New York Times*, June 23, 1973, 1; "Nixon Appoints Gov. Love as 'Energy Czar,'" *Los Angeles Times*, June 29, 1973, 2; Carroll Kilpatrick, "Gov. Love Is Named U.S. Energy Czar," *Washington Post*, June 30, 1973, A1.

18. EO 11726, 38 FR 17711 (June 29, 1973).

19. "Remarks Announcing Establishment of the Federal Energy Office," Dec. 4, 1973, in 1973 Pub. Papers 990; Edwin L. Dale Jr., "William Simon: The First Real Energy Czar," *New York Times*, Dec. 9, 1973, 26; "Changing of the Czars," *Wall Street Journal*, Dec. 4, 1973, 26; Hobart Rowen, "The Future of the Energy Czar," *Washington Post*, Feb. 14, 1974, A23; "Nixon picks Wall Street millionaire as power czar," *Chicago Tribune*, Dec. 5, 1973, B13.

20. EO 11748, 38 FR 33575 (Dec. 4, 1973).

21. Rowland Evans and Robert Novak, "Energy Czar Sawhill's Common Cause," *Washington Post*, April 28, 1974, C7; "Fuel for a Trip to Absurdity," *Los Angeles Times*, Aug. 28, 1974, C6; Leonard F. Perkins, "Favors Higher Gas Tax," *Chicago Tribune*, Sept. 19, 1974, A2; "Energy Czar Denies Pressure to Resign," *Los Angeles Times*, Oct. 22, 1974, 2.

22. 88 Stat. 96, 97 (1974).

23. Linda Charlton, "Nixon Designates Shultz to Guide Economic Policy," *New York Times*,

Dec. 2, 1972, 1; Courtney R. Sheldon, "Shultz: The Money Czar in New Nixon Cabinet," *Christian Science Monitor*, Dec. 2, 1972, 1; Tom Wicker, "Shultz: Cabinet's New Czar," *Palm Beach Post*, Dec. 5, 1972, A10; Rowland Evans and Robert Novak, "From George Shultz, a Whiff of Protectionism," *Washington Post*, Feb. 11, 1973, D7.

24. Shultz served as secretary of treasury during this time.

25. 62 Stat. 672 (1948); 3 U.S.C. § 106 (1970). See also 1972 Pub. Papers Appendix E-5 (Dec. 1, 1972).

26. Bill Anderson, "Demand for Economic Czar Rises," *Chicago Tribune*, May 23, 1974, 18; Bill Neikirk, "Rush Is Likely Economy Czar Choice," *Chicago Tribune*, May 24, 1974, 7; Hobart Rowen, "Rush Chosen as Coordinator of Nixon Economic Advisers," *Washington Post*, May 25, 1974, A1.

27. 62 Stat. 672 (1948); 3 U.S.C. § 106 (1970). See also 1974 (Book I) Pub. Papers 462 (May 29, 1974).

28. George W. Liebmann, *The Gallows in the Grove: Civil Society in American Law* (Westport, CT: Praeger, 1997), 217; M. A. Farber, "Veterans Still Fight Vietnam Drug Habits," *New York Times*, June 2, 1974, 1.

29. 86 Stat. 65, 85 (1972).

30. Rowland Evans and Robert Novak, "Energy Czar Sawhill's Common Cause," *Washington Post*, April 28, 1974, C7; "Fuel for a Trip to Absurdity," *Los Angeles Times*, Aug. 28, 1974, C6; Leonard F. Perkins, "Favors Higher Gas Tax," *Chicago Tribune*, Sept. 19, 1974, A2; "Energy Czar Denies Pressure to Resign," *Los Angeles Times*, Oct. 22, 1974, 2.

31. 88 Stat. 96, 97 (1974).

32. Rowland Evans and Robert Novak, "Ford's Energy Showdown," *Washington Post*, June 29, 1975, C7; Rowland Evans and Robert Novak, "Zarb Makes His Mark on the Hill," *Washington Post*, April 12, 1975, A11; Jack Anderson and Les Whitten, "Zarb Weighs Bid to Break Up Big Oil," *Washington Post*, Dec. 2, 1975, D14.

33. 1974 (Book II) Pub. Papers 286–287 (Oct. 11, 1974); 1974 (Book II) Pub. Papers 245, 248 (Oct. 9, 1974).

34. Rowland Evans and Robert Novak, "Confusion on the New Energy Council," *Washington Post*, Nov. 2, 1974, A15; George C. Wilson, "Public-Interest Groups Criticize Energy Team," *Washington Post*, Nov. 5, 1974, A3; Casey Bukro, "Morton Predicts Economic Upturn," *Chicago Tribune*, Feb. 6, 1975, 7.

35. During this time Morton was the interior secretary. Act establishing Interior Department, see 9 Stat. 395 (1849).

36. Presidential designation.

37. 88 Stat. 1233 (1974). See also EO 11814, 39 FR 36955 (Oct. 16, 1974). Act establishing Interior Department, see 9 Stat. 395 (1849).

38. "Carter Drug Unit Nominee Opposed," *Washington Post*, March 2, 1977, A9; Alexander Cockburn and James Ridgeway, "Bourne: Is the Case Closed?" *Village Voice*, Aug. 21, 1978, 15.

39. Office abolished.

40. 90 Stat. 241, 242 (1976).

41. Thomas O'Toole, "A Man without Airs," *Washington Post,* Dec. 24, 1976, A7; "Energy Czar," *Los Angeles Times*, May 26, 1979, A1; "Cabinet Members' Resignations and Carter's Replies," *New York Times*, July 21, 1979, 8.

42. 91 Stat. 565 (1977).

43. Stephen E. Nordlinger, "Shift from Schlesinger to Duncan Puts a Businessman at Energy Helm," *The Sun* (Baltimore, MD), July 21, 1979, A5; Richard Halloran, "Carter's Choice for

Energy Czar," *New York Times*, July 29, 1979, F1; Rowland Evans and Robert Novak, "Jordan Purges Tito Funeral List," *The Victoria Advocate* (Victoria, TX), May 11, 1980, 3.

44. Art Pine and James L. Rowe Jr., "Strauss Urges 'Toughest' Program on Wages, Prices," *Washington Post*, Sept. 20, 1978, A2; Rowland Evans and Robert Novak, "The Anti-Inflation 'Czar,'" *Washington Post*, April 14, 1978, A17; Hobart Rowen and Art Pine, "Strauss Dons Inflation Warrior's Helmet," *Washington Post*, April 15, 1978, A8.

45. 88 Stat. 1978, 1999 (1975).

46. 92 Stat. 2445 (1978).

47. Bill Neikirk, "Carter Names Kahn as His New Price Czar," *Chicago Tribune*, Oct. 26, 1978, 1; James L. Rowe Jr., "Kahn to Roam throughout the Economy," *Washington Post*, Nov. 10, 1978, D1; "Inflation Czar? Kahn's Powers Are a Bit Less Than Royal," *Milwaukee Journal*, Nov. 13, 1978, 10; Carole Shifrin, "Kahn: He's the Top Banana in Administration," *Washington Post*, Dec. 6, 1978, E5.

48. 88 Stat. 750 (1974).

49. 92 Stat. 2445 (1978).

Table 8

1. 84 Stat. 2085 (1970).

2. On March 2, 1974, Congress required Senate confirmation for the OMB director. See 88 Stat. 11.

3. The position ceased to be a czar when Congress passed the Drug Abuse Treatment Act of 1972. See 86 Stat. 65, 85 (1972).

4. EO 11599, 35 FR 11793 (June 17, 1971).

5. Served as secretary of treasury at the time.

6. Presidential designation.

7. EO 11615, 36 FR 15727 (Aug. 15, 1971).

8. Served as secretary of treasury at the time.

9. EO 11615, 36 FR 15727 (Aug. 15, 1971).

10. Abolished by EO 11788, 39 FR 22113 (June 18, 1974).

11. Abolished by EO 11695, 38 FR 1473 (Jan. 11, 1973).

12. EO 11627, 35 FR 11627 (Oct. 15, 1971).

13. Abolished by EO 11695, 38 FR 1473 (Jan. 11, 1973).

14. EO 11627, 35 FR 11627 (Oct. 15, 1971).

15. Shultz served as secretary of treasury during this time.

16. 62 Stat. 672 (1948); 3 U.S.C. § 106 (1970). See also 1972 Pub. Papers Appendix E-5 (Dec. 1, 1972).

17. Butz served as secretary of agriculture during this time.

18. 62 Stat. 672 (1948); 3 U.S.C. § 106 (1970). See also 1973 Pub. Papers 2, 4 (Jan. 5, 1973).

19. Weinberger served as secretary of health, education, and welfare during this time.

20. 62 Stat. 672 (1948); 3 U.S.C. § 106 (1970). See also 1973 Pub. Papers 2, 4 (Jan. 5, 1973).

21. Lynn served as secretary of housing and urban development during this time.

22. 62 Stat. 672 (1948); 3 U.S.C. § 106 (1970). See also 1973 Pub. Papers 2, 4 (Jan. 5, 1973).

23. EO 11726, 38 FR 17711 (June 29, 1973).

24. EO 11748, 38 FR 33575 (Dec. 4, 1973).

25. 62 Stat. 672 (1948); 3 U.S.C. § 106 (1970). See also 1974 (Book I) Pub. Papers 462 (May 29, 1974).

Table 9

1. 1981 Pub. Papers 386–387 (April 27, 1981); Robert D. Hershey Jr., "The Czar in Charge of Nuclear Arms," *New York Times*, Dec. 12, 1981, 20.

2. 91 Stat. 565, 570 (1977).

3. 1984 (Book I) Pub. Papers 558 (April 18, 1984); Michael Weisskopf, "Defense 'Procurement Czar' Named," *Washington Post*, July 6, 1985, A7; Michael Weisskopf, "At Work: Pentagon's New Troubleshooter," *Washington Post*, July 16, 1985, A13; Michael Weisskopf, "'Procurement Czar' Loses Mandate," *Washington Post*, Dec. 6, 1985, A8.

4. 97 Stat. 614, 686 (1983).

5. Marjorie Williams, "Insult and Injury as 'Weapons Czar' Assumes New Post," *Washington Post*, Oct. 6, 1986, A13; Clarence A. Robinson Jr., "Will the Bloated B-1B Be a Drag on the Stealth Bomber?" *Los Angeles Times*, Dec. 1, 1986, B5; John H. Cushman Jr., "Pentagon Tightens Its Buying Rules," *New York Times*, Dec. 28, 1986, E4.

6. 100 Stat. 1783-130 (1986).

7. Tim Carrington, "Meanwhile, Back at the Pentagon, Nominee to Top Weapons Job Sets Sights," *Wall Street Journal*, Sept. 25, 1987, 31; John H. Cushman Jr., "Pentagon Nominee Stresses Efficiency," *New York Times*, Sept. 28, 1987, D2; Malcolm Gladwell, "Are Defense Contracts Worth Cheating For?" *Washington Post*, July 10, 1988, 21; "The New Regime," *Washington Post*, June 19, 1989, A7.

8. Joel Glenn Brenner, "Ford Motor Executive Seen as Favorite for Defense Job," *Washington Post*, June 24, 1989, C1; Steven Pearlstein, "Incoming at Pentagon: A 'Czar,'" *Washington Post*, May 22, 1991, A19.

9. 100 Stat. 1783-130 (1986).

10. "Yockey to Act as USD/A until Replacement Confirmed," *Defense News*, Dec. 14, 1990, 1; Steven Pearlstein, "Incoming at Pentagon: A 'Czar,'" *Washington Post*, May 22, 1991, A19; "The Contest for the 2nd Seawolf," *Daily Press* (Newport News, VA), June 23, 1991, A4.

11. 1989 (Book I) Pub. Papers 224 (March 13, 1989); Philip Shenon, "Nominee for 'Drug Czar' Has Tough-Talking Past," *New York Times*, Jan. 13, 1989, D17; Michael Isikoff, "'Drug Czar' Won't Be a Cabinet Member," *Washington Post*, Jan. 25, 1989, A19.

12. 102 Stat. 4181 (1988).

13. 1991 (Book I) Pub. Papers 315 (March 28, 1991); Paul M. Barrett, "Bob Martinez, Bush's Proposed New Drug Czar, Is Criticized as Lacking Some Key Qualifications," *Wall Street Journal*, Feb. 25, 1991, A10; Bill McAllister, "Questions for Drug Policy Nominee," *Washington Post*, Feb. 27, 1991, A23.

14. "Ryan in Wings as Savings & Loan," *Los Angeles Times*, March 9, 1990, D2; "Thrift Czar Earns Respect after Rocky Start," *Pittsburgh Post-Gazette*, July 8, 1991, B6; Tim W. Ferguson, "Hopes Born in Korea Snag on U.S. Thrift Law," *Wall Street Journal*, Oct. 27, 1992, A17.

15. 103 Stat. 183, 278 (1989).

16. Otto Kreisher, "Company Anxious about C-17 Fate Stakes Are High for McDonnell Douglas," *San Diego Union-Tribune*, Aug. 5, 1993, C1; Laurel Kenner, "Air Force Secretary Has 'Different Sensitivities,'" *Daily Breeze* (Torrance, CA), Aug. 27, 1993, A1; Tim Weiner, "Man in the News: John Mark Deutch; Reluctant Helmsman for a Troubled Agency," *New York Times*, March 11, 1995, A8; John J. Fialka, "Pentagon Helps Contractors Pay Merger Costs with a Plan Opponents Call 'Payoffs for Layoffs,'" *Wall Street Journal*, July 22, 1996, A16.

17. 100 Stat. 1783-130 (1986).

18. Eric Schmitt, "Pentagon Divided by Radar Jammer," *New York Times*, July 6, 1995, A1; "DOD Approves Production of Longbow Apache Attack Helicopter," *Defense Daily*, Oct. 16,

1995, 1; Thomas E. Ricks, "Deal Would Test Pentagon Policies about Competition," *Wall Street Journal*, Dec. 17, 1996, A3; Tim Smart, "Fighting for Foreign Sales," *Washington Post*, Feb. 17, 1999, E1.

19. 107 Stat. 1547, 1728 (1993).

20. Sheila Foote, "After Delay, Panel Approves Gansler Nomination for Buying," *Defense Daily*, Oct. 31, 1997, 1; Anne Marie Squeo and Thomas E. Ricks, "Pentagon Seeks to Manage Competition," *Wall Street Journal*, Nov. 30, 1999, A3; "World-Wide," *Wall Street Journal*, Nov. 30, 1999, A1.

21. Joseph B. Treaster, "Ex-Commissioner of New York Named Drug 'Czar,'" *New York Times*, April 28, 1993, A15; Whitman Knapp, "Dethrone the Drug Czar," *New York Times*, May 9, 1993, E15; "Lee Brown Becomes Drug Czar," *New York Times*, July 2, 1993, A11.

22. 102 Stat. 4181 (1988).

23. 1997 (Book I) Pub. Papers 397 (April 7, 1997); Christopher S. Wren, "New Drug Czar Is Seeking Ways to Bolster His Hand," *New York Times*, March 17, 1996, 18; Christopher S. Wren, "Scouting Trip Brings Drug Czar No Easy Answers," *New York Times*, April 29, 1996, A18.

24. Samuel Francis, "The Radical Ambitions of Our New Housing Czar," *Washington Times*, March 1, 1994, A17; Eric Siegel and JoAnna Daemmrich, "Schmoke Stands behind Henson, Despite HUD Audit," *The Sun* (Baltimore, MD), Sept. 23, 1994, B1; Jeff Dickerson, "Why Rebuild a Center for Crime and Poverty?" *Atlanta Journal-Constitution*, June 4, 1996, A8.

25. 79 Stat. 667 (1965).

26. Spencer Rich, "Clinton Names Health Ex-Official First AIDS Policy Coordinator," *Washington Post*, June 26, 1993, A2; Christopher H. Foreman Jr., "What the AIDS Czar Can't Do," *New York Times*, July 14, 1993, A19.

27. See statements made discussing the office, 1993 (Book I) Pub. Papers 932 (June 25, 1993); 1993 (Book II) Pub. Papers 1641 (Sept. 30, 1993).

28. "Remarks on the Appointment of Patsy Fleming as National AIDS Policy Director and an Exchange with Reporters," 1994 (Book II) Pub. Papers 2060–2062 (Nov. 10, 1994); Joyce Price, "New AIDS Czar Claims Power to Achieve Results," *Washington Times*, Nov. 11, 1994, A4; "Clinton Appoints New AIDS Czar," *San Francisco Chronicle*, Nov. 11, 1994, A3.

29. 1997 (Book I) Pub. Papers 397 (April 7, 1997); Paul Bedard, "Clinton to Name New Czar for AIDS," *Washington Times*, April 7, 1997, A1; Susan Okie, "AIDS Policy Director Puts Stress on Science," *Washington Post*, April 22, 1997, A17.

30. Martha Sherrill, "The Health Czar, at Her Other Job," *Washington Post*, Jan. 27, 1993, D1; Grady Sandy, "A Cure for America's Hillary Jitters," *Atlanta Journal-Constitution*, Jan. 27, 1993, A11; Abigail Traford, "Public Perceptions and Expert Opinions," *Washington Post*, Feb. 16, 1993, Z6; Maureen Dowd, "Hillary Clinton Says She Once Tried to Be Marine," *New York Times*, June 15, 1994, B8.

31. Presidential designation.

32. Statement made by the president can be found at 1993 (Book I) Pub. Papers 13 (Jan. 25, 1993).

33. Blair S. Walker, "Healthcare Compare Loses Favor," *USA Today*, April 1, 1993, B3; Michael K. Frisby, "Dueling Initiatives: NAFTA vs. Health Care," *Wall Street Journal*, Sept. 3, 1993, A10; Carolyn Lochhead, "Health Czar Sees Plan's 'Land Mines,'" *San Francisco Chronicle*, Dec. 14, 1993, A6; Editorial, "Slouching toward Ira," *Wall Street Journal*, May 22, 1996, A22; Tony Snow, "Clinton's 'Kids First' Hatched 4 Years Ago," *USA Today*, March 5, 1997, A13.

34. 92 Stat. 2445 (1978); 3 U.S.C. § 105 (1988).

35. Lisa Hoffman, "Clinton Passes over Celeste for Health Care Reform Czar," *Cincinnati*

Post, Dec. 23, 1993, 5A; Robin Toner, "Washington at Work New Health Care Czar Preparing for Long Leap," *New York Times*, Jan. 24, 1994, A12; "Health Czar's Mission," *New York Times*, Jan. 24, 1994, A1; Mike Royko, "Health Czar Doesn't Need to Know Health Care," *The Sun* (Baltimore, MD), Jan. 28, 1994, 2A; "Ickes Enters Legislative Fray," *Rocky Mountain News* (CO), June 12, 1994, 85A.

36. 92 Stat. 2445 (1978); 3 U.S.C. § 105 (1988).

37. 34 Weekly Comp. Docs. 2391 (Nov. 30, 1998); Thomas W. Haines, "Magaziner Sees Net Revolution," *Seattle Times*, Oct. 17, 1997, E1; Eric Sorensen, "Forum Focuses on Net Regulation," *Seattle Times*, Jan. 8, 1998, A8; Max Schulz, "Coveted Internet Cash Cow," *Washington Times*, Jan. 30, 1998, A19; Jon Swartz, "A Web of Conspiracy Theories," *San Francisco Chronicle*, Nov. 16, 1998, B1.

38. 92 Stat. 2445 (1978); 3 U.S.C. § 105 (1994).

39. Valerie Alvord, "Bersin Is Expected to Become 'Border Czar,'" *San Diego Union-Tribune*, Oct. 14, 1995, A19; Anthony Depalma, "Mexico and U.S. to Patrol Border Trouble Spots," *New York Times*, Oct. 27, 1995, A14; Steve Fainaru, "Mexican Drug Lords Thrive at San Diego's Doorstep," *Boston Globe*, Sept. 1, 1996, A1.

40. During this time Bersin was the U.S. attorney for southern California.

41. 28 U.S.C. § 541 (1994); 80 Stat. 378, 617 (1966).

42. Attorney General appointed.

43. Judith Miller and William J. Broad, "Exercise Finds U.S. Unable to Handle Germ War Threat," *New York Times*, April 26, 1998, A1; M. J. Zuckerman, "Anti-Terror 'Czar' to Coordinate $7B Effort," *USA Today*, May 4, 1998, A1; Joseph Perkins, "Feel Like You're Being Watched?" *Washington Times*, Sept. 15, 1999, A18.

44. Bill Clinton, Presidential Decision Directive 63, May 1998, http://clinton2.nara.gov /WH/EOP/NSC/html/documents/NSCDoc3.html.

45. John H. Cushman Jr., "Clinton Hones Sales Pitch on Global Warming Pact," *New York Times*, Oct. 4, 1997, A10.

46. During this time Stern served as the White House Chief Negotiator for the 1997 Kyoto Protocol.

47. 92 Stat. 2445 (1978); 3 U.S.C. § 105 (1988). See also U.S. Government Manual (1995), 92; U.S. Government Manual (1996), 91; U.S. Government Manual (1997), 91.

48. 92 Stat. 2445 (1978); 3 U.S.C. § 105 (1988). See also 1998 (Book I) Pub. Papers 1112 (March 11, 1998); U.S. Government Manual (1998), 91.

49. Matthew L. Wald, "Few Answers on Monster of All Cyberbugs," *New York Times*, March 19, 1998, A19; Jim Landers, "John Koskinen," *Dallas Morning News*, Nov. 29, 1998, J1; Philip Shenon, "Washington's Man in the Middle of Millennium Madness," *New York Times*, Dec. 13, 1999, A16; John Simons, "For Clinton's Y2K, No Bubbly, No Panic Either," *Wall Street Journal*, Dec. 30, 1999, A14; Marc Fisher, "Something to Celebrate: A Return to Normalcy," *Washington Post*, Jan. 2, 2000, A9.

50. EO 13073, 63 FR 6467 (Feb. 4, 1998).

51. 92 Stat. 2445 (1978); 3 U.S.C. § 105 (1994).

52. Jonathan S. Landay, "Senate Oks New Security Chief for Nation's Nuclear Arsenal," *The State* (Columbia, SC), June 15, 2000, A12; John Diamond, "Missing Nuclear Lab Secrets Spark Call to Tighten Classification Rules," *Chicago Tribune*, June 15, 2000, 8; Stacey Zolt, "Energy Pick Is Likely to Be Grilled about Lack of Nuclear Experience," *Albuquerque Tribune*, Jan. 4, 2001, A6.

53. 113 Stat. 953 (1999).

Table 10

1. 92 Stat. 2445 (1978); 3 U.S.C. § 105 (1982).

2. The assistant to the president for national security affairs appointed.

3. 61 Stat. 495, 497 (1947).

4. Council members appointed.

5. 101 Stat. 482 (1987).

6. Quayle served as vice president during this time.

7. Presidential designation.

8. Ede Holiday, Secretary of the Cabinet, "Memorandum for the Cabinet and Agency Heads," June 13, 1990. This memo announced the formal creation of the Council. See Charles Tiefer, *The Semi-Sovereign Presidency: The Bush Administration's Strategy for Governing without Congress* (Boulder, CO: Westview Press, 1994), 66.

9. Council members appointed.

10. 101 Stat. 482 (1987).

11. During this time, Bersin was the U.S. attorney for Southern California.

12. 28 U.S.C. § 541 (1994); 80 Stat. 378, 617 (1966).

13. Attorney general appointed.

14. EO 13073, 63 FR 6467 (Feb. 4, 1998).

15. 92 Stat. 2445 (1978); 3 U.S.C. § 105 (1994).

Table 11

1. Jonathan S. Landay, "Senate Oks New Security Chief for Nation's Nuclear Arsenal," *The State* (Columbia, SC), June 15, 2000, A12; John Diamond, "Missing Nuclear Lab Secrets Spark Call to Tighten Classification Rules," *Chicago Tribune*, June 15, 2000, 8; Stacey Zolt, "Energy Pick Is Likely to Be Grilled about Lack of Nuclear Experience," *Albuquerque Tribune*, Jan. 4, 2001, A6.

2. Position dates to Bill Clinton's administration.

3. 113 Stat. 953 (1999).

4. Keay Davidson, "Nation's Nuclear Lab Chief Loses Job: Linton Brooks Asked to Resign over Security and Management Issues," *San Francisco Chronicle*, Jan. 5, 2007, http://www.sfgate.com/cgi-bin/article.cgi?f=/c/a/2007/01/05/NUKE.TMP.

5. Thomas P. D'Agostino biography, WhoRunsGov website, http://www.whorunsgov.com/index.php?title=Profiles/Thomas_P._D%27Agostino.

6. Bob Deans, "Bush Offers Budget Plan, Steps Up Tax-Cut Crusade," *Atlanta Journal-Constitution*, March 1, 2001, A1; Sue Kirchhoff, "Uphill Battle—US Budget Czar Fighting to Control Spending amid Declining Revenues," *Boston Globe*, May 30, 2002, E1; Bob Deans, "Bush, Congress Brace for $200 Billion Deficit," *Atlanta Journal-Constitution*, Aug. 25, 2002, A5; Craig Linder, "Rocky Relations Mark Daniels' Time," *Post-Tribune* (IN), May 11, 2003, A3.

7. 35 FR 7959; 84 Stat. 2085 (1970). See also 31 U.S.C. § 501 (2006).

8. Editorial, "Act Now to Curb Deficits," *Christian Science Monitor*, Oct. 16, 2003, 10; Bob Deans, "Federal Budget," *Atlanta Journal-Constitution*, Feb. 3, 2004, A4.

9. Jessica Holzer, "Bush Trades Portman for the Budget," Forbes.com, April 18, 2006, http://www.forbes.com/2006/04/18/portman-trade-budget_cx_jh_0418portman.html; Lynn Sweet, "'Reform' Isn't Stopping Earmarks," *Chicago Sun-Times*, July 20, 2006, 31.

10. "Briefs: Sinkhole Fix Ruled Out in Bridge Failure," *Journal Gazette* (Fort Wayne, IN), Sept. 5, 2007, A7; John T. Bennett, "Is DoD Building a Full 2010 Budget?" *Defense News*, June 16, 2008, 4.

11. Craig Welch, "Hanford Bonuses Paid Out Despite Overruns," *Seattle Times* (WA), Sept.

20, 2002, B1; Lisa Stiffler, "Hanford's Unfinished Business," *Seattle Post-Intelligencer*, April 18, 2002, A1.

12. 91 Stat. 565 (1977). In Nov. 1989, the Energy Department created the Office of Environmental Restoration and Waste Management (later renamed the Office of Environmental Management). 54 FR 47259 (Nov. 13, 1989).

13. Annette Cary, "Hanford Cleanup Czar Plans to Visit Tri-Cities," *Tri-City Herald* (Kennewick, WA), Aug. 17, 2006, B1; Rispoli Resigning as DOE Cleanup Czar," *The Energy Daily Network,* Nov. 6, 2008, http://www.theenergydaily.com/hottopics/nuclear_security/Rispoli-Re signing-As-DOE-Cleanup-Czar_1664.html.

14. Eric Pianin and Bradley Graham, "Ridge Is Tapped to Head Homeland Security Office," *Washington Post*, Sept. 21, 2001, A1; Marianne Means, "Homeland Security Czar Needs Practical Power," *Seattle Post-Intelligencer*, Oct. 23, 2001, B4; Alison Mitchell, "A Nation Challenged," *New York Times*, March 5, 2002, C8.

15. EO 13228, 66 FR 51812 (Oct. 8, 2001).

16. 116 Stat. 2135 (2002). See also 6 U.S.C. § 111 (2006).

17. Bob Barr, "Homeland Security Job Just Too Big," *Atlanta Journal-Constitution*, Feb. 22, 2006, A13; Phillip Matier, "Governor's Republican Forgiveness Finds Some Room on the Bench," *San Francisco Chronicle*, Aug. 2, 2006, B1; Editorial, "Immigration, Outsourced," *New York Times*, April 9, 2008, A24.

18. Thomas E. Ricks, "V-22 Osprey to Face 'Make or Break' Tests," *Washington Post*, Dec. 25, 2002, A14; Richard Whittle, "Osprey May Win Its War," *Dallas Morning News*, May 19, 2003, 1D; Bob Cox and Maria Recio, "Pentagon Weapons Chief Reportedly Keeps V-22 Osprey Alive," *Fort Worth Star-Telegram* (TX), May 21, 2003, 1.

19. 107 Stat. 1547, 1728 (1993).

20. Andrew Chuter, "U.S. Logistics Work: Open to Europe's Bids," *Defense News*, Nov. 1, 2004, 3; Andrew Chuter, "Pentagon Scans Market for Logistics Solutions," *Federal Times*, Nov. 8, 2004, 12; Bill Gertz and Rowan Scarborough, "National inside the Ring," *Washington Times*, June 24, 2005, A5.

21. The Senate never confirmed Wynne. He served as "acting" procurement czar for eighteen months.

22. 113 Stat. 512, 717 (1999).

23. Bob Cox, "A Fort Worth Fix," *Fort Worth Star-Telegram* (TX), Sept. 23, 2006, C1; John T. Bennett, "U.S. Acquisition Czar Wants FYDP Overhaul," *Defense News*, April 2, 2007, 6.

24. John T. Bennett and Vago Muradian, "DoD's Next Procurement Chief?" *Defense News*, May 14, 2007, 16; Donna Borak, "Decision Delayed on Future of Raptor," *Daily Press* (Newport News, VA), Feb. 28, 2009, C3.

25. Dick Durbin, "Graham Flunks the Cost-Benefit Test," *Washington Post*, July 16, 2001, A15; Michael Grunwald, "Business Lobbyists Asked to Discuss Onerous Rules," *Washington Post*, Dec. 4, 2001, A3; Henry Miller, "Death by Regulation," *Washington Post*, May 18, 2002, A22.

26. 94 Stat. 2812, 2814 (1980). See also 44 U.S.C. § 3503 (2006).

27. Editorial, "Recess Abuse," *Washington Post*, April 6, 2007, A20.

28. "Remarks Announcing the Nomination of John P. Walters to Be Director of the Office of National Drug Control Policy," May 10, 2001, in 2001 (Book I) Pub. Papers 506; Christopher Marquis, "Tough Conservative Picked for Drug Czar, Officials Say," *New York Times*, April 26, 2001, E20; William J. Bennett, "A Superb Choice for Drug Czar," *Washington Post*, May 7, 2001, A19.

29. 102 Stat. 4181 (1988).

30. Rick Weiss, "Bush Unveils Bioethics Council," *Washington Post*, Jan. 17, 2002, A21; Stephan Herrera, "Profile: Daniel Callahan," *Nature Biotechnology* 22 (Dec. 2004): 1496.

31. EO 13237, 66 FR 59851–59854 (Nov. 28, 2001).

32. At the time Lyon was the Chief of the Child Development and Behavior Branch of the National Institute of Child Health and Human Development at the National Institutes of Health.

33. Charles Ornstein, "Reading Research Gets Respect," *Dallas Morning News*, June 17, 2001, A4; Mary Gail Hare, "'Reading Czar' Has Talk with Educators," *The Sun* (Baltimore, MD), Sept. 17, 2002, B1; Diana Jean Schemo, "Now, the Pressure Begins for Bush's Reading Expert," *New York Times*, Jan. 19, 2002, A14; Steven Goode, "Bush's Reading Czar Visits School," *Hartford Courant* (CT), May 5, 2005, B5.

34. EO 13227, 66 FR 51287 (Oct. 2, 2001). The Commission's archived website can be found at http://www2.ed.gov/inits/commissionsboards/whspecialeducation/index.html.

35. "Statement by the Press Secretary: President to Nominate Director of Office of Science and Technology and Assistant Secretary of Education for Civil Rights," June 25, 2001, http://www.presidency.ucsb.edu/ws/?pid=78934; Glenn Roberts Jr., "Science Czar Brings Lab Good Tidings," *Tri-Valley Herald* (Pleasanton, CA), Feb. 21, 2002, 1.

36. 90 Stat. 459, 463 (1976).

37. Bennett Roth, "Bush's Choice of AIDS Czar Faulted: Evertz First Gay GOP Nominee," *Houston Chronicle*, April 15, 2001, A7; Carolyn Lochhead, "Bush's AIDS Czar Departing for Post with Global Focus," *San Francisco Chronicle*, July 19, 2002, A4.

38. 92 Stat. 2445 (1978); 3 U.S.C. § 105 (2000). See also 1993 (Book I) Pub. Papers 932; 1993 (Book II) Pub. Papers 1641.

39. Lochhead, "Bush's AIDS Czar Departing," A4; Sheryl Gay Stolberg, "White House Aides Confer with 200 Gay Republicans," *New York Times*, May 10, 2003, E16.

40. Matthew Bajko, "Groups Push National AIDS Strategy," *Bay Area Reporter*, Nov. 27, 2008, http://www.ebar.com/news/article.php?sec=news&article=3531.

41. Thompson would be the last occupant of the AIDS office during Bush's presidency.

42. 2001 (Book I) Pub. Papers 26–27; George W. Bush, "Remarks on Signing Executive Orders With Respect to Faith-Based and Community Initiatives," http://www.presidency.ucsb.edu/ws/index.php?pid=45707#axzz1GLKdY61o.

43. EO 13199, 66 FR 8499 (Jan. 29, 2001).

44. Larry Lipman, "Faith-Based Initiatives Czar Has History of Helping," *Palm Beach Post*, Feb. 9, 2002, 4A; Iffat Idris, "Rise of the Christian Right in US Politics," *Pakistan Journal of American Studies* 24 (Spring 2006): 11; Joseph Curl, "Faith-Initiative Chief to Leave Post in June," *Washington Times*, April 19, 2006, A6.

45. "Jay Hein: Deputy Assistant to the President and Director of the Office of Faith-Based and Community Initiatives," http://georgewbush-whitehouse.archives.gov/government/fbci/dir hein.html.

46. Jeff Pillets and Adam Lisberg, "Terrorism Czar's Mandate Unclear," *The Record* (NJ), Oct. 2, 2001, A1; Elisabeth Bumiller, "A Nation Challenged," *New York Times*, Oct. 10, 2001, E6; Ann McFeatters, "Turf Fight Lies Ahead for Ridge," *Pittsburgh Post-Gazette*, Sept. 30, 2001, A18.

47. http://clinton2.nara.gov/WH/EOP/NSC/html/documents/NSCDoc3.html.

48. "New Counter-Terrorism and CyberSpace Security Positions Announced," Oct. 9, 2001, http://georgewbush-whitehouse.archives.gov/news/releases/2001/10/20011009-4.html; Elizabeth Becker, "A Nation Challenged: Homeland Security," *New York Times*, Oct. 1, 2001, A6; Adam Bernstein, "Gen. Wayne Downing: Deputy National Security Adviser," *Washington Post*, July 19,

2007, http://www.washingtonpost.com/wp-dyn/content/article/2007/07/18/AR2007071802679
.html.

49. 92 Stat. 2445 (1978); 3 U.S.C. § 105 (2000). See also "New Counter-Terrorism and Cy-berSpace Security Positions Announced," Oct. 9, 2001, http://georgewbush-whitehouse.archives
.gov/news/releases/2001/10/20011009-4.html.

50. "New Counter-Terrorism and CyberSpace Security Positions Announced," Oct. 9, 2001, http://georgewbush-whitehouse.archives.gov/news/releases/2001/10/20011009-4.html;   Ariana Eunjung Cha, "For Clarke, a Career of Expecting the Worst—Newly Appointed Cyberspace Se-curity Czar Aims to Prevent 'Digital Pearl Harbor,'" *Washington Post*, Nov. 4, 2001, A10; Ross Kerber, "Cyber-Structure Still At Risk—Effort to Prevent 'An Electronic Pearl Harbor' Is Lag-ging," *Boston Globe*, June 25, 2002, D1; Sherwood Boehlert, "An Electronic Maginot Line," *Wash-ington Times*, Dec. 3, 2002, A19.

51. EO 13231, 66 FR 53063 (Oct. 16, 2001).

52. 92 Stat. 2445 (1978); 3 U.S.C. § 105 (2000). See also "New Counter-Terrorism and Cy-berSpace Security Positions Announced," Oct. 9, 2001, http://georgewbush-whitehouse.archives
.gov/news/releases/2001/10/20011009-4.html.

53. "Bush Picks Online Safety Czar," *Press Democrat* (Santa Rose, CA), March 20, 2008, A3; Joseph Menn, "Ex-Cyber Security Czar to Head ICANN," *Financial Times* (UK), June 26, 2009.

54. DHS Secretary appoints. Rod Beckstrom's resignation letter, March 5, 2009 [author's files].

55. Ellen Nakashima, "Bush Order Expands Network Monitoring," *Washington Post*, Jan. 26, 2008; Siobhan Gorman, "Outsider to Run Cyber-Security Initiative," *Wall Street Journal*, March 20, 2008.

56. Kevin Fagan, "Bush's Homeless Czar Is a Man on a Mission," *San Francisco Chronicle*, Jan. 14, 2004, A1; Kevin Fagan, "San Francisco—Newsom Wants Social Workers to Hit Streets—Every Day," *San Francisco Chronicle*, April 9, 2004, B4; Editorial, "Our Opinion: Homeless Find Support on Solid Ground," *Atlanta Journal-Constitution*, Aug. 16, 2004, A10.

57. 101 Stat. 482 (1987).

58. Editorial, "Taking AIDS Seriously," *Washington Post*, Sept. 28, 2003, B6; Thomas H. Maugh II, "AIDS Czar Defends U.S. Steps," *Seattle Times*, July 15, 2004, A10; Sabin Russell, "In-ternational AIDS Conference," *San Francisco Chronicle*, July 15, 2004, A3.

59. 117 Stat. 711, 721 (2003); 22 U.S.C. § 2651a (2006).

60. David Benkof, "Best President on AIDS? W!" *Philadelphia Daily News*, July 9, 2008, 19; Editorial, "A Bad Start on AIDS," *San Francisco Chronicle*, Jan. 30, 2009, B8.

61. 2004 (Book I) Pub. Papers 1172; Molly Ivins, "An Administration of Cronies," *Buffalo News*, Nov. 18, 2005, A13; Erika Lovley, "Czar (n): An Insult, a Problem Solver," *Politico*, Oct. 21, 2008, http://www.politico.com/news/stories/1008/14751.html; Jeremy Scahill, "Germ Boys and Yes Men," *The Nation*, Nov. 9, 2005, http://www.thenation.com/article/germ-boys-and
-yes-men.

62. Congress passed the Pandemic and All-Hazards Preparedness Act establishing the position of the "Assistant Secretary for Preparedness and Response" and transferring to it the functions of "Office of the Assistant Secretary for Preparedness and Response." 120 Stat. 2831, 2833–2834 (2006).

63. 67 FR 48903 (July 26, 2002); 67 FR 71568 (Dec. 2, 2002). See also 42 U.S.C. § 3501(a) (2000).

64. 92 Stat. 2445 (1978); 3 U.S.C. § 105 (2000).

65. Jeffrey Sparshott, "Frink Tapped to Be Manufacturing Czar," *Washington Times*, April 9, 2004, C10; Marilyn Geewax, "Manufacturing Czar Wants Taxes, Red Tape Cut," *Atlanta Journal-*

Constitution, June 9, 2005, E1; Mike Verespej, "New Manufacturing Czar Pledges Support," *Plastics News*, Oct. 1, 2007, vol. 19, 5.

66. 118 Stat. 3, 65 (2004). See also "Press Gaggle with Scott McClellan," March 11, 2004, http://www.presidency.ucsb.edu/ws/?pid=64831.

67. "Bush Picks Ex-Admiral as Advocate for Manufacturers," *Tulsa World*, May 5, 2007, E2; Mike Verespej, "New Manufacturing Czar Pledges Support," *Plastics News*, Oct. 1, 2007, vol. 19, 5; Chris Knape, "Factory Tours Showcase Ecofriendly Operations," *Grand Rapids Press* (MI), Sept. 4, 2008, C1.

68. John Nichols, "Bush's Win Proved Karl Rove Right," *Capital Times* (Madison, WI), Nov. 4, 2004, A12; Carolyn Lochhead, "Immigration Bill Faces Tough Foe," *San Francisco Chronicle*, May 27, 2006, A8.

69. Carolyn Lochhead, "The Stage Is Set—Battle Lines Drawn—GOP to Campaign on National Security, Democrats the Economy," *San Francisco Chronicle*, Sept. 5, 2004, A1; Carolyn Lochhead and Zachary Coile, "How Gay GOP Group Lost Its Faith in Bush," *San Francisco Chronicle*, Oct. 10, 2004, A1.

70. 92 Stat. 2445 (1978); 3 U.S.C. § 105 (2006).

71. Position established within HHS.

72. Michael Romano, "Of Capital Importance," *Modern Healthcare*, Aug. 22, 2005, vol. 35, 6; Jonathan D. Epstein, "Test Set for Electronic Health Insurance Payment Plan," *Buffalo News*, Sept. 4, 2006, B7; Gilbert Chan, "CalPERS Out to Tame Health Fees," *Sacramento Bee*, June 5, 2007, D1.

73. HHS Secretary appointed "in consultation with the President or his designee."

74. EO 13335, 69 FR 24059 (April 27, 2004).

75. Editorial, "An Intelligence Czar Choice, Diplomat Faces Toughest Test," *USA Today*, Feb. 18, 2005, A10; Editorial, "A New Intelligence Czar," *Buffalo News*, Feb. 23, 2005, A6; David Ignatius, "A Czar's Uncertain Clout," *Washington Post*, March 4, 2005, A21.

76. 118 Stat. 3638, 3644 (2004).

77. Christopher Beam, "Exit Strategies," *Washington Post*, Jan. 7, 2007, B3; Mark Mazzetti, "Intelligence Chief Finds That Challenges Abound," *New York Times*, April 7, 2007, A10; Bill Gertz, "Inside the Ring," *Washington Times*, June 26, 2008, B1.

78. Jim Hoagland, "Twisting in Their Own Windiness," *Washington Post*, Feb. 4, 2007, B7; Scott Lindlaw, "Congress Wants Answers on Tillman's Death," *Charleston Daily Mail* (WV), July 25, 2007, P5C.

79. 92 Stat. 2445 (1978); 3 U.S.C. § 105 (2000).

80. Jim Ruttenberg, "Adviser Who Shaped Bush's Speeches Is Leaving," *New York Times*, June 15, 2006, http://www.nytimes.com/2006/06/15/washington/15gerson.html?_r=2&scp=7&sq=michael%20gerson&st=cse; Andrew Sullivan, "Too Tired to Think: Team Bush Loses Its Way," *Sunday Times* (London, England), March 19, 2006, 4.

81. 92 Stat. 2445 (1978); 3 U.S.C. § 105 (2000). See also "Personnel Announcement," Feb. 8, 2005, http://www.presidency.ucsb.edu/ws/?pid=81651; 2005 (Book I) Pub. Papers 1106.

82. Lara Jakes Jordan, "Bush Names Recovery Chief—Powell Is FDIC Chair," *Sun Herald* (Biloxi, MS), Nov. 2, 2005, B7; Adam Nossiter, "Anniversary Brings Out the Politics of Commemoration," *New York Times*, Aug. 28, 2006, A12; Matthew L. Wald, "Bush's Czar to Rebuild Gulf Coast Is Resigning," *New York Times*, March 1, 2008, A14.

83. EO 13390, 70 FR 67327 (Nov. 1, 2005).

84. Glenn Kessler, "Hughes Reaches Out Warily in Cairo," *Washington Post*, Sept. 26, 2005, A16; James J. Zogby, "Shameless Political Posturing Insults Arabs and Americans," *The Sun*

(Baltimore, MD), Feb. 28, 2006, A11; Al Kamen, "Being There," *Washington Post*, Dec. 12, 2007, A27.

85. 112 Stat. 2681-761, 2681-776 (1998).

86. Michael Moran, "Losing the Cold Peace," *Star-Ledger*, July 20, 2008, 23; Al Kamen, "Get Thee to an Airport!" *Washington Post*, June 11, 2008, A17.

87. Robin Wright and Glenn Kessler, "Bush Administration Probes Syria's Future with Assad's Opposition," *Washington Post*, March 26, 2005, A11; Robin Wright and Al Kamen, "U.S. Outreach to Islamic World Gets Slow Start," *Washington Post*, April 18, 2005, A2.

88. Assistant Secretary of State appointed.

89. The State Department created the "Division of Near Eastern Affairs" in 1909 and retitled it the "Bureau of Near Eastern Affairs" on Oct. 3, 1949. See the history for "Assistant Secretaries of State for Near Eastern Affairs" at the U.S. Department of State, Office of the Historian website, http://history.state.gov/departmenthistory/people/principalofficers/assistant-secretary-for-near-eastern-affairs. The Secretary of State has general authority to "prescribe duties for the Assistant Secretaries and the clerks of bureaus, as well as for all the other employees in the department" under 22 U.S.C. § 2664; 18 Stat. 85, 90 (1874).

90. Michael McAuliff, "WTC Medical Czar Gets Swift Kick," *New York Daily News*, Sept. 8, 2006, 7; Nicole Bode, "Hill Warns 9-11 Health Budget Losing Its Life," *New York Daily News*, Dec. 19, 2006, 45; Heidi J. Shrager, "Sick 9/11 Heroes Face Cut-off of Treatment," *Staten Island Advance* (NY), Dec. 19, 2006, A1.

91. HHS secretary appointed.

92. 84 Stat. 1590 (1970).

93. Nate Legue, "Mine Safety Czar in Rockford," *Rockford Register Star* (IL), Jan. 11, 2007, D1; Editorial, "Something to Stew Over," *Lexington Herald-Leader* (KY), Aug. 23, 2007, A10; Lionel Van Deerlin, "Mine Safety 'Oversight' Is Right Word," *Monroe Evening News* (MI), Sept. 1, 2007, A4.

94. 91 Stat. 1290, 1319 (1977). See also 29 U.S.C. § 557a (2006).

95. Editorial, "A Transformation at State?" *Washington Post*, Jan. 22, 2006, B6; Roya Wolverson, "Influence: The New Bush Politics of Aid," *Newsweek*, Sept. 15, 2007, http://www.newsweek.com/2007/09/15/periscope-influence-the-new-bush-politics-of-aid.html.

96. 75 Stat. 424, 624a (1961). See also EO 10973, 26 FR 10469 (Nov. 3, 1961); 22 U.S.C. § 2384a (2006).

97. Amanda Schaffer, "The Family Un-Planner," *Slate*, Nov. 21, 2006, http://www.slate.com/id/2154249/; Andreas Estes, "Doctor Who Quit U.S. Post Was Warned by State," *Boston Globe*, April 7, 2007, http://www.boston.com/news/local/articles/2007/04/07/doctor_who_quit_us_post_was_warned_by_state/.

98. HHS Secretary appoints. "FDA Commissioner Announces New Food Protection Position," http://www.fda.gov/NewsEvents/Newsroom/PressAnnouncements/2007/ucm108903.htm.

99. 84 Stat. 1504 (1970).

100. Jonathan D. Rockoff, "'Food Safety Czar' Named," *The Baltimore Sun* (Baltiimore, MD), May 2, 2007, A1; Steve Hirsch, "FDA Chief Vows to Boost Food Inspection," *Washington Times*, July 18, 2007, C8; Mike Hughlett, "Tracking the Bug in Tomatoes," *Chicago Tribune*, June 18, 2008, 1.

101. FDA Commissioner appointed.

102. "FDA Commissioner Announces New Food Protection Position," May 1, 2007, http://www.fda.gov/NewsEvents/Newsroom/PressAnnouncements/2007/ucm108903.htm.

103. William Douglas, "Bush Names Army Man War Czar: Bush Selects War Czar,"

Virginian-Pilot (Norfolk, VA), May 16, 2007, A5; Charles A. Stevenson, "'War Czar' Requires Scrutiny," *The Sun* (Baltimore, MD), May 25, 2007, A19; Peter Baker and Robin Wright, "To 'War Czar,' Solution to Iraq Conflict Won't Be Purely Military," *Washington Post*, May 17, 2007, A13.

104. 94 Stat. 2835, 2849 (1980); 10 U.S.C. § 601 (2006). See also 43 Weekly Comp. Docs. 635 (May 15, 2007).

105. Michel S. Rosenwald, "The Financial Crisis," *Houston Chronicle*, Oct. 10, 2008, A3; Wailin Wong, "The Rapid Rise of Bailout Czar," *Chicago Tribune*, Oct. 13, 2008, 25; David R. Sands, "Bailout Boss Buoys Banks," *Washington Times*, Oct. 14, 2008, A11.

106. Treasury Secretary Henry Paulson designated Neel Kashkari as Interim Assistant Secretary of the Treasury for Financial Stability as provided for under the Emergency Economic Stabilization Act of 2008. "Kashkari Appointed Interim Assistant Secretary for Financial Stability," Oct. 6, 2008, http://www.financialstability.gov/latest/hp1184.html.

107. 122 Stat. 2765, 3767 (2008).

Table 12

1. EO 13228, 66 FR 51812 (Oct. 8, 2001).

2. EO 13199, 66 FR 8499 (Jan. 29, 2001).

3. In 2004, Congress changed the title of the council from "Interagency Council on the Homeless" to "United States Interagency Council on Homelessness." 118 Stat. 394 (2004).

4. Council members appointed.

5. 101 Stat. 482 (1987).

6. Congress passed the Pandemic and All-Hazards Preparedness Act establishing the position of the "Assistant Secretary for Preparedness and Response" and transferring to it the functions of "Office of the Assistant Secretary for Preparedness and Response." See 120 Stat. 2831, 2833–2834 (2006).

7. 67 FR 48903 (July 26, 2002); 67 FR 71568 (Dec. 2, 2002). See also 42 U.S.C. § 3501 (2000 suppl. 3).

8. 92 Stat. 2445 (1978); 3 U.S.C. § 105 (2000).

9. HHS Secretary appointed "in consultation with the President or his designee."

10. EO 13335, 69 FR 24059 (April 27, 2004).

11. EO 13390, 70 FR 67327 (Nov. 1, 2005).

12. HHS secretary appointed.

13. 84 Stat. 1590 (1970).

14. FDA Commissioner appointed.

15. "FDA Commissioner Announces New Food Protection Position," May 1, 2007, http://www.fda.gov/NewsEvents/Newsroom/PressAnnouncements/2007/ucm108903.htm.

Table 13

1. David E. Sanger, "Obama Faces Different World 2 Years after Campaign Began," *New York Times*, Jan. 18, 2009, A1; Rajiv Chandrasekaran, "Civilian, Military Officials at Odds over Resources Needed for Afghan Mission," *Washington Post*, Oct. 8, 2009, A1.

2. Position dates to George W. Bush's administration.

3. 94 Stat. 2835, 2849 (1980). See also "Statement on the Appointment of Lieutenant General Douglas Lute as Assistant to the President and Deputy National Security Adviser for Iraq and Afghanistan," May 15, 2007, 43 Weekly Comp. Docs. 635–636.

4. Bob Cox, "Lockheed Could Agree to Share in the Risks of Higher F-35 Costs," *Fort Worth Star-Telegram*, Nov. 29, 2009, D1; John T. Bennett, "Pentagon Acquisition Nominee Draws High Praise," *Federal Times*, Aug. 17, 2009, 14.

5. 113 Stat. 512, 717 (1999).

6. Mike Dorning, "Loosely Defined, but Czars on the Rise," *Chicago Tribune*, June 14, 2009, 3; Michael A. Fletcher and Brady Dennis, "Obama's Many Policy 'Czars' Draw Ire from Conservatives," *Washington Post*, Sept. 16, 2009, A6.

7. EO 13498, 74 FR 6533 (Feb. 5, 2009). See also George W. Bush's original EO establishing the office, EO 13199, 66 FR 8499 (Jan. 31, 2001).

8. Tracie Cone, "Interior Secretary Assigns Deputy as State Water Czar," *Redding Record Searchlight*, June 28, 2009, A1; "Still More Action Needed on Water Issues," *Fresno Bee*, June 30, 2009, B5; "More Action Needed on Water Issues," *Merced Sun-Star*, July 1, 2009, B3.

9. 104 Stat. 1427, 1454 (1990). Position originally established "Under Secretary." 49 Stat. 176, 177 (1935). See announcement of Hayes's appointment to coordinate "the federal response to California water supply," http://www.doi.gov/archive/news/09_News_Releases/062809.html.

10. David A. Fahrenthold, "Bay Group Is Urged to Gird for Battle," *Washington Post*, Dec. 17, 2009, B1; David A. Fahrenthold, "Bay Backers Call EPA Plan Weak," *Washington Post*, Dec. 31, 2009, B1; "J. Charles Fox Biography," http://www.epa.gov/history/admin/opr/fox.htm.

11. Environmental Protection Agency Administrator appointed.

12. Siobhan Gorman, "White House Cybersecurity Chief Quits," *Wall Street Journal,*, Aug. 4, 2009, A4; Shaun Waterman, "Cyber Security Strategy Unveiled," *Washington Times*, May 30, 2009, A1.

13. 92 Stat. 2445 (1978); 3 U.S.C. § 105 (2006). See also "Remarks by the President on Securing Our Nation's Cyber Infrastructure," May 29, 2009, http://www.whitehouse.gov/the_press_office /Remarks-by-the-President-on-Securing-Our-Nations-Cyber-Infrastructure/.

14. Ellen Nakashima, "Obama to Name Former Bush, Microsoft Official as Cyber-Czar," *Washington Post*, Dec. 22, 2009, A4; Gregg Carlstrom, "Obama Likely to Name 'Cyber Czar' Soon," *Federal Times*, Nov. 9, 2009, 8.

15. Martha Minow, "Keeping Stimulus Spending in Check," *Boston Globe*, March 1, 2009, 9; Dave Michaels and Robert T. Garrett, "Obama to Speed Stimulus Spending," *Dallas Morning News*, June 9, 2009, A1; Dorning, "Loosely Defined, but Czars on the Rise," 3.

16. Devaney has been the Interior Department Inspector General since 1999.

17. Law stipulates that the president can appoint any federal officer who was already appointed by the president to a position that required Senate confirmation.

18. 123 Stat. 115, 289 (2009).

19. Helene Cooper and Mark Landler, "For Obama's Iran Plan, Talk and Some Toughness," *New York Times*, Feb. 4, 2009, A11; Amanda Carpenter, "Culture Hot Button," *Washington Times*, June 15, 2009, A18; Daniel L. Gardner, "It Continues to Be about the Economy," *Starkville Daily News* (MS), July 19, 2009, A4.

20. 92 Stat. 2445 (1978).

21. Louise Story, "In Merrill's Failed Plan, Lessons for Pay Czar," *New York Times*, Oct. 8, 2009, B1; Tomoeh Murakami Tse, "U.S. Pay Czar Says Renegotiating AIG Bonuses Is a 'Top Priority,'" *Washington Post*, Oct. 29, 2009, A16.

22. Treasury Secretary appointed.

23. 74 FR 28394 (June 15, 2009). Regulation based on "Emergency Economic Stabilization Act of 2008," 122 Stat. 3765 (2008); "American Recovery and Reinvestment Act of 2009," 123 Stat. 115, 516 (2009).

24. Dorning, "Loosely Defined, but Czars on the Rise," 3; Fletcher and Dennis, "Obama's Many Policy 'Czars' Draw Ire," A6.

25. 116 Stat. 2135, 2178 (2002). Name changed by Reorganization Plan Modification for the Department of Homeland Security, March 1, 2003. H. Doc. No. 108-32, 108th Cong., 1st sess., in 6 U.S.C. § 542 (2006).

26. "Secretary Napolitano Highlights Illegal Immigration Enforcement, Appoints Alan Bersin as Assistant Secretary for International Affairs and Special Representative for Border Affairs," April 15, 2009, http://www.dhs.gov/ynews/releases/pr_1239820176123.shtm.

27. Homeland Security Secretary appointed.

28. 116 Stat. 2135, 2144 (2002). Reorganization Plan Modification for the Department of Homeland Security created the Office of International Affairs, March 1, 2003. H. Doc. No. 108-32, 108th Cong., 1st sess., in 6 U.S.C. § 542 (2006).

29. "Secretary Napolitano Highlights Illegal Immigration Enforcement."

30. Chuck Neubauer, "Obama 'Czar' Earned Millions from Legally Troubled Firms," *Washington Times*, Dec. 8, 2009, A1; Robert Pear and Jeff Zeleny, "On Health, President Takes Team Approach," *New York Times*, March 3, 2009, A14.

31. EO 13507, 74 FR 17071 (April 8, 2009).

32. 92 Stat. 2445 (1978).

33. Cheryl W. Thompson, "Obama, Mexican Leader Discuss Drug Cartels," *Washington Post*, Aug. 10, 2009, A8; David Mastio, "Putting Politics before Science—It's Standard Procedure for Climate Czar Carol Browner," *Washington Times*, Dec. 3, 2009, A23.

34. "President-Elect Barack Obama Announces Key Members of Energy and Environment Team," Dec. 15, 2008, http://change.gov/newsroom/entry/president_elect_barack_obama_announces_key_members_of_energy_and_environmen/.

35. 92 Stat. 2445 (1978).

36. "Jeffrey S. Crowley Will Join Domestic Policy Council as Top Advisor on HIV/AIDS Issues," Feb. 26, 2009, http://www.whitehouse.gov/the_press_office/PresidentObama-Selects -Health-Policy-Expert-to-Head-Office-of-National-AIDS-Polic/; Tim Murphy, "The Activists' Wish List," *The Advocate*, May 1, 2009, 14.

37. 92 Stat. 2445 (1978).

38. Fletcher and Dennis, "Obama's Many Policy 'Czars' Draw Ire," A6.

39. 118 Stat. 3638 (2004).

40. William Yardley, "In a Likely Obama Pick, Some Find Hope for a Shift in Drug Policy," *New York Times*, Feb. 16, 2009, A13; Matthew Daly, "Kerlikowske Describes How He'd Approach Drug-Czar Job," *Seattle Times*, April 2, 2009, B1.

41. 102 Stat. 4181 (1988).

42. Dorning, "Loosely Defined, but Czars on the Rise," 3.

43. 122 Stat. 3765, 3767 (2008).

44. Cindy Skrzycki, "The Rule Czar's Balancing Act," *Washington Post*, Jan. 13, 2009, D2; Neil King Jr., "Sunstein's Ideas at Work in US Policy," *Wall Street Journal*, July 6, 2009, A4.

45. 94 Stat. 2812, 2814 (1980). See also 44 U.S.C. § 3503 (2006).

46. Louis Mayeux, "Q & A on the News," *Atlanta Journal-Constitution*, July 15, 2009, A2; French Maclean, "Obama's Embrace of 'Czars' a Bad Thing for Democracy," *Herald & Review* (Decatur, IL), July 31, 2009, A4.

47. EO 13228, 66 FR 51812 (Oct. 8, 2001).

48. Laura Meckler, "U.S. News: 'Czars' Ascend at White House," *Wall Street Journal*, Dec. 15, 2008, A6; Amanda Carpenter, "Culture Hot Button," *Washington Times*, June 15, 2009, A18.

49. EO 13503, 74 FR 8139 (Feb. 19, 2009).

50. Kim Hart, "D.C. Tech Chief Headed for White House Slot," *Washington Post*, March 5, 2009, D1; Amanda Carpenter, "Culture Hot Button," *Washington Times*, June 15, 2009, A18; "President Obama Names Vivek Kundra Chief Information Officer," http://www.whitehouse .gov/the_press_office/President-Obama-Names-Vivek-Kundra-Chief-Information-Officer/.

51. Dorning, "Loosely Defined, but Czars on the Rise," 3.

52. 116 Stat. 2899 (2002).

53. Fletcher and Dennis, "Obama's Many Policy 'Czars' Draw Ire," A6; Lisa Lerer, "GOP Czar Revolt Scores Its First Win as Van Jones Resigns," *Politico*, Sept. 7, 2009, http://www.politico .com/news/stories/0909/26781.html.

54. This act created the Department of Environmental Quality in which Jones officially held his post.

55. Kim Hart, "Local Tech-Savvy Duo Steps onto Federal Stage," *Washington Post*, April 27, 2009, A12; Aneesh Chopra biography, White House website, http://www.whitehouse.gov /administration/eop/ostp/about/leadershipstaff/chopra.

56. 90 Stat. 463 (1976).

57. David Harsanyi, "Science Fiction Czar," *Denver Post*, July 15, 2009, B11; "Czar 54, Who Are You?" *Investor's Business Daily* (Los Angeles, CA), July 21, 2009, A10.

58. 90 Stat. 463 (1976).

59. EO 13226, 66 FR 50523 (Sept. 30, 2001).

60. Ed O'Keefe, "Who Are Jeffrey Zients and Aneesh Chopra?" *Washington Post*, April 18, 2009, http://voices.washingtonpost.com/federal-eye/2009/04/obama_names_chief_perfor mance.html; Jeffrey Zients biography, White House website, http://www.whitehouse.gov /administration/advisory-boards/pmab/members/jeffrey-zients; Jeffrey Zients biography, WhoRunsGov website, http://www.whorunsgov.com/Profiles/Jeffrey_D._Zients.

61. 104 Stat. 2838 (1990).

62. Peter Lattman, "Rattner, Possible 'Car Czar,' Faces Questions," *Wall Street Journal*, Jan. 13, 2009, C7; Peter Whoriskey and Brady Dennis, "UAW, Ford Cut Deal on Health Benefits," *Washington Post*, Feb. 24, 2009, D1; Fletcher and Dennis, "Obama's Many Policy 'Czars' Draw Ire," A6.

63. Treasury Secretary appointed.

64. Editorial, "Damage Control," *Detroit News*, Sept. 9, 2009, A14; Editorial, "Unplugged," *Washington Post*, April 18, 2010, A16; Ron Bloom biography, WhoRunsGov website, http://www .whorunsgov.com/Profiles/Ron_Bloom.

65. "Geithner, Summers Convene Official Designees to Presidential Task Force on the Auto Industry," Feb. 20, 2009, http://www.whitehouse.gov/the-press-office/geithner-summers -convene-official-designees-presidential-task-force-auto-industry.

66. 92 Stat. 2445 (1978). "President Obama Names Ron Bloom Senior Counselor for Manufacturing Policy," Sept. 7, 2009, http://www.whitehouse.gov/the_press_office/President-Obama -Names-Ron-Bloom-Senior-Counselor-for-Manufacturing-Policy/.

67. John Flesher, "Great Lakes Czar Has Long Record as Advocate," *Journal Gazette* (Fort Wayne, IN), June 5, 2009, C4; John Flesher, "Obama Appoints Czar for Great Lakes Cleanup," *USA Today*, June 5, 2009, http://www.usatoday.com/tech/science/environment/2009-06-05 -great-lakes_N.htm; Dan Egan, "Obama Names Overseer for Great Lakes," *Milwaukee Journal Sentinel* (WI), June 4, 2009, A1.

68. Environmental Protection Agency Administrator appointed.

69. Stephen T. Watson, "Schumer Wants Return of Delphi Plants to GM," *Buffalo News*, May 5, 2009, B7; David Shepardson, "Auto Czar Montgomery Resigns for Post at Georgetown University," *Detroit News*, June 15, 2010, B6.

70. "Geithner, Summers Convene Official Designees."

71. EO 13509, 74 FR 30903 (June 23, 2009).

72. Gilbert Sperling biography, Cleantech website, http://events.cleantech.com/newyork /sperling-gilbert.

73. Position dates to George W. Bush's administration.

74. Energy secretary appointed.

75. 123 Stat. 115 (2009).

76. Weatherization and Intergovernmental Program, Organizational Chart, http://www.eere.energy.gov/wip/pdfs/wip_org_chart_112010.pdf.

77. "Vice President Biden Announces Appointment of White House Advisor on Violence against Women," June 26, 2009, http://www.whitehouse.gov/the_press_office/Vice-President-Biden-Announces-Appointment-of-White-House-Advisor-on-Violence-Against-Women/.

78. Vice president appointed.

79. 92 Stat. 2445 (1978).

80. "Appointment of Special Envoy on Climate Change Todd Stern," Jan. 26, 2009, http://www.state.gov/secretary/rm/2009a/01/115409.htm.

81. Secretary of State appointed.

82. Thomas Mitchell, "A Czar for Every Harm—Including Media Bias," *Las Vegas Review-Journal*, Sept. 20, 2009, D2; Amanda Carpenter, "Diversity Czar Takes Heat over Remarks," *Washington Times*, Sept. 23, 2009, A1.

83. Linda Douglass biography, WhoRunsGov website, http://www.whorunsgov.com/Profiles/Linda_Douglass.

84. HHS Secretary appointed.

85. EO 13507, 74 FR 17071 (April 8, 2009). See also "Secretary Sebelius Announces HHS Office of Health Reform Personnel," May 11, 2009, http://www.hhs.gov/news/press/2009pres/05/20090511a.html.

86. Howard Kurtz, "Obama Meets the Press," *Washington Post*, Feb. 9, 2009, C1; David Ignatius, "Quiet Tiger at the Fed," *Washington Post*, May 28, 2009, A19.

87. EO 12835, 58 FR 6189 (Jan. 25, 1993).

88. Tom Hamburger and Christi Parsons, "White House Czars' Power Stirs Criticism," *Chicago Tribune*, March 5, 2009, 10; Dale McFeatters, "Czarist Washington," *Deseret News* (Salt Lake City, UT), Sept. 17, 2009, A16.

89. EO 13501, 74 FR 6983 (Feb. 6, 2009).

90. Dave Weber, "Education Czar Vows to Work with State," *Orlando Sentinel*, April 2, 2009, B1; Maureen Magee, "Education Chief Wants Merit Pay Considered," *San Diego Union-Tribune*, July 3, 2009, B1.

91. 93 Stat. 668 (1979).

92. Tracey Planinz, "Will Obama's New Food Czar End Organic Farming?" *Examiner.com*, Aug. 10, 2009, http://www.examiner.com/x-11401-Orlando-Alternative-Medicine-Examiner~y2009m8d10-Will-Obamas-new-Food-Czar-end-organic-farming; "Cash for Clunkers Wastes Usable Cars," *Herald-Journal* (Spartanburg, SC), Aug. 14, 2009, A6.

93. Food and Drug Administration Commissioner appointed.

94. 74 FR 41713 (Aug. 18, 2009); 75 FR 7490 (Feb. 19, 2010). See also "Office of Foods: Overview and Mission," http://www.fda.gov/AboutFDA/CentersOffices/OC/OfficeofFoods/ucm196720.htm.

95. "President Obama Announces More Key Administration Posts," White House website, May 12, 2009, http://www.whitehouse.gov/the_press_office/President-Obama-Announces-More-Key-Administration-Posts-5-12-2009/; Arturo Valenzuela biography, WhoRunsGov website, http://www.whorunsgov.com/Profiles/Arturo_Valenzuela.

96. 58 Stat. 798 (1944). See also Department of State History, "Assistant Secretaries of State for Western Hemisphere Affairs," http://history.state.gov/departmenthistory/people/principalofficers/assistant-secretary-for-western-hemisphere.

97. Antony Bruno, "Will Obama's Copyright Czar Help Save the Music?" Reuters, Nov. 15, 2008, http://uk.reuters.com/article/idUKTRE4AE10J20081115; David Kravels, "Obama Appoints Scholar as New Copyright Czar," *Wired*, Sept. 25, 2009, http://www.wired.com /threatlevel/2009/09/obama-taps-new-copyright-czar/.

98. 122 Stat. 4256 (2008).

99. Editorial, "5 Myths on Health Care's Electronic Fix-It," *Washington Post*, April 26, 2009, B3; Marjianne Kolbasuk McGee, "Physicians Question Health IT Stimulus Requirements," *InformationWeek*, Nov. 23, 2009, http://www.informationweek.com/news/healthcare/policy/showAr ticle.jhtml?articleID=221900779.

100. HHS Secretary appointed "in consultation with the President."

101. EO 13335, 69 FR 24059 (April 27, 2004).

102. Editorial, "Queering Our Schools—More Dangerous Ideas from Obama's 'Safe Schools Czar,'" *Washington Times*, Oct. 16, 2009, A20; Jim Rutenberg, "Behind the War between Fox and Obama," *New York Times*, Oct. 23, 2009, A16.

103. Education secretary appointed.

104. 115 Stat. 1425, 1734 (2002). Under the general reorganization authority provided by Title 20, section 3473 of the U.S. Code, the education secretary could create the Office of Safe and Drug-Free Schools. See 20 U.S.C. § 3473 (2006). See also "Paige Announces Formation of Two New Offices," Sept. 17, 2002, http://www2.ed.gov/news/pressreleases/2002/09/09172002.html.

105. "Remarks by the Vice President at the Swearing-in of United States Trade Representative Ron Kirk," March 20, 2009, http://www.whitehouse.gov/the-press-office/remarks-vice -president-biden-swearing-united-states-representative-ron-kirk; Jim Abrams, "Kirk Says as Trade Czar He Would Enforce Rules," *Houston Chronicle*, March 10, 2009, B6.

106. 88 Stat. 1978, 1999 (1975); 19 U.S.C. § 2171 (2006).

107. Not an official title.

108. Jeffrey H. Birnbaum, "The No-Win Presidency," *Washington Times*, June 17, 2010, B3; "BP to Set Up Huge Fund for Claims," *St. Louis Post-Dispatch*, June 17, 2010, A1.

109. Mabus served as navy secretary during this time.

110. Presidential designation.

111. For a statement by Obama, see "Remarks by the President to the Nation on the BP Oil Spill," June 15, 2010, http://www.whitehouse.gov/the-press-office/remarks-president-nation-bp -oil-spill.

112. Joel Achenbach and Steven Mufson, "Oil-Well Partner Lashes Out, Says Fault Is All BP's," *Seattle Times*, June 19, 2010, A1; Cristina Silva, "Claims Czar Visits Florida," *St. Petersburg Times*, July 2, 2010, B9.

113. The exact appointment mechanism used to name Feinberg as the BP Claims Fund head has never been clearly stated by the Obama administration. Our best estimation is that Obama and BP executives jointly appointed Feinberg.

114. Dan Egan, "Corps Says Barrier Won't Stop All Carp: Power in Canal Too Low to Repel Smallest Fish," *Milwaukee Journal Sentinel*, March 27, 2011, B1; Nathan Hurst, "Corps: Electric Barriers Work against Asian Carp," *Detroit News*, March 26, 2011, A1; Jerry Zremski, "Asian Carp Threat to Great Lakes Prompts Naming of Federal 'Czar,'" *Buffalo News*, Sept. 9, 2010, A7.

115. 92 Stat. 2445 (1978).

116. Editorial, "A Food Czar? Really?" *Investors Business Daily*, July 16, 2010, A16; "Obama Family Cook Named Policy Adviser," *Corruption Chronicles*, July 14, 2010, http://www.judicial watch.org/blog/2010/jul/obama-family-cook-named-policy-adviser.

117. 92 Stat. 2445 (1978).

118. Peter Nicholas, Jim Puzzanghera, and Don Lee, "With Shake-Up, Obama Plays to His

Base," *The Sun* (Baltimore, MD), Sept. 24, 2010, A14; Editorial, "Fixing Ms. Warren's Shop," *Boston Herald*, May 29, 2011; Patrice Hill, "Hill Fight Intensifies over Consumer Czar," *Washington Times*, May 30, 2011, A1.

119. 92 Stat. 2445 (1978).

Table 14

1. EO 13498, 74 FR 6533 (Feb. 5, 2009). See also George W. Bush's original executive order establishing the office, EO 13199, 66 FR 8499 (Jan 31, 2001).

2. EPA Administrator appointed.

3. 92 Stat. 2445 (1978).

4. Treasury Secretary appointed.

5. 74 FR 28394 (June 15, 2009). Regulation based on "Emergency Economic Stabilization Act of 2008," 122 Stat. 3765 (2008); "American Recovery and Reinvestment Act of 2009," 123 Stat. 115, 516 (2009).

6. EO 13507, 74 FR 17071 (April 8, 2009).

7. 92 Stat. 2445 (1978).

8. "President-Elect Barack Obama Announces Key Members of Energy and Environment Team," Dec. 15, 2008, http://change.gov/newsroom/entry/president_elect_barack_obama_an nounces _key_members_of_energy_and_environmen/.

9. 92 Stat. 2445 (1978).

10. EO 13503, 74 FR 8139 (Feb. 19, 2009).

11. 83 Stat. 852 (1969).

12. Council members appointed.

13. 101 Stat. 482 (1987).

14. Treasury Secretary appointed.

15. 92 Stat. 2445 (1978). "Geithner, Summers Convene Official Designees to Presidential Task Force on the Auto Industry," Feb. 20, 2009, http://www.whitehouse.gov/the-press-office /geithner-summers-convene-official-designees-presidential-task-force-auto-industry.

16. "President Obama Names Ron Bloom Senior Counselor for Manufacturing Policy," Sept. 7, 2009, http://www.whitehouse.gov/the_press_office/President-Obama-Names-Ron-Bloom -Senior-Counselor-for-Manufacturing-Policy/.

17. EPA Administrator appointed.

18. "Geithner, Summers Convene Official Designees."

19. EO 13509, 74 FR 30903 (June 23, 2009).

20. FDA Commissioner appointed.

21. 74 FR 41713 (Aug. 18, 2009); 75 FR 7490 (Feb. 19, 2010). See also "Office of Foods: Overview and Mission," http://www.fda.gov/AboutFDA/CentersOffices/OC/OfficeofFoods /ucm196720.htm.

22. HHS Secretary appointed "in consultation with the President."

23. EO 13335, 69 FR 24059 (April 27, 2004).

24. The exact appointment mechanism used to name Feinberg as the BP Claims Fund head has never been clearly stated by the Obama administration. Our best estimation is that Obama and BP executives jointly appointed Feinberg.

25. 92 Stat. 2445 (1978).

26. 92 Stat. 2445 (1978).

27. 92 Stat. 2445 (1978).

INDEX